Pittsburgh Series in
Social and Labor History

D0169018

Killing Time

*Leisure and Culture in
Southwestern Pennsylvania, 1800–1850*

Scott C. Martin

University of Pittsburgh Press
Pittsburgh and London

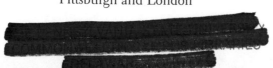

Published by the University of Pittsburgh Press, Pittsburgh, Pa. 15260
Copyright © 1995, University of Pittsburgh Press
All rights reserved
Manufactured in the United States of America
Printed on acid-free paper

Designed by Jane Tenenbaum

Library of Congress Cataloging-in-Publication Data

Martin, Scott C., 1959–
    Killing time : leisure and culture in Southwestern Pennsylvania,
1800–1850 / Scott C. Martin.
        p.   cm. — (Pittsburgh series in social and labor history)
    Includes bibliographical references and index.
    ISBN 0-8229-3916-9 (cloth)
    1. Leisure—Pennsylvania—History—19th century. 2. Pennsylvania—
Social life and customs. I. Title. II. Series.
F138.M37   1995
306.4'812'09748—dc20   95-23604
                                                                CIP

A CIP catalogue record for this book is available from the British Library
Eurospan, London

I say we had best look our times and lands searchingly in the face, like a physician diagnosing some deep disease. Never was there, perhaps, more hollowness at heart than at present, and here in the United States. . . . The great cities reek with respectable as much as non-respectable scoundrelism. In fashionable life, flippancy, tepid amours, weak infidelism, small aims, or no aims at all, only to kill time. In business, (this all-devouring modern word, business,) the one sole object is, by any means, pecuniary gain.

—Walt Whitman
Democratic Vistas, 1871

Contents

Preface

IN THE PAST THREE DECADES, scholars in a variety of disciplines have turned their attention to leisure as a significant social and cultural phenomenon. In the 1960s and 1970s, much of the academic study of leisure relied on structuralism for its theoretical underpinning, as sociologists and other scholars sought to define and categorize nonwork time and activities. More recently, philosophers and poststructuralist theorists have manifested an interest in leisure, often questioning the equation of leisure with "free" time, especially in societies shaped by industrial capitalism. Feminist studies of leisure have emerged as well, frequently insisting on the importance of an unequal distribution of leisure between men and women and the implications of this inequality for gender roles. Historians, especially those who study England and the United States, have produced excellent studies that focus on class and leisure, most of which explore the relationship between leisure activities and working class culture and consciousness.

The present work owes a great deal to all these perspectives. I approach early nineteenth-century leisure in southwestern Pennsylvania from the standpoint of a cultural historian, but my concerns reflect those of other scholars and historians as well. Defining leisure in the context of nineteenth-century U.S. society, I view it as contested cultural space, in which ideas about ethnicity, class, and gender were articulated and developed. Rather than focusing on one class or social group — the working class, for example — I have chosen to examine the leisure of southwestern Pennsylvanians in general during a period of rapid and tumultuous change in the region. What this method sacrifices in depth, it more than compensates for in breadth. Though studying the leisure of one segment of the population yields important insights into that group, examining areas of conflict and agreement among different elements of a society allows a broader picture of social and cultural dynamics to emerge. In the following chapters I show how a variety of people and social groups in southwestern Pennsylvania used leisure as a cultural palliative for and response to the pressures generated by their changing and industrializing society.

Throughout this book, when quoting from books, letters, diaries, and newspapers of the period, I have preserved original spelling and construction. Rather than repeated use of *sic* after misspellings and the like, I include this general note to inform the reader that misspellings in quotations are reproduced unchanged from the original document.

In the course of writing a dissertation and transforming it into a monograph, I have incurred numerous debts, both intellectual and personal. Special thanks are due to Sam Hays, my principal adviser, for moral support, insightful comments, and valuable advice. On that score, I would also like to thank Van Beck Hall, Elizabeth Johns, William Stanton, and John Markoff. Maurine Greenwald, Joan Hedrick, Sharon Salinger, and Richard Godbeer kindly read and commented on earlier versions of all or parts of the manuscript. Others offered encouragement and conversation during various stages of the project: Joe White, Piotr Górecki, and Randy Head, as well as other colleagues and fellow graduate students. In addition, Marilyn Holt and the staff of the Pennsylvania Room at the Carnegie Library of Pittsburgh provided needed assistance, as did Marcia Grodsky at the University of Pittsburgh's Darlington Library. Fred Hetzel at the University of Pittsburgh Press expressed early interest in and support for the book. Most of all I would like to thank my family, who provided emotional support through the whole process: my parents, Magdalene and Edward McGuire; my son, Nathaniel Duntley Martin; and especially my wife, Madeline Duntley, who read the manuscript and offered invaluable comments and suggestions. All of these people contributed materially to whatever merits the book has; its shortcomings are, of course, solely my own responsibility.

Killing Time

1

Introduction

IN MARCH OF 1846, Joseph Buffum moved to Pittsburgh, Pennsylvania, from Keene, New Hampshire, in the hopes of establishing a bottling factory with his brother. After a year of "pretty hard scratching," the business flourished, and the twenty-two year old Buffum "came off the gainer." With his financial prospects favorable, he decided to quit business and pursue his fondest ambition, a college education. Though always an avid reader, Buffum had received only sporadic schooling as a boy: "I was very much attached to my books, getting along mostly without instruction, having learned much by piecemeals by night and at leisure." Now Buffum hoped to remedy his deficiencies in Latin and Greek so that a year later he could "go to College in good standing" with a "right good knowledge of the languages." To this end, the budding scholar purchased textbooks, engaged "Mr. Bradley of Allegheny City, a graduate of Yale College"[1] as his tutor, and began keeping a journal to chart his progress and activities.

Buffum's journal reveals a Franklinesque passion for self-improvement, community service, and ceaseless activity.[2] Like many nineteenth-century emulators of Poor Richard, Buffum became obsessed with time and resolved to use it wisely and efficiently. "I will now keep a dayly record of my time and progress," he wrote early in his journal, "and am deter-

3

mined that a day shall not pass without my doing some good not only to myself but to my fellow man. . . . I am now determined to value time as it passes and improve it."[3]

Buffum paid special attention to valuing and improving time during his leisure hours. He preferred to spend free time poring over Latin, Greek, or history texts instead of indulging in "fictitious reading," which he considered to be "injurious." When not studying, Buffum participated almost compulsively in a variety of social reforms, scientific fads, and voluntary associations. Universalism, temperance, "eclectic" medicine, phreno-magnetism, and dietary reform occupied his free time, while membership in the Sons of Temperance, a debating club, and the New England Society provided useful outlets for his seemingly boundless energy.[4] Fear of idleness and frivolous activity permeates his journal; even time lost to illness provoked guilt and self-recrimination. Unable to study Greek because of fever and headaches, Buffum scolded himself for not taking better care of his health. "Don't like to lose time this way," he fretted to his journal, "but it is mostly my own folly which I must guard against in the future."[5]

Sometimes this self-imposed discipline and the anxieties it generated proved onerous, even for as serious a young man as Buffum. Though constantly vigilant, he often felt the lure of pleasant but trivial leisure activities. The opposite sex was a particularly vexing distraction.

> Came down this evening in company with Miss Maria Ramaley, had a very pleasant time of it indeed: walked home with her last Sunday evening and received from her a beautiful purse, knit by her own hands, for which I am truly grateful; and I almost ought to have been there tonight, but instead I am here writing. Oh the works of fate! It seems that education must take the foreground to the exclusion of everything else on earth.

Soon thereafter he resolved to be more attentive to his studies and health. The following day, however, his protestations continued: "Have improved my time pretty well today. Got a long Latin and Greek lesson. Could not avoid going home tonight with the girls. Oh, what a bother! I am getting more and more interested in my studies and must leave more of my company."[6]

The Dangers of Unoccupied Time

Buffum's anxieties about time and leisure were far from idiosyncratic, for similar sentiments resonated throughout antebellum society and culture. To understand these sentiments, we must recognize that leisure meant something far different to early nineteenth-century Americans than it does to us. At the turn of the nineteenth century, leisure did not represent necessarily a period for recreation and entertainment. Rather, it connoted unoccupied time, or time free from obligations. An 1810 dictionary defined leisure simply as "freedom from business," or "convenience." The *Oxford English Dictionary* gives an expanded but essentially similar meaning: freedom or opportunity to do something specified or implied; time which can be spent as one pleases; free or unoccupied time. Conceiving leisure in this way, many Americans expressed deep misgivings about its potential for abuse, worrying that free time would be wasted in frivolous or depraved amusements. Typically, pessimists articulated their concerns in discussions of the proper usage of time. Reflecting an intellectual heritage that combined both the jeremiads of Puritan divines and the aphorisms of Poor Richard, reformers and social critics urged Americans to improve, rather than waste, time during their leisure hours. Failure to do so, they warned, imperiled both individuals and American society.

> Kill time today, and to your sorrow,
> He'll stare you in the face tomorrow;
> Kill him again, in any way,
> He'll plague you still from day to day;
> Till, in the end, as is most due,
> Time turns the tables, and *kills you*.[7]

Among the guardians of American leisure, clergymen and moralists evinced a special urgency, for they believed that misspent time threatened one's spiritual existence. Presbyterian minister George Bethune, for instance, cautioned that wasting leisure time denied the imperative of moral and spiritual improvement. "Leisure strictly signifies unoccupied time. . . . In this nice sense of the term, we can have no leisure; for the truly virtuous and faithful will find occupation for every moment. Living in a world of so many wants, and with an immortality before us so full of reward, we can never lack an opportunity of doing good to others and profiting ourselves." In a more strident vein, South Carolina minister T. Charlton Henry blasted hedonists who squandered precious time in popular amusements, rather than using it to seek salvation. "To say that we were sent into the world merely to enjoy ourselves in its pleasures, is to utter the language of grossest sensuality . . . the very design of popular recreations is to make us insensible to the lapse of time, or in other words, to prevent it hanging heavy on our hands." By blinding people to the possibility to sudden death and divine condemnation, Charlton urged, misspent leisure threatened one's immortal soul.[8]

Others put matters even more bluntly. Pursuing "vain amusements" like "stage plays, balls, horse-racing, and gambling" not only "suppress[ed] the voice of the understanding and the dictates of the conscience" but might also provoke a swift and unexpected divine judgment. This was the message of a father-son dialogue published in Pittsburgh in 1815. The pamphlet concerned a famous fire in a Richmond, Virginia, theater four years earlier. The solicitous father viewed this "woeful calamity," which killed sixty-one people, as "a sign of the displeasure of the Almighty against plays and gambling." Vain and "trifling" amusements are evil, the father assured his son, because they "waste precious time and property. You well know," he added, "that play-actors, puppet-show masters, winners in horseraces, and in gambling, live in idleness, and often in pride and luxury." The Richmond fire was but one of many "heavy judgments" to come if people failed to mend their errant ways and continued to use their leisure time irresponsibly. As a women's magazine put it, "Let us never engage in a conversation, or amusement, or business in which we would not be willing to be found when summoned to the bar of the Eternal."[9]

In contrast to religious writers, secular admonishers cautioned against the temporal, rather than the eternal, consequences of leisure wasted in idleness. A spirit of restless industry pervaded the antebellum United States, rendering free time extremely problematic for anyone concerned with efficiency and economic progress. Americans' desire to develop and improve their new nation — not to mention their individual fortunes — made them wary of killing time in nonproductive pursuits. An "Old Merchant" writing to a Pittsburgh newspaper in 1839, for example, urged young men to exercise equal caution during their leisure and work hours:

> Be industrious, prudent, honest, and persevering — and studious to advance the permanent and best interests of your employer by strict attention to business during all the regular business hours. On the Sabbath, the 4th of July, and at all leisure times, be *prudent*, *abstemious*, sober, and strive by occupying every moment — like Dr. Franklin and other great and useful men — to improve your mind by reading good books, attending church and moral and literary societies, & c., or when mingling in society, let it be *select*, *choice*, prudent, remembering at all times the golden proverb from the best of books, "I, *Wisdom*, dwell with *Prudence*."[10]

Nor could any amount of sophistry place idleness in a better light. "In no conceivable respect," physician Daniel Drake warned a Philadelphia audience, "can idleness be a parent of virtue. All its tendencies are to vice. The *idler* is a prey to every folly. None is so much exposed to temptation: None yields himself up with so little resistance. He is the sport of circumstances. He walks into the snare, because he is too lazy to go around it." Contrasting industry and idleness, Drake reached a triumphant crescendo: "*Idleness* abridges life, and renders the longest unproductive of happy results. Finally, INDUSTRY is money, is credit, is power, is *time* itself!"[11]

Drake's harangue reflected an eighteenth-century notion of leisure that persisted well into the next century. For many Americans, leisure did not automatically mean a period reserved for fun or amusement. In fact, Americans frequently used their free time for activities we might consider to be tedious work: planting a garden, mending clothes, taking a second job, even writing a scholarly article. During the late eighteenth and early nineteenth centuries, then, leisure simply meant free time; an opportunity to engage in whatever activity, and at whatever pace, one wished, provided that one used time wisely.

The Changing Face of Work and Play in an Industrializing Society

Though freedom, opportunity, and choice were central to eighteenth-century notions of leisure, widespread concern that people might misuse their free time emerged only in the early nineteenth century. Previously, powerful constraints on individual behavior inherent in traditional agricultural society limited Americans' options and curbed their excesses. Scarce resources, abundant hard work, and communal surveillance prevented most individual abuses. In small, closely knit preindustrial towns and villages, foolish or disapproved uses of leisure risked social ostracism and exclusion from group activities.[12]

As customary restraints on free time faded with the extension of market relations and the gradual transition from agricultural to industrial society, the potential abuse of leisure became a pressing problem. Moralists and reformers found the growth of commercial amusements particularly troubling in this regard, for it severed the customary relationship between work and play. Harvest dinners, barn raisings, husking bees, and other traditional festivals encompassed both work and leisure, legitimizing play and amusement as rewards for productive labor rather than ends in themselves. Commercial amusements made it possible to enjoy leisure activities that were completely divorced from both work and communal regulation. Severing work and play, critics warned, could only lead to trouble. Cast adrift without the moral compass of family or community to guide them, the young and weak-minded could easily be corrupted by novel and provocative amusements. Or worse, the entire population might be seduced and led into idleness and vice. This possibility appeared very real, as antebellum Americans increasingly devoted their leisure to enjoyment and excitement rather than usefulness and edification.[13]

The dual processes of urbanization and territorial expansion accelerated this development. Each allowed Americans to escape the communal regulation of behavior: one, through the social distance engendered by urban anonymity; the other, through the spatial distance produced by wilderness isolation. "The burgeoning interior and the burgeoning cities," historian Paul Boyer notes, "both represented massive challenges to the established social order, and fears about the menace of the city were reinforced and intensified by the parallel menace of the wilderness." Travelers' accounts attested that frontier drunkenness, blood sports, and gambling rivaled or surpassed the excesses of urban leisure. Far from the moderating influence of civilized society, mountain men, Indian fighters, boatmen, and frontiersmen adopted raucous, violent pastimes that reflected the uncertainty and danger of their lives.[14]

Tales of frontier depravity notwithstanding, most Americans reserved their strongest condemnation for urban leisure, recounting a litany of alarming problems. Theaters, taverns, brothels, and gambling dens proliferated, concerned citizens noted ominously, providing increasing opportunities for abusing free time. Reformers considered the problem of urban leisure particularly acute because it threatened young men, the supposed lifeblood of the republic. Especially in the northeast, where land shortages constricted agricultural opportunities, country boys flocked to towns and cities in search of employment during the 1830s and 1840s. Unfamiliar with the snares of urban life, and innocent of the ways of vice, they seemed easy prey for the "heavy assaults of temptation" they inevitably encountered. The erosion of the craft system made matters worse, for it meant that apprentices and employees no longer lived under the authority and supervision of their master's household. Indignant urban dwellers pointed to young men's abuse of leisure as the dangerous consequence of increasing amounts of unsupervised free time. Bands of jobless young toughs roamed the streets, they complained, harassing passersby and fighting rival gangs. Even gainfully employed young men caused problems: groups of unmanageable apprentices congregated on street corners after work, insulting respectable citizens and making it difficult for ladies to walk the streets unescorted. "If there ever was a country in which the character of its young men was worthy to be an object of national solicitude," the Pittsburgh Young Men's Society warned in 1833, "ours is that country; and if there ever was a time when this country had reason to feel a special solicitude on this subject, that time is the present."[15]

Concerns about young men's leisure were only part of a larger reaction to genuine problems confronting American society. Drunkenness, poverty, vice, and crime did increase during the early nineteenth century, and reformers often linked them to idleness and the misuse of free time.[16] But Americans' anxiety about leisure also cut to the very heart of larger fears about their rapidly changing society and culture. When moralists railed against frivolous and immoral uses of free time, they expressed dismay at a nation that no longer conformed to eighteenth-century standards of social behavior. Americans' propensity for unruly, disorderly leisure, they feared, manifested a disregard for authority and a lack of deference and portended social disintegration. When denizens of a theater's pit pelted their social betters in the boxes with fruit and other debris, for example, or when journeymen refused to celebrate the Fourth of July with their employers, community itself seemed threatened. Leisure thus became a bellwether for much larger concerns about the transformation of the United States to an industrial society.[17]

A Growing Acceptance of Recreation and Amusement

Two developments helped to assuage these worries. First, Americans realized by the 1830s that overwork could be as destructive a vice as idleness. The compulsive drive to get ahead that accompanied nineteenth-century industrialization and economic growth made it increasingly difficult to think of anything but making money. This unyielding devotion to business extended even into Americans' leisure. Alexis de Tocqueville, for example, found it surprising that the rich, who had time to spare, nonetheless shunned inactivity or repose. He noted that "a wealthy man thinks that he owes it to public opinion to devote his leisure to some kind of industrial or commercial pursuit or to public business. He would think himself in bad repute if he employed his life solely in living." Tocqueville's countryman, Michel Chevalier, agreed. Writing of Pittsburgh, he noted that

> Nowhere in the world is everybody so regularly and continually busy as in Pittsburg; I do not believe there is on the face of the earth, including the United States, where in general very little time is given to pleasure, a single town in which the idea of amusement so seldom enters the heads of the inhabitants. . . . there is no interruption of business for six days in the week, except during the three meals, the longest of which hardly occupies ten minutes, and Sunday in the United States, instead of being, as with us, a day of recreation and gaiety, is . . . consecrated to prayer, meditation and retirement.

Or, as a Pittsburgh almanac put it in 1836, "Recreation is not being idle, but easing the wearied part by change of business."[18]

Some social critics believed that treating leisure as an extension of work encouraged people to equate the accumulation of wealth with the successful improvement of time. By the 1820s, many Americans worried that unceasing work and the pecuniary rewards it promised were becoming an unhealthy obsession in their society. In 1821 "Philadelphius" warned his countrymen against the unbridled love of money.

> For it is usually the case with those who are under its dominion, to become so infatuated with the fair exterior of worldly greatness, and the influence which the undiscerning part of mankind attach to men of wealth — instead of worth, that their energies are directed to this attainment, as that alone which is capable of imparting happiness, and exalting its possessors to the summit of human felicity.

Inattention to anything but money-making, Philadelphius warned, would turn the world "into a habitation of cruelty, where neither the rights of God or our fellow men are objects of regard."[19]

Making money to the exclusion of all else, Philadelphius and others recognized, threatened to distract people from worthier goals that might be pursued during leisure time. Samuel Nott, a popular lecturer in the 1830s, admonished "men of business and toil" not to let preoccupation with their work deprive them of leisure time. Nott enjoined the "weary farmer or mechanic, and more certainly the weary man of business" to devote at least an hour a day to "study and improvement," promising that leisure well spent not only promoted intellectual and spiritual improvement, but also enhanced one's ability to work.[20]

George Bethune also urged people not to allow industriousness and ambition to enslave them. Focusing on financial gain could easily turn a person into "a mere idolator of his own purse" and render him incapable of appreciating the "far higher ends" of one's spiritual life.

> Commerce, then, or any pursuit which is usually called business, is unworthy of being considered the proper occupation of life. It is only necessary to provide or to procure the means of living. The time devoted to it should be considered as a tax upon our immortal being, laid upon us by the necessities of that curse which sin brought with it into our world. If so, *leisure* which the necessities of business allow, becomes incalculably more precious, as being the only season when we can devote ourselves mainly and exclusively to the great end of our being.

Though reformers still worried about the social effects of immoral amusements, they recognized that excessive labor could have dire consequences beyond the impoverishment of one's spiritual life. Depleting mental capacities in the relentless pursuit of wealth overstimulated the mind and warped the judgment as surely as did idleness. Both forms of excess engendered unhealthy appetites for "vapid amusements" and "vulgar debaucheries," making proper respect for leisure essential to individual and social well-being.[21]

When juxtaposed with the cupidity and materialism that too often characterized Americans' working lives, leisure given to fun and amusement no longer appeared in such a negative light by the 1830s. If judiciously regulated, enjoyable recreation might even do more good than harm. "Let innocent amusements be invented," Daniel Drake pleaded, if only to prevent the rising generation from acquiring bad habits. Purveyors of commercial recreation capitalized on this grudging acceptance of amusement. As commercial leisure expanded without the predicted collapse of public morals, entrepreneurs argued that "moral" dramas, uplifting concerts, and educational exhibitions of curiosities provided salutary alternatives to vicious and degraded pastimes. P. T. Barnum, for example, quieted critics of his much-maligned American Museum by querying whether they would rather see work-weary citizens patronize his establishment or nearby taverns, gambling halls, and other haunts of vice.[22]

The second development that calmed Americans' fears was a growing recognition that leisure — even leisure divorced from work — could help people adapt to unprecedented social and economic developments. During the first half of the nineteenth century, Americans witnessed a number of revolutionary changes: the expansion of the market; the democratization of politics; the reformulation of gender roles, and so on. Living in a nation that denigrated traditionalism and rejected European cultural models,[23] Americans had to formulate identities and recast social relationships with little guidance. In this fast-paced and sometimes confusing cultural milieu, Americans embraced new forms of leisure to help them make sense of their changing world. Leisure thus served as the subjunctive mode of culture: inherently creative and potentially subversive.[24] It might buttress the status quo or engender alternative ideas and concepts for new and different social or political relationships. Clubs, voluntary associations, private parties, and public gatherings provided contexts in which people redefined themselves and their relationship to the larger society. Mingling with strangers at plays and concerts, judging for oneself the authenticity of "Feejee mermaids" and other humbugs, assuming leadership roles in social or civic organizations, exchanging ideas and opinions at lectures, lyceum meetings, and debates[25] — all these allowed Americans to experiment, at least temporarily, with new roles and different social arrangements. In leisure, bewildered Americans found one way to create a culture better suited to their altered social reality.

By the 1850s, the cultural transformation of leisure was already well advanced. Older conceptions of leisure as unoccupied time to be used wisely and productively were fading. In their place emerged a growing acceptance of amusement and recreation as proper uses of free time. Even Joseph Buffum eventually softened his Spartan stance on free time, though not without some reservations. Perhaps allowing himself to enjoy pastimes that amused without educating was a function of his growing affection for Maria Ramaley, whom he married, after a somewhat stormy courtship, in August 1848. More likely, the allure of new and exciting leisure activities captivated Buffum, as it did many other Americans. Circuses, menageries, plays, concerts, panoramas, balls, demonstrations of mesmerism and animal magnetism, and a host of other amusements vied for his time, attention, and money. Unable to resist their enticements but unwilling to abandon his convictions about using time wisely, Buffum faced a quandary. He, like many other Americans, resolved it by reconceptualizing leisure, ascribing value to amusement and enjoyment. After a two-month gap in his journal, Buffum revealed this change of heart: "I have been as attentive at my studies as my health would permit and have made rapid progress in them. During my leisure hours I have enjoyed different kinds of recreation and amusement as occasion presented in which I think every one ought to indulge themselves to a proper degree on account of its beneficial effects upon the wearied mind and body." Buffum came to believe that leisure — even amusing leisure — provided a necessary complement to work by alleviating its deleterious effects. Now he could improve his time even in previously questionable pursuits. "I have also heard the great tragedian [Edwin] Forrest. One does not lose time seeing him play Damon and Pythias or any of those great plays. I like very well to see a good play. I think it very instructive." Once opened, however, this Pandora's box proved difficult to close. After this somewhat strained defense of the drama, Buffum made no excuses for seeing "little

Tom T. Smith and the Sable Harmonists and the great Diorama of the funeral of Napoleon, a grand painting indeed." Two weeks before his wedding, the transformation of Buffum's attitude about leisure was all but complete: "Miss M. R[amaley] and I took a walk to the Monster Circus. They perform pretty well. Dan Rice is the greatest clown I ever saw. I laughed enough to do me a good deal of good I know."[26] Like many of his peers, Buffum came to realize that leisure could offer recreation in both senses of the word: a pleasant diversion from the demands of a bustling society, and the opportunity to create oneself anew.

Southwestern Pennsylvania in the Early 1800s

This study examines the meanings, uses, and dynamics of leisure in the lives of Americans like Joseph Buffum between 1800 and 1850. Its focus, a four-county area in southwestern Pennsylvania comprising Allegheny, Fayette, Washington, and Westmoreland counties (see map 1), offers several advantages.[27] First, the region was settled relatively late in the eighteenth century and was by 1800 still in many respects a frontier area. After the Revolution, many officers and their families settled on land grants received for military service. These predominantly Scots-Irish settlers engaged successfully in agriculture and commerce, becoming the region's first elite. After overinvesting in trade and simple industries before the War of 1812, this elite suffered economically during the postwar depression. By the 1820s, newly arrived entrepreneurs challenged the first elite's dominance by exploiting the region's abundant supply of coal, iron ore, and other raw materials. This entrepreneurial element prospered in industry and trade, and its merchants and manufacturers formed the basis of a middle class. In the process, they set southwestern Pennsylvania well on the road to an industrial society. With the advent of steam and improved roads, increasing numbers of immigrants and laborers poured into the region, swelling the working class. In short, what had been an isolated trade link to the west in 1800 became by 1850 a vibrant industrial and commercial center. This relatively rapid settlement and economic development provides a stark contrast between traditional and modern uses of free time, underlining the link between leisure and cultural change. Using 1850 as an endpoint is somewhat arbitrary, but it limits the study

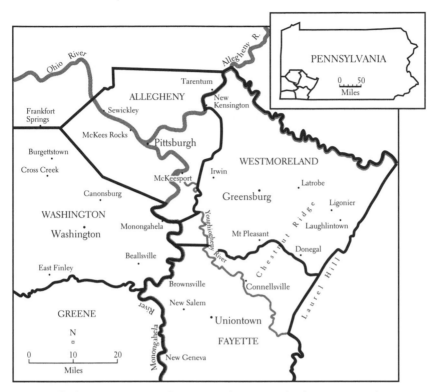

Map 1. Allegheny, Fayette, Washington, and Westmoreland Counties, with Major Towns and Landmarks

to the period before railroads again transformed the region, as the canal and turnpike booms had done two decades earlier.

Southwestern Pennsylvania's mixture of rural and urban areas offers a second advantage. Urban forces emanating outward from Pittsburgh and smaller cities like Washington and Uniontown influenced the rest of the predominantly rural area early in the century. Juxtaposed with the countryside, these centers of industry, commercialization, and demographic change highlight new developments in leisure, culture, and social relations. Further, southwestern Pennsylvania's towns and cities served as transportation centers and layovers for travelers, many of whom kept diaries and journals of their trips.[28] These sources provide a variety of perspectives on nineteenth-century Pennsylvania society and leisure.

A final, related advantage concerns the enormous demographic, economic, and political changes that occurred in southwestern Pennsylvania during the first half of the nineteenth century. Because these changes, which for heuristic purposes might be called the Market Revolution,[29] were so rapid and pronounced in the region, they place concurrent social and cultural developments in high relief. As we shall see, residents experienced and reacted to these changes in their leisure as well as their work. Indeed, people often used ideas, concepts, and values generated in and through leisure to help them to understand and react to their times. Southwestern Pennsylvanians' responses to rapid and extensive change, then, reveal the imbeddedness of leisure in other social and economic processes as well as its potential for reciprocal influence on those processes.

The body of this study consists of six chapters and an epilogue. The next chapter outlines the pattern of leisure in southwestern Pennsylvania at the turn of the nineteenth century and compares it to the customary depiction of communal pastimes in the preindustrial world. Chapter 3 examines the transformation of leisure between 1800 and 1850, demonstrating how the period's rapid changes generated or accelerated trends toward communal fragmentation, commercialization, and privatization. The following chapter uses a specific leisure activity, the celebration of the Fourth of July, to illustrate these trends over time. Chapter 5 discusses leisure and class, demonstrating the malleability of leisure as both a source of dominant ideologies and an expression of resistance to them. Leisure's importance for shaping gender roles and ideologies is the subject of chapter 6. Chapter 7 discusses attempts by various groups to regulate leisure and contends that an historical account of the changing meaning of leisure is more useful than a class-based social control model for understanding reform. Finally, a concluding chapter uses Jenny Lind's 1851 visit to Pittsburgh to sum up the study's findings and suggest some implications.

2

Cohesion and Diversity in Southwestern Pennsylvania Leisure

ANY ATTEMPT TO UNDERSTAND THE COMPLEXITY OF LEISURE in early nineteenth-century Pennsylvania must first take into account the image so often advanced by historians and social theorists of traditional agricultural society as a closely knit, relatively conflict-free community. Writing of the Pennsylvania frontier, for example, Albert Bushnell Hart contends that unanimity of feeling and neighborliness were the hallmarks of this earlier society.

> That was one of the great virtues of the frontier — the feeling of brotherhood. . . . There was a strong sense of common enterprise and a common interest which nowadays is much diminished. The pioneers knew no rivalry or frantic hatred between employers and employed; envied no undesirable plutocrats; experienced little friction between race elements.[1]

According to such accounts of traditional society, leisure activities served as a necessary social cement that bound communities together. Limited by the seasonal rhythms of an agricultural economy and relative isolation from the larger American society, preindustrial people like turn-of-the-century southwestern Pennsylvanians would have experienced a pattern of leisure in which cooperative festivals and communal amusements loomed large. Farm families could not accomplish many crucial agricultural tasks, like harvesting or barn-raising, unaided, making cooperation in work essential. At the same time, limited contact with the outside world made community-based companionship and leisure highly desirable. During Washington County's early years, one historian remembered, friends and neighbors met together and entered with "hearty good will . . . into the spirit of social amusement." Another commentator observed that southwestern Pennsylvania's first settlers were "extravagant in the noisy sports of the chase, the raising, the harvest and the husking, but frugal of all the means of quiet fireside enjoyment."[2]

The Myth of Communal Leisure and Social Harmony

However attractive and realistic this account of communal leisure and traditional agricultural society appears to be, closer scrutiny reveals it to be an oversimplification. The idyllic vision sketched in the foregoing quotations owes its influence and authority to an almost nostalgic attachment to a better, more harmonious (or at least simpler) society. For our purposes, then, the image of communal leisure in a harmonious traditional agricultural society may provide a starting point from which to explore fault lines in the community.

To begin with, accounts of all-inclusive communal festivals as cornerstones of coherent, unified traditional societies seldom mention that some elements of local society were not always welcome at these occasions. Religious, ethnic, racial, and economic divisions pervaded agricultural societies like early nineteenth-century southwestern Pennsylvania, and often found expression in leisure activities. Scots-Irish farmers may not have invited their German or African-American neighbors to a corn-husking or harvest festival, but members of both those groups had probably witnessed or participated in some form of those occasions during their lifetimes. The coexistence of these groups with the dominant Anglo-American society never necessarily reflected cohesiveness or unanimity. Southwestern Pennsylvania's relatively sparse population served to mask, though not eliminate, these differences and conflicts as late as the 1820s.

As we see in this and succeeding chapters, leisure examined in all its complexity can yield important insights on power and social dynamics in southwestern Pennsylvania's communities. Within the broad pattern of communal leisure sketched by scholars and participants, distinct leisure styles and practices not only promoted cohesion within ethnic, religious, and occupational groups but also served to differentiate those groups from others, thereby providing a sense of self-identity. The idyllic vision of traditional society and communal leisure masks this complexity. In so doing, it also hides the power relations that underpinned agricultural societies. One of the reasons that many accounts of traditional leisure highlight unanimity and social harmony was that dominant groups told the story, ignoring or suppressing any information that did not fit their desired pattern.

More than this, however, the traditional image distorts our understanding by minimizing the amount of option and complexity available in leisure. Structuralist scholars like Joffre Dumazedier, for example, contend that leisure did not even exist in societies whose work rhythms were dictated by the seasons. In this view, seasonal respites from work like the long period of inactivity during winter did not afford leisure in any meaningful sense: "Inactivity under such circumstances [winter], was something to be endured; followed (as it too often was) by a train of misfortunes, it certainly had none of the characteristics of leisure as we understand it today." Close examination of the evidence does not bear out this contention. A wealth of contemporary material attests that the seasons did not exercise total control over southwestern Pennsylvanians' free time. Nor was it the case that summer held greater pleasures, or that local residents dreaded the cold months as periods devoid of leisure.[3] Rather, they welcomed winter as a time free from hard farm work during which people could indulge their preferences for socializing, resting, reading, or other activities. Early settlers "hailed [winter] as a jubilee," for it meant both a cessation of work and freedom from the threat of Indian attacks. A local poet, for example, celebrated winter's long nights of "friendly glee":

> No brighter moments have I known, Than those which winter can
>   bestow,
> When friendship draws her circling zone, 'Mid lakes of ice, or fields
>   of snow.

"A Winter's Song" also captured this affection for winter as leisure time. The 1809 poem records an imaginary conversation between two weary lumberjacks who welcome Old Man Winter to their cabin after a hard season of lumbering.

> The louder his storms blow — the louder our mirth;
> He shall hear all our jokes while we sit round the hearth;
> Thus we'll welcome dark winter as long as he stays,
> Till his old frosty face shall look bright as the blaze.
>
> By degrees he grew merry, but still he kept sober,
> Until we had quaff'd our twelfth jug of October;
> Then reeling he roars out — "My hearties well done!
> Be my season henceforward, the season of fun."[4]

The enjoyment of winter leisure extended beyond those directly engaged in agriculture to the community at large. An 1835 almanac, for example, urged families to spend winter evenings enjoying books and domestic companionship. It enjoined the young in particular to use this free time to "read and reflect," thereby engaging in "some occupation that will give growth to the mind as well as the body." A Pittsburgh editor advised both farmers and mechanics:

> While winter lays an embargo on your operations, and shuts you up in your dwelling, let your fireside be a paradise, and let the long evenings be consumed in doing good to your fellow men, in profitable conversation, or in the pursuit of useful knowledge, especially of that knowledge which is the principal thing; that knowledge which has reference not merely to time but to eternity.[5]

Like free time during the rest of the year, winter leisure could be used wisely or squandered. The *Western Literary Messenger* contrasted the pleasures of the "the virtuous and reflecting mind" with those of the "gaudy butterflies of creation," noting that winter evenings offered opportunities for enjoyment to both. Some writers suggested ways to turn winter relaxation and leisure to one's economic advantage. Playing on Americans' desire for financial gain, the *Western Address Directory* urged anyone eager to meet prominent merchants and businessmen to travel in "THE WIN-

TER—a season when those, with whom his business was to concentrate, would have more leisure to converse, and to impart information."[6]

Nostalgia for an Idyllic Past

If the conventional image of communal leisure and traditional agricultural society ignores evidence of social divisions, masks power relations, and fails to conform to the facts, why has it retained such vitality? One answer is that it continues to seem plausible because contemporaries often painted a similar picture. Thomas Ashe, an early traveler through southwestern Pennsylvania, depicted leisure in the Pittsburgh of 1806 as simple and communal: "As for the amusements here, they are under the domination of the seasons. In winter, cariolinging or sleying predominates. . . . The summer amusements consist principally of concerts, evening walks, and rural festivals held in the vicinity of clear springs and under the shade of odiferous trees."[7]

In addition to descriptions of uncomplicated, almost innocent leisure like Ashe's, one also often encounters nostalgia in the observations of contemporaries. Writing in 1826, for instance, Pittsburgher Samuel Jones described turn-of-the-century leisure in accord with the now familiar image of an uncomplicated, unified, and harmonious agricultural society:

> The long winter evenings were passed by the humble villagers, at each others homes, with merry tale and song, or in simple games; and the hours of night sped lightly onward, with the unskilled, untiring youth, as they threaded the mazes of the dance, guided by the music of the violin, from which some good humoured rustic drew his Orphean sounds. In the jovial time of harvest and haymaking, the sprightly and active of the village, participated in the rural labours and the hearty pastimes, which distinguish that happy season. The balls and merry makings, that were so frequent in the village, were attended by all, without any particular deference to rank or riches.

Compare this glowing account with Jones' commentary on the city in 1826:

> The days of simple happiness, which were once enjoyed upon the banks of our two, aye, three pleasant streams, are gone, and it would be very silly to mourn over them. Still, we cannot help looking back, with sorrowful heart, on that time of unaffected content and gaiety, when the unambitious people

who were domiciled in the village of "Fort Pitt," or the yet unchartered town of Pittsburgh, were ignorant and careless of all the invidious distinctions, which distract and divide the inhabitants of overgrown cities.[8]

Harking back to an idyllic past must have seemed attractive to early nineteenth-century Pennsylvanians, who struggled with the rapid changes their society experienced. For people like Jones, positing a prelapsarian community offered a comforting point of reference in an uncertain world.

Unfortunately, scholars have too often viewed this nostalgic longing uncritically and accepted it as an accurate memory. For historians or social scientists eager to place differences between earlier societies and our own in high relief, the vision of close-knit, simple, and harmonious communities bound together by rustic festivals and cooperative amusements held obvious appeal. In addition, the simplistic image of traditional society recommended itself to scholars because it did make sense of *some* of the facts. Within the matrix of seasonally influenced leisure, communal festivities and neighborly amusements did play major roles. And if all individuals and groups did not join in these activities equally, all recognized and participated in variants of them. The rest of this chapter examines how well the image of communal leisure describes the situation in southwestern Pennsylvania, where it fails to render an accurate recounting of the past, and why. Many local residents' activities and experiences fit nicely into this broad pattern; even more revealing are those cases that do not.

Traditional Communal Leisure

With the foregoing caveats in mind, we can begin to examine the familiar picture of traditional communal leisure that excluded few and served the interests of all. County histories, newspaper articles, travelers' accounts, and other contemporary sources attest to the simplicity, inclusiveness, and popularity of work-related recreation and amusement. Cooperative labor undertaken in the spirit of neighborly conviviality transformed difficult tasks into "picturesque social occasion[s], not merely arduous work" and constituted an essential part of community life. The social aspect of communal work was crucial for ensuring broad participation in necessary labor and for promoting social interaction and enjoyment. Everyone in the community looked forward to a variety of these admixtures of work and play, commonly known as bees or frolics: mowing, reaping, chopping, hauling, and manuring for men, and sewing, quilting, flax pulling, scutching, and apple butter making for women. To outsiders, the leisure aspects of communal gatherings sometimes seemed to predominate, often leaving less than favorable impressions of rural life. Poet and traveler Sally Hastings, for instance, recalled her experiences at a corn-husking frolic on Chestnut Ridge in 1808: "they devoted the night to Dancing, Singing, and other Exercises, the names of which my Ear did not communicate. . . . From the Noise and Discord, which the Ballroom exhibited, we began to fancy ourselves in the neighborhood of Pandemonium."[9]

Work-related frolics were so interwoven in the fabric of southwestern Pennsylvania life that residents seldom mentioned them unless something untoward occurred. In 1816 the *Washington Reporter*, for example, recounted an accident in Amwell Township during a corn-husking frolic. In the course of "throwing the shoulder stone," a test of strength similar to the shot put, a man died after being "hit in the chest by a stone thrown by Mr. H. Vankirk's blackman (Caesar)." Similarly, the *Greensburg Gazette* reported in 1828 that Tobias Byers was killed by a falling log at a barn raising in Westmoreland County's Derry Township.[10]

Mishaps sometimes proceeded from using whiskey, that "essential element" at gatherings of all sorts, as a lubricant for work and leisure. Laborers expected their hosts to treat them to frequent draughts from the "green-glass, long-knecked quart bottle," which one historian claims enjoyed the status of a "kind of a household god . . . present at nearly every occasion." This reliance on liquor to foster the raucous fun associated with cooperative labor could produce tragic results. At an 1823 manure-hauling frolic in Washington County, for instance, William Crawford became enraged at his stepson Henry over a long-standing family dispute. After drinking with some friends, Crawford shot and killed the young man.[11]

Not all leisure occasions, tragic or otherwise, were related to work. Numerous communal celebrations enlivened the routine daily life of southwestern Pennsylvanians: weddings, funerals, and infrequent hangings never failed to draw large crowds. Weddings offered an opportunity

for merrymaking and a show of community support for its members; perhaps ironically, funerals played a similar role in community life. When
an entire family died suddenly of food poisoning in Fayette County, an
unusual throng of relatives and strangers, estimated at between 1,000 and
1,500, attended the funeral. Between eight and fifteen thousand people
gathered to witness the execution of William Crawford. The large crowd
became so unruly that the militia was required to keep order.[12]

Patriotic occasions and militia muster days also provided opportunities for communal celebration and leisure. The Fourth of July, always an
important festival, is discussed in chapter 4. Lesser patriotic occasions also
called for observance. A public dinner at Simon Drum's inn in Greensburg honored returning war hero Captain Markle in 1813; an illumination
of Pittsburgh in 1814 commemorated U.S. land and naval victories against
the British. In 1825, General Lafayette's visit to southwestern Pennsylvania
produced parades, dinners, and celebrations throughout the region, often
sponsored or orchestrated by local militia units wishing to honor their
revolutionary hero.[13] Militia units also fostered communal leisure
through their sponsorship of muster days. Ostensibly training days, musters were community festivals devoted more to dancing, courting, and
drinking than to drills and martial exercise. Sometimes producing larger
gatherings than even the Fourth of July celebration, muster days were
major leisure occasions. Booths erected around the parade ground sold
food and refreshments, bands played for the entertainment of the crowds,
and soldiers and civilians alike engaged in arguments, fistfights, and af-
frays to settle differences and let off steam. To the uninitiated, this good
fun sometimes appeared to be the unruly actions of a belligerent, drunken
mob. Sally Hastings, fresh from her encounter with the pandemonium
of a corn-husking frolic, witnessed a militia muster in Greensburg the
following day. That "being the day of a Public Review," Hastings recorded
in her journal, "the Town was full of riotous People." She disdained the
heavy drinking that characterized the proceedings, attributing to it the
eventual brawling of Greensburg's citizen-soldiers.[14]

Another much anticipated communal celebration was the annual
round of horse racing, which usually took place in the fall after the harvest
season. Despite the activity's proscription by state law, many localities in
the region hosted horse races. McKeesport in Allegheny County held

races as early as 1800, and the irrepressible Sally Hastings attended public races in Greensburg eight years later. Many race sponsors flouted the law and advertised their events in the newspapers: the Pittsburgh races in 1800 and the Williamsport races in 1809 were both advertised, as were the 1814 races in New Geneva and Uniontown in Fayette County. Ignoring their illegality, southwestern Pennsylvanians greeted races as festivals offering excitement and entertainment for the entire community.[15]

Henry Marie Brackenridge recorded the communal spirit excited by horse races in his reminiscences of turn-of-the-century Pittsburgh. The annual races, held at the foot of Grant's Hill, were

> Then an affair of all-engrossing interest, and every business and pursuit was neglected during their continuance. The whole town was daily poured forth to witness the Olympian games, many of all ages and sexes as spectators, and many more either directly or indirectly interested in a hundred different ways. The Plain within the course, and near it, was filled with booths as at a fair, where everything was sold, and eaten or drunk — where every fifteen or twenty minutes there was a rush to some part, to witness a *fisticuff*— where dogs barked and bit, and horses trod on men's toes, and booths fell down on people's heads![16]

Despite changes in form and setting, horse racing continued to fascinate southwestern Pennsylvanians throughout our period. Whether sponsored by a group of local sportsmen, a locality, or a tavern, horse races persisted as an important community focal point.[17] Though not everyone had a direct interest in the outcome of the race itself, the entire community benefited from an opportunity to gather, socialize, and interact in a leisure setting.

Such was also the case with agricultural fairs, school examinations, and spelling bees. Not everyone had a prize farm animal, a college-aged relative, or a child in grammar school, but most local residents concerned themselves with the outcome of the annual plowing match, literary contest, and spell-off. These events allowed individuals to express a competitive spirit, either by direct participation or through moral (and sometimes vocal) support of favorite contestants, all in the supportive milieu of community solidarity. Agricultural fairs in particular were pivotal leisure events for many localities. In Washington, for instance, not even the exigencies of the harvest could dampen enthusiasm for the fair. At the 1822 fair there was good attendance by ladies and farmers, despite it being "the busy season of the year." For Washingtonians, the agricultural fair affirmed community spirit and social harmony: an account of the 1823 fair proudly contrasted it with the rancor and divisiveness of party politics, which, unlike the fair, were "conducted by the Many for the Benefit of the Few."[18]

School examinations, literary contests, debates, and spelling bees also enhanced people's sense of community by exhibiting the intellectual attainments of local young people while allowing friendly partisanship and competition. School examinations were the least competitive of these occasions in that they pitted students more against their examiners than each other. Usually held in the fall or spring, they were always local favorites that drew considerable crowds. Though ostensibly for students' friends and family, large segments of the community often became involved. At a public exhibition of Latin scholars in Greensburg in 1802, for instance, the militia turned out to provide music for the audience that had gathered to witness the proceedings. Four years later, when Sally Hastings attended the commencement of Jefferson College in Canonsburgh, Washington County, she noted that "the Streets are crowded, and all is Life and Activity." In Claysville, Washington County, frequently there was not even standing room available in the packed examination hall. At a lower educational level, spelling bees and youth debate clubs garnered much interest and support. Spelling bees that pitted one school against another usually attracted the most spectators. These popular events occurred in the Pittsburgh area early in the nineteenth century, and spread to Greensburg, Adamsburg, Irwin, and other parts of Westmoreland County as early as 1825.[19]

Women's Leisure

In addition to communal leisure, individual leisure activities also engaged southwestern Pennsylvanians. Though not directly dependent on the community, individual leisure often reproduced patterns and divisions found in group leisure. Division by gender, which was central to the work-play pattern of frolics and bees, also characterized solitary leisure. Typically, the home provided a focal point for women's leisure, just as it did for women's work.[20] Whether it was self-improvement through music, art, and handicrafts, or merely socializing with female friends, women's leisure revolved around their roles as homemaker, wife, and mother. Domestic work and daily chores usually kept women busier than did the labor of their male counterparts, limiting their leisure time even further. Any free time would likely be devoted to family-based leisure that not only celebrated the domestic unit but also displayed it for others to admire. Henry Marie Brackenridge remembered that around the turn of the century, Pittsburgh's Grant's Hill was "the favorite promenade in fine weather, and on Sunday afternoon. It was pleasing to see the line of well-dressed ladies and gentlemen, and children, nearly the whole population, repairing to this beautiful green eminence."[21] The task of insuring that this sort of leisure was "pleasing to see" — that the family was well dressed, fed, and the like — fell largely to women.

The dual imperatives of housework and self-improvement occupied most of a woman's time, making formal leisure activities with other women difficult to fit in. Beyond quiltings and occasions when "a large company of women would meet to welcome a new accession to the family," gatherings of women alone were rare. Women had to content themselves with informal socializing during the course of their everyday activities, though the women of two families might occasionally exchange visits.[22] The routine of everyday life made solitary leisure more feasible for many women: needlepoint, knitting, or filigree work could be pursued in odd moments not occupied by other domestic or familial duties.

Unmarried women had perhaps more free time than wives, but their leisure, too, was linked to the home in that it centered around courtship, marriage, and family. Promenades, walks, dances, and concerts allowed young women to meet and socialize with men outside their homes, but these activities were usually directed toward finding a marriage partner and, ultimately, starting a household and family. In Elizabeth, Allegheny County, Rairden Spring provided medicinal waters and a picnic spot, "the destination of many lovesick young couples in their evening rambles." If young people desired less secluded leisure and courtship, they might opt for a buggy or sleigh ride to a country inn. At the Fayette Springs Hotel in Fayette County, for instance, "merry parties of young folks from Uniontown and elsewhere were accustomed to assemble and enjoy a hearty supper, engage in the dizzy mazes of the dance, and when it was all over 'go home with the girls in the morning.' " Likewise in Washington County, parties of young men and women drove to taverns as distant as ten miles from town to eat, dance, and socialize.[23]

Men's Leisure

If women's leisure was closely linked to the home, men's leisure was often separate from it. Though men engaged in the family-based and communal leisure that included both sexes, they also carved out a distinctly male preserve that excluded women. Men could make this division seem natural and necessary with reference to the cultivation of frontier skills like hunting, fishing, and other sports that preserved a society's vitality even after the recession of the wilderness. Militia service, too, required the maintenance of shooting, tracking, and riding skills. These activities, which men argued were necessary (at least early in the century) for protection and the destruction of predators, were thought to be simply too rigorous for women.

In southwestern Pennsylvania as elsewhere, hunting and shooting were always popular male pastimes. Travelers testified to the region's suitability for this staple of male leisure, heaping praise on its abundant hunting grounds. Writing of Finkle's Inn at the summit of Laurel Mountain in 1809, Joshua Gilpin observed that the "forest and stream round this house abound with every thing which can render it the favorite spot for a Sportsman to repose. The streams are full of fine trout, & the woods have plenty of Deer, Bear, & Turkies." Philip Nicklin, another traveler, also commented on the fine hunting and fishing in and around Fayette County in the 1830s. In Westmoreland County, locals and travelers seeking field sports frequented Jones's Mills, an area rich in game.[24]

Hunting, shooting, and fishing promoted male camaraderie partly because they sparked interest and conversation and bound together assemblies of men even after the actual activities were finished. Skill and prowess in field sports could be compared, discussed, and disputed, all in the context of male sociability and good fellowship. The *Pittsburgh Gazette* remarked in 1812, for example, on a large sunfish caught in the

Allegheny and put in a pond for the "angling fraternity" to inspect. Debates over marksmanship were doubtless common at the Sun, Moon, and Seven Stars Tavern in Greensburg, for the establishment maintained a patch of sloping land to the south called the Bullet Ground, as a site for shooting matches.[25]

Men made taverns, inns, reading rooms, and stores into centers of this kind of male sociability. Here they regaled their fellows with hunting and fishing stories, argued politics, and discussed community affairs. These local gathering points provided all-male havens for reading, drinking, talking, and enjoying a variety of diversions and entertainments without the distractions of wives and children. In Canonsburgh, Washington County, the shaded arbor behind Henry Westbay's Black Horse Tavern became a "favorite resort for convivialists," while in Claysville, the local barroom hosted the "village senate" long into the fifties. These establishments offered their predominantly male clientele a variety of entertainment ranging from billiards, cards, and cockfights to live music and collections of reading material. The spectrum of activities was striking: Greensburg's Bunker Hill Tavern gave "riotous men" the opportunity to "indulge in the sport of cock-fighting and other sports of doubtful character," while Boyle Irwin's Pittsburgh Coffee Room offered patrons "a selection of the best news-papers, novels, histories, and works of literature and taste."[26]

Much of the male sociability at inns and taverns revolved around drinking. Whiskey, rum, ale, and beer lubricated men's tongues and added hilarity to otherwise mundane affairs. The Prospect Hill Tavern in Uniontown, for example, allowed neighborhood residents to enliven their otherwise routine existences with evenings spent drinking and gossiping. If liquor made the mundane seem exciting, it also made the banal seem profound. Samuel Young remembered the back room of Kennedy McKee's Pittsburgh grocery store, where "day after day and night after night," the neighborhood's "choice spirits" assembled. After "loading up with the pure juice, [they] would open arguments on various important subjects." Overindulgence in the "pure juice" sometimes turned philosophical discussions ugly. In 1818 James Flint witnessed three fights in Bayardstown, a village just outside Pittsburgh:

These originated from private quarrels in taverns. The combatants sallied from them to the street, where the battles were fought in the presence of the passengers. There are five taverns in this place; of course only two of them escaping being scenes of action. This is not in perfect agreement with the character of sobriety, absence of dissipation and gross vices, that a late describer of Pittsburgh has given its people.

Sometimes alcoholic excess had far worse consequences. Drunkenness frequently produced "great disorder and much tumult, amounting almost to riot," at a tavern on Washington County's Egg Nog Hill. On one particularly egregious occasion, a melee among patrons became so serious that the Washington county militia had to be called in to restore order.[27]

Men also established formal leisure organizations and clubs to augment, and perhaps to curb the excesses of, their informal sociability. Many southwestern Pennsylvanian men found Freemasonry especially attractive. Ancient York Masons chartered a lodge in the region as early as 1785, and the Free and Accepted Masons followed suit by 1798. In many ways, the Masonic lodge was the quintessential all-male retreat. Freemasonry served both work and leisure interests, providing business connections and an excuse to leave the domestic sphere on a regular basis for monthly meetings and annual celebrations on St. John the Baptist's and St. John the Evangelist's feast days. In addition, membership in a lodge offered male fellowship in a secure environment, and the excitement of secret ritual.[28] By 1815 Pittsburgh boasted four Masonic organizations; lodges also sprang up in Washington, Uniontown, Monongahela City, Greensburg, and several other towns and villages in the region.[29]

Freemasonry was not the only organized male leisure: debating, literary, scientific, and even theatrical societies enjoyed varying degrees of popularity during the early nineteenth century. Because of its population and wealth, Pittsburgh became a center for these organizations, though other towns also garnered their share of clubs and associations. As early as 1802, the "young gentlemen" of Washington banded together to perform amateur theatricals for charity; in Pittsburgh, two societies, one composed of "students of law," the other of "respectable mechanics," produced entertainments. For the more refined, the Pittsburgh Chemical and Physiological Society invited "Lovers of Science" to a lecture on nitrous oxide in 1814, while a "dozen gentlemen of the town" formed the Pittsburgh

Apollonian Society to perform instrumental music for "respectable" spectators. Trade, civic, and professional groups with leisure functions also proliferated. After belonging to a literary society during his Jefferson College days, Henry Marie Brackenridge formed a legal debate society with "the younger members of the bar and the students" in 1807. Similar organizations of manufacturers, called mechanical societies, flourished in Pittsburgh, Washington, and elsewhere.[30]

Commercial Leisure

Some commercial leisure supplemented communal and individual activities, but southwestern Pennsylvania's relative isolation in the early years of the century limited both its variety and quantity. In most parts of the region, public entertainment was rare and mostly for men, women being either excluded or segregated in many commercial amusements. This gender division further diminished women's already meager access to leisure but also impoverished the male experience: small towns could not offer large enough audiences of men to attract traveling performers. Greensburg, the largest town in Westmoreland County, for example, received visits from only two commercial entertainments before 1815. Sol Smith, a traveling actor who toured southwestern Pennsylvania in the early 1820s, shed light on the reason for this dearth of entertainment. While in Pittsburgh, Smith and some companions made a side trip to Greensburg to present songs, dramatic recitations, and scenes from *Richard III*, in the hope of earning some extra money. To their dismay, the audience was so small that they earned only enough to pay for "lights, lodging and supper."[31]

In larger population centers like Pittsburgh and Washington, the story was somewhat different, but transportation problems and small audiences still limited commercial entertainment to itinerant actors, acrobats, and performers. Commercial theater began in Pittsburgh as early as 1803, when touring actors stopped there to give performances; in Washington, traveling thespians offered comedy and farce by 1812. Because their stopping points usually lacked formal theaters, peripatetic entertainers often used public buildings for their exhibitions. Henry Marie Brackenridge remembered that Pittsburgh's old courthouse, the third story of William Irwin's tavern, served as an improvised stage:

> Nor was this attic region exclusively appropriated to the administration of justice; it was also the village theater where Punch and Judy, and the Babes in the woods were exhibited to an admiring audience — where feats on the tight rope and slack wire were performed, and where, wonderful to tell, the performer spouted flames from his fiery mouth.[32]

Circuses, animal shows, and menageries also drew sizable crowds. An elephant was exhibited in Pittsburgh and Greensburg in 1808; in 1810 Pittsburghers could view an Asian tiger at a local tavern. By 1814, animal exhibitions had become more elaborate. A traveling showman displayed his "Museum of Living Animals" to astonished Pittsburghers for a mere twenty-five cents (children half-price). The museum's owner bowed to public opinion by reserving a separate show times for ladies, so they could avoid the noise and disturbances caused by his male patrons.[33]

For the more intellectually minded, lectures and concerts were sometimes available, both from local and distant orators. In Pittsburgh, Doctor Aigster, a professor at the Pittsburgh Academy, offered a public lecture series on chemistry by subscription in 1811; the Reverend John Taylor presented a lecture series on astronomy for five dollars per quarter the following year. Traveling orators and singers also occasionally visited southwestern Pennsylvania. In 1813 local papers excitedly reported the arrival of a Mr. Ogilvie, a popular and well-known orator, while in 1820 lovers of music looked forward to vocal concerts by Mr. Garner, who had recently toured the principal eastern cities. For those in active pursuit of refined diversions, a growing number and variety of teachers offered lessons in music, dance, and fencing. Like other purveyors of commercial leisure, these instructors often segregated or excluded women from male pursuits. Doctor Bainbridge, a Pittsburgh music teacher, restricted his students to "gentlemen," and Uniontown dancing academies routinely established different times of instruction for men and women.[34]

Ethnic and Religious Differences

From the forgoing it might be tempting to assume that gender differences in leisure were the major divisions in an otherwise coherent, unified pattern of individual and communal leisure. But this would ignore the diversity of leisure practices and leave unexamined the simplistic image of traditional society discussed above. As noted earlier, ethnic, religious, and occupational groups used leisure to promote cohesion within their own ranks and to foster a sense of self-identity by distinguishing their group from others. This dual process of cohesion and differentiation becomes clear upon consideration of ethnic and religious differences in leisure. Four groups deserve special attention because of their numbers and relative importance in the region: the Scots-Irish; Germans; Irish; and African Americans. Each of these groups developed ethnic organizations with significant leisure functions.

An important example was the militia company. Because of their early preeminence in the region, the Scots-Irish often established and controlled military units that, though ostensibly representative of the entire community, were in fact ethnically homogeneous. As other ethnic groups populated southwestern Pennsylvania they followed suit, frequently dropping the pretense of communal inclusiveness in favor of a more overt celebration of their heritages and values. The coexistence of ethnic militia companies in the close proximity of a town or village sometimes produced rivalry rather than harmony. Thus, in Washington, two militia companies engaged in (usually) mock battles on muster days: "Almost yearly a battle occurred between the [Scots-Irish dominated] Blues and the Dutch company out in what is now part of Wade Avenue. The marching and counter-marching, the strategy of the respective commanders, received the approval of the boys"[35] and other spectators.

Ethnic militia companies also emerged in Pittsburgh. The German Grays joined the Pittsburgh Light Artillery for a Fourth of July celebration in 1829; two decades later, German militia membership had grown to the extent that a German battalion was formed. Nor were the Irish inactive in military matters. Pittsburgh was home to the Irish Greens and the Hibernian Greens, among other Irish companies. Often these military units would be organized with the help of a local tavern owner, especially where, as in Greensburg, different taverns catered to Irish and German patrons.[36]

Southwestern Pennsylvania's German population used leisure activities and practices to maintain their language and cultural identity. This inclination was readily apparent to travelers. In 1802, F. A. Michaux noted that the Germans living near Greensburg "assist each other in their harvests, live happy among themselves, always speak German, and preserve as much as possible, the customs of their ancestors, formerly from Europe." Sixteen years later James Flint observed that although most Germans in Adamsburg could speak English, their "conversation with one another is in German, and a clergyman in the neighborhood preaches in that language." Leisure aided in this preservation of German culture by offering Germans a sense of identity and a place in the community. The Turner movement, for example, gave Germans an ethnically based leisure activity that won the admiration (and often imitation) of the larger community.[37]

Ethnic music was another extremely popular activity, and German bands abounded. Teachers specializing in German music and coffeehouses catering to Germans provided entertainment and a sense of solidarity within the group, while appearances by German performers in public concerts and civic functions promoted a sense of identity within the community. In 1837, for instance, a "band of German musicians" from Pittsburgh amused traveler Lucy Ann Higbee and her companions during their trip on a canal boat. German bands apparently found widespread acceptance and approval: in 1848, a large procession headed by a local German band greeted volunteers returning to Pittsburgh from the Mexican War.[38]

The Irish too developed distinct leisure activities and practices. In contrast to the Germans, who maintained relatively informal leisure organizations until the 1840s, the Irish established formal ethnic clubs early in the century. In 1802, Pittsburgh's Irish residents met to consider a constitution for the formation of a Hibernian Society; in 1808, a "Meeting of Naturalized Irishmen" took place at Moses Williams's house. The Sons of Erin also originated around that time, while the Erin Benevolent Society arose somewhat later. All these organizations allowed Irish men to socialize and celebrate together, thereby promoting group solidarity and ethnic unity. At the same time, ethnic leisure also helped the Irish to work out their place in American culture. Saint Patrick's Day celebrations, for instance, were ideal times to both celebrate Irish traditions and develop ideas about Irish-American patriotism. Toasts at these occasions often lauded Irish heritage and American patriotism while condemning the common enemy, Britain.[39]

Leisure also allowed the Irish to mediate divisions and disagreements within their own ranks. Recent immigrants and long residents of Irish descent sometimes saw their relation to the larger community and society differently. How strident should public anti-British sentiment be among Irish-Americans, and how should it be expressed so as to avoid alienating large segments of the community? Leisure provided the means and context for addressing these problems. In 1807, both the Sons of Erin and the Sons of Hibernia commemorated St. Patrick's Day with dinners in Pittsburgh. The Sons of Erin, a group more sympathetic to the political mainstream, met at the Sign of President Jefferson, which also served as the wigwam for the local chapter of the Tammany Society. The Sons invited everyone to their celebration, presenting themselves as members in good standing of the local community:

> Men of generous feelings of all nations were invited — the American, the German, the Frenchman, the Scotchman and the Englishman, associated with the Irishman, to celebrate the day. All distinctions, political and religious, were melted down into that of good citizen and brother.

In contrast, the Sons of Hibernia celebration appears to have been more exclusively Irish, and much more anti-British.[40] The celebratory form, then, allowed different groups to develop their own ideas of what it meant to be Irish in America, and to articulate notions of self-identity, ethnicity, and community.

Like the Irish and Germans, southwestern Pennsylvania's black population used leisure to define themselves and their place in the community. The region in general, and especially Pittsburgh and Washington, contained a substantial free African American population early in the nineteenth century. Though organized black leisure emerged somewhat later than its white equivalent, African Americans fashioned for themselves many of the same leisure organizations and practices from which whites excluded them. African-American leisure ranged from informal "Negro balls" (in the predominantly black suburb of Pittsburgh called Hayti) to church picnics, ladies' fairs, and Christmas "Soirees" sponsored by black congregations. Like their white counterparts, black men organized Masonic lodges that offered a chance for male sociability and fraternization without the interference of women.[41]

Black Masonic lodges and church groups served the needs and desires of their constituencies, but they also demonstrated to the white community African Americans' ability to live respectable lives in both work and leisure. Though their reliance on and imitation of white middle-class models was perhaps misplaced, African Americans realized that their leisure behavior and choices influenced white perceptions of them. This consciousness of their visibility was especially clear in black organizations geared toward providing respectable leisure. As early as 1823, Washington's black population considered sobriety to be crucial to a respectable public image. The organizers of an "African Camp Meeting" forbade "spirituous drink within 3 miles" of the event to reduce the risk of drunkenness. African Americans also established temperance societies on the model of white organizations but with a distinctive urgency and mission. The Temperance Society of the Coloured People of Pittsburgh, for example, rehearsed all the standard temperance arguments for sobriety but added that it was especially important for free blacks to be sober, industrious citizens because they had to serve as examples to the white community of the worthiness of *all* African Americans for freedom.[42]

The dual imperative of promoting group solidarity and defining the group's place in the community also led all four ethnic groups to celebrate holidays differently. The Scots-Irish, for example, celebrated all the standard civic holidays, usually taking prominent positions in the committees of arrangement. In addition, they observed occasions important primarily to them. H. M. Brackenridge remembered fondly that among the "inhabitants of Pittsburgh were some [of] Scottish origin or descent, who on the anniversary of St. Andrew, (30th of November) were accustomed to celebrate the festival." Robert Burns's birthday was another holiday for the Scots-Irish; in 1832 Burns's admirers in Pittsburgh sponsored a dinner in his honor.[43] We have already seen how the Irish observed St. Patrick's Day as part of their ethnic heritage; they also celebrated American civic holidays in a distinctly Irish manner. Irish "repealers" chose to commemorate the anniversary of American independence with strident calls for the repeal of the union between Ireland and Britain, often pressing Irish militia units into the service of the cause. African Americans and Germans also imparted their own flavor to civic celebrations. Though joining in general electoral victory celebrations, Germans also held their own ethnic festivities if the victory was especially auspicious for their group or favored candidate. African Americans were in a difficult position on civic holidays because of their lack of access to the political system. How could they celebrate the equality of all men on the Fourth of July, when Pennsylvania denied the franchise to every black man, free or slave? Some black Pennsylvanians did celebrate Independence Day, emphasizing their patriotism even if they were excluded from white civic exercises. Others deemphasized the Fourth as a cause for black celebration, choosing instead to celebrate August 1, the anniversary of West Indian emancipation.[44]

Ethnic culture and custom also imbued religious holidays and informal leisure occasions with different meanings and flavors. German gatherings, for instance, were much less restrained in drinking, laughter, and gaiety than their Scots-Irish counterparts. Germans emphasized different bees and frolics than did the Scots-Irish (the apple butter bee was an especial German favorite), and the groups' commemoration of religious holidays also differed. The staunch Scots-Irish Presbyterians of southwestern Pennsylvania proscribed celebrations of Christmas, Easter, and New Year's because they considered them to be "popish" practices. In Claysville, Washington County, the "people were too Scotch-Irish to attach any significance to Christmas. A New Year's call was a thing unheard of. Still, both Christmas and the New Year were recognized by big dinners and often by the traditional country ball." Individual congregations also kept their own traditions. At Beulah Presbyterian Church near Pittsburgh, communion season held special meaning. After fasting on the preceding Thursday and attending a Saturday service, Beulah's congregation celebrated the sacrament in a lengthy Sabbath-day service. They spent the following Monday visiting, socializing, and celebrating.[45]

For some Scots-Irish Presbyterians, the contrast to German leisure extended even further. Particularly strict congregations permitted harvest festivals, Thanksgiving dinners, and family visits but believed that balls and dances smacked of frivolity and moral laxity. The Presbyterian Synod of Pittsburgh condemned both "ardent spirits" and "balls and other places of fashionable amusement," concluding that "attendance upon balls, dances, routs, theatrical exhibitions, and other vain amusements, is censurable in the members of our church." Presbyterians took this condemnation of fashionable amusements to heart. The elders at Beulah Presbyterian Church forbade horse races, card playing, and cockfighting and urged pious church members to report infractions to the session. Even Pittsburgh's fashionable First Presbyterian Church disciplined liquor selling and theater attendance as late as 1834, also taking a stand against "card parties and dancing."[46]

Occupational Differences

Like religious and ethnic divisions, occupation also generated distinctive leisure patterns and practices. Trade groups sponsored parades and processions; steamboat owners banded together for trips and celebrations; and professional groups composed of doctors and lawyers met to socialize and discuss their respective callings.[47] Working class patterns of leisure highlighted differences among occupational groups. Stage drivers and boatmen, for example, evolved two distinct leisure styles, even though both worked in the transportation business and both enjoyed consuming large quantities of whiskey in their free time. The drivers, known as "pike boys," frequented taverns like Brown's Tavern in Fayette County. Brown's, a popular resort for "dancing and revelry," had the added advantage of being close to Jockey's Hollow, a spot renowned for its frequent cockfights and horse races. The Sheep's Ear and Bull's Head Inns in Fayette County also catered to wagoners and stage drivers who wanted to "while away" the long winter evenings in drinking and socializing. The pike boys apparently eschewed gentility, as a reference in an 1826 almanac to "Solomon Lightcap's *Crack-loo* Wagon tavern, alias the *Lion's Den*" suggests. For all their drinking and carousing, however, they maintained both good humor and good reputation. Samuel Young recalled that there "was no class of men engaged in any special calling that enjoyed it more than the jolly, hard-working and constantly exposed drivers of the popular, old Conestogas." This "jolly set" of carefree workers enjoyed talking, singing, demonstrations of magic and ventriloquism, and practical jokes as much as drinking.[48]

Boatmen, too, established distinct patterns of leisure and frequented their own gathering places. Andrew Fulton's bell and whistle shop on the Pittsburgh waterfront became the steamboatmen's favorite haunt. Fulton reserved a spacious room in his building especially for boatmen, who congregated there when in port. In contrast to the pike boys, however, boatmen found it difficult to retain either good humor or good reputation. The boatman's life was difficult and dangerous, often alternating long spells of indolence with short periods of intense labor and hardship. As Timothy Flint put it, the boatman's "peculiar way of life has given origin not only to an appropriate dialect, but to new modes of enjoyment, riot, and fighting."[49] The boatmen's penchant for drunkenness, boasting, and violence, exemplified in the larger-than-life figure of Mike Fink, led travelers and locals alike to a poor opinion of boatmen and their leisure pursuits. Accounts of brutal violence were common. Samuel Young remembered that many "ugly fights happened along the canal; but the most severe struggles were frequent along the Monongahela wharf," where boatmen and draymen fought. Young himself was involved in a riot along the wharf, and the Pittsburgh press often reported savage fights among boatmen, some of which led to fatalities. Not surprisingly, respectable society held boatmen in low esteem. Mrs. Houston, a British traveler who journeyed on the Pennsylvania Canal in the late 1840s, noted that boatmen were "generally lawless, reckless characters, and bear but an indifferent reputation for honesty and the rest of the social duties." Similarly, a historian of Sewickley, an Allegheny County town on the Monongahela River, observed that the old names of the town, "Dogtown, Contention, and the Devil's Race Track are regrettable memories reminiscent, probably, of the days of the keelboatmen and squatters along the river who once formed a considerable part of the community. These 'hardy frontiersmen,' as we delight to call them, were in reality a lawless, roistering, and illiterate lot."[50]

A distinction similar to the one drawn between pike boys and boatmen also characterized the leisure of journeyman and common laborers. Journeymen and mechanics sometimes celebrated extravagantly, travelers noted, but on the whole their leisure activities were not destructive or morally reprehensible. While in Pittsburgh in 1817, Henry Fearon discovered that "mechanics in every occupation met at Carey's Porter House" to socialize and discuss politics, work, and current affairs. Fearon added that they were "chiefly English, and all discontented with America." Perhaps to soothe this discontent, some journeymen overindulged in recreation and amusement. Morris Birkbeck noted in 1817 that many Pittsburgh journeymen "are improvident, and thus they remain journeymen for life. It is not, however, in absolute intemperance and profligacy, that they in general waste their surplus earnings; it is in excursions and entertainments. Ten dollars spent at a ball is no rare result of the gallantry of a Pittsburgh Journeyman." Despite this failing, journeymen and mechanics formed trade associations and purely social organizations to promote both fellowship and economic interest. Pittsburgh carpenters, for example, formed a journeymen's association that met at various coffee-houses to socialize and discuss labor matters. Monongahela City mechanics established a band that served as a social club and an informal benevolent society that provided mournful music at the funerals of its members.[51]

In contrast, the common laborer's leisure consisted (or so it seemed to observers) of drunkenness and brutish revelry. John Palmer observed in 1817 that smoking "segars, and whiskey and cherry bounce drinking, is a habit to which the working class are considerably addicted." While Palmer's censure may have applied to mechanics as well as laborers, most observers reserved special condemnation for workers who occupied the lowest rung on the economic ladder, the Irish and free blacks. James Flint reported that both groups swore freely. He lamented that the general industriousness of these populations did "not prevail to [bring about the] extinction of dissipation." According to Flint, some southwestern Pennsylvanians affirmed that the "low Irish are the most immoral of the population." Birkbeck also considered the low Irish prone to whiskey drinking and little better than the free blacks of the region. While foreign travelers' comments obviously reflect their class and ethnic biases, as well as those of their informants, there is some reason to believe that the leisure of the poorest segments of the working class did reflect badly on that population, even in the eyes of their American contemporaries.[52]

Cultural Redefinition and Experimentation Through Leisure

This variation in leisure style and practice points to a community vastly different from those usually associated with either traditional agricultural

society or small-town America. Though a broad pattern of customary leisure comprised of bees, frolics, muster days, school exams, and the like
provided a common ground for a variety of groups, diverse practices,
forms, and emphases developed within that pattern. Leisure served not
to join the community together in a seamless social garment but rather
to allow a number of social, occupational, ethnic, religious, and gender
groups to define themselves and their place in the community. Not all
groups could use leisure activities as effectively as others: women, African
Americans, the Irish, and elements of the working class experienced grave
social and economic disabilities that leisure alone could not remedy. Yet
leisure at least offered the possibility of resistance to social stereotypes and
dominant ideologies through cultural redefinition and experimentation.[53]
This potential became increasingly important as waves of demographic,
economic, and social change swept over southwestern Pennsylvania in
the early decades of the nineteenth century.

3

The Transformation of Leisure

Commercialization, Fragmentation, and Privatization

SURVEYING PITTSBURGH IN 1826, Samuel Jones noted the many improvements and benefits that the city enjoyed as a result of its transition from a trading town to an industrializing city. Pittsburghers "stoutly maintain[ed]," Jones averred, that

> when the projected water-works, the national armory, and the grand canals shall be completed; when the obstructions in the Ohio, above Wheeling are removed, and when the contemplated indications of immense improvement, in and about the city are realized, we shall be the most manufacturing, commercial, and altogether flourishing community west of the mountains, not excepting *Wheeling*, Cincinnati, or Louisville.

"Yet what have we gained," Jones asked plaintively, "by our growth in wealth and population, in manufactures, trade, and all other desirable things, compared with the artless manners, and delightful amusements, which we have lost?" Where "are our pleasant, social tea-drinkings; our sturdy blind-man's bluff . . . the strawberry huntings; the unclassed balls; the charming promenades[?] . . . Many of us are, as a direct consequence, often sadly at a loss how to dispose of a leisure hour."[1]

Jones's comment reveals much about the transformation of leisure during the first half of the nineteenth century. First, it demonstrates a recognition that leisure had changed by the 1820s and that the transformation was linked to larger social and economic developments. Second, and perhaps more importantly, Jones's lament discloses the ambivalence many people felt about the far-ranging changes southwestern Pennsylvania experienced during the first half of the nineteenth century, especially as they touched on leisure. People often embraced the benefits of economic growth, technological progress, and financial prosperity, while rejecting their corollaries: the expansion of impersonal market relations and values, the erosion of a sense of local community, and the recession of traditional social practices. This ambivalence proved to be especially evident in leisure, as communal festivals gave way to commercial amusements, and customary pastimes languished in the face of more novel ways of spending free time.

The Transportation Revolution and the Market Revolution

In another sense, however, Jones's concerns seem overly nostalgic, if not maudlin. As we saw in chapter 2, the integrated, unified community whose loss Jones regretted never really existed in the first place. More than this, the disappearance of traditional leisure forms and activities was far from complete by 1826, or even 1850. Rather, the erosion of traditional leisure was a slow, irregular affair, not an abrupt disappearance of older forms. Indeed, some traditional leisure forms, like frolics, bees, cockfights, and the recreational activities of fire companies, retained their vitality throughout the period of this study and beyond.[2] In many respects, the pattern of leisure by 1850 had much in common with the "artless manners and delightful amusements" whose loss Samuel Jones lamented. Yet many residents like him idealized the recent past and yearned for the supposedly harmonious communal leisure of days gone by. How, then, do we make sense of the transformation of leisure, or of this puzzling reaction to it?

To resolve these questions, this chapter employs two related conceptual frameworks that historians have developed to characterize early nineteenth-century social and economic change. The first, developed some years ago by George Rogers Taylor, is the notion of a "transportation revolution." Much of the economic and social change Americans experienced during the nineteenth century, Taylor argued, resulted from technological advances in transportation and the expansion of the turnpike, canal, and rail network. According to Taylor, improved transportation made consumer goods cheaper, opened new markets for agriculture and industry, and powered economic growth. More recently, U.S. historians have subsumed Taylor's emphasis on transportation under the broader rubric of a "market revolution." Historians like Sean Wilentz, Harry Watson, and Charles Sellers have stressed the importance of expanding market relations and commercial values in motivating the growth of transportation, stimulating new and innovative economic activities, and transforming traditional social relationships.[3]

Both of these frameworks illuminate the transformation of leisure and southwestern Pennsylvanians' reactions to it. Attention to the region's increasing linkage to broader social and economic networks through its expanding transportation system helps to explain many of the changes in leisure activities and opportunities. Focusing on market expansion sheds light on the slow, uneven pace of the erosion of traditional forms by commercial leisure and provides insight into the ambivalence evident in Jones's observations. Market historians rightly observe that the progress of the market was not uniform and that not all Americans embraced its new practices and values. A conflict arose in American society between those who welcomed the new ways and those who rejected them.

Leisure emerged as a prominent battleground in this conflict. Many Americans coped with the disturbing social and economic change prompted by market expansion by imagining an archetypal past in which unifying, communal leisure bound society together into a harmonious whole. That this communal past never really existed did not stop Pennsylvanians from using it as a reference point from which to interpret, and sometimes denounce, their troubling present. Though market-influenced leisure did not completely supplant customary pastimes, it did alter the context in which they could be pursued. Improved transportation and the spread of commercial values changed the style more than the substance of leisure — not necessarily *what* one did with one's leisure, but where, how, and with whom. The emergence and progress of three related trends in leisure illustrate this transformation: commercialization, fragmentation, and privatization. Before we examine these trends in detail, however, it is necessary to outline the developments that underpinned them.

In the first fifty years of the nineteenth century, southwestern Pennsylvania experienced a number of tumultuous changes, all of which helped to reshape customary patterns of leisure. Not the least of these developments was far-reaching economic change. The region's strategic location and network of navigable waterways suited it to trade, and its commercial prosperity grew steadily as the nineteenth century unfolded. The 1820 federal census recorded that 567 persons were engaged in commerce in our four-county area; by 1840 that number had grown to 1,462, with most of the gains coming in Allegheny and Westmoreland Counties. Significant as commerce was, it was soon surpassed by manufacturing. In 1820, 6,684 people worked at manufacturing various goods in the four counties; by 1840 that number had risen to 10,843,[4] again largely due to gains in Allegheny and Westmoreland Counties.

Pittsburgh stood at the forefront of these changes. Production of iron, glass, textiles, and other products changed the city's preindustrial pattern of work early in the century, and by 1830, manufacturing outstripped commerce or trade in economic importance. Pittsburgh's example encouraged primitive industry in other parts of the region as well: Connellsville and Uniontown emerged as important iron-producing areas in Fayette County, and many of the region's growing towns and cities manufactured other products as well.[5] This nascent industrialization eroded customary patterns of work and leisure, speeding up production and rapidly transforming the relaxed pace of preindustrial labor. "Jonathan's Visit to Holdship's Paper Mill," an original poem published in the *Pittsburgh Gazette* in 1824, captured this transition. After commenting on the general bustle of activity that characterized Holdship's Pittsburgh operations, the author turned to the automation of the paper-making process:

> There too's the steam-things all kicking alive;
> The Ingine they call it, is a snorter;
> Lawd when they let on the steam, how it drives
> The rags round about, on the tip o' the water!

And then, what a darnation racket's kept on;
By golly I never could talk to a fellur;
Such roaring and puffing and hissing, I swan,
'Twas like forty great cats in a cellar.[6]

Linked to this transition of work and leisure through commercialization
and industrialization was the complex of technology, practice, and organization that George Rogers Taylor called the transportation revolution.
Primitive roads and turnpikes had linked western Pennsylvania to the east
since the mid-eighteenth century, but it was the turnpike and canal boom
of the early nineteenth century that truly alleviated the region's relative
isolation (see map 2). Among the roads constructed or improved by the
state of Pennsylvania during this period were turnpikes that would later
become the William Penn Highway, connecting Blairsville to Pittsburgh,
and the Lincoln Highway or Pennsylvania Road, linking Pittsburgh to

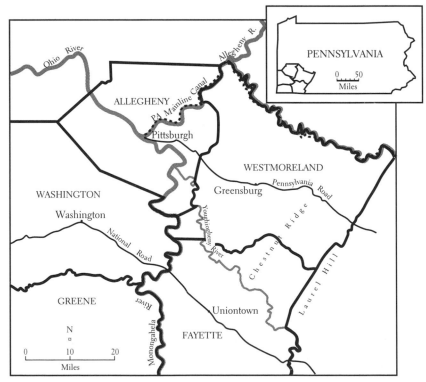

Map 2. New Transportation Routes in Southwestern Pennsylvania, 1800–1850

Philadelphia and the east. Building on previous Indian trails, provincial highways, and military roads, the 299 miles of the Lincoln Highway provided southwestern Pennsylvania with an important avenue for the transport of news, people, and goods across the state between 1818 and 1852.[7]

Even more important for connecting southwestern Pennsylvania with the rest of the country was the National Road. Known colloquially as the "Old Pike," the National Road opened officially in 1818. It ran through southwestern Pennsylvania, crossing the Maryland-Pennsylvania border in Fayette County and proceeded through Uniontown, Brownsville, Beallsville, and Washington, and on to Wheeling and points further west. The Old Pike proved to be especially important for western Pennsylvania because it brought a constant stream of travelers, a route by which exports and imports could flow, and a great impetus to economic and social development. Tavern and inns, which served as social centers for their surrounding areas, sprang up to meet the needs of ever-increasing passenger and freight traffic. Whole new towns materialized along the route: Beallsville and Centerville in Washington County, for example, were direct products of the Old Pike. Established towns also benefited from the social and economic invigoration of improved transportation. Pike traffic revitalized Uniontown, and in Washington no one doubted that the turnpike played a crucial role in the town's growth and prosperity.[8]

Canals as well as roads advanced economic and social development. The four-hundred-mile Pennsylvania Main Line Canal, completed in 1834, provided an easy, inexpensive route for passengers and freight from Philadelphia to Pittsburgh and the west. By allowing Pittsburgh to distribute eastern merchandise in the west and ship farm produce and its own manufactures, the canal fostered dissemination of leisure patterns and practices throughout the Ohio Valley. The economic stimulus offered by the canal, however brief it was, also provided necessary funds and population to support new forms of leisure. As smaller feeder canals and steam lines on the region's rivers supplemented the Main Line traffic, the spread of leisure goods, services, and customs proceeded with even greater rapidity.[9]

The effects on leisure of the transportation revolution and the expansion of the market should not be underestimated. Roads, turnpikes, and canals tied southwestern Pennsylvania to ever larger commercial networks, stimulating leisure both directly and indirectly. On the most direct level, improved transportation made travel itself as a form of leisure possible for the first time. Instead of enduring a bumpy, expensive journey by stage over indifferent roads across Pennsylvania, travelers could take the National Road to Brownsville and a steamer up the Monongahela River to Pittsburgh. Owing to its status as an engineering marvel, the Main Line attracted many travelers eager for the novelty of what we now consider tourist attractions.[10] Many European travelers preferred the Main Line to the Erie Canal or other western routes because of the Allegheny Portage Railroad's reputation as one of the most spectacular experiences available to North American travelers. But better roads and waterways did more than just increase the palatability of travel through the region. They also made excursions within the region easier and affordable and promoted market expansion through the dissemination of leisure goods and services from Pittsburgh.[11]

When travel as leisure became possible, so did various related activities and facilities: resorts, spas, pleasure gardens, inns, and taverns provided opportunities ranging from a day trip to an extended vacation. Nor were travelers the only ones to benefit from these new (or newly available) forms of leisure. For locals, the National Road decreased the region's isolation from eastern markets, introduced new types of amusements, and made an array of shows and attractions available for the first time. As we have already seen, taverns, inns and hotels served as social centers for local inhabitants as well as way stations for visitors. In Fayette County, for example, the Fayette Springs Hotel's tenpin alley, billiard tables, swing, and "other appliances of pleasure and comfort" made it a "favorite resort for visitors" to the Springs as well as a gathering spot for "merry parties of young folk" from nearby Uniontown. Likewise, the Summit House on the top of Laurel Hill was both a "fashionable and popular summer resort" and a place where the "yeomanry of the country came to make a harvest home, or celebrate an anniversary."[12]

Improved transportation affected leisure directly by making traveling amusements available to southwestern Pennsylvanians on at least a semi-regular basis. This process was especially apparent in Westmoreland County, one of the most isolated areas in the region at the turn of the century. Before the advent of the Pike, theater companies, menageries, circuses, and itinerant performers were relative rarities in the region.

When the turnpike was completed, however, numerous commercial amusements became frequent visitors. Traveling acting companies and bands of musicians were no longer uncommon, and the turnpike also brought the first "shows," or exhibitions of wild animals, to Westmoreland's citizens. Roadside taverns and inns promoted the development of commercial leisure by providing space for "jugglers, acrobats, ham actors and sly mountebanks" to astonish locals with recitations, gymnastic stunts, and sleight of hand. These exhibitions, like their counterparts in other counties, appealed to all classes and drew spectators from as far as twenty miles away. Westerners thronged these primitive shows, parting with so much money that by 1829 the National Road was carrying several sizable menageries and troupes of skilled performers.[13]

Stagecoaches and steamers brought a wide variety of amusements and services to southwestern Pennsylvania, including rope dancers, fencing masters, sword swallowers, ventriloquists, lecturers, dance teams, acrobats, and panoramas. Improved transportation made possible the dissemination of new cultural forms, like minstrelsy,[14] both within the region and beyond. By the 1850s, the new market in leisure, in the form of nationally renowned attractions and celebrities of an emerging mass culture, had penetrated even the most isolated parts of the region. Thousands gawked at Charles Dickens, delighted in the music of Olé Bull and Jenny Lind, marveled at Dan Rice's circus elephants, and puzzled at Tom Thumb and a Barnum menagerie "which even local church elders endorsed as a needed education for their children."[15]

In a more indirect manner, the transportation and market revolutions also promoted the development and transformation of leisure by providing a growing population desirous of amusement and recreation. Access to distant markets stimulated manufacturing and commercial agriculture, drawing workers into the region. The necessity of constructing, maintaining, and servicing the new roads and canals also swelled the population, building a clientele for newly available commercial recreations, amusements, products, and services. By stimulating manufacturing, the transportation revolution also created a wage-earning labor force that worked increasingly regular hours. As other historians of leisure have noted, money wages and regular hours were critical to the emergence of new leisure forms and practices.[16]

The Commercialization of Leisure

Inevitably, the growth of manufacturing, the expansion of the market, and the improvement of transportation transformed the traditional patterns of leisure described in the previous chapter. The most obvious effect was the growing commercialization of leisure, which proceeded as southwestern Pennsylvanians opted for new and exciting amusements offered for a price instead of the more familiar community-oriented leisure and recreation. As we shall see, population growth and diversification made traditional communal leisure difficult, but this was only half the story. Pennsylvanians did not purposefully reject or abandon familiar recreational activities. Rather, with novel forms of leisure penetrating western Pennsylvania, customary diversions and amusements simply held less appeal. Increasing leisure options diminished the popularity of traditional pastimes and transformed the ways in which people experienced them. The very fact that options existed as never before encouraged people to experiment with new leisure practices and forms: with menageries, musicians, dancing teachers, and lecturers regularly parading through the region, the husking bee and apple butter frolic were no longer the only games in town.

New Leisure Options and Opportunities

Southwestern Pennsylvanians embraced these new opportunities enthusiastically. Writing in 1847, for example, the usually serious Joseph Buffum evinced excitement at the spectacle of Raymond and Waring's Menagerie. Buffum admired the show's "musical chariot," a "splendid thing" that "cost five thousand dollars," but the

> best part of it all was to see Herr Drissbach enter the cage with the lions and tigers. He sported with them as he would with lambs. They seemed to be perfectly docile and fawned upon him like the house cat. He harnessed one of them into a chariot and rode through a long cage. They would hug him and kiss him like a true friend. They would all cower at the glance of his eye and obey him by motion of his hand. The tigers would leap over him and stand up on him. He is truly a king among them as king of beasts.[17]

Buffum was not alone in his fascination with commercial amusements, for Pennsylvanians spent both time and money on these new leisure activities at unprecedented levels. In 1837, for example, during the frightening days of the financial panic that gripped the nation, the Brown and Company traveling circus received eight hundred dollars in specie in Washington County at a time when bankers were circulating nearly worthless notes known as shinplasters because of the scarcity of silver.[18]

Commercialization altered irrevocably the scope and conduct of leisure, even in activities that retained some continuity with the past. Bees and frolics are a case in point. Women still gathered together to sew quilts and continued to invite men to a dancing party after the work was done. These parties, like the quilt making itself, celebrated communal spirit and nurtured feelings of mutuality because everyone made some personal contribution to the occasion: food, entertainment, labor, and so on. Commercialization altered the tone of these occasions by substituting market services for mutual assistance. Rather than making things themselves and relying on the unpaid aid of friends to help them, people could now purchase leisure goods and services from an impersonal marketplace. Joseph Buffum, for instance, engaged a "Mr. Burns of Allegheny to come out and play at a quilting frolic Thursday night for $4.00" in December 1847. This development did not invalidate the frolic as a social event — Buffum "had a pretty good time of it" at the party — but it does point to the transformation of customary patterns of leisure.[19]

Theater provides another example of this process. Before 1810, dramatics were largely the province of amateurs. Neighbors entertained each other, and even prominent citizens sometimes trod the boards. In Pittsburgh, young lawyers and professionals appeared on makeshift stages in the upper room of the courthouse and in William Morrow's tavern. Early in the century, Pittsburghers could occasionally view farces and comedies acted by these young men or perhaps hear "dramatic recitations" performed by itinerant actors. In either case, early theatrical activities provided a focal point for community interest and a topic for discussion and comment for weeks to come. Commercialization altered this pattern of close-knit sociability and neighborly amusement. By 1850, a profusion of commercial dramatic activity became available: Pittsburgh alone boasted eleven theaters and halls suitable for plays and exhibitions. The type of entertainment changed as well. At midcentury, Pittsburgh audiences enjoyed a diverse array of professional performers, and community-based theatricals had either disappeared or taken a back seat to their more polished counterparts. In July 1849, for instance, Pittsburghers could choose from a lecture on "Electrical Psychology" at Philo Hall, performances of the Western and Empire Minstrels at two local auditoriums, and musical entertainment at the Atheneum Ice Cream Saloon. The number of regularly scheduled commercial leisure activities increased so prodigiously by the late 1840s that the *Pittsburgh Gazette* no longer ran isolated advertisements but began collecting them together in an "Amusements" section.[20]

Commercialization proceeded slowly and unevenly but was clearly under way as early as 1820. Even after the completion of the National Road, commercial offerings were at first infrequent and often unsophisticated, like the French magician and sword swallower who appeared at the Pittsburgh theater in 1818. The difficulty of supporting regular amusements also continued to plague western towns. After praising a dramatic troupe that appeared at a local hotel, the *Greensburg Gazette* suggested that Mr. Scott, one of the actors, offer himself for a much deserved benefit performance, as "our population is not of that extent, to afford remuneration, such as the merits of the company claim." The increasing availability and appeal of commercial leisure, however, apparently motivated people to loosen their purse strings and make feasible more frequent visits by actors and performers. In 1824, one Greensburger seemed already jaded by the variety and number of commercial offerings. Writing to a local paper, "T." praised the histrionic talents of Mr. Pemberton, a traveling performer who recently stopped in the town. With the air of a seasoned critic, "T" noted Pemberton's superiority to the rest of "the *entire corps* of oratorical and dramaturgical pilgrims." As their exposure to a variety of commercial leisure grew, southwestern Pennsylvanians became more discriminating in their choices and judgments. In Pittsburgh, the *Statesman* remarked in 1830 that "we have lately had an unusual number and variety of public amusements," adding sadly that people turned to some, like the circus, for "pastime and amusement" in the absence of a regular theater.[21]

Cheaper, faster transportation gradually made a wide array of commercial choices available for southwestern Pennsylvania's amusement seekers. From the exotic to the bizarre, commercial offerings fed local residents' growing appetite for novelty and recreation. Beginning in the teens with visits by foreign musicians and exhibitions of European paintings, commercialization proceeded with increasingly elaborate and fantastic attractions. In Pittsburgh, Lambdin's Museum modeled itself on Peale's Philadelphia establishment, displaying permanent exhibits and featuring traveling attractions like Egyptian mummies, artificial fireworks, armless musicians, and dioramas of spectacular places and events ranging from the Great Fire of Moscow to the Battle of Waterloo. Pennsylvanians also manifested a taste for the unusual. Ah Fong Moy, a Chinese woman with bound feet, conducted well-attended "levees" at Pittsburgh's Musical Fund Hall in 1836, and city residents also turned out to see the "Great Novelty and Unprecedented Attraction" of the Albino Lady and the Irish Giant in 1838. In 1844, a tavern owner offered his patrons an opportunity to view two South Sea Islanders, brothers with "long claws on both wrists and ancles, resembling the sateral claws of an Eagle" for only twelve and a half cents.[22] Those wishing to see humbugs exposed could visit Zelim Kha Nourhina's 1842 display at Pittsburgh's Concert Hall, "Chaldean Miracles Exposed," that consisted "chiefly of illustrations of the pretended miracles attributed to the ancient magi, sorcerers, enchanters and necromancers."[23]

Amusement seekers who lived outside the region's cities could easily travel to see these attractions or partake of the commercial offerings that visited their own communities. For a paltry twelve and a half cents, a traveling museum offered Uniontown residents the chance to inspect a thousand-bladed knife, European musical instruments, a painting of the Treaty of Ghent, and automatons dubbed "musical androides." By the late 1840s, exhibitions of mesmerism, electricity, and Shaker music were making their way through Washington and Westmoreland counties. Menageries and circuses visited small and large towns in the region even earlier. A Grand Caravan of Living Animals stopped in Uniontown in 1829, Raymond and Ogden's Menagerie toured Washington County in 1834, and a menagerie and aviary visited Greensburg in 1840. Using improved roads and steamboats, other attractions reached even remote areas: ventriloquists, magicians, traveling museums, musicians, acrobats, and all varieties of lecturers were common visitors to the region's villages and hamlets.[24]

By the 1830s, improved transportation and consumers eager to purchase commercial leisure brought renowned attractions to southwestern
Pennsylvania. In 1833, for instance, Edwin Forrest, America's premiere
tragedian, played the Pittsburgh theater. James Hill, the celebrated co-
median and popularizer of the stage "Yankee" character also performed
that year, while the distinguished Irish actor Tyrone Power appeared a
year later. Nor was Pittsburgh the only site for nationally known attractions. Raymond and Waring's Grand Zoological Exhibition stopped at
Greensburg and three smaller towns in Westmoreland County in 1846;
Dan Rice's Circus performed in Washington in 1849.[25] By 1850, commercial leisure had penetrated every corner of southwestern Pennsylvania, building a devoted following of amusement seekers in the process.

A Leisure Industry Develops

With the development of a leisure-consuming public came the emergence of a leisure industry that provided goods and services to southwestern Pennsylvania's growing population. The decline in transport costs
and the increase in population made it profitable to devote labor and
capital to commercial leisure. Leisure goods became increasingly available as the region developed ever-stronger links to larger market networks.
Book sales and publishing, for example, became profitable businesses.
Zadok Cramer, James Johnston, William Burford, and others operated
bookstores and publishing houses in Pittsburgh; smaller concerns also
sprang up in other towns. By 1841, Pittsburgh boasted nine bookstores,
including two specialty shops devoted to German and Methodist subjects.
Bibliophiles could select from locally produced books, commercial publications shipped in from the East, and national periodicals like *Godey's
Lady's Book* and the *American Turf Register*. In the 1840s, customers of
Burford's Periodical Depository in Pittsburgh could choose from the *Ladies' Companion, Dollar Magazine, Robert's Semi-Monthly Magazine,*
and a host of others. Leisure entrepreneurs capitalized on public enthusiasm for all this newly available reading material. The Blairsville Keel
Boat Line, for example, offered a selection of papers and magazines to
its passengers as an inducement to prospective travelers.[26]

Music was another activity conducive to commercialization. Piano-
fortes were manufactured in Pittsburgh by 1813, and a Pittsburgh store

sold instruments and sheet music as early as 1819. *Harris's Directory* for 1841 lists four music stores in Pittsburgh, reflecting both an interest in musical goods and a larger population. Miscellaneous recreational goods also appeared on the market: billiard tables, fireworks, sportsmen's supplies, and ice cream all helped to satisfy the public's desire to spend time and money on leisure.[27]

Leisure services, especially instructional services, also emerged as popular commercial items. Southwestern Pennsylvanians supported dancing schools throughout the period, and their number increased as transportation and demand improved. The career of J. C. Bond, a Pittsburgh dancing teacher, illustrates the impact of heightened consumer demand on commercial leisure services. Beginning by offering dance classes in the 1820s, Bond elevated his school, at least in name, to a "Dancing Academy" by 1828. Realizing the potential for commercial dance instruction, Bond began holding his own cotillion parties, both to give his students a chance for practice (at a price, of course) and to stimulate business. By 1830, the enterprising Bond expanded further, opening "Bond's Concert Hall Garden," a commercial space he used for his own periodic "Promenade and Dancing Partys" and also as a rental property for other attractions. James Spratley, another Pittsburgh leisure entrepreneur, took a similar tack. In addition to hiring out his "Cotillion Band," Spratley also offered rooms to let, suitable for "Singing Schools, Debating Societies, private assemblies . . . Exhibitions of a Respectable Nature" and "private Balls."[28]

Art and music classes were widely available as well, catering to the public's desire for refined leisure pursuits. Music schools opened in Washington as early as 1816, while an artist offered portraits and art lessons there in 1817. By 1830, singing schools were in vogue: a Mr. Ely set up shop in Uniontown in 1831, and in 1834 Mr. McLain offered Greensburgers instruction in sacred music. Some instructors devoted themselves exclusively to artistic instruction: Thomas Cole, for example, opened a drawing school in Pittsburgh in 1823; William Staunton offered classes in music composition and performance. Others, motivated by economic necessity or expedience, combined artistic and instrumental instruction. A Uniontown girls' school, for example, offered instruction in painting and music to supplement its curriculum in domestic science, while Pittsburgh's Raub and Brown taught penmanship and bookkeeping as well as landscape painting in 1838.[29]

In the form of commercial relations, the market entered into all aspects of leisure, even those linked to religion. Camp meetings, usually occasions for socializing as well as devotion, lent themselves to commercialization because of the large crowds they drew. Once the province of strict religious observances, some camp meetings gradually took on the social ethos characteristic of horse races and militia musters. Though more restrained than secular occasions, camp meetings partook of many of the trappings of commercial leisure: food booths, liquor sales (if permitted, and sometimes in spite of prohibition), and wandering peddlers. Contrasting the camp meetings of later years with those of the early century, the Reverend Richard Lea recalled that "camp meetings, including preaching, praying, exhortation and communion, were held. One large tent, plenty of wagons, loaded with provisions. Nothing for sale. No visitors around the grounds." This pattern changed rapidly as entrepreneurs, and the meeting organizers themselves, realized the commercial possibilities of religious gatherings. In 1822, for example, the managers of a Methodist Episcopal camp meeting in Washington County notified the public that "the sale of spirits, beer, cider, bread, fruit, merchandize & c., within a limited distance of the camp ground, is prohibited, unless permission is given by the managers of the meeting."[30]

The Fragmentation of Community

With the commercialization of leisure and the diversity of choices that it offered came a fragmentation of community.[31] As chapter 2 describes, the ostensibly communal leisure of the early century encompassed divisions along racial, ethnic, gender, and economic lines. Population growth and demographic diversification made even this level of commonality in leisure difficult to sustain. Between 1800 and 1820, the total population in the four counties of this study increased from 86,270 to 132,684; by 1850 the total had grown to 274,067, more than double the 1820 figure. Pittsburgh expanded faster than any of the region's other towns and cities, especially during the 1830s and 1840s. Between 1800 and 1820, it grew from a mere 1,565 people to 7,428; in the following thirty years, however, the population increased to 46,601. Much of this growth occurred in the 1840s: Pittsburgh's population more than doubled in that decade, from 21,515 in 1840 to nearly 47,000 in 1850. Early in the century, city residents remarked upon the city's startling growth. Samuel Jones, hardly an unabashed proponent of change, noted in 1826 that the "population of our melancholy city, has within a few years, increased, beyond the greatest ratio, that is usually adopted in calculations relative to human accumulation."[32]

This "human accumulation" entailed ethnic and racial diversification as well as sheer numerical increase. With its commerce, industry, and transportation facilities expanding, southwestern Pennsylvania drew large numbers of immigrant settlers, "of almost all European nations, tongues and languages" to the region. Writing in 1818, John Wrenshall recorded in verse his impressions of the people he encountered on the road to Pittsburgh.

We bend our course now o'er those hills and vales,
Where emigrants in crowds, the eye assails;
Of various nations, sects, and colours too,
Europa's sons, with Africans and Jew.
The keen-eyed Yankey too, with carriage trim,
And well fed oxn, straining every limb,
To drag the pon'drous load, through mud and clay,
O'e rocks and hills, which stand athwart the way.
In crowds, the Germans too, of Swabian race,
Whose grotesque figure, and whose ruddy face,
Oft times excite involuntary smiles,
And not less oft, the tedious way beguiles.

Irish and German immigrants comprised the most significant minority groups. Pittsburgh contained relatively substantial populations of both groups, while Greensburg and Westmoreland County had large German populations. Free blacks, too, settled in significant numbers, especially in Pittsburgh and Washington. So extensive was the influx of immigrants that by the late 1830s native-born Americans accounted for less than 50 percent of Pittsburgh's population. A local almanac estimated the city's population at 60,000 in 1839; of these, 28,000 were "native Born Americans," 10,000 Irish, 12,000 German, 2,500 "African," and the rest English, Welsh, Scots, and French. Not surprisingly, this population influx eroded existing patterns of leisure and community and exacerbated the divisions already present. Commercialization further accelerated communal fragmentation through the proliferation of new leisure options. Participation in the new commercial leisure required only the price of admission, not membership in or identification with a unified community, however defined.[33]

The Partisan Exploitation of Traditional Leisure

But demographic and economic change were not the only sources of fragmentation. The emergence of mass politics also eroded the inclusiveness of traditional communal leisure, even within largely homogeneous social groups. The antebellum era's expanded suffrage forced aspiring politicians and party organizations to find effective ways of influencing and mobilizing a mass electorate. Political organizers and strategists often turned to familiar methods of promoting and maintaining group solidarity and unity — methods drawn from the leisure practices of earlier times. With the injection of politics into traditional leisure forms like barbecues, frolics, and raisings, however, the group solidarity and sense of community these forms fostered was no longer inclusive but, rather, fragmentary.

The partisan appropriation of communal leisure began with the disagreements between Federalists and Republicans but did not reach full flower until the advent of mass politics in the 1820s and 1830s. Scholars have devoted much attention to the *effects* of the campaign tactics of Jacksonians and Whigs[34] but little to the tactics themselves as leisure forms with a history all their own. In 1828, for example, Fayette County Democrats did not hold a mere political meeting or campaign rally. Rather, they enticed voters with a "Harvest Home and Jackson Barbacu." Playing on a tradition of communal leisure gatherings, the organizers announced that the "farmers of German and Springhill townships" would barbecue a five-hundred-pound ox in early August. Party regulars "respectfully" invited the friends of General Jackson "to come and dine with them, free of all expense. The usual entertainment on such occasions, may be expected." Democrats thus cast a political rally in the mold of a traditional harvest feast comprised of farmers and friends. Since no one charged friends admission, neither did the good Democratic farmers of Fayette County. Accounts of the event suggest that it was a great success: the "Barbacu" drew fifteen hundred people who listened to pro-Jackson speeches and toasts and dined on two oxen whose weight totaled eight hundred pounds. Nor was this celebration a mere plying of prospective supporters with food and strong drink. Partisan organizers emphasized the feast's links to traditional leisure practices. In accordance with customary practice, they insisted, moderation governed the proceedings, and "the steppings of that haggard monster, intemperance, [were not] seen upon the ground."[35]

The Democrats also used other traditional leisure forms to frame their increasingly partisan messages. By the 1840s, no Uniontown Democratic parade was complete without "Col. Ben Brownfield with his famous and popular string band." Democrats recognized that music, long a staple of communal leisure, made their divisive, often abrasive partisan credo more palatable to voters unaccustomed to the bitter strife of mass politics. The Democrats did not hesitate to change with the times, however, if new forms promised to attract voters. As horn music came into vogue, for example, they sponsored "Democratic" brass bands to augment traditional fiddle and guitar music.[36]

The Democrats were not alone in their partisan exploitation of traditional leisure forms. Though relative latecomers, the Whigs in many respects were the true masters of that gambit. Whig politicians reached even further back into the preindustrial past to imbue partisanship with an aura of communal cooperation and artless fun by drawing on the traditional linkage of work and leisure. A classic example was the raising of a log cabin for use as local campaign headquarters.[37] Whig organizers conducted the raising like a community project on the frontier: they encouraged local farmers, workers and "neighbors" to help and rewarded them with the customary meal and hard cider. Local participants, like their frontier predecessors, obtained a sense of accomplishment and communal solidarity. Whig politicians assured them that the raising, both of the cabin and the Whig party, could not have proceeded without their unified effort and neighborly support. Cabin and pole raisings thus utilized a popular affection for traditional leisure forms to disguise the divisive effects of partisan battles on the community. In the process, however, politics infused those communal leisure activities with exactly that divisiveness.

The fiction of communal solidarity could not long withstand the corrosive effects of party politics, and the contrivances of partisan raisings and barbecues soon rang hollow. In 1835, for example, Pittsburgh and Allegheny City Whigs held a "Jubilee," their answer to the Jacksonian's harvest home celebration. The Whigs offered the customary food and hard cider but abandoned the charade of communal inclusiveness. The *Allegheny Democrat* charged that ticket holders were required to renounce Jackson at the door to gain admittance to the feast. As party battles heated up, the partisan use of traditional leisure forms as facades became increasingly transparent. The Whigs' "Jubilee" of 1835 amounted to little more than a political meeting at which a ticket was nominated; the leisure aspects of it were mere window-dressing.[38]

The intrusion of mass politics into leisure changed traditional forms and practices by enlisting them in fragmenting instead of unifying causes. Partisan politics altered people's expectations of public leisure by associating it with divisiveness and rancor rather than harmony and neighborliness. The forms of specific leisure activities themselves — barbecues, picnics, dinners, lectures — changed but little. Their linkage to issues and personalities that divided the community, however, permanently transformed their social and cultural meaning. No longer did leisure minimize differences and integrate distinct groups into the larger community, as did the ethnic celebrations discussed in chapter 2. Nor did people necessarily expect it to do so. Now leisure often defined and emphasized the communal divisions engendered by political discord.

The fragmentation resulting from politicized leisure extended even to the relatively homogeneous group of white males actually eligible to vote. This process was apparent in Westmoreland County by the late 1830s, when barn raisings, formerly a bastion of neighborliness and communal leisure, became occasions for political discussion and partisan dispute. At Abraham Eichar's barn raising in 1838, participants conducted a straw poll of his neighbors' preferences in the upcoming gubernatorial contest, as did attendees of two other local raisings. All three favored David Porter over Joseph Ritner in the election, and this greatly perturbed Ritner partisan Henry Null, a local farmer known to his detractors as the

"Great High Priest of Anti-masonry." Upon contemplating a raising on his property, Null found the prospect of a pro-Porter poll so odious that he ignored the usual protocol for conducting the event: "He despatched messengers to the four adjoining townships of South and North Huntingdon, Hempfield and Mountpleasant, inviting only such as were known to have supported Ritner on a former occasion, and leaving even his nearest Democrat neighbors uninvited."[39]

Politics fragmented leisure in homogeneous communities like the Pennsylvania German population as well. Despite a shared language and culture, German residents too experienced communal divisiveness through the politicization of their leisure forms. Though Germans probably celebrated ethnic holidays and festivals together without regard to party affiliation, politics made significant inroads into the solidarity of the German population. In Greensburg, for instance, two Germans kept taverns that served as Democratic gathering points. Frederick Rohrer owned the Westmoreland House, long the Democratic headquarters for Greensburgers of all ethnic backgrounds. In "Dutch Town," a German named Kuhns kept another tavern, the favorite haunt of the German Democrats. Frederick Mechling, the proprietor of "The Federal Springs," located his establishment in "Irish Town," perhaps because he opposed Kuhns's politics, though in both houses the predominant language spoken was Pennsylvania Dutch.[40] Politics in leisure, then, fragmented even groups with strong traditions of cultural solidarity; its effects on groups without a unifying culture and language were still more pronounced.

Politics Fragments the Celebration of Washington's Birthday

This process occurred even in activities generally acknowledged as unifying and nonpartisan. The celebration of Washington's Birthday is a case in point. Americans of all political and ethnic persuasions revered Washington; pride in his accomplishments was the common property of all citizens. In 1811, for example, Pittsburghers of every political stripe braved snowy weather to parade in honor of their hero, further saluting him with a dinner and patriotic speeches by the "Sons of Washington."[41] Patriotic Americans treated the anniversary of Washington's birth as a sacred occasion when they could forget petty differences, community divisions, and partisan squabbles and join together in common veneration of their national hero. Yet by the 1830s, even this hallowed occasion divided the community as political issues permeated the celebratory process. Early in the decade, community celebrations included many groups: the trades, militia units, government leaders, clubs, and various local organizations. In Pittsburgh's 1832 celebration of the centennial of Washington's birth, a large procession of military companies, societies, and trade groups paraded through town, ending up at the Methodist Church for an oration and worship service. Underlying this apparent unity of purpose, however, were divisive tendencies. The mechanics met separately to arrange their procession, insisting on their autonomy in an era of labor unrest and spurious "working men's" parties. Further, after the church services, the procession broke up into many smaller groups for balls and parties, which were neither unifying or inclusive. For the elite, a ball at Mr. Gleims's boasted attendance by surviving revolutionary veterans; other could attend the less prestigious affair at the Exchange Hotel.[42]

Five years later these divisive tendencies had proceeded further. In Pittsburgh, the trades, increasingly disenchanted with the volunteer militia and the politics that they represented, sponsored their own celebration, separate from the general military celebration. In Washington, a town noted for antislavery activity, the twenty-second of February became little more than an opportunity for an antiabolitionist minority to denounce their neighbors. The town's volunteer companies met early in the month to arrange a celebration and invite the citizens; they also arranged to join with Washington College's Washington Literary Society for the festivities. Belying the apparent inclusiveness of the affair, Major John Irons, a local militia leader and hotel owner, used his influence to have the requisite dinner at his hotel and turned it into a forum for antiabolitionist sentiment. Linking the celebration to a local "Convention of the Friends of the Integrity of the Union," Irons opposed abolitionism as anti-union, promoting instead colonization as the appropriate policy for Washington's heirs. Partisan fervor even made the celebrants oblivious to their hero's message: after reading the isolationist Farewell Address aloud, the group endorsed toasts encouraging intervention in the Texas revolution.[43]

Political issues colored Washington's Birthday celebrations throughout the 1830s. Pittsburgh Democrats held an extremely partisan celebration in 1839 at Armstrong's Washington Coffee House; even when they honestly attempted to be nonpartisan, the best they could muster were pro-Democrat instead of anti-Whig celebrations. Issues other than politics also made unified celebrations difficult in the 1830s. Reacting to what one critic termed "military foolery and whiskey drinking," teetotalers began holding separate observances. In 1843, the twenty-second in Pittsburgh was "celebrated generally by the military, and also by a large temperance procession."[44]

By 1840, Washington's Birthday bore little resemblance to the patriotic festival that the public-spirited had originally intended. Partisan celebrations disillusioned Americans who yearned for patriotic unity; many people stopped attending such festivities. One observer remarked on flagging attendance at Washington's Birthday celebrations, decrying partisan influence in the process:

> The *democrat* may rejoice over the glorious victory at New Orleans — the *whig* may celebrate the battle of the Thames — but in these there are party prejudices and party principles, and they alloy the pleasure. But on the 22nd of February our whole land can meet in one happy social band. They can sit around the same table, and chaunt in the same voice the name of the greatest man who ever lived.

By 1840, this plea for unity was more nostalgic than realistic. In Washington, the Whigs and Democrats greeted the upcoming anniversary of their hero's birth with large partisan processions through the town, emphasizing not unity but division through the celebratory forms of leisure.[45]

The Privatization of Leisure

This fragmentation was linked to a third major trend, the privatization of leisure. In the small agricultural communities of turn-of-the-century southwestern Pennsylvania, the spirit of neighborliness and the necessity of mutual aid made public leisure a communal activity, at least for some segments of society. But by the 1820s, social fragmentation and partisan divisiveness began to sever the link between public space and communal leisure. In the face of disorderly crowds and political rancor, southwestern Pennsylvanians could no longer find the satisfactions of communal leisure in a public setting. Consequently, they increasingly began to seek social enjoyment and a sense of belonging in smaller, more select groups. In the process, they created a new cultural space for leisure: the private sphere.[46]

Private leisure encompassed many of the same activities pursued in familial contexts earlier in the century: solitary free time and occasions spent with close relatives and intimate friends. In these private settings Pennsylvanians hoped to recapture the closeness and congeniality that they believed previous generations had once found in communal leisure. Thus, they excluded from their homes and social circles those divisive issues and troublesome strangers that were so prevalent in public settings. Yet this withdrawal into the private sphere eroded further the remaining link between communal leisure and public space. What emerged in the 1830s was a redefined notion of leisure and community. Once denoting a unified whole, in conception if not in fact, community now referred to a fragmented collection of coexisting social groups. Southwestern Pennsylvanians now sought feelings of belonging (that they previously expected from communal leisure) in smaller groups — groups differentiated along racial, ethnic, partisan, gender, and class lines.

Though it affected the entire population, the transition to privatized leisure was particularly apparent in the region's middle class. Participation in communal leisure once afforded doctors, lawyers, landowners, and merchants positions of leadership and social authority. They were able to enjoy a sense of community with their perceived inferiors because everyone, regardless of rank or station, tacitly agreed upon the necessity of hierarchy and abided by its rules. The advent of mass politics and new demographic diversity presented a double challenge to the preeminent social position of the middle class. No longer could middle class Pennsylvanians ensure their own leadership in community festivals and celebrations. Nor could they always dictate standards for participation and behavior in public leisure. New rivals for social authority emerged: immigrants, workers, and social climbers. One way the middle class responded was by opting for leisure in the private sphere, where their authority could not be questioned or contested. Private leisure gave the middle class a safe alternative to chaotic public recreation and amusement.

Private leisure also gave members of the middle class a sense of group solidarity by allowing them to develop their own distinct styles of using free time. They upheld their leisure choices as exemplars of propriety and refinement, creating new standards of social and cultural authority. In essence, the middle class claimed that leisure time could be spent wisely and virtuously only by adherence to their prescribed standards of decorum. Even outside the private sphere, middle class Pennsylvanians sought ways to assert this new authority. The plethora of clubs, societies, and voluntary associations established during the antebellum era reflect attempts to demarcate a semiprivate sphere. Though ostensibly public and open to everyone, these organizations restricted membership and guaranteed respectability through expensive entrance fees, steep dues, and elaborate rules for behavior. In this desire to impose standards of private behavior on public events, southwestern Pennsylvania's middle class was no different than its counterparts elsewhere. As Karen Haltunnen, Lawrence Levine, John Kasson, and others have shown, middle class Americans used a variety of methods to distance themselves from the disturbing aspects of public leisure while simultaneously attempting to remake it according to their own standards.[47]

Commercial leisure activities contributed to the move toward privatization as well. It might seem that commercialization would mitigate rather than foster privatization by bringing people together in public. To some extent this did occur, but the public leisure created by commercialization was problematic for two reasons. First, public commercial amusements were a far cry from communal leisure. Theaters, halls, streets, and pleasure gardens were scenes of the very disorder and divisiveness that had driven people from public contexts to begin with. Also, commercial leisure did not produce the sense of camaraderie that southwestern Pennsylvanians craved, for these leisure activities did not require a communal ethos to function. Gathering with others at a play or concert did not necessarily generate the same satisfaction as communal leisure, for such amusements could be performed for and enjoyed by an audience of total strangers. On the other hand, a husking bee and butchering frolic relied heavily upon the familiarity and harmony of a close-knit community for their success, if not their existence. People did come together in public for commercial leisure, but they often had little more in common than the price of admission. This type of social interaction, unlike that found in communal leisure, hardly provided the building blocks of community.

Commercialization also fostered privatization by drawing people away from the communal leisure activities that nevertheless persisted well into the century. With more options available for solitary and group leisure, individuals no longer had to depend on the larger community as the primary venue for amusement and recreation. Instead, they could seek social enjoyment in smaller groups of family members or like-minded friends. Or they could eschew group leisure altogether and seek solitary pleasures in private or in the anonymity of a mass audience. These new forms of leisure were perhaps better suited to southwestern Pennsylvania's changing society. Yet the transition to privatized leisure also evoked in the region's residents a nostalgic longing for their supposedly communal past.[48]

Not surprisingly, in 1826 Samuel Jones commented on the privatization of leisure in just these terms. In Pittsburgh's early days the city was "conspicuous for its hospitality"; the homes of even the most prestigious citizens were open to all visitors, and community interaction was "unclouded by fashionable doubts and refined prejudices." Surveying the city's emerging class and political divisions, Jones could not "but regret that those good old times of liberal feeling and social intercourse ha[d] gone by, and given way to those cold and heartless formalities that distinguish[ed] the present day." The formalities that Jones had in mind often revolved around privacy and exclusivity in leisure pursuits. By the 1840s, social intercourse in the public eye no longer held the appeal it once had. Writing on the "Peculiarities of Social and Domestic Life" in 1842, an anonymous Pittsburgh critic observed that the "safest way of coming into communion with mankind is through those of our own family."[49] No longer was public sociability of prime value in leisure; as public recreations and celebrations grew less satisfactory, privacy assumed greater importance.

An Emerging Ideology of Domesticity

This retreat from public leisure into the privacy of home and family dovetailed with the emerging ideology of domesticity. As the marketplace became more threatening and difficult, men increasingly looked to the home for refuge. Women became the guardians of that refuge and, in the process, promoters of private leisure. Contemporary sources attest to women's role as leisure providers in the home. With her grace and charm, a wife could enliven her husband's "feeling from the languor of his necessary avocations," render the home "agreeable to him," and "receive him with open arms, and cheerful looks."[50] A poem published in Pittsburgh in 1822 expressed this vision of home as sanctuary:

Oh! the best spot on earth for delight to be found,
Is at home, where with joy our affection is crowned;
Where the wife of our bosom still meets us with smiles,
And the mirth of our children each sorrow beguiles.
In the walks of ambition, with pow'r and with fame,
We may shine in full pomp, and establish a name,
But the flow'r of content in the soul will not bloom,
Unless it first springs from our comforts of Home.[51]

By making the home a place for leisure and social enjoyment, men and women could avoid reliance on public leisure.

Commercialization played a dual role in the privatization of leisure. On the one hand, the commercial leisure industry offered a wide range of consumer products suitable for use in home leisure: inexpensive books, newspapers, and periodicals, sheet music and instruments, ice and exotic foods for cooking and entertaining, and so on. On the other hand, by providing cheap public entertainment for a mass audience, commercialization promoted many of the excesses that made many people yearn for a more privatized, exclusive leisure. As the theater, circus, menagerie, and tavern became available to everyone, an increasingly rowdy, indecorous audience emerged, much to the dismay of respectable folk of all ages and classes. In short, the allure of hearth and home attracted people toward private leisure, just as the threat of unruliness and disorder drove them away from public leisure.

Rowdiness in Public Leisure

This concern over the behavior of participants in mass public leisure was not entirely misplaced. Newspaper accounts and crime reports indicate that public leisure was growing increasingly fractious as the decades passed. "Loafers" played cards and fought cocks in public places, tippling houses and doggeries expelled quarrelsome drunks onto the streets, and fights at taverns and ball alleys were alarmingly frequent events. Holidays were especially disturbing. On the Fourth of July, any number of people were usually "led into the excesses of the day . . . disturbing the peace by their disorderly conduct," and Washington's Birthday was no different. Military exercises often suffered from poor discipline and intoxicated soldiers. In 1842, for example, a company of German militiamen caused havoc all day, finally inciting a riot (complete with drawn swords) after they had "finished their patriotic celebrations of the Glorious 22nd."[52]

Commercialization also posed problems of order and decorum in public leisure. As commercial leisure moved into the financial reach of most people, it became increasingly susceptible to disturbances and declining quality. The necessity of pleasing a mass audience led some consumers to reject public leisure on aesthetic or intellectual grounds. Pittsburgh lawyer Robert McKnight found demonstrations of animal magnetism, for example, "a grand humbug and a mere catchpenny." He also objected to the low comedy and melodramatic spectacle often available in local theaters, sighing "Alas for the legitimate drama!" to his diary.[53]

Even those who enjoyed the available fare found cause for dissatisfaction with public leisure. The behavior of theater audiences, never models of deportment, appears to have deteriorated through the 1830s and 1840s. Drunks on both sides of the footlights were common sights; sometimes police intervention was necessary to remove insouciants from the theater. Henry B. Fearon attended the Pittsburgh theater in 1817: "The acting was equal to the audience, perhaps superior. A son of the celebrated Lewis performed Horatio: he was dead drunk, and extremely dirty." Boisterous spectators were another problem: whether swelled by visiting volunteer militiamen, transient boatmen, or unruly locals, Pittsburgh audiences often evoked complaints of "clamor and confusion" from more restrained patrons of the arts.[54]

The rowdiness of public leisure was often more than just unpleasant, for the threat of violence was always close at hand, especially when liquor was consumed. Loafers congregating on street corners and insulting passersby were bad enough; sometimes drunkenness led to mayhem and murder. Intoxication led to at least one Pittsburgh murder in 1838; frequently violence in taverns and bars spilled into the streets, threatening innocent pedestrians. In 1842, Frank Dravo's Pittsburgh tavern was the site of a riot involving forty to fifty drunken people. The tavern was scheduled to be razed the following day, and its devoted patrons threw a farewell bash, designating a bottle of whiskey as the price of admission. Once the potable admission fees were used for refreshment, the affair proceeded to its violent and predictable conclusion.[55]

The possibility of violence in public leisure was not confined to any class or geographic area. Young men of prominent families were arrested and fined for drunken serenades and fights just like their working class counterparts. Charles B. Scully recorded one such occasion of upper class violence: in 1843, several young men from Pittsburgh's first families congregated at a local hotel for a banquet. After hours of drinking, the party degenerated into a drunken brawl in the wee hours of the morning, much to Scully's disgust. Nor was violence in public leisure solely an urban problem. A Fayette County jury tried a murder case in 1831 originating from an assault after "a party from Brownsville and Bridgeport went a pleasuring on a steam boat" equipped with a well-stocked bar.[56]

The Growth of Private Recreation

Under these conditions, it is perhaps hardly surprising that many southwestern Pennsylvanians spent larger portions of their leisure time in private rather than public pursuits. Both Robert McKnight and Charles B. Scully continued to patronize public theaters and concerts, but much of their leisure revolved around solitary pursuits like reading, writing, and gardening, or socializing with their peers at private gatherings. Scully was disappointed when some aspects of his privatized leisure took on the characteristics of public amusement. He chose not to celebrate St. Patrick's Day with the Catholic Institute of which he was a member, noting that he had "great respect for the memory of Ireland's St ('Patrick') but [did not] wish to partake of a public discussion on the 17th." Dwindling attendance at the Catholic Institute's meetings turned Scully away from the organization, "which from the non-attendance of a quorum for the last few evenings ha[d] resolved itself into a 'free and easy club.'"[57]

Though some of Scully's and McKnight's discomfiture with public leisure might be attributed to their middle and upper class backgrounds, evidence suggests that privatization did not respect class bounds. Theater and popular amusements were hardly communal events; by charging admission and segregating spectators by sex, race, and class, they emphasized privacy and communal division instead of unity.[58] Working class clubs and organizations like volunteer fire departments also could be called community organizations only with reservations. Though they served an instrumental function and often participated in public celebrations, fire companies evolved into private social clubs (some said gangs) with which outsiders interfered only at their peril. Privatization, then, affected the working as well as middle and upper class, albeit in slightly different ways and to varying degrees. But by 1839, even a "practical mechanic with a large family" pursued the "intelligent" course of subscribing to eight "select" newspapers and keeping a quantity of good books on hand as a "cheap and profitable" way of keeping his family at home.[59]

By midcentury it was obvious that the communal pastimes of earlier years were gone forever. Many southwestern Pennsylvanians preferred retreating into the privacy of their homes and families rather than braving the altered conditions of public leisure. Combined with trends toward the commercialization and fragmentation of leisure, privatization transformed the leisure practices and forms characteristic of the turn of the nineteenth century. All three trends were interrelated, each acting separately and in concert with the others to change the conduct and style of leisure in the region. What emerged by 1850 was vastly different from, yet still related to, the leisure of a traditional agricultural society. To better understand this transition, and the forces of commercialization, fragmentation, and privatization that motivated it, we next look at the transformation of a single leisure practice over time: the celebration of the Fourth of July.

4

The Fourth of July
in Southwestern Pennsylvania

No SINGLE EVENT BETTER ILLUSTRATES TRENDS in southwestern Pennsylvania leisure from 1800 to 1850 than does the celebration of the Fourth of July. Like the communal pastimes discussed in chapter 2, Independence Day supposedly unified communities but, in practice, often revealed more about divisions than shared values. The Fourth's transition from a communal, patriotic observance to a recreational holiday depicts in high relief the changes wrought by the commercialization, fragmentation, and privatization of leisure discussed in chapter 3. Perhaps most importantly, examination of the Fourth of July over time highlights the creative aspects of leisure activities. As we see in this chapter, the Fourth was contested cultural space from which a variety of ideas, values, and models of behavior emerged in response to new social, economic, and political circumstances. Clearly, partisan politics played a major role in the Fourth's commemoration, and people often held purely political celebrations. But the range and complexity of Fourth of July observances extended far beyond the realm of politics. To appreciate the role of leisure in this complexity, we must examine the Fourth not merely as an occasion for partisan debate or communal affirmation, but as an opportunity for the development, articulation, and display of differing visions of community and society.

A Ritual of National Patriotism or Factional Rivalry?

The Fourth of July has long been depicted, both in popular and scholarly parlance, as a celebration of American republicanism, emphasizing the values of unity, communal spirit, and patriotism. A recent compilation of American holiday traditions defined the Fourth as "a political holiday and a community enterprise traditionally observed with fireworks, parades, band concerts, oratory, picnics, public entertainment, and especially sporting events." Another account asserted that during the 1830s, formal public ceremonies in honor of the day enlivened small towns and large cities alike. No less an historian than Merle Curti observed that, despite the efforts of some groups to "capture the day for their own ends, by and large the Fourth brought Americans together without reference to their differences." In a similar vein, Thomas Bender contended that "rituals of national patriotism" like the Fourth "had the effect of invigorating the sense and experience of community in town after town."[1]

Yet some historians have noted that early partisan differences some-times made the Fourth a divisive rather than a unifying occasion. Charles Warren asserted that, beginning "in 1788, in many parts of the country, the celebration became strictly political and partisan, and separate party celebrations of the day continued for over thirty years." William Cohn elaborated on this theme, noting that while widely celebrated by 1801, the Fourth was not really a national festival but rather a dramatic reflec-tion of the factional rivalries then emerging in American politics. Cohn argued that factional divisiveness on the Fourth receded only after 1826, when the deaths of Jefferson and Adams on Independence Day made it more of a community celebration. After 1826 the "Fourth of July as a festival to affirm a national purpose, evolved into a uniform ritual."[2] Clearly, the vision here is of communal solidarity and harmony on an important patriotic holiday.

Diverse Celebrations Follow a Typical Pattern

A close look at the Fourth in southwestern Pennsylvania from 1800–1850 reveals a far different picture. Although attractive as generalizations, pre-vailing views of the Fourth rely too heavily on data from New England, impeding an accurate account of the day's meaning and complexity in specific social contexts. Any account of the Fourth that establishes a dichotomy between a "national" and a "partisan" celebration minimizes the range of social, cultural, and political values articulated by various participants. Southwestern Pennsylvanians organized celebrations around a number of themes, issues, and values, including: military celebrations, moral or religious festivals, economic celebrations, "out-group" gatherings, artistic and intellectual groupings, social observances, and political meetings.

Data gleaned from southwestern Pennsylvania newspapers, diaries, and other contemporary sources between 1800 and 1850 reveal the Fourth's diversity. Although the form of the celebration[3] remained roughly constant, Fourth of July observances presented a kaleidoscopic picture, for any celebration might be colored by a number of different themes and orientations. An Irish militia company, for example, might emphasize not only the Fourth's revolutionary associations but also the contributions of Irish immigrants to the republic, as well as the economic or occupational positions of the celebrants. In 1843, for instance, Pittsburgh's Hibernian Greens militia company paraded through the city in the morning, highlighting military and revolutionary associations. In the afternoon, however, they joined with the stridently anti-British Repealers for a celebration in Gazzam's Grove that focused on their shared ethnicity.[4]

In spite of this complexity, Fourth of July celebrations all followed a basic pattern that varied only slightly no matter what group organized the affair. Most celebrations began with participants assembling at a prearranged point, often a courthouse, church, or tavern. Opening exercises consisted of a prayer, oration, or address, depending on the nature of the celebration. The group then departed, usually in procession, for the site of the dinner and festivities. Frequently, organizers served the customary feast in a "shady grove" outside of town or on the property of a prominent celebrant. The dinner also followed a pattern common to nearly all celebrations. The company appointed (rather than elected) a president, one or more vice presidents, and a secretary, often by unanimous acclamation. An officer or appointee read the Declaration of Independence, and patriotic orations by prominent citizens or guests sometimes followed. The company then sat down to dinner, with officers and distinguished guests seated at a head table. After dinner, the "cloth" was removed, and the company prepared for toasting. Participants offered two types of toasts: regular toasts, which an organizing committee prepared in advance; and volunteer toasts, which ordinary participants proposed spontaneously. Music, cheers, and musket or cannon fire accompanied both types of toasts. Typically, American unity, the bravery and selflessness of the founding fathers, and other patriotic issues or themes of particular interest to the company received the lion's share of toasts.

Military Celebrations

Observance of the Fourth most commonly revolved around the military and patriotic values emerging from the Revolution. The military festival often began with cannon fire at dawn, followed by a parade, military "evolutions" or maneuvers, and a dinner sponsored by one or more militia companies. After-dinner toasts celebrated national unity, the Revolution's military heritage, and the continuing vigilance of the republic's citizen-soldiers. On July 4, 1818, for example, the Pittsburgh City Guards and Washington Guards met on Grant's Hill in Pittsburgh to celebrate the day: "No party animosity was agitated; all sentiments appeared to harmonize when they reflected on the glorious event they were then met to commemorate." After firing a twenty-gun salute and partaking of the "elegant entertainment" prepared for them, the companies offered toasts to the day, the flag, General Washington, and the military. Emphasizing the underlying patriotism of Americans, the companies offered a toast to "Party Spirit. — Though we are divided into *sections*, we are ready to form the *line* when danger threatens." Similar sentiments prevailed in Greensburg, Westmoreland County, in 1823, where the Greensburg Blues' celebration emphasized "utmost harmony and good feeling." Joined by the Westmoreland Artillery and Jackson Blues, the Blues assembled in a church to hear the Declaration of Independence read, then marched to a grove for dinner ("all of the best, and all made at *home*") and the attendant toasts: "The meeting seemed composed of brothers of the same family — all was hilarity, mirth and good humor. No wrinkled brow of care was seen, no squinting suspicion. It was a joyous burst of pleasure at the remembrance of a great day that gave birth to an independent people."

One of the regular toasts captured the tone of the day: "The United States of America. 'E Pluribus Unum.' *Unanimity.*"[5]

Though some militia celebrations fell prey to the influence of partisan politics in the 1830s and 1840s, others succeeded in preserving a nonpartisan spirit throughout the antebellum era. At Robbstown, Westmoreland County, in 1839, for instance, a "large number of people" (an observer gave a rather high estimate of two thousand) met in a specially constructed bower with three hundred uniformed militiamen. After the Declaration of Independence and a patriotic oration the company sat down to a dinner provided by three local innkeepers: "There was nothing of partyism in any proceedings. It was truly a celebration of *freemen* of the country, in which all were at liberty to join."[6] As these examples illustrate, the military celebration served as a focal point for enunciating the "American" values of republican unity and military virtue. The emphasis on unity and the consequent condemnation of factionalism sometimes reached a frenetic pitch, attesting to both the importance of the bond all Americans supposedly felt on the Fourth and the celebrants' anxiety over threats to this shared heritage.

Economic and Occupational Group Celebrations

Economic or occupational groups also observed Independence Day. In the early years of the century, economic celebrations often displayed the wealth of a local patrician who extended hospitality to less fortunate neighbors as a way of articulating a superior position in the community. At the Collins estate in Whitehall, Allegheny County, neighbors routinely gathered on the Fourth to witness a flag raising and drink a glass of wine to "Freedom and Union." Similar scenes occurred at the McCandless house in Aliquippa and at Adamson Tannehill's Grove Hills, where citizens met on the Fourth "to hail with joyful hearts" the anniversary of independence. In a similar vein, William Foster hosted a "grand barbecue" in 1826 at Foster's Grove in Lawrenceville including speeches, cannon and musket fire at the nearby federal arsenal, and bountiful tables waited on by "Negro slaves and bond servants."[7]

Other economic celebrations might be sponsored by an employer, a union, or an occupational association to commemorate the contribution of a particular group to the nation's prosperity, promote harmony between employer and employees, enhance the solidarity of an occupational association, or offer a vision of the ideal republican socioeconomic order. The Fourth of July at Humphreysville, Washington County, in 1810, "an exhibition that for novelty, utility and patriotism, probably stands unrivaled in the records of all preceding festivals," illustrates all these aspects of the economic celebration. "The farmers, shepherds, mechanics and manufacturers in col. Humphrey's employ having beforehand solicited to be usefully occupied on this day," were treated to a ploughing match and the construction of a shepherd's lodge on Humphrey's farm. Beginning at the crack of dawn and working at breakneck speed, Colonel Humphrey's laborers completed their tasks by early afternoon. In the spirit of the day, Humphreys entertained the company with

> a variety of fermented and distilled liquors. From thence they were invited to sit at the table, which was well furnished with Merino mutton, beef, poultry, puddings, & c. the products of his [Humphrey's] farms. The proprietor did the honors of the table; and the following sentiment alone was given after dinner: — "*Independence.* Deeds — not words. — Let those who wish to appear to love their country, prove it by actions rather than by toasts and declarations."[8]

Though Colonel Humphrey's patriotic vision seems inextricably linked to the improvement of his real estate, his celebration offered a model for preindustrial economic and labor relations nonetheless. The nobility and value of agriculture as "useful" occupation; the loyal and hardworking republican laborers who shunned idleness even on a festival day; the beneficent proprietor, mindful of his superior position but still solicitous of the happiness and welfare of his workers: all these elements represented in graphic display the harmonious preindustrial economic relations that many Americans hoped would continue in the new republic. With Jeffersonian warnings against the rise of an industrial work force of economic dependents still echoing, the Humphreysville Fourth bespoke stability, virtue, and firm ties with the agrarian past. Not surprisingly, this celebration shared many features of the traditional preindustrial harvest feasts in which the lord of the manor rewarded his servants for their hard work with a rich feast.[9]

    As the southwestern Pennsylvania economy shifted away from agriculture and toward industry, new economic values that emerged were represented and developed in Fourth of July celebrations. In 1823, Pittsburgh's Phoenix Cotton Factory "exhibited the singular spectacle" of some of the city's "most distinguished and respectable gentlemen" celebrating with the "superintendents and hands of that establishment, both male and female."

> We say singular, because, however creditable, the cordial feeling of sociability with which respectability and rank there united with honest industry, and modest worth, the prejudices of feudal times, aristocratic notions, and commercial wealth, have hitherto held themselves above such associations. We are proud of them because, while they cannot degrade, any citizen, however elevated, they introduce manufacturers to that rank in social life which the development of mind in the mechanical pursuits of modern days, determines shall be the *first*.[10]

In contrast to the Humphreysville celebration, which left the proprietor's preeminent social and economic position unquestioned, the Phoenix dinner presented a very different picture of labor relations. Though still affirming the importance of socioeconomic distinctions ("respectability and rank" united with "honest industry" and "modest" worth), the celebration's toasts praised manufacturers (i.e., artisans and laborers) and immigrants, even allowing the laborers themselves, through the vehicle of volunteer toasts, a forum for expressing their feelings. Whatever the reality may have been, the Phoenix celebration depicted relations between employer and employed as cooperative and democratic by using the Fourth to articulate social ideas and values appropriate to changing economic circumstances.

Many economic and occupational groups asserted their value to American society on the Fourth. Pittsburgh's Snag Marine, an association of steamboat captains, officers, and owners, observed the Fourth by dining together and toasting the contributions of steam transportation to the nation's growing prosperity: "Pittsburgh and her Operatives — Owners, Masters and Men — They can furnish the Manufacture, we can find the Market."[11] Similarly, celebrations sponsored by artisans and mechanics emphasized the value of their occupations to the republic's freedom and dignity. Humorously defending their observance of the Fourth to an assembly of the prestigious Pittsburgh Light Artillery,

A deputation from the society of Journeyman Shoemakers, who were celebrating the day in the neighborhood presented the following sentiment: "The
Pittsburgh Light Artillery: May they be charged with the *soles* of true republicanism, and *primed* with the best American *uppers*, always *ram home* European invaders." Tune — St. Patrick's Day in the Morning.[12]

Immigrant workers also proclaimed their devotion to their new country,
using the Fourth to affirm their rights and abilities as republicans. Immigrant participation set the tone for the Trade Union celebration held
in Pittsburgh in 1836. Accompanied by the German band, the celebrants
marched in procession from the courthouse to George Hatfield's garden,
one mile from the city. The celebration, which followed the standard
form, aimed at promoting solidarity for equal rights among working men,
and toasts revealed strong Irish as well as German participation. Doubtless
to combat stereotypes, a spokesman pointed out "a fact creditable to this
company, which is, that, unlike celebrations in general of this day, the
company drank but a very small quantity of ardent spirits."[13] The Trade
Union celebration thus presented an image of temperate, virtuous workers eager to participate in the American republic and justifiably insistent
on their right to do so.

Moral and Religious Group Celebrations

As the antebellum period progressed, moral and religious as well as economic groups claimed a place in the celebration of national independence. These groups insisted upon the importance of religion, temperance, or morality to the establishment and maintenance of the American
republic. If the Fourth happened to fall on a Sunday, religious observances took clear precedence during the antebellum years. Any festivities
would occur the day before or after, thereby preserving the Sabbath's
sanctity and dignity. Episcopal minister Sanson Brunot took little heed
of the Fourth at all in 1830. The day being a Sunday, Brunot traveled to
a small church eight miles from Pittsburgh to preach, perform five bap-
tisms, and minister to the spiritual needs of "about eighty or a hundred
people," all of whom were "very serious and attentive . . . during prayers
every knee was bent." After dining with "a Christian man and hospitable
farmer," Brunot spent the evening listening to a sermon at a nearby Methodist church, foregoing any patriotic celebration of the day.[14]

Other religiously minded celebrants attempted to demonstrate explicitly the dependency of republican virtue on religion. As early as 1819, Pittsburgh's Francis Herron sponsored a religious observance of the Fourth in his prestigious First Presbyterian Church. Herron emphasized gratitude to God for aiding the American cause in the Revolution as the only proper mode of celebrating the national festival. This theme of thanks to God on the Fourth also surfaced early in Washington County, where some citizens reacted with alarm to the worldliness and profligacy of Fourth celebrations. "A Friend to the Celebration of the 4th of July, 1776" lamented in 1821 that

> our newspapers continue to be barren this year as former years, of any account of expressions of thanks and gratitude to Almighty God upon the late celebration of the 4th of July, as the author of our national mercies and privileges. . . . All nations, christians, Jews and Mahometans, Turks and even heathens ever had, and still have thanksgivings and praise to Almighty God or their imaginary deities — in their national festivals, in remembrance of mercies received.

A year later, a "Friend of Gospel Religion" again scolded Washingtonians, declaring their current mode of celebration "more inexcusable" than previously, because they had "many good examples of the last year, and numerous admonitions" on the subject. Raucous, intemperate observances, the "Friend" complained, had "now become almost universally disgusting to the friends of gospel religion and republicanism."[15] For these champions of religious virtue, the Fourth was a time for gratitude and reflection on God's role in creating and sustaining the republic, not merely an opportunity for feasting, toasting, and saber rattling.

Later in the period, Sabbath school celebrations expanded and developed this theme, asserting that Christianity and religious education were the bulwarks of republicanism. The celebration at Pigeon Creek, Washington County, in 1843 was a case in point. After assembling in the Presbyterian church, the Sabbath school and "many citizens" joined in an opening prayer. A sermon to the children and choir music initiated the festivities, followed by an address to the parents and guardians on "the importance of [a] well regulated system of instruction & c." and a collection for the school library. After retiring to a grove for refreshments, the company, "amounting to some hundreds," heard the Declaration of Independence read before returning to the church for more prayer, music, and a temperance oration. Before closing the day's observance with prayer, papers were "circulated through the house, [and] a respectable number attached their names to the rolls of the Temperance society."[16] In exercises characterized by their religious overtones (the only overtly patriotic aspect of the day was the recitation of the Declaration), the Pigeon Creek Sabbath School insisted on the centrality of moral and religious values to the maintenance of the republic.

Temperance societies also sponsored celebrations in their own right, often comparing freedom from the thralldom of drunkenness to the political independence commemorated by the Fourth. This was the message of the 1847 Sons of Temperance celebration in Washington. After assembling at the Masonic Hall the Sons proceeded, in full regalia, to the courthouse. Following the Declaration and two temperance-oriented patriotic addresses, the ladies of Washington presented the young men of the society with a Bible. The order's spokesman admitted that some might think the Sons' celebration not as exciting as other Fourth observances but quickly discounted this objection: "Although no noisy mirth betrayed the over-excited feelings, it was evident that those who participated, were rejoicing in a better freedom — a freedom not alone from foreign shackles, but, from a more deadly and dangerous foe to man."[17] For temperance organizations, like other moral and religious groups, the Fourth served as a powerful symbol for relating a specific moral issue to the life of the republic.

Out-group Celebrations

Out-groups, or those excluded from most civic celebrations, also found in the Fourth an opportunity to promote a sense of belonging, however limited, to the patriotic community. Out-group celebrations allowed women, young people, and minorities to foster group solidarity and to prove that they, too, could be good republicans. Though not characteristic of all Fourth celebrations, gender and age segregation was common throughout the antebellum era. In 1801 in Greensburg, Westmoreland County, a group of women excluded from the men's celebration met separately to commemorate national independence and were toasted by the Westmoreland Cavalry at the militia celebration. Sometimes men were willing to forgo all-male festivities to spend time with their families on the Fourth. In 1818, Pittsburgh men who did not believe that "patriotism is the exclusive prerogative of the male part of the creation" gathered with their wives to "engraft" the "sacred principles which led to our national independence" onto the "young and tender minds" of their children. This inclusiveness was far from the norm, however, and in 1845, women and young people still asserted their capacity for republican celebration through separate Fourth observances. At Dr. Reed's schoolhouse in Canton Township, Washington County, the pupils and ladies of the vicinity "concluded that as they were excluded by dust, noise and public opinion from the more gorgeous celebration in the Borough, they would have a picnic among themselves, where they might discharge their superabundant patriotism, and love of fun without restraint."[18]

Young men as well as women and children were also sometimes excluded from the holiday observances of their more established elders. In 1818 "a small party of young men of this city [Pittsburgh], anxious to participate in the festivity of this day," assembled on the banks of the Monongahela River "for the purpose of commemorating 'the most memorable epocha' in the history of America." Their celebration followed exactly the form of their elders' Fourth celebrations, attesting to the youngster's ability to participate properly in the republican festival. College students often sponsored their own Fourth celebrations, proving their civic maturity and asserting the importance of learning and scholarly attainment to the republic. In 1815, for instance, Washington College students arranged an anniversary meeting and patriotic oration at a local tavern. The Tusculum Association, a student organization at Canonsburgh's Jefferson College, celebrated the Fourth in 1836 with a "feast of reason and a flow of soul" that emphasized temperance, morality, and scholarly values.[19]

Minority groups also attested to their republicanism by holding Fourth celebrations. African Americans held separate celebrations that followed the same form as those of their white counterparts, demonstrating their eagerness to commemorate the patriotic occasion. These efforts at participating in patriotic observance were sometimes the target of derision by whites, as a satiric account of a black Fourth of July in Washington County demonstrated: a "priva parta of us fashonebal kolored gemman, dissembled at de cool spring on de forth Jule, in detension of shulen de felins onde alter hour contres fre liberte." Black women also partici-pated in the Fourth, holding church fairs similar to those hosted by white women on or around the Fourth. In 1848, the women of Pittsburgh's African Methodist Episcopal Church held a "grand entertainment" on the Fourth, and Allegheny City's "colored Wesleyan church" sponsored a ladies' fair two days earlier.[20] These celebrations, like those of other out-groups, allowed African Americans to demonstrate their ability and will-ingness to be good Americans and provided an opportunity for black people to feel part of a larger celebration, albeit in a limited way.

Catholics, another target of public hostility, often observed the Fourth separately as well. By the 1840s the Catholic population of Pittsburgh was large enough to support a sizable celebration at St. Paul's Orphan Asylum, the proceeds of which benefited the orphans. Catholics observed the Fourth with a dinner, oration, and toasts, as did their Protestant counter-parts, but also used the occasion to articulate a vision of their place in a society suspicious of the Church's hierarchy and tradition. In 1845, for example, recent convert Orestes A. Brownson delivered an oration before the Catholic Institute at the Orphan Asylum. Brownson contended that Catholicism bolstered rather than threatened republican government. Virtue, he asserted, was necessary to a republic, and true virtue resided in obedience to God. As the Catholic Church was the only reliable au-thority on God's will, the "only safeguard for our Republic will be found in the wide-spread dissemination of the doctrines of that Church." Again in 1847 the Reverend John Lancaster, pastor of St. Paul's, took up the subject of Catholicism and the republic, arguing that priests did not in-terfere in the politics of their congregations and condemning political proscription on religious grounds.[21] Like other out-groups, Catholics used the Fourth to claim a place in republican society and to demonstrate their loyalty and patriotism.

Specialized Group Celebrations

More specialized groups also observed the Fourth, for social as well as patriotic reasons. Intellectual or artistic organizations met on the Fourth, as the Pittsburgh Harmonic Society's boat trip in 1818 illustrates. After meeting at Davis's Ferry on the Allegheny River at 10 A.M., the company boarded an "elegant barge" and proceeded up the river to Foster's ferry, their trip "enlivened by the music of amateurs (members of the society)." After an oration and recitation of the Declaration of Independence, the society dined and, later, toasted the usual patriotic themes as well as literature and the fine arts. Despite the social aspects of the outing, the Harmonic Society also used the occasion to make a statement about the value of art and high culture to the life of the republic. Participants toasted the fine arts ("Their encouragement stamps a character upon nations and distinguishes the civilized from the savage"), literature ("The source, the honour, and solace of civilizations"), and music ("The Sons of Harmony") as cultural signposts and repositories of wisdom useful in determining the nation's future course. The society's expansiveness inspired an effusion of "hilarity" and "unanimity," leading members to toast the Irish, immigrants generally, and the heroes of the new South American republics.[22]

Many people met on the Fourth for purely social purposes, treating the day as a holiday. Sportsmen, for example, sometimes pursued their avocation on Independence Day. In 1820, fourteen Washington county hunters joined together for a hunting party on the Fourth; in 1826, the fiftieth anniversary of the Declaration of Independence, jubilant Pittsburghers gathered at the foot of Grant's Hill for horse racing.[23] Another popular Fourth activity was the social party. Pittsburgh merchant Henry Sterling described a youthful Fourth of July party in 1819 notably devoid of patriotic feeling:

> While some around the chirries shared,
> And others eating, others talking,
> And others swinging, others walking,
> And others on the Ladies gazing,
> A number, down the sparkling wine
> Were swilling, like so many swine
> 'Till every thing to them amazing,
> In their rolling eyes appeared.
> And as the Ladies mounted high [i.e., swinging]
> Up in the air, young Jack, 'tis said
> A wicked notion in his head
> The rascal took that he would stare
> At garters tied the knees below
> And stockings white as wool or snow

Which clasp the limbs of Ladies fair
Between the ancle and the thigh.[24]

Samuel Young remembered a Fourth dinner around 1828 that gave the appearance of a patriotic gathering but was in reality as much a social occasion, the banquet's food occupying the attention of many participants more than the speeches and orations. A group of well-to-do young Pittsburghers who met at the country estate of Samuel Frew in 1835 to eat, drink, and converse with the opposite sex gathered with the express purpose of avoiding the tiresome oratory of regular Fourth dinners. This group preferred convivial socializing to the "political dinners, inflammatory speeches and red-hot toasts, delivered by the energetic and warm advocates of party strife and discontent" then current in Pittsburgh.[25]

Yet even social gatherings on the Fourth articulated ideas and values about American society and culture. Sponsored by a clergyman and his wife, a "glorious little celebration, by the young gentlemen and ladies of Monongahela City," Washington County, in 1843 illustrates this point. In contrast to the military and political observances of the Fourth, this celebration emphasized the role of white women in maintaining the republic.

> The ladies, God bless them! who does not feel that get-out-of-the-way-go-aheadiveness, which distinguishes Anglo-Saxon energy when they are "on hand," and mingle in the rites and ceremonies of a Nation's holy-day? . . . Yes! while Americanized Anglo-Saxon blood dilates our veins, and the smiles of the virtuous fair, who are destined to become the mothers of true republicans, continue to hover around the festive board, where the freemen's prayers ascend to the God of battles, and where the shouts of their lips go out "like a thunder roll upon the banners of the air" — we may deem our liberties secure and firm as the everlasting hills, and continue to show the world, as we have already done, that mankind is capable of self-government.

The celebration, which included the "usual *tete a tete,*" a procession and "promenade" through town, and a cold water banquet, served as a social gathering for young people and, in an offhand way, as an affirmation of the nativist ideology already finding its way into politics. In claiming an important role for women in the "rites and ceremonies of a Nation's holy-day," the organizers of this social gathering implicitly excluded anyone not born of "Americanized Anglo-Saxon blood" from the ranks of "true republicans." Rather than affirming democracy, this "glorious little celebration" proposed a social and political hierarchy based on the assumed superiority of British ancestry. This tribute to Anglo-Saxon excellence and virtue delighted the forty to fifty men and women in attendance. "The only regret uttered on the occasion was, that the Fourth of July comes but once a year."[26]

Partisan Politics Transforms the Fourth

Treating the Fourth as contested cultural space reveals the complexity and diversity of the festival but does little to highlight change over time. Fourth of July observances in southwestern Pennsylvania changed considerably from 1800 to 1850, both in mode of celebration and type of celebrant. While the demographic, economic, and social changes detailed in the previous chapter obviously played a role in altering the celebration of independence, a primary cause of the transformation of the Fourth was the introduction of partisan politics into American life. The disruptive effects of partisanship on an ostensibly communal and unifying occasion promoted the fragmentation, privatization, and commercialization of the day. Though interrelated, these developments each express a significant aspect of cultural change from 1800 to 1850. We can begin to understand these changes and their effects on leisure by examining the impact of partisan politics on the Fourth of July.

As other historians have noted, the Fourth was from the start a profoundly political occasion. Newspaper accounts attest to the plethora of competing celebrations sponsored by opposing factions. At least in the early years of the century, this political fragmentation did not necessarily detract from the communal or unifying aspect of the day. Opposing factions could agree to disagree, even celebrate separately, while still respecting the opinions and patriotism of their rivals. Such was the case in Uniontown, Fayette County, in 1815, when Federalists and Democrats exchanged cordial toasts from their respective places of celebration.[27]

As the vehement partisan struggles of the Second Party system emerged in the 1820s, Fourth observances changed from a celebration of republican community to a litany of Americans' political antagonisms.

Celebrants proposed angry, partisan toasts at Fourth dinners, excluded persons of opposing political sentiments from supposedly public celebrations, and denied vehemently the patriotism, morality, and republicanism of their opponents. At a celebration in Burgettstown, Washington County, in 1823, citizens favorable to the election of Andrew Gregg for governor delayed toasting until the room was "cleared of some persons of opposite sentiments, who had intruded by mistake." The company toasted Gregg, and then the opposition candidate: "John Andrew Schulze — without talents, political knowledge, or experience in public affairs, he attempts to ride into office on the pack horse of party — down with him." Democrats enacted a similar scene at Ligonier, Westmoreland County, in 1840: their festivities began only "after all those who preferred to go to the hard cider [i.e. Whig] celebration had left their ranks." The two to three hundred Democrats present erected a liberty pole after dinner and railed against Whiggery in the traditional festive toasts. In the same year, Uniontown Democrats avowed that "there cannot be a Republican heart that does not beat high at the very mention of the Fourth of July!" and urged attendance at the celebration of "a day which should be kept as the Sabbath of our Liberties." The Democrats used this "Sabbath" to condemn the "rough sea of Whiggery, the deep dead sea of Federalism, floating with 'log cabins and hard cider' to the port of Democracy."[28]

Nor were the Democrats alone in putting the Fourth to partisan uses. Whigs and a variety of factions regularly used the day to deride their opponents. Andrew Jackson became a frequent target of indignant toasts at these celebrations. A dinner organized by the Greensburg "Friends of the Constitution opposed to Usurpation by the Federal Executive" in 1834 hailed the usual objects of patriotism but also urged that the presidency "never again be occupied by any other than a man duly qualified to exalt its dignity" and protect the Constitution. Volunteer toasts were less reticent: Dr. W. R. Speer praised republican government, hoping it would survive despite "the schemes and machinations of our present Executive, and his sycophantic, aristocratic coadjutors." James F. Rainey proposed a volunteer toast to one such "coadjutor": "Wm. Barry — the honest and faithful slave of Gen. Jackson, who has suffered the political friends of the General to swindle the citizens of the United States out of $800,000, for political purposes, by way of Reform."[29]

Recognizing the possibilities presented by a large gathering, Pittsburgh Whigs nominated an electoral ticket at their blatantly partisan Fourth celebration in 1835. This elicited a venomous blast from Neville B. Craig, the Antimasonic editor of the *Pittsburgh Gazette*, who complained that "there never was an occasion on which such a disregard for public opinion and republican usage were displayed." Craig's indignation highlighted the multiplicity of patriotic meanings and values generated in the Fourth's contested cultural space. Partisanship was highly appropriate as long as it served patriotism and true republicanism; problems arose because the Fourth was a cultural arena in which competing and divergent visions of patriotism and republicanism were engendered. Thus Craig's *Gazette* had praise only for the large Antimasonic rally that he attended on the Fourth, despite the vituperatively partisan rhetoric of Thaddeus Stevens, the featured speaker. Antimasons in Westmoreland County looked askance at the whole process: their gubernatorial candidate, Joseph Ritner, didn't need to drum up support on the Fourth, they boasted smugly, for the "Old Farmer and his friends felt no such lack of excitement" as to need a dinner in 1835.[30]

As the partisan strife of the Second Party system deepened, many Americans feared that politics would destroy the original patriotic meaning of the Fourth. Complaints about exploitation of the day for self-serving purposes became more common as the years passed. As early as 1828, dissatisfaction with the partisanship of Jacksonian celebrations surfaced in Westmoreland County. A letter to the *Greensburg Gazette* objected that the toasts at Jacob Eichar's lionized Jackson at the expense of the founding fathers:

> While in but *one* volunteer toast the name of *Washington* is even mentioned, *fifteen* toasts are given to *General Andrew Jackson*. . . . there are besides this one, 364 days in the year, Sundays excepted, to indulge in party rancor without this day (which ought to be a jubilee and on which all good citizens might unite in its celebration without regard to political party feelings or attachments,) being prostituted to such a purpose.[31]

John Butler, the *Pittsburgh Statesman*'s editor, expressed similar sentiments a year later, when Leonard Johns of the *Allegheny Democrat* attempted to organize a large Democratic celebration. Butler objected that

"The occasion is commemorative of a common event — which produced effects and blessings common to all! It should be celebrated as our National Jubilee! It should be the festival of an *Empire* of a PEOPLE, and not of a *Party*!!" Butler accused Johns of using the names of prominent men without their knowledge or approval "to profane and prostitute the sacred day of our National Celebration, by converting it into a scene of contention and discord."[32]

Another such incident occurred in 1835, when southwestern Pennsylvania politicians of various stripes attempted to court the laboring class by holding "Working Men's" celebrations. In Pittsburgh an anti–Van Buren faction sponsored a Working Men's Party celebration headed by lawyers, politicians, and professionals. One celebrant offered a toast to: "The mechanics and working men of Pittsburgh — too wise, too virtuous and too independent to be made the dupes, and wear the collar, of political aspirants, especially of men who subvert the principles for which the Fourth of July has been revered, and convert them to base designs." Elements of the working class led by Richard Phillips organized a competing celebration, denouncing the Working Men's Party dinner as an insult "emanating from a batch of political speculators, who are desirous of attaining their objects by imposing on an unsuspecting community."[33] Concerned observers like Phillips feared justifiably that parties would use the powerful symbolism of the day for partisan purposes, deceiving gullible voters and corrupting the Fourth itself.

Individuals as well as parties sought to turn the Fourth to their advantage. Tom Neal, an Allegheny County politician who in 1837 organized a self-serving celebration in Tarentum, claimed that its praise of him represented the will of the people. An angry denial in the *Pittsburgh Gazette* insisted that Neal tried "to secure to his interest those who might not have the moral honesty enough to detest, or the intelligence to discern, his real motives. It was to this man that the Fourth was prostituted in Tarentum."[34] By the 1830s it became uncomfortably clear that the Fourth, an important symbol of American unity and republican virtue, was all too vulnerable to exploitation and misuse by unscrupulous politicians concerned only with the powerful legitimating function of "patriotic" observances on Independence Day.

The National Republicans, precursors of the Allegheny County

Whigs, illustrated graphically the potential for exploitation of the potent symbolic associations of the Fourth with their 1831 celebration. The "Friends of Colonel James Johnston" agreed in June to hold a Fourth of July celebration "in a manner best calculated to do honor to our Revolutionary worthies," with "special reference to the valor and services of our ancestors." The meeting deemed the observance of "our National Anniversary as a practice promotive of patriotic feelings and sentiments" that should be dedicated to "grateful expressions of our thankfulness toward living Revolutionary patriots" and consecrated to the memory of the dead.[35] Though the organizers invited all surviving revolutionary veterans as guests of honor, they made the elderly Colonel Johnston the centerpiece of the celebration. Not coincidentally, Johnston was also the National Republicans' candidate for the Senate. The party obviously hoped to capitalize on the enormous respect and prestige accorded revolutionary veterans by running Johnston as a candidate. They attempted to enhance this appeal by framing his candidacy with the powerful ritual of the Fourth of July, thereby adding a further luster of symbolic patriotism to an already sentimentally attractive candidate.

This attempt to cloak partisanship in the sheep's clothing of patriotism emerges clearly in the celebration itself. Colonel Johnston's "Friends" portrayed him as the patriotic choice for the Senate; a candidate who, by virtue of his revolutionary experience, could rise above party strife and unite his fellow Americans under the banner of true republicanism:

> All present seemed linked together by the great bands of one national fraternity. No different party interests here came in collision; no political animosities received an utterance or; for a moment, intervened to mar the harmony or interrupt the warm glow of feelings which should preponderate over all other considerations on such an occasion.

Sitting among the other surviving revolutionary veterans at the head table, the venerable Johnston epitomized American patriotism. The company's toasts rapidly revealed, however, that the patriotism of James Johnston bore a striking resemblance to the emerging Whiggery of Henry Clay.

> The American Revolution and the American System — By the former we achieved our political liberty, by the latter we sustain our national independence.

By a Quondam Jackson Man who was prevented from attending by sickness: Gen. A. Jackson — The Hero "who filled the measure of his country's glory" at New Orleans; but alas! has emptied the measure since his residence at Washington.

By Wm. Hamilton: Our Next President — May he be made of no worse materials than American *Clay*— and may he deliver us from the sway of petticoat Government!

By R. N. Koneche: Col. James Johnston — The old Revolutionary veteran, his virtues are engraven on our hearts, may the recollection of them, induce us to secure his elevation to the Senate, by a "pull, a strong pull, and the pull together."

Reveling in the legitimacy afforded them by Colonel Johnston, his National Republican "Friends" sent a delegation to offer a sarcastic toast to the Jacksonians celebrating on Stewart's Island: "The Tariff of 1828 — May it not be nullified till we get a better."[36] The Johnston celebration is a clear example of how the Fourth, as well as the Revolution it commemorated, could be put to blatantly partisan use.

Some concluded that partisan politics itself was the culprit in this debasement of the Fourth. Looking fondly back on the communal festivals of his youth, one editor observed that

Old General Jackson stopped all this fun, unconsciously, of course; in 1827, the first party celebration took place; there were no ladies, and what was worse for us and our companions, there were no boys there; and then the toasts; when all met together, no man on that day thought of obtruding his politics on his neighbor, and every sentiment breathed patriotism — now, all of one political faith, each exhibits his orthodoxy, by his extra party fury. The whole thing was spoiled — the happy Fourths were ended.[37]

Though an obvious romanticization of bygone days, this comment highlights an important aspect of changes in the Fourth. Partisan politics altered the meaning and conduct of the day; rather than unifying Americans, it fragmented them.

Beyond Partisan Politics

Issues as well as parties threatened to divide Americans on the national Sabbath. As abolitionism emerged as a political issue, its disruptive im-

plications for the Fourth became clear. Abolitionists considered the celebration of independence in a nation that tolerated slavery to be outright
hypocrisy and used the Fourth to denigrate the morality and patriotism
of their countrymen: "Can those who profess to be true friends of liberty
and the sincere haters of slavery, join in the popular celebrations of our
National Independence, as it is called? . . . The shouts of liberty and the
cannon's roar are mockery in the ear of God."[38] Many abolitionists chose
the Fourth, with its association with freedom and liberty, as the occasion
for their annual meeting. The Pittsburgh Antislavery Society, for example,
stipulated in its constitution that "The Society shall hold its Annual Meeting on the Anniversary of Our National Independence, at which time
the Annual Report shall be read, appropriate addresses delivered, and the
officers elected" for the coming year. To quiet anyone skeptical of the
necessity and urgency of linking the Fourth to the abolitionist cause,
antislavery advocates pointed to shameful incidents of attempted kidnap
of runaway slaves and free blacks alike during the nation's commemoration of freedom and inalienable rights.[39]

The corrosive effect of partisanship on an ostensibly national, unifying festival troubled many Americans. Observers complained that celebrations were too political, that Americans paid insufficient attention to
patriotic and religious reflection on the day, and that the Fourth had
departed from the happier "times when we were a boy — when dinners
were served up on an extensive scale, and none were excluded from
partaking." Increasingly, customary forms of leisure failed to unify communities experiencing rapid growth and change. Even attempts to adapt
old forms to new circumstances proved unsuccessful. A militia celebration in Westmoreland County, for example, confronted the problem of
destructive partisanship at Fourth celebrations in 1839 by altering the
toasting ritual: "The celebration of the day being neutral as regards party
politics; both parties having cheerfully united on the occasion, it was
resolved to have none but regular toasts prepared by a committee consisting of an equal number of persons from each party appointed for that
purpose."[40]

Toward Moral and Religious Celebrations

This stopgap measure failed miserably, and local residents soon looked
for new modes of celebration. Concern for preserving the Fourth's integ-

rity as a patriotic festival fostered two developments: a rejection of public celebration in favor of private observance, which is discussed below; and a shift in the orientation of Fourth celebrations away from political concerns and toward moral and religious values. As noted above, the Fourth could be a vehicle for relating piety, temperance, and morality to the establishment and maintenance of the American republic. Moral and religious observances linked the republic to God and Christian virtue, avoided divisive partisan issues, and included women and children in the patriotic festival. One might object to the stridently partisan procession of the Sons of Democracy through Uniontown in 1840, but it was harder to object on patriotic grounds to the Sons of Temperance parade through Washington in 1847. The temperance cause took the Fourth by storm, especially in population centers increasingly troubled by the social dislocation caused by drunkenness. Commenting on the large temperance processions in Pittsburgh and Allegheny in 1842, the *Spirit of Liberty* observed that the "friends of temperance seem to have quite a monopoly on the celebration of the Fourth."[41]

Most people applauded this recession of partisanship. In 1843 Pittsburgh's *Morning Chronicle* hailed the apparent absence of political dinners:

> Heretofore, long before the day arrived, all the leaders of the different political parties of our city were busily engaged in making preparations to celebrate the Anniversary of American Independence in their own selfish and anti-American manner. But this year we have heard of no such preparations. . . . a majority of our citizens have seen the absurdity of sacrificing all their better feelings on the altar of some political party, just because a few unprincipled men command them to do so.[42]

Associating moral issues with American independence proved so powerful that moral and religious celebrations had, by the 1840s, subordinated other celebrations to themselves.[43] This was particularly true of military celebrations. Military parades were still considered appropriate Fourth observances but were increasingly overshadowed by moral and religious exercises. In 1843, for example, the Pittsburgh Blues volunteer company signed the temperance pledge en masse before joining the Washington Total Abstinence Society and the Jackson Independent Blues, another temperance company, for a boat trip to a temperance celebration six miles from the city. In the same year the military and citizens of Monongahela City met at Carrollton, Washington County, for a cold water (i.e., no liquor allowed) Fourth: "*This* is an achievement of the great moral revolution that has absolved these states from all allegiance to 'King Alcohol' — a greater tyrant than was ever King George."[44]

Sabbath school as well as temperance celebrations eclipsed the military. Westmoreland County's Phoenix Guards, which previously had sponsored or participated in military celebrations, became by 1847 an auxiliary to the Methodist Episcopal Sabbath School celebration. The guards escorted the school to their place of celebration and provided music for the procession. Later they joined in adopting resolutions that affirmed the necessity of religion to republican government:

"*Resolved,* That patriotic feelings incites to worthy and noble action, and that a professed regard for the religion of the Bible, is anti-hypocritical and real, in those only, who . . . labor to keep them [i.e., republican institutions] free from weakening innovations and unholy and anti-Republican connections"[45]

Birmingham, in Allegheny County, witnessed a similar phenomenon in 1847. After turning out at "an early hour," the town's "Guards" and the "Blues" escorted the Methodist Episcopal and Associated Reformed Sabbath Schools to a grove where the German Lutheran Sabbath School had already begun a celebration.[46] In using the day to promote group solidarity, to articulate a vision of their place in American society, and to develop a dominant form of public celebration, moral and religious groups demonstrated how symbolically powerful and how malleable the Fourth could be.

Even this move away from the divisiveness of partisan celebrations had a fragmenting effect, however. Ethnocultural issues came into play in moral and religious celebrations, dividing celebrants along ethnic, religious, or cultural lines. Sabbath schools of the same denomination might celebrate the Fourth together, but Methodists, Presbyterians, Episcopalians, and Catholics usually celebrated separately, as did members of black churches. Temperance advocates agreed on the evils of drinking but divided on questions of moral suasion versus coercion and total abstinence versus renunciation of hard liquor. Religious advocates of antislavery ran afoul of their fire-eating political counterparts on the issues of abolitionism and colonization. Evidence also suggests that this division was a partial product of the Old Light-New Light schism in the Presbyterian church in the late 1830s.[47] The emergence of moral and religious celebrations on the Fourth alleviated some of the discomfort produced by partisan fragmentation but could not prevent completely the clash of values, ideals, and interpretations of patriotism in a rapidly changing society.

A More Private Holiday

Linked to this transition from a partisan to a religious Fourth of July was a trend away from any public observance of the holiday at all. Though more people than ever observed the Fourth as 1850 approached, an increasing number chose to forgo public celebration and its attendant divisiveness in favor of a more private holiday. Often southwestern Pennsylvanians spent the day in small parties, on picnics, or in the quiet company of friends and family. The diaries of Charles B. Scully and Robert McKnight illustrate this retreat from public celebration. Scully and McKnight spent their Fourth holidays in the 1840s not at political or religious celebrations but at social gatherings and private amusements. Scully played tenpin with friends in Allegheny City and paid evening social calls on the Fourth in 1843; McKnight viewed fireworks displays, visited local amusements, and attended dancing parties in 1842 and 1846. Though aware of the public celebrations (McKnight remarked indignantly that a noisy militia parade awakened him at an early hour in 1846), neither took part in them or, apparently, felt obligated by patriotism to do so. Neither did the harried editor of the *Morning Chronicle*. After enumerating the various activities and amusements available in 1842, he revealed his plan to spend the day in "retirement," sitting "among reams of unopened exchanges, sipping some of the delicious Peach Syrup, which Mr. I. Harris furnishes temperance folks, quietly puffing one of Cooke's excellent cigars!"[48]

For those spending the Fourth privately, the day had become a time for amusement, recreation, and the enjoyment of one's social and familial circle. Even organizations that previously participated in public, patriotic observances had by the 1840s inclined toward a recreational Fourth. In

1838 Pittsburgh's Vigilant Fire Company rejected an invitation from the Neptune Company to join in a citywide firemen's dinner on the Fourth, commenting that "many of the members of this company are attached to military and other associations that have already made arrangements for the celebration of the coming Fourth." This proliferation of social gatherings by military and other groups accelerated the trend toward privatization by providing smaller, more selective venues for celebration. In 1842, for example, a Washington County tavern owner informed the *Washington Reporter* that a previous notice of a general celebration with a militia company at his tavern was in error: his preparations were only for the company; the general public should unite with the local Sabbath School celebration. Similarly, in the 1840s Pittsburgh's Duquesne Fire Company sponsored a yearly Fourth of July picnic, replete with sack races and egg tosses, rather than participating in other public gatherings. Joseph Buffum arranged a Fourth dinner for his Sons of Temperance division at Shakespeare Gardens in East Liberty in 1848, but only ten Sons and their dates journeyed on the omnibuses provided by the Gardens' management for what turned out to be "a pretty jolly day."[49] This trend toward privatization led a Washington County editor to lament in 1843:

> No preparations for feasting are going on. The fatted calf is permitted to chew its cud unmolested in the stall, and the poultry is secure in the barn yard. Shady groves are not now visited, as of old, by "select assemblies," nor cannons fired to wake the hill sides with their echoes, as they hail the dawn of a nation's jubilee. . . . Times are sadly changed! The Fourth of July will soon cease to be remembered in any public or peculiar demonstration. True, it will be celebrated at particular *places*, and by particular *persons*. But we desire to see *all* parties, sects, ages, sexes and conditions, unite in an offering of gratitude, with pure hearts, for this purpose, to the Giver of every good and perfect gift.[50]

Commercialization

Commercialization also contributed to the decline of common observances on the Fourth. As the population of southwestern Pennsylvania increased, a sizable market for recreation, amusement, and holiday goods developed. This led to the commercialization of the Fourth and its further transition from patriotic festival to recreational holiday. Like private celebrations, commercial amusements allowed people to distance themselves from partisan strife and social fragmentation. As suggested in chapter 3, commercial entertainments were usually public events but not necessarily communal activities. No one could reasonably expect a menagerie or minstrel show to unify Americans as the community festivals of bygone days supposedly had. By eliminating the expectation of communal unity on Independence Day, commercial leisure mitigated feelings of unrequited patriotism and helped to redefine the occasion as a recreational holiday.[51]

If some Pennsylvanians ceased attending civic celebrations because they were disenchanted with their tone and conduct, others simply found the growing number of commercial amusements a more attractive way of spending the Fourth. With the advent of steam, regular packet lines transported southwestern Pennsylvanians up and down the region's rivers to pleasure gardens that catered to the holiday trade. In the Pittsburgh area, Greenwood, Rosedale, and Manchester Gardens drew many holiday amusement seekers with special events and attractions. In 1849 Rosedale Gardens in Manchester offered its patrons "an exhibition of fireworks, prepared expressly to commemorate the anniversary of American Independence," while Greenwood Gardens, "a place so pretty it almost exceeds description" promised its expected "five thousand visitors" a 3.5-acre garden consisting of "nearly three miles of walks, with numerous summer houses, shady bowers, & c. all ornamented with Flowers both native and exotic." For those wishing to range farther afield, steamboat pleasure excursions to rural towns provided opportunities for bucolic enjoyment. In 1848, for example, Pittsburghers could choose from the "fast running steamer LAKE ERIE" that made a pleasure trip to Beaver and back with "a fine band of music" on board, or the "splendid and fast running steamer CAROLINE" that left Allegheny City for the Sons of Temperance convention in McKeesport.[52]

Traveling amusements like circuses, equestrian troupes, vocalists, performers, and curiosities scheduled their arrival in Pittsburgh, the largest population center in the region, to coincide with the Fourth. Often, these commercial attractions scheduled additional performances to accommodate the large number of spectators. Public enthusiasm for Fourth of July amusements sometimes pushed attendance beyond safe limits. So many eager spectators packed the Pittsburgh Amphitheater to watch a balloon ascension in 1835 that the seats collapsed under their weight, causing several injuries. In 1839 a traveling menagerie took advantage of the holiday crowd by exhibiting Master Nellis, a boy without hands "whose feats with his toes are astonishing," adjacent to the giraffe, in a separate exhibit that allowed the collection of a second admission charge.[53] Commercial recreations proliferated in the 1840s: in 1843 a "Fakir" gave two exhibitions in Concert Hall, and by 1846 a circus, a menagerie, a theatrical performance, and a vocalist at the Eagle Ice Cream Saloon competed for Pittsburghers' Fourth of July patronage. Joseph Buffum reported the uneven quality of some of these commercial amusements. In 1848 he went to "Apollo Hall to hear the Vermont Troups of singers, some cream but the singing was not good."[54]

Commercial amusements even catered to their patrons' desire for patriotic remembrance on the Fourth. To prevent squabbling about the content of attractions from driving audiences away, leisure entrepreneurs presented unabashedly filiopietistic amusements that were unlikely to offend most patrons. In 1849, for example, Spalding and Roger's North American Circus added a dramatic troupe to the company for its engagement in Pittsburgh "for the purpose of getting up every night the grand Heroic and Patriotic Spectacles of GENERAL WASHINGTON, 'OLD PUT,' AND 'MAD ANTHONY WAYNE.'" Promising to commemorate "the gallant deeds of the *Heroes of '76*," the show concluded with a "grand National Tableaux of *Gen. Washington* mounted on a noble charger, *borne on the shoulders of his brave continentals*." The troupe performed four times on the Fourth, insuring citizens maximum availability of the "patriotic Spectacle."[55] Even religious groups contributed to the commercialization of the Fourth. At its Fourth of July fair in 1843, Pittsburgh's First Evangelical Lutheran Church exhibited the war tent in which General Washington supposedly slept at Valley Forge. Commenting on the occasion in his diary, Charles B. Scully noted that a "procession passed through our city this evening with the Military escorting Gen'l. Washington's War Tent borrowed from Mr. GWP Custis, his relative of Arlington, Va. This is certainly humbugerous," Scully complained, "— it is brought here on a speculation to be used on the 4th of July to raise money for a Church."[56]

Merchants stocked specialized items in the 1840s as southwestern Pennsylvanians viewed the Fourth increasingly as a recreational holiday. The Methodist Episcopal Sabbath School celebrations in Pittsburgh and Allegheny in 1839 presented attending children with books chosen specifically for the occasion. The custom of giving gift books to children on the Fourth apparently became common in the next decade. "A holiday Salute and Fourth of July XPounder, containing the Declaration of Independence and Twenty large and beautiful engravings" was available at Patterson's for six and one-half cents in 1844, and in 1846 Pittsburgh merchant C. E. Miner advertised "articles, which, on each return of our National Birthday, the juvenile class, also the youth, expect to procure and receive for their amusement," consisting of games, books, cards, paints, and the like. A year later Miner evidently expanded his selection of Fourth of July wares, offering "Yankee Doodle, Brother Jonathan, &c. &c., mammoth sise and full of Pictures, got up expressly for the Anniversary of National Independence." Anyone who wished to remember friends was advised to go to Miner's and "obtain a Fourth of July paper to send them." The *Chronicle* of 1847 reminded its readers that McKenna's Auction Rooms had a large lot of books for sale, and that "some are suitable for 4th of July presents, among which are the Boudoir Annual for 1817, fine plate, Kriss Kringle, rare show plates."[57]

Fireworks also became a Fourth of July staple in the 1840s. Firecrackers appealed to all ages and social groups. The *Pittsburgh Daily Dispatch* noted in 1848 that stores "will be crowded with purchasers of fireworks, the little urchins who desire to 'raise thunder' at night," while the young attorney Charles B. Scully exasperated a hack driver in 1843 by frightening his horses with crackers on a trip to Allegheny City. Merchants promoted this taste for pyrotechnics, offering a variety of explosive goods. According to the *Gazette*, C. Yeager stocked crackers, pinwheels, torpedoes, triangle wheels, and a "large assortment of other Fire Works, too numerous to mention." B. Bown advertised in the *Daily Dispatch* that he sold "Fire Works and Sundries for the Fourth" that included pinwheels, serpents, rockets, and Roman candles. Firecrackers became so prevalent and bothersome that proprietors of steamboats and pleasure gardens warned patrons that their use would not be tolerated on the Fourth. Pittsburgh's city government considered the problem serious enough by the late 1840s to merit increasing police protection to crack down on Pittsburgh boys' abuse of firecrackers.[58]

Caterers too responded to holiday demand. Pittsburgh's Lease and Brown stocked extra confections, ice cream, and citrus fruit for Fourth of July picnics. B. Bown carried coconuts, loaf sugar, rock candy, licorice, and dates expressly for the holiday trade. Pittsburgh butchers Shaffer and Flannegan offered "A Fine Bullock for the Fourth" purchased from the Harmony Society at Economy, as well as veal and mutton in 1843. Charles Kent and Andrew Graham advertised "PRIME BEEF! FOR FOURTH OF JULY DINNERS" in 1847, promising to slaughter two prime Pennsylvania steers being "determined that [their] customers should have the best for their independence dinners."[59]

A Recreational Fourth

Commercialization depended on the creation of a market for leisure goods and services, which in turn required widespread cessation of work on the Fourth. Some employers allowed their workers time off for celebration as early as the 1820s, but many merchants and manufacturers routinely conducted business on the Fourth. In 1826, for instance, George Anschutz shut down his Pittsburgh rolling mill and Christopher Cowan paid off his men and eased down the fires in his furnace, but shipping activity on the river wharves remained brisk. As time passed, however, Pennsylvanians, like other Americans, worried about the deleterious effects of overwork. They came to view preoccupation with business on the Fourth as mean-spirited, especially among employers who forced their workers to toil on a national festival day. By the mid-1830s stores and businesses began to work shortened hours or close completely on the Fourth, allowing workers to spend the day as they wished.[60] Increased free time not only promoted the development of commercial amusements but also fostered the idea of the Fourth as an appropriate occasion for recreation and amusement. A letter from "An Old Merchant" to the editor of the *Pittsburgh Gazette* in 1839 recommended as a "matter of economy and justice" that business cease on the Fourth to give "clerks, young men, and all hands, a little time to turn out and participate in the happiness and enjoyment of the day." The merchant reminded employers that a good and faithful clerk, apprentice, a worthy lad, or a smart, intelligent young man, who attends well to business and to the interest of his employer, ought to be occasionally indulged, not only on such a day as the 4th of July, but also by times in the evenings to attend religious meetings, literary and moral societies & c. The good old proverb, "All work and no play, makes Jack a dull boy," may fairly be applied to the matter in question. In our apprenticeship, we and many other young men were confined too closely, and it was attended with bad consequences.[61]

Editor Isaac Harris hailed the transition from work to play on the Fourth, noting approvingly in 1839 that many "cheerful groups" would assemble for sheer enjoyment, with "no other intention than to spend the day in joyful harmony — exchanging and interchanging feelings and sentiments, improving acquaintance and binding still closer the strong ties of friendship."[62]

As Pennsylvanians opted for a recreational Fourth during the 1840s, participatory and spectator sports became increasingly popular holiday events. To some extent, sports had always been favorite holiday activities. In 1818, for instance, young men "eager for victory in the race, the throw, the leap, and the fall" congregated on a hill outside Pittsburgh, and we note above that horse racing was held on the Fourth in 1826. But participation in sports and physical recreation increased as the Fourth changed from an occasion for patriotic reflection to a time for fun and amusement. *Harris's Intelligencer* remarked in 1839 that many people spent the day in the country hunting and fishing. In 1842 Pittsburgh's Regatta Club organized a Fourth of July Regatta at Berry Hall in which, among other races, six one-man skiffs competed for a silver watch. By 1844 even the highbrow Marshall Literary Institute surrendered to the sporting impulse: their Fourth celebration in East Liberty's Shakespeare Gardens included a morning of "pleasant ramblings" and "sports of the field," the newspapers reported, before the customary dinner and literary exercises.[63] The popularity of sports as a Fourth of July pastime grew throughout the 1840s. Local marksmen sponsored a shooting match for an expensive rifle behind the Western Penitentiary in Allegheny City in 1845, and sportsmen deemed Independence Day 1850 an appropriate occasion for the first meeting of the Pittsburgh and Allegheny City cricket clubs.[64]

From Republican Festival to Raucous Celebration

What emerged from these changes was a Fourth of July barely recognizable to those who pined for the simpler, more patriotic observances of their youth. The Fourth was transformed or, in the view of some, transmogrified from a republican festival and national Sabbath to a raucous celebration of idleness, excess, and commercialism. By 1847 the Fourth had gotten so out of hand in Pittsburgh that the mayor added police to contain the "bustle and excitement" attending " 'Fourth of July times.' " The press applauded this prudent move because there were "many men, as well as boys who grow entirely too patriotic on such occasions."[65] The *Pittsburgh Weekly Telegraph* of July 10, 1847, captured the tone of the new "bustle and excitement" on the Fourth in a report of the day's festivities:

> The streets were crowded by a general turnout of our citizens and by a great number of people in from the country. The Circus, theatre, Eagle Saloon and ice cream establishments did a great deal of business. And we are sorry to say, from the considerable number of persons whom we saw on the streets in a very independent condition, that some other establishments must have done a considerable business. We saw one fellow so drunk that he mistook Wilkins' marble manufactory for a grave-yard and begged that somebody would bury him there, and raise a monument over him. A constable complied with a part of his wish by taking him to the Tombs.[66]

The Fourth's transformation resulted in large measure from the fragmentation, privatization, and commercialization of leisure we observed in southwestern Pennsylvania between 1800 and 1850. As in other areas of leisure, demographic increase, ethnic diversification, the emergence of mass politics, and economic change combined by 1850 to transform irrevocably patterns of celebration that were characteristic of traditional agricultural society. In the process, however, Pennsylvanians used new leisure forms and options to redefine their notions of patriotism and community, to meliorate the social tensions generated by partisanship, and to create a culture more consonant with their changing lives and experiences.

5

Leisure, Culture, and the Creation of Class

THOUGH LEISURE ONCE SERVED THE ESTABLISHMENT and maintenance of communal solidarity in southwestern Pennsylvania's traditional agrarian society, it could also be profoundly divisive. As chapters 3 and 4 discuss, changing patterns of leisure led to communal fragmentation and privatization. This divisiveness stemmed from leisure's imbeddedness in larger social processes: population increase, ethnic and religious diversification, political change, and economic growth. In one sense, then, leisure both shaped and was shaped by these developments, and its effects were not the direct product of deliberate calculation or choice by any individual or group. People could, however, enlist leisure in the cause of consciously directed social differentiation. Leisure served exactly this function in the formation of social classes during the early nineteenth century. Socio-economic groups eager to establish social preeminence and display cultural authority used leisure activities in two ways: to promote solidarity and their own sense of identity, and to differentiate themselves from other social formations. At the same time, promulgating ideologies of class superiority through leisure activities raised the possibility of contesting or resisting those assertions using similar tactics.

Three Classes in Nineteenth-Century Pennsylvania

Class is a notoriously difficult and slippery concept. Few historians and social scientists agree on a single definition or unitary theory of class.[1] For our purposes here, class should be understood as a complex phenomenon that encompasses more than just economic and political factors: kinship, education, lifestyle, and other cultural variables also play major roles in defining social class.[2] The following discussion of leisure and class adopts a tripartite division as a heuristic device: an upper class; a "middling" or middle class; and a lower or working class. Admittedly, this division is imperfect. It is as viable as any other, however, and because it would have been recognizable to nineteenth-century Pennsylvanians,[3] it does as little violence as possible to the evidence.

Even this simple scheme requires some elaboration. In the following discussion, *upper class* refers to large landowners, prominent members of the learned professions, owners of substantial commercial enterprises, and influential politicians. Wealth was a crucial, but not the only, factor in determining upper class membership in southwestern Pennsylvania. Most members of the patrician class had also descended from or been closely associated with the region's early settlers. "It so happened," Henry Marie Brackenridge explained, "that after the revolutionary war, a number of families of the first respectability, principally officers of the army, were attracted to this spot [Pittsburgh]," imparting the area with "a degree of refinement, elegance of manners and polished society" unusual on the "extreme frontier." Colonel John Neville of Pittsburgh epitomized southwestern Pennsylvania's upper class. Neville was "indeed the model of an accomplished gentleman, as elegant in his person and finished in his manners and education as he was generous and noble in his feelings. His house was the temple of hospitality, to which all respectable strangers repaired."[4] Though wealth certainly loomed large in the ascription of upper class status, cultural factors like refinement, manners, education, and hospitality also played major roles. Consequently, as used here, *patrician* denotes families who combined wealth and lineage as the benchmark of upper class status. For this group, refined and genteel leisure loomed large in demarcating the social boundaries of class.

The *middle* or *middling class* included landowners and farmers with moderately sized holdings, prosperous merchants and, especially after the War of 1812, industrialists and manufacturers. Well-off but undistinguished professionals, particularly lawyers, also belonged to the middle class. As early as 1810, Fortescue Cuming complained that lawyers "arrogate[d] to themselves the title or epithet of esquire," filled through "intrigue" many political offices, and "assume[d] to themselves a consequence to which they are in no other way entitled." Financial prosperity elevated the middle class to a respectable status, but newcomers could seldom match the cultural attainments, social prestige, or professional reputation of their patrician counterparts. Lawyers proliferated in Pittsburgh, Samuel Jones noted in 1826, but "with a few exceptions" they bore no "comparison to those who flourished" in the "olden time," when patricians dominated the legal profession.[5] Though middle class lawyers, politicians, and civic functionaries were not patricians, they, like the upper class, constituted an elite of sorts. Here, *elite* refers to an overlapping upper and middle class group with some form of social distinction, political authority, or cultural prestige. Thus, middle class Pennsylvanians might share elite status with patricians based on education or occupation without actually being a member of the upper class.

Southwestern Pennsylvania's working class numbered artisans, mechanics, laborers, and landless agricultural workers among its members. The region's economic development spurred the growth of a working class early in the century. Its network of navigable rivers made the area a commercial nexus between east and west and generated work for boatmen, dock workers, and draymen. The construction of roads and turnpikes produced more jobs for construction laborers, coach drivers, teamsters, and transportation workers. When manufacturing grew in importance, lower class men and women entered factories and shops as industrial workers. Not surprisingly, the lower class commanded little social authority or respect from the middle or upper classes. Workers lacked financial resources and distinguished family roots and pursued lifestyles that their social "betters" considered rude and uncultivated at best, dissolute and boorish at worst. Despite increasing middle class disapproval of drinking, gambling, and killing time in relaxation and idle conversation, however, workers insisted on spending their free time as they saw fit. The working class contrasted their independence, informality, and unrestrained enjoyment of free time to what they often perceived as the stultifying conventionality of "respectable" leisure.[6]

A Few Caveats on Class

This depiction of class division and composition requires a few caveats. First, the foregoing divisions were not hard and fast, particularly at the interstices between classes. Small proprietors, for example, who were ostensibly members of the middle class — struggling shopkeepers or marginally successful yeoman — had much in common with the lower class: hard work, little extra cash, and comparable day-to-day experiences. Much the same was true of the upper middle and upper classes, particularly for those patricians who fell on hard times and were "reduced from a more affluent situation, by misfortune."[7] Both groups enjoyed comfortable, sometimes even elegant lifestyles, and moved in similar social circles, despite the upper class's claims to superior bloodlines. This points to a second caveat: even though Pennsylvanians recognized class boundaries, they often ignored social and economic differences and interacted with people of different backgrounds. Despite Samuel Jones's contention that there existed between the classes "lines of demarcation . . . wide, distinct, and not to be violated with impunity," cross-class socializing did occur. Samuel Young, for example, gained access to prestigious literary circles in spite of his working class roots. Mingling of upper and upper middle class neighbors was even more common, and even religious and ethnic differences did not prevent it. Robert McKnight and Charles B. Scully, for instance, shared acquaintances and pursued similar leisure activities, even though the former was an upper class Protestant and the latter an upper middle class Catholic.[8]

A third caveat concerns the exaggeration of class differences by upper and middle class Pennsylvanians. We must remember that class is, after all, the artificial creation of human beings, and not a "natural" phenomenon, as the upper classes sometimes urged. To add a pleasing cultural facade to disturbing economic and political inequality, southwestern Pennsylvania's elites often attempted to portray class differences as the inevitable product of superior refinement, gentility, and intelligence, rather than the other way around. This obfuscation sometimes betrayed itself, especially when upper and middle class Pennsylvanians confronted the specter, if not the actuality, of social mobility. Patricians sought to protect their cultural authority by denying that wealth alone made a person fit to join the upper class. Similarly, the middle class attempted to distance itself from the working class by emphasizing respectability and superior morality as its defining qualities. Anxiety about retaining one's elevated position and the consequent necessity of pulling up the cultural ladders to foil social climbers engendered developments that highlighted the artificiality of class distinctions. Often, this anxiety about maintaining class divisions centered on how and with whom one spent leisure time.

Middle and Upper Class Distinctions

Middle class Pennsylvanians took great pains to distinguish themselves from the working class, perhaps because the social distance between the two was often quite small. Though their money afforded them significant prestige, middle class parvenus attempted to cement their claims to social and cultural authority by adopting a "refined" style of leisure and social intercourse. This style emphasized propriety, respectability, and exclusion of the unworthy from polite society. In practice, middle class refinement frequently led to complaints about how inhospitable southwestern Pennsylvanians could be. Fortescue Cuming noted that Pittsburghers were too busy making money and practicing politics to be good hosts. New Englander Timothy Flint concurred. Flint and his family met a Pittsburgh minister "whose stately mansion and fine furniture, gave us an impression of the opulence, if not the hospitality of the owner." The homesick Flint pined for "the simple, unaffected, and ample hospitality, which constitutes so delightful a trait in the character" of New England clergymen. For the middle class, polite society, swelling coffers, and an affected refinement promised distance from the working class and the hope of climbing higher in the social order.[9]

Among the upper class, fear of middle class social climbing generated a compulsive, almost morbid, interest in genealogy and family lineage as determinants of gentility and prestige. To bolster their claims of refined lineage and cultural authority, patricians excluded anyone of inferior bloodlines from their social circle. Native Pittsburgher Samuel Jones disdained the "cold and heartless formalities that distinguish the present day." Refinement had its virtues, Jones allowed, but not as a mask for pretension and arrogance.

> *That* refinement which compels a stranger, on his introduction, when he pulls off his hat with one hand, to thrust out his pedigree with the other, while the whispering interrogatories of "who is he," "what is he" and "what is he worth," are echoed from the cellar to the garret with lightnings' rapidity, is as ridiculous as it is contemptible. And *that* refinement which excludes from the assemblies of the rich, because their possessor is poor, or because he is not even remotely allied to some distinguished family, is despicable, as creating distinctions altogether foreign to that simplicity which should characterize the American people.[10]

This genealogical obsession reached its zenith at the exclusive spa at Bedford Springs, which employed a "master of ceremonies" to interrogate young men about their bloodlines. Only after passing muster with the genealogist would the aspirant be admitted to the ballroom and introduced to upper class daughters.[11]

These contrivances did not deceive everyone. Traveler Fortescue Cuming derided status-conscious Pennsylvanians, both the upper and middle class varieties. Even those in southwestern Pennsylvania's upper class, Cuming noted, were relative newcomers to patrician status. Though they styled themselves "*Well born* to distinguish themselves from the not so wealthy," some "could not tell who had been their ancestors in the second generation." They were merely fortunate enough to gain land and wealth early in the region's settlement. Like many people who suddenly gained money and status, Cuming observed perspicaciously, the upper class "wish[ed] to seem as if they had always been in the same situation." To this end they affected "the manner and appearance of the great," and "assum[ed] airs of superiority." The bottom line, Cuming insisted, was that even southwestern Pennsylvania's first families used wealth to compensate for their lack of "descent, and all the virtues and accomplishments."[12]

Samuel Jones offered a similar critique of middle class pretensions, pointing out that money opened doors even in "polite circles." Despite social divisions as rigid as "the most scrupulous Hindoos maintain, in the defence of their religious prejudices," wealth "is held in high honour, and is a most potent agent in bringing down the hills, and filling up the vallies

of etiquette." Few middle class Pittsburghers could boast of "noble lineage," Jones observed, even if that meant merely being related to a revolutionary officer. To compensate for this "deficiency," Jones railed,

> they unrol their deeds, or those of their ancestors, (not in *arms*, but) con-
> taining their *titles*— to boundless tracts of land in the country adjacent, or
> to lots in town, with the appurtenances. They speak modestly, of their stock
> in bank, and stock in trade; for it is considered no derogation from family
> consequence, to be concerned in trade, in this palpably trading commu-
> nity.[13]

Leisure as Social Differentiation

To divert attention (their own as well as others') away from the economic
basis of their pretensions to cultural authority, the upper and middle
classes turned to leisure as a means of social differentiation. Patricians
and parvenus alike expressed class differences through both the style and
substance of their leisure activities, though obviously there was some over-
lap in these two categories.[14] All classes gathered for dance parties, for
instance, but their forms and styles differed markedly. An informal barn
dance attended by working folk differed in both style and substance from
the elaborate upper class balls held at estates or country homes. Similarly,
the genteel social interaction in a reading room or coffee house set its
middle class patrons apart from workers who enjoyed the easygoing atmosphere of a tavern or beer cellar. Participants in these activities cultivated such differences as representations of class membership.

Even public events and community leisure activities demarcated
class lines. The division of labor and responsibility in common leisure
pursuits replicated and validated the socioeconomic hierarchy: upper and
middle class participants occupied leadership roles, while the working
class filled subordinate positions. This reproduction of class hierarchy in
a social and cultural rather than a strictly economic sphere pointed to
the "naturalness" of social divisions. In essence, class-based leisure provided a cultural concomitant for the economic divisions that southwestern Pennsylvanians experienced on the job or in the market. Two aspects
of this process are especially revealing. First, the development and en-
trenchment of class-specific activities illustrates how leisure enhanced

social differentiation and promoted class identification. Second, the division of activity in common leisure pursuits demonstrates how the upper and middle classes attempted to extend their authority beyond the economic sphere to social and cultural realms. As we shall see, leisure was an effective means of class differentiation but a less than satisfactory tool of class domination.

Upper Class Leisure

The emergence of class-specific activities was nowhere more apparent than in patterns of visiting and social gatherings. Each class developed a distinct style of social interaction, based on availability of resources and group preferences. The upper class, composed mostly of southwestern Pennsylvania's traditional elite, favored exclusive private parties and formal social gatherings more than did the middle or working classes. In part this preference reflected the availability of large houses and estates suitable for lavish entertainments. But it also stemmed from the upper class's desire to differentiate itself from the raucous leisure styles of the working class and the "respectable" amusements of the aspiring middle class. Large landowners, wealthy merchants, and the scions of patrician families used exclusive social gatherings to foster an image of gentility far removed from the banal public leisure of their perceived social inferiors. Upper class visiting also drew on a wider geographic area: visitors and guests from outside the region socialized with southwestern Pennsylvania's upper crust, linking elites in one locale to another and offering a sense of cosmopolitanism unavailable to their social inferiors. Easterner Lucy Ann Higbee recorded visits to two prominent Pittsburgh families on her journey west in 1837. In June she and her party stopped at The Meadows, James Ross's mansion, where Ross entertained his guests with pet deer, walks through his extensive grounds, and an "astral lamp," a device akin to a magic lantern. Higbee next visited the Widow Collins, who maintained "one of the most cultivated residences on the river," complete with a greenhouse and a glass "bee palace."[15]

This emphasis on genteel hospitality and social refinement based on wealth, education, and polite manners had two purposes. On the one hand, refined socializing and elegant entertainment promoted upper class solidarity by providing a set of shared experiences and a sense of common identity. On the other, participating in polite society set members of the upper class apart from those below and certified their claims to social superiority by allowing them to portray their class as exemplars of cultural attainment. Posarach, an 1840 correspondent to the *Literary Messenger,* an upper class literary journal, made this point explicitly. "Every community contains three classes of society — the higher, or richer; the middling, or those in ordinary circumstances; and the lower, or extremely poor class. To the first of these has been awarded the honor of retaining politeness in its legitimate form."[16]

Southwestern Pennsylvania's upper class extended and refined this distinction, taking pains to impress upon social climbers that patrician status depended on more than just money. In an era of startling, if not widespread, economic growth and social mobility, the upper class realized that even wealth alone was insufficient to insure gentility, for many of the middling class were accruing it. Using leisure to claim social distinction and cultural authority rested on genteel style as well as financial substance, and the patrician descendants of early settlers claimed that only they had sufficient social connections, education, and refinement to define that style. Ellen Blythe, the wife of a Pittsburgh minister, noted this distinction: "There is a dashing, fashionable set, much like the same class elsewhere, but of these I know little. The middling classes are mostly merchants & manufacturers, who came here to grow rich, & they are succeeding."[17]

The genteel style of upper class leisure depended on more than the consumption of leisure commodities and services unavailable to others. It also required large amounts of time free from work in which to enjoy and display that consumption. Thus only a gentleman of leisure could learn the "fashionable" art of fencing, or patronize traveling professors of music who offered lessons and performances for upper class families ("private parties entertained at their house, $5 per night"). Politician and novelist H. H. Brackenridge, for example, "bestowed" the "usual accomplishment of dancing" on his son Henry Marie, as well as instruction in "fencing with the small sword." Neither time nor money could discourage the elite from pursuing their distinctive style of leisure: despite a wartime tax on "playing and visiting cards — fifty per centum ad valoreum," there is no evidence that their use declined in elite social circles. Only the "dashing, fashionable set" had time and money to rent Gideon Gray's "Steam Pleasure Boat" that sailed the Monongahela River attending "pleasure parties & those who may wish to sail it up and down for the purpose of fowling and fishing & c."[18] Cultivating this upper class style of leisure allowed participants to display publicly their refinement, gentility, and education, thereby demonstrating their elevated social position.

The diaries of Robert McKnight and Charles B. Scully, two young Pittsburgh attorneys, reveal the contours of upper class leisure in the 1840s. Both attended a constant round of parties, balls, and elite social gatherings. Scully, for example, reported frequent visits to Homewood, the estate of influential jurist and politician William Wilkins. The young man rhapsodized about the parlor games, music, and conversation he enjoyed at Homewood, the "headquarters of hospitality." McKnight recorded several visits to Deer Creek, the rural retreat of the socially prominent Denny family. In 1842 he described the arrival of guests at a cotillion party; approximately sixteen young ladies and twenty or more gentlemen from the Pittsburgh area's first families comprised the company: "next came four musicians, & we soon formed a cotillion on the green in front of the house. . . . We sat down to dinner about 3 O'clock — & afterwards danced away on the piazza. . . . Supped about 6 after which they got to dancing in the parlours." The Dennys also exhibited refined hospitality by entertaining at their home in Pittsburgh. In 1847 McKnight "called at Mr. Denny's where were about 20 ladies & gentlemen assembled to hear the musical soiree. Had good music (La Somnambula, Love not, Vive la France &c.) from Misses Mary Irwin, Anderson, Julia Murray & E. O. H. Denny, & Mess. Nevin and Kleber, leader."[19]

Middle Class Leisure

The splendor of cotillion parties on the green and musical soirees contrasted sharply with the less elegant social occasions attended by middle class Pennsylvanians. Joseph Buffum, a middle class young man who aspired to great things, attended a number of dances, balls, and dinners in Pittsburgh during the late 1840s. Some pleased him with decorous surroundings and enjoyable companions: a New England dinner on Thanksgiving 1847 in "the dining hall of the spacious St. Charles" and a ball at "Ingolby's temperance house" in December won his approval.

Others disappointed him with poor food and rude company. Buffum managed to enjoy himself "very well" at a dancing party, for example, despite reservations about "some bad company there." The "Mercy Soiree," a "charity ball for the purpose of erecting a hospital," dismayed Buffum even more: "There was a large company between 1 and 2 thousand tickets $2.00. Was not well pleased with it, too crowded. Supper poor."[20]

If the middle class could not match the glamour of upper class socializing, it was not for want of trying. Their efforts represented more than mere pretense. They, like the patricians jealous of their elevated status, recognized that leisure's usefulness for defining class boundaries also implied its exploitability in obliterating those demarcations. Portraying class as partly a function of gentility, education, and intellectual cultivation in leisure engendered the possibility of social climbing through the acquisition of these qualities. If elite status and social preeminence rested on acquaintance with art, literature, dance, and genteel sports, obtaining this knowledge could serve as an entrée into elite circles. At the very least, it could undermine upper class pretensions to social and cultural superiority.[21]

The desire to exploit these possibilities stimulated middle class interest in women's social education. Upper class families could afford to send daughters to local seminaries or to hire private tutors to teach them music, elocution, embroidery, and art, all desirable social skills. To avoid feelings of inferiority, middle class parents also emphasized ornamental and artistic education for young women. Leisure entrepreneurs provided a more public, less expensive commercial alternative to the middle class: permanent schools and itinerant teachers offered their services as instructors of young middle class women. Mr. and Mrs. Baker, for instance, moved their school from Washington to Pittsburgh in 1817. Mr. Baker offered pianoforte lessons, while his wife instructed young ladies in "the ornamental branches of education such as Embroidering, Fillagree, Drawing, Painting of Flowers, Fringe Netting, & c."[22]

In other areas of leisure as well, a burgeoning commercial industry catered to the middle class desire to cross class barriers. Dancing schools proliferated, especially after repeated civil unrest in France loosed a plethora of dance masters on the world. Other schools and teachers offered patrons instruction in music, art, and languages. By the 1840s, commercial leisure instruction had expanded to the point where entrepreneurs could lower prices to capture a mass rather than just an elite market. Middle and even working class parents willing to make financial sacrifices could now send their sons and daughters to private tutors, commercial schools, or local seminaries to acquire leisure skills that would suit them for polite society. Inexpensive commercialized instruction made possible a blurring of class distinction in leisure; by the 1840s it was not always easy to distinguish "country bumpkins" from "city gentlemen" at militia musters or to recognize the ill-bred "country loafers" at literary gatherings, as had been the case earlier in the century.[23] Sometimes the desire for refined leisure led to mere ostentation. A local wit, for example, chided those of "moderate income, who, by attempting to vie with the wealthy in splendour and etiquette" incur ruinous debts. Even minor excesses provoked disapproval. One middle class Pittsburgher scolded his compatriots for displaying gratuitously the visiting cards of guests in their parlors as proof of their frequent hospitality and widespread popularity.[24]

Not all of southwestern Pennsylvania's middle class attempted to imitate upper class leisure, however. Many rejected upper class pretensions to cultural superiority and created a distinctive middle class culture with leisure activities and styles all its own. Like its upper class counterpart, middle class leisure fostered group identity and defined participants in relation to other classes. Middle class visiting, for instance, substituted propriety and respectability for elegance and gentility. For intimate socializing at home, the middle class parlor served as a bastion of decency and decorum and a bulwark against the immorality and ferment of the outside world. Outside the home, middle class men and women created public and semipublic contexts for respectable fellowship and decorous sociability. Middle class men established Masonic and Odd Fellows lodges as well as other fraternal and professional organizations to provide forums for social interaction. Middle class women welcomed religious and church societies as opportunities for social interaction. Female Mite societies, church sewing circles, and ladies' fairs offered middle class women a chance to socialize and visit outside the home in the socially approved context of religious benevolence. Both sexes interacted in middle class temperance organizations, which served, as Brian Harrison has argued about England, as counterparts to the tavern-based popular culture. Religious societies, junior temperance organizations, and specialized moral and educational clubs allowed young men and women to mingle in settings informed by middle class values. In Pittsburgh, for example, the staunchly middle class Young Men's Society sponsored regular lectures, debates, and cold water (temperance) celebrations.[25]

Though middle class families rarely had the space or resources to throw balls or large parties in their own homes, they could club together and hire public facilities for group entertainment. Young men and women, for example, patronized balls held by temperance hotels and commercial dance teachers or sponsored cotillion parties on their own behalf by selling subscriptions. These occasions illustrate not only the development of a distinctly middle class approach to leisure but also the importance of commercialized leisure in that process. Anyone attending a cotillion had to have some knowledge of dance, often obtained from a relatively costly teacher. Mr. Boudet, a popular teacher in Pittsburgh during the teens, charged a five dollar entrance fee to his school and ten dollars per quarter tuition, though he offered reduced rates to those with previous training. Boudet also gave practice balls and cotillions, insisting on a measure of decorum that pleased a status-conscious middle class. In 1817 he conducted a ball at the Pittsburgh courthouse "as they are in our populous cities, viz — the ladies to be invited, the gentlemen to pay one dollar on their admission." Boudet ensured that his male patrons would be respectable by stipulating that men seeking admission be known by or introduced to him through a mutual acquaintance. He specified further that "no gentlemen [would be] allowed to dance in boots," thereby insuring his customers a refined dance experience and attesting to middle class taste and respectability.[26]

Working Class Leisure

The working class, too, developed a distinctive style of leisure, one which largely rejected the middle and upper class values and practices discussed above. In part, this reflected a lack of financial resources. Workers, both urban and rural, pursued leisure activities that required little money. Often, these activities partook of traditional, informal patterns of amusement and sociability rather than newer forms of leisure that emphasized consumption and display. Though they also attended circuses, menageries, and museums, as their means allowed, the working class continued to participate in the bees, frolics, play parties, and informal visits characteristic of small agricultural communities well into the nineteenth century. Robert McKnight observed one such occasion in 1846, when he returned from an evening social call to find his family's servants having a bee: "Found a party in full blast in our kitchen being the sequel to a quilting. Witnessed the amusements, playing & kissing — Juniper tree & c. They kept it up to my impatience until after 12."[27] Despite McKnight's impatience with the relatively unsophisticated leisure of his social inferiors, his comments reveal recognition and acceptance of the distinct difference between upper and lower class patterns of leisure.

This difference did not go unnoticed by McKnight's contemporaries, whatever their class. Even if they had wanted to, the working class could not ape upper class sophistication like the middle class; resources were simply unavailable. Working class attempts to appear sophisticated by adopting leisure forms beyond their means invariably appeared ridiculous rather than threatening or rebellious. Sleighing, in which groups of young people took horse-drawn sleds to outlying taverns for an evening of merrymaking, was a prime example. In 1835, a Washington County newspaper printed "Courting Below," a satiric dialogue between Sally, a maid, and Obadiah, her clumsy suitor. In language replete with slang and spoonerisms, Obadiah feigned sophistication in asking Sally to go sleighing with him. Sleighing, primarily a winter pastime of the middle and upper classes, was clearly beyond Obadiah's means, making his awkward attempts to seem worldly an indication of the social disability of his class.[28] Sleighing appealed to the middle and upper classes in part because its high cost — renting or owning a sleigh and team, plus buying drinks and dinner at a tavern — displayed their resources and excluded most working people from participating. Though some observers, like the author of the dialogue just mentioned, portrayed sleighing's exclusivity as a function of taste and gentility, others recognized it as a question of resources. In 1841, for example, a struggling Greensburg editor extolled the pleasures of sleighing, noting that "we are almost tempted to leave our three-legged stool and join the merry throng. But no — we can't come it," he lamented. "We're O.O.O.K. — *Oltogether out of Kash.*" Resolving to endure the drudgery of work while others played, he finally exclaimed "Zounds! — we'd go sleighing. Who'll lend us a good horse and sleigh?"[29]

Poverty did more than merely exclude working people from upper class amusements, however; it also changed their entire outlook on leisure and sociability. As noted in chapter 2, Pennsylvanians often greeted winter as a season for sociability and friendship. Cold weather and confinement indoors promoted exactly the types of traditional, informal sociability and leisure the working class might be expected to enjoy. In reality, the scarcity of food and warmth only served to highlight their class's disadvantages, in leisure and otherwise. As an 1844 poem observed, enjoyment of winter sociability depended on shelter and warmth, and these were often the province of the well-to-do, not the working class:

> We do not love old winter, when he rides his merry blast,
> To make belles' gay feathers stream, like penons from a mast.
> The tune he whistles in her ear, is incense to her pride; While he howls a
>   gush of anguish to the ragged wretch beside.[30]

Working class difference from middle and upper class leisure became a disability in a number of ways, some highly ironic. In 1842, Edwin Forrest, the United States' first matinee idol, visited Pittsburgh for a theatrical engagement. Forrest, a self-conscious symbol of and spokesman for the American "common man," captured the imagination of all classes but was especially beloved by the working class. When theaters increased the price of seats from twenty-five to seventy-five cents for Forrest's engagement, however, they largely excluded his working class supporters from witnessing his acting. As an indignant observer noted, when the pit became the "Parquette," the working class could no longer afford seats.[31]

Despite their inability to participate in many middle and upper class leisure activities, the working class maintained a vital leisure style of its own. Workers often felt little envy of respectable or genteel leisure, spending their free time reading, casually discussing the issues of the day, engaging in convivial drinking and gaming, or simply resting in contented repose. Nor were they necessarily impressed by upper class styles of leisure. Their social "betters' " efforts to accrue cultural capital through conspicuous consumption often yielded few dividends. Workers resisted cultural domination by denying the class distinctions implicit in upper and middle class leisure activities. Working class Pittsburgh, for example, did not defer to elite opinions on theater, rejecting actors and plays that seemed foppish, restrained, or pretentious. Francis Wemyss noted that in 1833, Pittsburghers' "judgment in theatrical matters was most singular. . . . They selected the worst actors as their especial favorites, and even hissed poor Spencer, (who afterwards perished with Fanning, like a hero, in Texas), from the stage, because he dressed like a gentleman, and would persist in wearing white kid gloves in the street."[32] Viewed in the context of leisure and class, this affection for the "worst" actors and hostility toward a "gentleman" emerges not as mere lack of working class refinement but rather as a rejection of upper class pretensions and elite aesthetic standards. Many workers idealized not the cultivated gentleman of leisure but the independent working man who enjoyed work and play to the fullest. Samuel Young wrote fondly of wagoners who plied the National Road, for example, noting that "there was no class of men engaged in any special calling that enjoyed it more than the jolly, hard-working and constantly exposed drivers of the popular, old Conestogas. . . . The wagoners were a jolly set, who had no cares to bother them, or at least did not allow them to do so."[33] Young chronicled the wagoners' affection for conversation, drink, magic tricks and ventriloquism, practical jokes, and other forms of good-natured fun.

Nor did all working folk aspire to nonmanual occupations or the learned professions; many valued physical labor and the lifestyle that underpinned it. Samuel Jones deprecated the "roguery" of prosperous mechanics who pushed their sons to "become a candidate for civic honors — a follower of Hippocrates, or a novitiate for holy orders."

> We say *roguery*, because by devoting these youths to those professions, the mechanic's shop is often cheated out of many an able bodied man, who in the line of his father's business might have done credit to the manufacturing interests of his country; whereas on the other hand, in pursuing the studies necessary to make a lawyer, doctor, or a minister, how many are there, who becoming sensible of their incapacity to arrive at eminence, or even at a respectable mediocrity, retire in disgust, and lead a life of uselessness, if not of dissipation.

A mechanic himself, Jones denied that the sons of professional men were any "less thick-skulled, or possess greater capacities than those of mechanics" but considered it "ridiculous and absurd" that "every man who follows a laborious occupation, by which he has accumulated considerable wealth, should consider son too good to pursue that business to which his life had been devoted."[34]

Especially around Pittsburgh, workers defended tenaciously not only their occupations but also their right to leisure. Labor activism generally, and particularly the movement to reduce the working day, expressed the workers' desire for increased free time. Pittsburgh carpenters struck for a ten-hour day in 1831; a similar walkout occurred in 1836. During the 1840s, both male and female textile workers agitated for shorter hours and more leisure. They chose July 4, 1846, to declare the independence from the "Oppressive manufacturing power" that threatened their free time. Throughout our period, workers jealously guarded their leisure, insisting on their right to possess and use free time as they saw fit.[35]

Working class leisure reflected this pride and frequently revolved around occupational groups and trade associations. Trade or craft societies often met on holidays to celebrate and march in procession, alone or in conjunction with larger community observances. William G. Johnston remembered witnessing one such trade procession in his early childhood, on the centennial of Washington's birth in 1832. A large procession of trades "employing symbols of their respective occupations" moved through the streets. The banner of his father's printing firm, which depicted a printing press, particularly impressed the young Johnston. Other spectators commented approvingly on the large collection of militia units, societies, and other trades comprising the procession.[36] In 1837 a similar trades' procession commemorated Washington's Birthday but, this time, the trades marched independently of the militia parade. Individual trades also periodically sponsored processions without any special occasion. In 1842 the Pittsburgh Victuallers marched in procession with four examples of their skill and craftsmanship: "The four immense beefs were slaughtered in the forenoon and the meat drawn in procession in twenty-two neatly decorated wagons, followed by nearly one hundred butchers, attired in white aprons trimmed with ribbons." Another account noted that the procession "was very large, reaching nearly the whole length of Wood

St., and the regalia of those who took part in it had a very handsome appearance."[37] Where middle and upper class sociability celebrated restraint and sophistication, working class leisure emphasized the public, communal aspects of social interaction and enjoyment.

Leisure Accommodations and Class Segregation

Class differences in leisure depended on space as well as style. Whether formal or informal, class segregation in leisure space was obvious to all who cared to look. Commenting on the opening of M'Guire's Washington Coffee House, a working class Irish establishment, the *Pittsburgh Statesman* observed in 1829:

> There is not perhaps, in the Union, a City that abounds with so great a number, and such a variety of grades, of places of "entertainment for man and horse," as our own. We have them, from one story high, (and frequently that is below ground!) to five stories above the ground, and containing from one room to one hundred. Thus, it must be admitted, that we can accommodate all classes, *high* or *low*, rich or poor, sumptuously or otherwise, as may suit the taste of our travelers.[38]

This division of public accommodations along class lines occurred in towns throughout southwestern Pennsylvania. In Greensburg, Simon Singer's first-class Greensburg and Pittsburgh Hotel catered to the carriage trade, while the Sun, Moon, and Seven Stars Tavern, Kuhn's Tavern, and the Dublin House provided entertainment for less elevated locals. The dregs of Greensburg society congregated at Bushfield's Tavern on Bunker Hill, so named because of the "full scale fights" at the inn. "This tavern was a favorite place for stage drivers. It did not take much, if anything to start a fight there. Dogs fought, cock fights were held and men fought, sometimes for money and sometimes they just fought. These battles kept on until someone remarked that more heads were broken at the Bushfield Tavern than at the Battle of Bunker Hill."[39]

Upper class leisure spaces included the best taverns, inns, and coffee houses, as well as reading rooms, private libraries and clubrooms, and hotel parlors that served refreshments and stocked a variety of magazines and newspapers. In Pittsburgh the Exchange and Mansion House catered to the upper and middle classes; in Washington, the Sign of the Globe offered refined surroundings for its genteel patrons. William G. Johnston remembered his father's Pittsburgh bookstore as "a well-known rendez-vous for many gentlemen of leisure," while Anthony Bonville's coffee-house on Front Street provided a place "where gentlemen (wishing to spend a leisure hour, or discuss the political matters of the day) will at all times find the best assortment of LIQUORS, together with a general selection of newspapers without respect to party."[40]

The middle class patronized similar establishments as their means allowed, but they usually frequented less exclusive commercial and pub-lic spaces. Middle class women were more likely than their upper class counterparts to be present at public or commercial amusements, so pro-priety and respectability assumed paramount importance. In Washington, the public square was a favorite resort, especially in the summer. "Hither the fair ones of our borough resort," rhapsodized the *Reporter*, "upon summer evenings, to regale themselves in the balmy air; and here, too, the 'Mozart Band' ('Oft in the stilly night') discourse their sweet music." To provide the middle class with wholesome entertainment, temperance hotels and ice cream saloons sprang up in all major towns. In 1843 Major Thomas Irons's Green House Temperance Hotel in Washington, for ex-ample, displayed the "Night Blooming Ceres," flowers that bloomed after dark and died before dawn, to a "throng of citizens of both sexes, and troops of the more juvenile classes."[41]

The working class was both more constrained and freer than the middle and upper classes in acquiring leisure spaces for socializing. Fi-nancial considerations excluded them from all but the least expensive commercial accommodations, but freedom from the dictates of middle class respectability opened up a wide variety of informal, sometimes il-legal, leisure spaces. Beer cellars, brothels, unlicensed tippling houses, and gambling dens supplemented more respectable working class estab-lishments. Though less elegant than upper class facilities, working class leisure spaces offered their patrons informality and conviviality at a cost within their reach. During a visit to Pittsburgh in 1815 the actor Noah Ludlow recorded his favorable impressions of a Pittsburgh beer cellar's easy informality. Ludlow enjoyed a singer who performed for the crowd, remarking that he had never "heard a better uncultivated voice." The young actor's admiration of working class informality increased when, after a companion ran out before paying the check, the cellar's proprietor trusted him to return the following day to pay his bar bill. Throughout the region, working people valued the congeniality and unpretentiousness of lower class leisure establishments. Middle class Greensburgers may have disdained Mrs. Bignall's Sun, Moon, and Seven Stars Tavern as a second-rate establishment, but the local working class considered it "a very hilarious place." Sometimes working class hilarity had its disadvantages. Samuel Young recorded stopping unknowingly in a "questionable resort" for a drink and escaping arrest with the thieves and prostitutes he found there only by climbing out a side window during a police raid.[42]

Some establishments catered specifically to workers' tastes. Pittsburgh's Mechanic's Retreat, for example, which opened opposite Jelly's cotton factory in 1816, offered laborers an assortment of liquors along with turtle soup on Wednesday and Sunday. Carey's Porter House also attracted a working class clientele. In later years Pittsburgh's coffeehouses became popular congregating places for workers, both for informal socializing and formal meetings. In the early 1830s the Mechanic's Hall and Masonic Hall Coffeehouses were frequent meeting places for working men, especially the journeymen carpenters.[43]

Class-Specific Leisure Facilities

Recreation facilities as well as gathering spaces offered opportunities for class differentiation, especially as the century wore on. By the 1830s, summer homes and fashionable resorts accelerated the move toward class-specific leisure facilities. Early in the century, wealthy Pittsburghers found the "noise and soot of the growing industrial town"[44] oppressive and unhealthy. Families with sufficient funds began to build summer homes along the rivers or leave the city altogether during the hot months. For the upper class, a summer vacation at an exclusive, expensive, and prestigious resort distant from urban clamor and heat articulated their social preeminence and attested to their elevated tastes and bountiful resources. The spa at Bedford Springs, approximately one hundred miles from Pittsburgh, became a favorite summer refuge for southwestern Pennsylvania's elite. James Ross, a well-known lawyer, politician, and social luminary, thought so highly of the Springs that he composed a paean (originally in Latin, of course) in its honor: "Let the sons of leisure, and votaries of amusement, on these health preserving waters regale themselves."[45] An 1842 visitor observed that the Springs offered something for everyone, vacationers, invalids, and sportsmen alike. "The lovers of comfort, and ease, and good living," he continued, "are stowed away indiscriminately, and find the dining and bar rooms, at all proper times, teeming with good things for their especial accommodation." Two years later the *Iron City* reported in mid-July that many "citizens are now about leaving town on their different excursions for the summer" and that Bedford Springs was a frequent destination.[46] Accounts of the arrival of these "citizens" at the Springs leaves little doubt about their class: "Then came the chariots and horse, desirable young men riding on horseback. Papas and mammas with lovely daughters drawn in coaches attended by coachmen, footmen and maids. Then the harp resounded to knights and ladies bright, while the dance swept on."[47] By the late 1840s, the annual visit to the Springs had become a staple of upper class leisure. It offered patricians the opportunity to distance themselves both geographically and symbolically from their social inferiors. To satisfy their longing for a lost system of deference and social hierarchy, upper class vacationers represented their class as the last vestige of medieval pageantry and splendor.

> Above all delights of fancy dress ball and tableau vivant, there came the tournament, when some twenty-five knights rode at a ring for the honor of their ladies. This was really a beautiful spectacle. Each knight had selected a lady and received from her a token, glove or ribbon which he wore on his breast. The knights wore medieval dress and aiming at a ring, suspended in the roadway, galloped fiercely on their quest. He who secured the iron ring three times on the point of his spear had the privilege of crowning his lady "The Queen of Love and Beauty," while all the other ladies walked with their knights as escorts to the Queen at the Ball, which followed at night.[48]

This kind of display and consumption assured the upper class a sense of difference from its social inferiors. The cost of taking the waters at Bedford put a visit beyond the reach of most middle class families, and the closest the working class would ever get to the elegant spa was gawking at a diorama of the Springs exhibited by the Pittsburgh Museum for a quarter.[49]

For those members of the upper class unwilling or unable to travel to Bedford, exclusive spas closer to home provided a suitably refined vacation. Fayette Springs near the Youghiogheny River in Fayette County attracted vacationers because of its proximity to the mountains, which were "much visited" in the summer because of their cool temperatures and suitability for hunting, rural sports, and rustic parties. Frankfurt Springs in nearby Beaver County was another upper class haunt. This resort offered "so many attractions of scenery and accommodations [that it] entirely supplies the wants of the '*upper ten*,' and whenever the hot weather comes and the brick walls begin to glow with a fiery redness, they are glad to exchange the filth of the city, for the refreshing breezes and wild flowers of 'Frankfurt Springs.'" Pittsburgh's young and aspiring elite favored Frankfurt Springs: both Charles B. Scully and Robert McKnight recorded visits there. During Scully's two-week stay at Frankfurt in 1843 he and friends enjoyed fishing, cards, tenpins, and parties with the first families of Pittsburgh. McKnight's brief visit in 1846 involved a similar round of elite socializing, dancing, and conviviality.[50]

Middle class families who could not afford an expensive excursion to a distant resort frequented taverns, inns, and guest houses in pleasant rural areas surrounding towns and cities. William G. Johnston remembered two summer vacations at local resorts during his boyhood in the 1830s. In 1838 he spent part of the summer at the Mount Emmet Tavern in Allegheny, a hotel patronized by some of Pittsburgh's most respectable families. The next summer found Johnston among similar clientele at the Point Breeze Tavern near Pittsburgh. Though less elegant than Bedford or Frankfurt Springs, these local resorts offered the middle class a bucolic setting and a variety of healthful activities: tenpins, riding, and similar sports for the men; and needlework, conversation, and socializing for the women.[51]

For the most part, lack of resources relegated the working class to the "filth of the city" that the upper and middle classes escaped. Not owning a horse and carriage limited the distance into the countryside that workers and their families could venture. As time passed, however, the commercialization of leisure provided working class families with opportunities for day trips in the summer. Especially around Pittsburgh, the region's economic and population center, commercial pleasure gardens, recreation areas, and inexpensive conveyances offered the working class an affordable day in the country. As early as 1831, Saxe-Hall Gardens, three quarters of a mile from the city, furnished working people with a rural recreational space outside the hot, sometimes unhealthy urban environment. That year "the flower of the young mechanics of the city" chose Saxe-Hall Gardens for a Fourth of July celebration. Greenwood and Rosedale Gardens, each about a mile from Pittsburgh on the Monongahela River, also boasted facilities for picnics, strolls, outdoor sports, dancing, and other recreations for a nominal admission price. These establishments often provided transportation by steamboat from Pittsburgh and Allegheny and allowed patrons to redeem their admission tickets for refreshments. Several steamboat lines offered inexpensive day trips to patrons living along the Allegheny River; in 1838, one company ran regular excursions to rural Sharpsburg throughout the summer. Local recreational facilities within financial reach of the working class provided some relief from the heat to those unable to leave home. By 1850, for example, a concrete-bottomed, spring-fed bathing pond, complete with bath house, opened in Washington.[52]

Like varying styles of socializing and visiting, leisure spaces segregated social groups and defined class differences. Exclusive resorts, tasteful coffeehouses, and elegant ballrooms allowed the upper and, to some extent, the middle class to articulate symbolically their cultural power. A double movement was at play here. On the one hand, the upper and middle classes distanced themselves from the working class through the conscious segregation of leisure spaces. On the other, they represented class differences in leisure as (they claimed) the natural consequence of possessing superior gentility, elegance, and refinement of taste, instead of the artificial product of abundant resources. Wealth and social position did not produce gentility, they could claim, but rather, natural gentility suited one to wealth and position.

Southwestern Pennsylvania's elites were not alone in urging this ideological construction on the rest of society. In antebellum American society generally, the notion that natural genius overcomes all obstacles emerged forcefully in many areas of cultural production. Sentimental novels, for instance, frequently depicted worthy heroes ascending to wealth and gentility by dint of hard work and natural aptitude. John Cawelti has noted that "it is almost invariably the case in [sentimental] novels of this kind that, above all, nature teaches the traditional deportment and attitudes of the upper class gentleman."[53] To southwestern Pennsylvanians, the implications for leisure of this vision of class were clear. Individual inclinations and aspirations, not wealth and opportunity, differentiated the spectators of a dogfight at the Bushfield Tavern and a medieval tournament at Bedford Springs. The refined gravitated toward improving their time in tasteful leisure, the unrefined toward killing time in mindless or brutish amusements.

Clubs and Societies Segregated by Class

The emergence of class-specific clubs and societies illustrates how the upper and middle classes sought to glamorize their own activities as the natural product of intelligence and genteel taste. Music was a case in point. All classes enjoyed playing and listening to music, but only the upper and middle classes made musical enjoyment a mark of taste and refinement. Working class music stressed informality and fun, while the middle and upper classes treated music as serious business. Early in the century, Pittsburgh's Apollonian Society, composed of "a dozen gentlemen of the town," performed "with a degree of taste and execution" unusual in "so remote a place." The group did include at least one working man, a German glassworker named Mr. Gabler, whose virtuosity on the violin apparently made him acceptable to his social betters. On the whole, these "several musical amateurs" emphasized propriety and refinement, however, admitting only "respectable" audience members and musicians to the society. Another musical group, the Pittsburgh Harmonic Society, also aimed for respectability. In 1818 the society eschewed the more raucous Fourth of July celebrations in favor of a dignified barge trip up the Allegheny River. Instead of celebrating Independence Day in drunken debauchery, the elite "amateurs" of the Harmonic Society spent the day saluting their country with music and feasting, all in an appropriately decorous manner.[54]

By forming musical societies, the middle and upper classes differentiated their style of music making from what they viewed as the undisciplined, often cacophonous efforts of the working class. The patrician Washington Musical Society, for instance, numbered the town's most important citizens among its members. The society assembled for an elegant "Evening of the Week" to play music and conduct business, much of which centered on maintaining the group's standards. The group's constitution stipulated that new members were to be elected by ballot, but "only those who have some previous knowledge of the principles of music excepting those whom the society may think proper to invite" were eligible for membership. As the society's membership included a virtual who's who of elite Washington society, it is apparent that the group thought it proper to invite only the upper crust into their circle.[55]

Pittsburgh's Associated Singing Society, a predominantly middle class group, took similar measures to preserve respectability, decorum, and distance from lower class leisure forms. The society, formed out of the subscribers' consciousness "of the propriety of performing vocal music, in a harmonious manner," limited membership to fifty and established an elaborate organizational hierarchy to keep order. The society's constitution noted that the group's "sole design" was to "acquire a science, whereby they may be enabled to praise their creator in a becoming manner." Thus the society expected each member to "have a deportment, during the time of singing, tending to accomplish the object in view"; expulsion was the penalty for "behaving disorderly." Contrast this with the image of working class music provided by Charles B. Scully in 1843: "The Diamond is now the abode of muse of every wind and stringed instrument. A band is playing a part of "Norma" in one house, while a neighbor hard by & it would seem enviously, is blowing at the top of his lungs on a dry clarinette a tune that is commonly known as 'Shirt tail out & the wind a'blowin' sufficient to tear that nether garment to tatters."[56] Scully's dry humor pointed not only to a perceived difference between the working class and his own, but also to music and leisure as a representation of that difference.

In addition to decorous music, the upper and middle classes also vigorously promoted intellectual, artistic, or scientific organizations as a mark of social distinction and educational attainment.[57] Pittsburgh's Horticultural Society, for example, aimed at the "improvement and promotion of Horticulture, as well ornamental as useful, by the establishment of a Library, and a Garden." Its 1834 list of members included two Pittsburgh mayors, a congressman, several members of the city council, and a number of prominent citizens. The society's library and gardens provided space for upper class meeting and socializing in a refined atmo-

sphere. Its constitution guaranteed members a dignified and genteel atmosphere by mandating expulsion for anyone who disobeyed the bylaws
or "defame[d] the Society, [was] guilty of any breach of honor or mis-
conduct, or [did] anything to the dishonor of the Society."[58]

Established upper class and aspiring middle class citizens especially
favored literary societies as emblems of class and status. By the 1840s a
virtual literary subculture had developed in the upper strata of southwestern Pennsylvania society. In Washington County, literary societies
and debate clubs attached to Washington and Jefferson Colleges provided
intellectual stimulation, and similar organizations connected to Uniontown's Madison College offered refined and uplifting leisure. W. T. Wiley, for example, argued in an anniversary address before Madison's Apollonian Literary Society in 1842 that "The Basis of All Real Happiness,
As Well as all true Honor and Glory" is the principle and practice of
virtue. Clearly, those who lacked any of these qualities had simply failed
to practice virtue.[59]

In Pittsburgh, literary societies proliferated, producing by 1840 a journal, the *Literary Messenger,* as their unofficial forum. The *Messenger's*
editor devoted the publication to obtaining "the benefits of refined society" and securing "the stability of our government" through literature and
the cultivation of "intellectual faculties." Pittsburgh's literati considered
belletristic endeavors to be an upper class preserve, as the composition of
the *Messenger's* audience attests. The Philological Institute, perhaps Pittsburgh's most prestigious literary society, was "composed of young men,
among whom it numbers some of our most talented merchants, manufacturers, physicians, lawyers, editors and gentlemen in the various walks
of life." At the institute's twelfth anniversary meeting, the audience included a supreme court justice, several clergymen, and "a number of our
most respectable ladies and gentlemen." An enumeration of its members'
occupations revealed eleven manufacturers, twenty-eight merchants,
twenty lawyers, six doctors, and fourteen editors. The Wirt Institute, no
less prestigious, routinely drew Pittsburgh's upper crust to its lectures, both
as speakers and audience. Wirt members' prominence sometimes caused
difficulties: in 1841, two prospective lecturers had to be excluded from the
program because their political rivalry raised fears of partisanship in the
supposedly pristine atmosphere of intellectual detachment.[60]

Literary societies in Pittsburgh ranged from the Olympian heights of the Philological and Wirt Institutes down through less influential middle class organizations and finally to working class debate and library societies. Samuel Young served as vice president of the Franklin Literary Society, which was "formed by [the] voluntary subscription" of twenty-five members in 1843. Though access to a library was one of the chief attractions of belonging to a society like the Franklin, workers also had access to book collections through other means. The Neptune Fire Company, for example, maintained a library for its members' use. In 1845 the Neptune's librarian maintained "362 volumes[,] books & 54 numbers of Living Age belonging to the Co., 319 of which is now in their possession, the remaining 43 charged to different members of the company." The Young Men's Mercantile Library and Mechanic's Institute also maintained a library and reading room, as well as a cabinet of models and minerals, and organized popular lectures on the sciences. Though the institute's one dollar initiation fee and four dollar annual dues were substantial, they were much more affordable than membership in a more prestigious society.[61]

Sometimes working class clubs originated from upper and middle class efforts to manipulate the lower orders. The Keystone Association, a supposedly nonpartisan society formed by local Democrats in 1842, met ostensibly "for the purpose of discussing the leading political principles on which our institutions are founded" and offered lectures intended to "draw large audiences of men of all parties." By playing on the popular ideology of self-improvement during leisure, the Keystone Association's managers apparently hoped to drum up political support. They betrayed their intentions in hoping to see "the Hall crowded with men of all parties who desire correct information in relation to the principles of Democracy. Let Farmers, Mechanics and Laborers attend. Seats Free!"[62]

Though the upper classes encouraged working class literary and intellectual activity, they did so with a sneering condescension. Speakers at the prestigious Tilghman Literary Society's nineteenth anniversary meeting thus differentiated "college bred and Franklin taught" young men, praising both yet observing that the latter could hardly be expected to match the former in literary attainment. Elite literary associations took pains to distinguish themselves from working and middle class clubs. An

1844 newspaper piece on literary societies in Pittsburgh contrasted the useful associations, where those who felt "so inclined can spend a quiet evening in their hall, with a Library worthy of the name," with mere "Debating societies where the loftiest flights of oratorical display do not extend beyond mere excited and affected declamation." As with musical societies, the upper class portrayed the sophistication and erudition of elite societies as the determinant rather than the product of social class. Reporting on a Philological Institute meeting in 1837, *Harris's Intelligencer* made this connection explicitly. "We observed the worthy Mayor of our city, and a number of our most intelligent young merchants, manufacturers, lawyers, & c., engaged in the literary contest, and as its members [i.e., the Philological Institute] are generally young men of great promise in the several walks of life, it at once opened to us the secret of their rising generation." Middle and upper class observers were quick to point out that any young man, regardless of wealth or occupation, had the opportunity to rise in society through literary accomplishment and study. Though less prestigious than the Philological Institute, societies like the Marshall Institute opened their doors to worthy young mechanics desirous of improving their minds. The twenty-five young mechanics who comprised the Marshall's membership in 1839 had, in the estimation of one Pittsburgh editor, "done much toward exposing the folly of those who think that mechanics cannot improve in the study of literature." If the working class was uneducated and unacquainted with the benefits of the intellectual life, the elite argued, it reflected apathy or character flaws, not lack of opportunity.[63]

Events sometimes belied this smugness. Writing to the *Pittsburgh Mercury* in 1839, "An Operative" recounted his efforts to join in the Wirt and Philological Institutes. Preferring the Wirt Institute, this self-described mechanic expressed his dismay at discovering that the twenty dollar initiation fee prevented his admittance: "I had not imagined that in a temple dedicated to Mercury I should find Plutus enthroned in the porch; nor that a society bearing the name of a dignified and classic teacher — an accomplished orator and profound jurist, should bar its door against all save those who could pronounce the 'open sesame' in the shape of a golden donceur." Turning to "the more pretending but really less inviting sister society[,] the Philological Institute," our astonished mechanic found that its initiation fee was fifty dollars: "Fifty dollars[,] I involuntarily exclaimed, for what?" Lamenting this effective exclusion from the city's literary elite, the mechanic concluded hopefully that "there are some persons in Pittsburgh, who would be willing to aid in the formation and conducting of a Society for mutual improvement, who could be satisfied with doing good to themselves and others without regard to the meretricious decorations and extravagant Senatorial machinery, and without the aristocratic exclusiveness that shuts the door in the face of an operative."[64]

Even in the supposedly egalitarian antebellum era, when any accusation of aristocratic sympathies cut deeply, detractors could dismiss peremptorily this literary aspirant's criticism. The *Mercury* responded icily that it could not see "why anyone has a *right* to complain of this as a grievance unless these societies positively monopolize all the polemical capacity of the city. The writer can doubtless find congenial spirits willing to attain improvement in a less luxurious mode than appears to be the fashion at Philo Hall."[65]

If these "congenial spirits" of the working class failed in their literary endeavors, the *Mercury* implied, then the fault lay with their own incapacity and lack of interest, not with flaws in the opportunity structure of intellectual leisure. In this, elite Pittsburghers reflected larger cultural trends and ideologies. Propagandists for American social mobility contended that anyone willing to apply himself, work hard, and save for the future could attain wealth. Even unskilled workers might one day join the ranks of property owners if they only tried diligently to improve themselves and their fortunes.[66] The *Mercury* and other apologists for aristocratic leisure proposed a cultural corollary to this economic doctrine. It portrayed the superiority of elite literary societies not as aristocratic hauteur or the mere product of social and economic advantage but, rather, as a function of the natural moral predilections and intellectual abilities of their members. Anyone possessing a keen intellect could enter the best literary circles, they claimed, just as any hardworking laborer could eventually own a business. If anyone of humble origins failed to ascend to the ranks of owners, scholars, and gentlemen, it was his own fault. Skeptics could be reminded of the difficulties working class literary societies experienced in just surviving. Fayette County's Mechanic's Institute experienced persistent difficulties in attracting members. Small audiences at lectures threatened the institute's continued operations soon after its inception, and it appears that only upper and middle class support enabled the group to survive. Members of the Mechanic's Independent Literary Society in Washington met in 1847 to address a similar problem, resolving to decide in the face of scant interest "whether or not we shall continue our organization."[67]

As in other areas of leisure, upper and middle class attempts at class differentiation proved more successful than efforts at cultural dominance. Many young working class men evinced an interest in acquiring knowledge but rejected elite pretensions and prescriptions. Members of Pittsburgh's Young Men's Mercantile Library and Mechanic's Institute valued its library and lecture series but apparently made little effort to mimic the genteel manners so often associated with elite societies. The institute's bylaws stipulated that a modicum of propriety be maintained in its rooms, enjoining members to whisper in the library and mandating that they resist the urge to "smoke, spit on the floor, damage or injure the furniture thereof, or [engage in] conduct in any way inconsistent with decorum."[68] Patricians who hoped that plebeians would respect and emulate their refined style of literary leisure appear to have been foiled by the persistence of working class informality even in the intellectual realms the elite supposedly defined and dominated.

More than this, upper and middle class attempts at class differentiation and domination through intellectual and literary pursuits contained within themselves the possibility of their own transcendence. To make the fiction of social mobility through literary attainment at all believable or palatable, it had to contain some element of truth, if only for a small number of working or middle class aspirants. Like instruction in art, music, and dance, literary and intellectual pursuits offered a particularly promising avenue into elite circles. A bright youth from humble origins could gain prestige and win influential friends through study and membership in the proper literary and debate societies. The literary societies attached to local colleges were especially suited to this end. A historian of Jefferson College noted that literary society members tried to attain "mental and moral improvement, mutual friendship, and habits of system and good order in their exercises, deliberations and business transactions."

Nor were literary society members necessarily the sons of rich men. Remembering the common habit of rising "an hour or two before day," Henry Marie Brackenridge remarked in his memoirs that many fellow students and society members at Jefferson College "were not young men of fortune, who came to obtain some gentlemanly accomplishments — they came to get the worth of their money in useful knowledge."[69]

Even those without the benefit of a college education might use literary society membership as an aid to success and social mobility. This appears to have been the goal of Henry Sterling, a Pittsburgh merchant who joined the Pittsburgh Quintillian Society in the late teens. Aware of his own lack of formal schooling, Sterling hoped that membership in the PQ Society would improve his public image and enhance his social position. Profusely thanking the members for admitting him to the society in his introductory address, Sterling praised the PQ's emphasis on public speaking, debate, recitation, and composition. This education, he noted, would make young men enlightened and useful citizens. Sterling asserted that "Improvement in knowledge generally and particularly in the art of speaking correctly being the principal object I had in joining. . . . The collection of a most valuable Library and the concentration of the wisdom and talents of so many ornaments of Society will have a more powerful effect on opening the genius, informing the mind and communicating instruction than the most tedious and labored collegiate studies."[70] Clearly, Sterling viewed literary attainment as a path to social mobility and cultural prestige, and he hoped to become an "ornament of society" in his own right through association with the PQ Society.

Other middle and lower class Pennsylvanians shared these aspirations. Robert Galloway, for example, dabbled in poetry and drama during his youth and was elected secretary of the Cookstown (Fayette County) Debating Society in January 1837. Galloway's literary and intellectual endeavors apparently stood him in good stead. Though not from an elite family, he ran successfully for the Pennsylvania House of Representatives in 1845. Even the working class used literary societies as a vehicle for social mobility, as the career of Samuel Young demonstrated. Beginning life as a laborer, iron puddler, and dock worker, Young educated himself and eventually became a successful writer, editor, and poet. He attributed much of his education and rise in status to Pittsburgh's Marshall Literary Society: "some of the brightest young men of the city were members of it, and the exercises were of the highest character. . . . That society was like a school and from it we derived many important benefits."[71] As a working class member who did experience significant social mobility in his own lifetime, Young was clearly atypical. But his successful crossing of class lines using literary societies — a form of leisure intended to highlight upper and middle class superiority — points to the difficulties of using leisure for cultural domination.[72] Literary societies and intellectual leisure pursuits may have given upper and middle class Pennsylvanians a sense of their own identity and importance, but the working class did not always defer to the resulting claims of social precedence or cultural prestige.

Cross-Class Social Interaction

Similar patterns prevailed in other areas of leisure, particularly those that involved cross-class social interaction. Upper and middle class Pennsylvanians attempted to divide tasks in common activities along appropriate class lines. In civic organizations and at public celebrations, elite citizens typically assumed leadership positions, often relegating the working class to supernumerary status. On the Fourth of July, Washington's Birthday, and other patriotic occasions, prominent, usually wealthy, men served as officers of the day, speakers, and organizers. A perusal of existing city directories reveals the extent of upper and middle class control of civic organizations. In the early teens, Pittsburgh's Permanent Library Company numbered among its members a virtual who's who of the city's civic and social elite. In Washington a similar situation prevailed: elite citizens controlled and directed organizations ranging from temperance societies to volunteer fire companies.[73]

Usually the working class accepted their inferior status with little resentment, less from deference than disinterest. Sometimes, however, workers excluded from decision making in civic functions and celebrations expressed their indignation. In 1825, for example, Pittsburgh's city government sponsored a celebration and reception for General Lafayette, who was then touring the United States. The city used $214 of taxpayers' money to fund the celebration, which included a lavish dinner and elegant ball. An angry letter in the *Allegheny Democrat* denounced this use of tax money, protesting in the name of "laborers" who were not present — indeed, who had not been invited to this "aristocratic occasion."[74]

Volunteer Fire Companies

Generally, this kind of exclusion did not occur in ostensibly common leisure activities. The classes each performed their assigned functions cooperatively, their relative harmony providing both the illusion of democracy and the reality of class differentiation. The volunteer fire department was a classic example of this arrangement. Fire companies, like militia units, resembled social clubs while also providing a crucial community service. All classes belonged to the various companies, but they performed distinct and often revealingly different functions. The upper and middle classes attended to administrative duties, while the working and, to some extent, middle classes undertook the dirty work of polishing the equipment, fighting with other companies, racing the engines, and extinguishing the odd fire.[75]

William G. Johnston's account of Pittsburgh's Allegheny Fire Company in the 1840s points to a class division within the company's ranks. Johnston's memoirs explain that "in every organization of firemen, a rowdy element managed to get a foothold, and it was ever the delight of this class to keep a pot of strife constantly boiling." This "rowdy element," usually drawn from the working class, required "numerous false alarms, and frequent incendiary fires" to preserve their "esprit de corps."[76] In some companies the rowdies got the upper hand, especially when the company tolerated excessive use of whiskey. One fireman remarked that Birmingham's Hydraulic Fire Company was by the 1840s "no fire company; it was just a lot of young rascals who ran with the machine, fought one another and the other companies, and squirted more water on the spectators for the fun of the thing than on the fire." Despite recognition of this rough element within the Allegheny's ranks, Johnston described the company as "largely composed of young businessmen, in high standing in the community." He also noted that "it seemed to be then understood that fighting was no small part of the duties of firemen, [but] the

gentlemen I have named [i.e., the young businessmen] did not so con-
strue their duties, and were not participants in the encounters referred
to."[77]

This division of labor maintained morale in the ranks and indicated
the superior refinement, taste, and manners of upper class fire fighters.
The young elite might aid in extinguishing a blaze — Charles B. Scully
recorded an instance where he, "a retired member of the 'Bully' Eagle,"
lent a hand to his old fire company — but would disdain taking part in "a
general and disgraceful fight" between companies. If respectable firemen
like Johnston and Scully believed that their social inferiors accorded them
prestige for their forbearance and judgment, however, they were often
sorely mistaken. Young working class men apparently preferred the rough
and tumble of fights and company rivalry to more sedate duties, and they
maintained a sense of independence and self-worth despite upper class
attempts to denigrate their approach to leisure and fire fighting. In the
period's popular culture, this dogged working class insistence on its own
value and distinctiveness generated Mose, the Bowery B'hoy and stalwart
fire fighter who was the hero of numerous plays; in popular politics, it
transformed volunteer firemen into powerful voting blocs that office-
holders and aspirants ignored only at their political peril.[78]

Fox Hunting

In some cross-class leisure activities, the working class rejected elite cultural dominance so completely that only rigid control or segregation by
class could preserve patrician dignity. Upper class patrons of sports, for
example, frequently found their assertions of leadership rejected and their
pretensions to authority ridiculed by those they considered to be social
inferiors. Fox hunting illustrates the problems the upper class encountered when it attempted to use leisure for both class differentiation and
cultural domination. Southwestern Pennsylvanians had hunted fox since
the region's settlement, but the fox hunt as a self-consciously elite activity
emerged only in the nineteenth century.[79] Until that time communities
hunted fox mainly as part of a larger effort to exterminate predators that
they believed threatened their livestock. They preferred the circular hunt,
in which local residents formed a large circle and converged on a central
point, killing any animals they encountered. Like other cooperative labor

events, these communal gatherings also involved sociability and recreation. Circular hunts were thus perfect opportunities for the upper class
to seize control of cross-class leisure: participants could be organized into
lines of attack and directed by upper class marshals and captains. Further,
the spoils of the hunt could be divided by the managers of the hunt
according to the "rules of hunting."[80] In essence, the class hierarchy that
originated in economic relationships could be reproduced through leisure in the social and cultural life of the community.

Theory proved tidier than practice, for working class hunters often
rejected this dignified testament to upper class superiority. Leisure did
provide opportunities for the upper class to claim cultural leadership, but
it also allowed the working class to undermine or invert social hierarchies
that elites hoped to establish. This proved to be especially true in the
rigidly structured common activities that seemed most conducive to class
differentiation and dominance. Instead of deferring to elite leadership
and prescribed standards of behavior, the hunt's foot soldiers often trans-
gressed the rules of the chase and poked irreverent fun at the pretensions
of their self-important superiors. Despite fierce injunctions to restrain
dogs and hold their fire until the marshals gave appropriate signals, working class hunters frequently broke ranks, fired prematurely, or otherwise
disrupted the order and precision of the hunt.

Such was the case at an 1827 hunt in Cross Creek Township, Washington County. Recounting the event for a local newspaper, "Tecumseh"
noted that "the whole militia of the township" agreed to participate in a
hunt that was supposedly organized along lines of strict military discipline. He ridiculed the self-important captains and marshals, whom he
referred to as Andrew Jackson, Lord Wellington, Henry Clay, and Lord
Packenham. "The whole corps [was] commanded by the emperor *Napoleon Bonaparte*, mounted on a double blonded horse, whose tail was
borne up by a *steam generator* placed in his rear." Despite the efforts of
this august officer corps to maintain order, the "troops" became over-
excited and charged General Reynard and his forces prematurely:

> Before any of our troops arrived at their proper stations the attack was com-
> menced by the regulars letting loose some of their dogs. The attack was
> partial at first, but in a short time became general — the blowing of horns,

yelling of men and dogs, and screaming of the killed and wounded, produced the most fearful concussions in the atmosphere, somewhat resembling the siege of Jericho. At this critical period our lines were thrown into disorder in many places, owing to the want of discipline in our troops, many of whom had never before seen an enemy and were off at the first sight.

Nor would the triumphant forces respect the rules of hunting in dividing the spoils. A young soldier attempted to escape with one of the prisoners before the booty was fairly divided: "The young beau acknowledged that he had no legal right to the prisoner, his only object was to get the fine flowing tail of the animal to decorate the lower story of his wig."[81]

This episode and others like it reflected an obstinate working class denial of elite authority, leadership, and pretensions. Despite attempts to increase control and discipline, the lower class continued to assert its own brand of leisure and reject the roles urged on it from above. "At the grand circular hunt in Donegal," a Westmoreland County paper reported in 1842, "they caught five foxes and had six fights. Quantity of liquor drank — not ascertained, as we have not time to calculate how much it would take to produce this amount of kicking, biting, and gouging."[82] Despite upper class attempts to impose order and exert leadership, fox hunting continued to lack the refinement and taste befitting an elite activity, smacking more of lower class brutality than genteel sport. As a latter-day historian observed, circular hunts could not be "construed as sporting events. . . . No event may be so classified when the quarry has little or no opportunity to escape with his life. This is game slaughter, pure and simple." For patrician hunters, the resolution of this problem was equally simple: make the *sport* of fox hunting an upper class preserve. Sponsors and organizers of hunts might invite everyone, but they restricted real participation to the elite. In 1840, for instance, Westmoreland County hunters invited all sportsmen to a fox hunt, but stipulated that only purebred fox hounds would be allowed in the chase. Elite fox hunting not only excluded the lower classes, but also allowed the wealthy to deploy items of conspicuous consumption: hounds, horses, riding gear, expensive guns, and the like. All this made elite fox hunts — like the one William G. Johnston remembered attending with the Whig gubernatorial candidate's son and some friends in the 1840s — much different from the rough sport of the Donegal hunt.[83] At the same time, by effectively excluding the lower classes from their leisure activities, southwestern Pennsylvania's elites abandoned their attempts to win direct affirmation of their superior cultural position. Though they could exert a measure of control over who participated, they could not convince or coerce the lower class to accept their preeminence in leisure activities as natural and worthy of respect. Instead, a sense of class identification based in exclusivity and patrician hauteur would have to suffice.

Horse Racing

Elite attempts to monopolize horse racing present a similar pattern. Moralists, clergymen, and reformers roundly condemned horse racing as morally reprehensible and corrupting of youth. Much of this stigma seems to have stemmed from the "undesirable" (and, by intimation, criminal) lower class spectators that races attracted. By taking the sport out of the hands of criminals and maintaining decorum at races, the upper class hoped to prove its gentility and social leadership. Patricians supposedly demonstrated their superior moral fiber by remaining uncorrupted by an activity that proved harmful to the lower orders of society. Because Pennsylvania officially outlawed horse racing, it had to be conducted on suitable private tracks, usually owned by wealthy landowners or under the protection of influential upper class patrons. In Fayette County, Thomas Clare's Uniontown farm included a popular race course; in Westmoreland County David Williams maintained a course on his Greensburg farm. But even upper class sponsorship and control had its pitfalls, for lower class spectators apparently viewed races as occasions for vocal partisanship and rambunctious fun rather than the desired deferential reverence for patrician munificence and cultural leadership. Though the upper class could control the worst excesses associated with horse races by eliminating criminals and disreputable gamblers from their courses, the presence of less than subservient lower class race fans made this sport an unsatisfactory means of gaining social and cultural prestige.[84]

As with fox hunting, patricians increasingly excluded the lower classes from their racing activities. By the 1840s a number of private courses catered to upper class turf enthusiasts, especially around Pittsburgh. In 1848 a course opened in East Liberty, and in 1850 another track began operations on the grounds of the Agricultural Association in Wilkinsburg. John Ormsby, a prominent Pittsburgher, maintained a private course at his 2,400-acre farm on the south bank of the Monongahela River, and by 1850 wealthy club members had built a one-mile course and clubhouse on the Glen Road near the Monongahela.[85] To further insure exclusivity, tastefulness, and class differentiation, upper class sportsmen developed and popularized trotting, a more genteel form of racing than the frenzied heats popular with the lower classes. Wealthy sportsmen held trotting matches "within the confines of the city on private courses" but did not publicize them. These races were "usually the outgrowth of a bet arising at a party or ball on the estate where the private course existed."[86]

Upper class race fans sought to distance themselves from the base passions of the lower class by justifying their interest in the turf on scientific and patriotic grounds. Elite race enthusiasts contended that they raced and bred horses only to improve the breed for the benefit of society. They backed these claims with exhibitions, shows, and time trials, all of which promoted class differentiation and attested to the progressive civic-mindedness of the events' sponsors. As early as 1831, Pittsburgher Isaac Hill sponsored horse shows and offered premiums "to encourage their improvement, and to introduce a more active and better winded horse for the saddle." A similar exhibition occurred a year later on John M'Ginnis's Troy Farm, eight miles from Pittsburgh on the Monongahela River.[87] While these activities produced something of the desired effects, they also illustrate the difficulties of achieving what some might call cultural hegemony.

Volunteer and Compulsory Militia Units

These difficulties extended even into leisure activities in which the upper class proved successful at establishing class-specific leisure organizations. Volunteer militia units, for example, offered men of similar social and economic backgrounds the chance to associate with one another. Pennsylvania law required service in either a volunteer or compulsory militia company until 1858. Though ostensibly a public service, militia duty, especially in the volunteer units, also played an important role in male sociability. After 1815, one historian noted, "the athletic and social-club aspect of the volunteers was clearly one of their principal attractions." Volunteer units appealed to upper class citizen-soldiers because of the possibilities for finery and display. Though they trained more than compulsory units, volunteer companies emphasized "pageantry and show, [and] they concentrated on the manual of arms and drilling to the neglect of rifle practice, marches, camping, maneuvers and general tactics."[88] Elite units sprang up early in the nineteenth century and persisted until Pennsylvania abolished the volunteer system in the 1860s. In Washington County, the Washington Light Infantry hoped in 1811 that "no member of the company will appear on parade without having their hair neatly powdered." The company urged "genteel young men" to join the unit at their next battalion muster. The Washington County Rangers also invited "genteel" recruits to enlist at the unit's Fourth of July celebration in 1812. In Allegheny County, too, the elite established their own militia companies. The Washington Cavalry of Bellevernon counted "the best men of the community" among its members by the 1840s, and in Pittsburgh, patrician companies brought the upper class together for training and socializing. Robert McKnight, for example, recounted an 1842 shooting match for prominent volunteers at the farm of Pittsburgh politician and militia officer Harmar Denny.[89]

Volunteer units offered the upper class a number of advantages. They allowed patricians to emphasize their superior taste and resources and to act as exemplars of civic-mindedness to the rest of the community. A prime instrument for this display was the uniform. Volunteer companies wore elaborate uniforms that reflected their members' affluence, while less wealthy recruits in the enrolled or compulsory units wore no distinctive dress at all. Recognizing that ornate apparel set them apart from those below, the upper class portrayed military raiment as a badge of its superior patriotism. It was, after all, up to the "Gentlemen of the Army" to set a republican example for all Americans, especially on festive occasions and national holidays. The upper class displayed its patriotic mettle to those below by rendering the uniform "useful as common wearing apparel upon Sundays, and days of festivity" and resolving to wear their "uniforms regularly on all convenient occasions."[90] In this view, anyone who still failed to procure a uniform simply demonstrated a lack of patriotic ardor.

Volunteer service also emphasized and enhanced the upper class's autonomy and choice in leisure activities. In contrast to compulsory units, volunteers could choose their own muster days, uniforms, and training methods. Volunteers also gained independence from the state militia bureaucracy, which sometimes interfered with upper class prerogatives. Conflicts of authority, command, and dress could lead to embarrassing court-martials for obstinate elite volunteers. An elite company in the 17th Regiment of the Pennsylvania Militia court-martialed and fined a soldier for wearing the state's official tricolor cockade on his hat instead of the black ornament favored by the Anglophilic unit. Much to the unit's chagrin, the regiment overturned the fine.[91] The state sometimes penalized aristocratic officers for refusing to muster their companies on the officially appointed day or for denying the state militia's authority over their troops. Patrician officers in the regular army might find their autonomy and prerogatives curtailed even more sharply. Thomas Butler, an illustrious Revolutionary War officer from Pittsburgh, ran afoul of his superior over a matter of personal fashion. General Wilkinson court-martialed Butler, the second highest ranking officer in Jefferson's army, because he refused to cut off his queue and wear his hair short, as per Wilkinson's order. Only Butler's death in 1805 from yellow fever ended what promised to be an ugly power struggle between two prominent officers.[92] Forming separate, independent, elite volunteer companies to avoid this type of annoyance promoted class solidarity and emphasized the elite's advantages over recruits in the compulsory units.

Independence and choice also attracted the middle class and those working class men able to afford uniforms and equipment to the volunteer system. For merchants, professionals, and prosperous artisans, volunteer duty combined patriotism with convenience: they could train when they wanted and remain close to home. Thus, staunchly middle class infantry units originated alongside elite companies. The Westmoreland Guards epitomized this development. The Guards, a volunteer company "composed principally of young men from this place [Greensburg], Youngstown and Adamsburgh," boasted among its recruits "17 lawyers and 7 printers."[93] The middle class gained choice and autonomy through volunteer units but, like the upper class, its primary motivation was also to avoid the stigma attached to compulsory service.

Denigration and ridicule of the compulsory militia was nearly universal in antebellum Pennsylvania. Newspaper accounts, public lectures, and common gossip portrayed compulsory units as a "corn-stalk" militia:

conglomerations of clumsy, ill-clad bumpkins, usually lower class and frequently drunk.[94] In Allegheny in 1842, for example, the "tallest kind" of militia muster, a "real 'rag, tag, and bobtail' affair" took place:

> Notwithstanding the temperance reformation, the "citizen soldiers" appeared in fine spirits, and it was with the greatest difficulty in the world that the officers could convince them that those who carried umbrellas should file off in the rear, and permit their friends who were armed with cornstalks, canes and switches to fill the front ranks. No one who saw the display, could refrain from throwing his cap in the air, and giving three cheers for the militia system.

Critics of the compulsory system frequently impugned the intelligence of working class recruits. An 1842 Mount Pleasant muster "would have made a fine appearance, were it not that many were without arms, and that a great difference of opinion existed among them as to which foot had the right of precedence in marching."[95]

The possibilities for class differentiation and cultural prestige here were immense. Any gentleman would certainly choose a volunteer unit; an industrious worker would also recognize the financial sacrifice necessary to avoid compulsory duty as a small price to pay for serving one's country. The only explanation for service in a compulsory unit was sloth, apathy, or lack of intelligent patriotism. Critics depicted the compulsory militia as ridiculous not because of its working class troops' poverty and lack of opportunity but because of their personal failings. Conversely, they praised elite volunteer units not because of the upper and middle class troops' abundant time and resources but because of their inherent superiority. Militia service, like other leisure activities, represented upper class superiority as the cause rather than the consequence of economic and social advantages.

Yet the working class, too, could use leisure to develop its own cultural patterns and values. Even in the apotheosis of hierarchy, the militia system, leisure allowed working class Pennsylvanians to reject established rules and elite authority. Perhaps better than other, less rigidly organized activities, militia service demonstrates that leisure was by no means a sure avenue for establishing class hegemony. At best, leisure was disputed cultural ground on which ideas, interpretations, and practices were contested, modified, and sometimes rejected outright. Workers used leisure to affirm a sense of their own identity. But leisure offered the working class much more than this, for it aided workers both to resist dominant ideologies and to formulate distinctive visions of social relations that were more than mere reactions to upper class initiatives.

On one level, working class members of compulsory or undistinguished volunteer units subverted the prestige accorded elite officers by parodying the practice of "electing" prominent men to command positions. As Thomas Phillips complained of militia election day in 1842,

> many an ambitious wight, who heretofore has toiled in the ranks, with no higher badge of military honor than a cornstalk, received permission to mount an epulet, and will on next "trainin' day" be found marching in his proper position with all the "pride, pomp and circumstance," of a Militia officer. The number of Colonels, Majors, Captains and officers of lower grade that was created last Monday, would form a good sized army themselves.[96]

In addition, working class citizen-soldiers often simply rejected the air of gravity and dignity with which elite officers hoped to imbue the most visible form of social display, the periodic muster day. Training days allowed volunteer officers to parade in all their grandeur and to display their refinement, gentility, and social authority. Subordinates undermined this pageantry by taking the occasion less than seriously. Thus, while flirting, fighting, gaming, and excessive drinking on muster day expressed working class joi de vivre, these activities also resisted and subverted behavioral rules and social roles prescribed by the elite. By treating muster day as a community festival, lower class militiamen and their families mocked not only militia discipline but also the social hierarchy and class divisions it represented. A three or four day encampment involving several companies brought together men and women of different classes, ethnic backgrounds, and political persuasions. The festive atmosphere of the bivouac allowed, even encouraged, participants to temporarily invert or suspend established rules and conventions and conceive of alternative social structures and arrangements. Encampments sometimes produced what anthropologist Victor Turner has called "communitas," a period of unmediated interpersonal communication and group solidarity. By its very nature, "communitas" undermined the class divisions the elite hoped to display and support through the militia system.[97]

Take, for example, the muster at Camp Fayette, on Pittsburgh's South Side (then Birmingham) in September 1842. The encampment, which assembled approximately 1,500 volunteers in more than twenty companies from surrounding counties, was much anticipated as an important social event. Though professedly intended to train the "citizen soldiers of the West" in "those manoevres which are so necessary for the defence of our country — our firesides — and those we love — from the enemies of freedom throughout the world," the scene quickly took on a festive character:

> The highway from the city to the Camp seemed literally covered with men, women and children, all pressing toward the busy scene. . . . Carriages, wagons, and conveyances of every description were passing and repassing during the whole day, and the four steamboats and ferry-boat, which were engaged in transporting our citizens to Birmingham, were crowded with passengers. . . . As this is one of the days set apart for the reception of the ladies, we presume the Camp will be visited by the youth, the beauty, and the fashion of our city. Let the soldiers beware! MARS is nothing in the hands of that little rascal CUPID![98]

Belying the gravity of the encampment's military mission and the class relations on which it was based, soldiers of different social and ethnic backgrounds fraternized, socialized, and played together:

> Some of the soldiers amused themselves by singing, dancing, wrestling, &c., around their camp-fires; while others were in the booths satisfying the cravings of an empty stomach. They all looked cheerful and happy. But at a local tavern, a goodly number of young men were spreeing it out at a great rate — drinking and hallooing as if they were so many Indians. . . . The fire works and the "learned pig," together with a swing and nine pin alley, and also several fights, were the chief amusements in the neighborhood.[99]

All this fun and good fellowship culminated in a burlesque parade, the ultimate rejection of upper class dignity and order.[100] The soldiers' ridicule of social hierarchy and pompous military display revolved around a six foot, eight inch "young mountain lad" who attended the encampment with his Uniontown company. His comrades nicknamed this unusually tall recruit the "Giraffe."

His principal amusement for the past week has consisted in taking the arm of some fat good-natured Dutchman, and gallanting him through the camp, the contrast between his tall body and the rotund "corporation" of the little German convulsing every beholder with side-splitting laughter. . . . some of his acquaintances procured some spotted saddle cloth, from which the neck and head of a giraffe were soon manufactured. . . . With the addition of a wooden frame and buffalo robe the animal was completed, and a pair of ears, operated upon by wires, gave an air of life to the whole apparatus.[101]

Adequately accoutered, the Giraffe led a "tall Parade" that mocked upper class claims to dignity, valor, and preeminence:

The fifty or sixty men dressed and painted like Indians, with a tallow candle in the muzzle of each of their muskets, paraded around, and were rather savage looking in their appearance. But the stuffed Giraffe that preceded them was the best of the joke. . . . No one could stuff us, however, that it was a living animal; and to satisfy our curiosity on the point, we lifted up its covering, and saw a blue coat tail, adorned with the military trappings, sticking "straight out." The affair did well to laugh at, and many improved the opportunity.[102]

With its juxtaposition of the "military trappings" of the elite and the ludicrous garb of the Giraffe, this burlesque parade effectively belied any notion of deference to upper class superiority based on military leadership. As with other attempts to gain cultural authority through leisure, the upper and middle classes found it easier to define themselves than to convince others of the definition's validity.

6

Engendering Leisure

WRITING TO HER MOTHER IN 1821, Eliza Swift described her daily activities as the wife of a Presbyterian minister in Pittsburgh. Eliza rose early and began knitting socks "fast an hour before light," pausing only to prepare breakfast for her still-sleeping husband Elisha. Having roused the man of the house, Eliza and the family commenced their daily devotions as soon as "it is light enough to see to read from the window." Eliza then served breakfast, cleared the dishes, and set her house in order. Though she sometimes had a hired girl to help with the housework, Swift preferred to rise early and do the work herself, thereby avoiding the expense and trouble of servants. "By this means," she told her mother, "we have our morning's work done and are ready to see company before they are perhaps ready to come." Most southwestern Pennsylvanians considered visiting friends and relatives an enjoyable use of leisure. Eliza, however, expressed some misgivings about the constant round of socializing she experienced as a minister's wife. "In town after nine or ten we may always calculate to have some one dropping in. This Mama," she confided, "you know I am sometimes willing to be excused from."[1]

Eliza Swift's account of her daily routine highlights the difficulty of applying conventional definitions of leisure to women's experience with free time. Much existing scholarship focuses exclusively on male leisure, even defining leisure in opposition to paid labor, the pattern of work that has been historically more the province of men than women. Feminist scholars have pointed out that this approach either ignores women completely or treats them as an aberrant case.[2] The definition of leisure adopted here — freedom from business, or time free from obligations — avoids these pitfalls somewhat, for it allows us to understand women's perceptions of leisure in their own terms. Though no one paid Eliza Swift for her labor, she certainly recognized her household chores as work and had a clear idea of what freedom from the "business" of being a housewife meant. Free time could be used for writing and reading letters, perusing books and tracts, taking walks, or engaging in church and missionary activities. "Again I find myself at leisure," Swift wrote her mother in 1820, "to take up my pen and presume it will be gratifying to my dear mama to hear more about our missionary friends." She went on to describe a sewing party she attended, and an unexpectedly exhausting walk up Pittsburgh's "Coal Hill[,] which is a steep mountain."[3]

Still, Swift's experience suggests further questions. For Eliza and most other women of her era, work and leisure were in many respects not sharply differentiated. Knitting and visiting might be pleasant diversions, burdensome chores, or a mixture of both, depending on the circumstances. Though Swift considered her "work" done before morning callers arrived, for instance, she clearly did not embrace the constant round of visitors as pure leisure. Considering the "mixed" quality of her activities, and the fact that the demands of her husband's profession determined her daily schedule, how free was her leisure time after all?[4] How much did her roles as wife and mother influence the range and type of activities open to her? And how did she respond? In broader terms, how did being a woman in southwestern Pennsylvania during the early nineteenth century affect one's perception, experience, and practice of leisure? To answer these questions, we must look carefully at leisure and its relation to gender roles. By examining the kinds of leisure activities that southwestern Pennsylvanians deemed appropriate for women, we can begin to understand how gender shaped the meaning and use of free time in women's lives. We can also learn much about how women used leisure to comment on their society's notions of acceptable female behavior. As we shall see, leisure in southwestern Pennsylvania served as a cultural arena in which both men and women articulated and contested varying ideas about gender.

In southwestern Pennsylvania's preindustrial communities, women's leisure, like their work, was most often linked to home and family. Though men too spent some of their leisure time at home with their wives and children, they also enjoyed a range of activities that excluded women and took place beyond the domestic sphere — hunting trips, political meetings, drinking parties, social clubs, and so on. In contrast, women found their leisure in the odd moments they snatched from their duties as wives, mothers, sisters, and daughters. Reading, visiting, informal socializing with female neighbors or relatives, and sewing and quilting alone or in groups comprised the bulk of women's leisure. Not only were these activities centered in and around the home, but they were also linked closely to work. Women's leisure intertwined amusement and recreation with the productive and instrumental tasks that comprised their daily labors. Sewing an elaborate article of clothing or piecing together an intricate quilt might provide opportunities for relaxation, artistic expression, and female socializing, but they also produced items both useful and necessary to the family. In this respect, it is often difficult to determine where women's work ceased and their leisure began.[5]

This difficulty reflected the differing conditions of men's and women's work, for the sexual division of labor contributed to gendered experiences of time and leisure. Plowing a field, repairing a fence, or building a barrel were discrete tasks with beginnings and ends; feeding, clothing, and caring for a family were open-ended and continuous occupations with no clear stopping points. Catharine Beecher recognized this pattern and advised her time-conscious readers accordingly. "With housekeepers, and others whose employments are various, and desultory," she urged, "much time can be saved by preparing employments for little intervals of leisure." Sewing, knitting, or reading, if kept close at hand, Beecher noted, would help housekeepers to find "employment for [the] odd intervals of time" between domestic tasks. To be sure, southwestern Pennsylvania's women shared with their men a conviction that time should be spent wisely. Eliza Swift, for instance, encouraged a female relative to write as

"often as you can and keep cheerful — the time will soon while away —
only improve it." Merely killing time, Swift warned, led one to "look back
and regret much wasted time[,] and the longer we live the more we
regret."[6] Despite this common ground, two important differences separated men's and women's experience of leisure.

Differences in Men's and Women's Leisure

First, the amount of free time available to men and women was not equal:
men had more leisure than women. Typically, women bore responsibilities for the family's welfare and the production of household goods for
consumption, barter, and sale. This expended more time than did the
limited and circumscribed tasks that fell to men. In addition, gender roles
as constituted in southwestern Pennsylvania made it unacceptable for
males to aid females in the conduct of "woman's" work. Jane Grey Swisshelm remembered that "Pennsylvania custom made it unmanly for a
man or boy to aid any woman, even mother or wife, in any hard work
with which farms abounded at that time. Dairy work, candle and sausage
making were done by women, and any innovation was met with sneers.
I stubbornly refused to yield altogether to a time-honored code, which
required women to perform out-door drudgery, often while men sat in
the house."[7]

Though men could refuse to do women's work, they expected women
to help with men's work if circumstances dictated. At harvest time, for
example, crops had to be gathered before they spoiled, and this sometimes
required the participation of every available person. Disregarding temporarily notions of female fragility and incapacity, men welcomed women
to the fields. For their part, farm women proved that they could wield the
sickle as skillfully as men.[8] But women's work in the fields did not excuse
them from their regular tasks and, in fact, added to them. Field workers
expected their employer to feed them, and meal preparation was a quin-
tessentially female job. Cooking for a large group might be exhausting
by itself, for it required numerous trips to a spring or well for water. "You
have so much of that to do in harvest," Jane Grey Swisshelm remarked
of the constant running for water, "for it is cook, cook, all the time."
Swisshelm resented deeply the unequal distribution of work and leisure,

railing against the "masculine superiority fever" that allowed men to loaf while women toiled in the fields and prepared harvest meals. Farm women, she commented bitterly, "did such work often, while the 'menfolk' pitched horseshoes to work off their surplus vitality."[9]

A second difference in male and female leisure followed from the first. Not only did women have less free time than men, but they also helped to produce surplus male leisure with their own labor. Though both sexes might gather for a harvest dinner or wedding celebration, women undertook the laborious task of preparing refreshments, serving meals, and cleaning up afterward. Gender roles thus shaped women's participation in and enjoyment of these common "leisure" events. Even celebratory occasions, which were outside the realm of everyday life, did not untangle women's work and leisure but, rather, highlighted their interconnectedness by juxtaposing them with male idleness and relaxation.

Southwestern Pennsylvania's preindustrial communities institutionalized this pattern in frolics, bees, barn raisings, and other social rituals that linked cooperative labor with communal celebration. At butchering frolics, for instance, men performed the unpleasant task of killing, boiling, and cleaning hogs in the morning, and women prepared the customary sumptuous noon meal. After dinner the men, their labor substantially finished, spent the afternoon engaged in "shooting at a mark or other sports and games." While their menfolk played, the women began the unpleasant, dirty, and presumably female work of rendering lard and making sausage.[10] This affirmation of community and neighborly assistance placed the sexual division of labor, and the gender roles that underpinned it, in high relief. If the day was half work and half leisure for men, the same could not be said for women.

Such was also the case at husking and quilting bees, which neighbors often held on the same afternoon. Men husked the corn crop while women joined together to sew a quilt as the prelude to a general communal dinner prepared, of course, by the women. Observers and historians have often portrayed such cooperative gatherings as necessary for the accomplishment of labor beyond the abilities of a single family, and for the preservation of communal solidarity and neighborliness. This account, however accurate, masks the ways in which gender roles shaped men's and women's experiences of work and leisure. If women had not been limited to the female tasks of sewing and cooking and had taken part in the male job of husking, would a large gathering have been necessary to process the corn crop? One account from Fayette County casts doubt on the absolute necessity of cooperative labor: "In quality, quantity and variety, that old table was spread with the best the season could afford and was the result of no small amount of work on the part of the hostess and her daughters. As one good old grandmother used to express it: 'It took longer to get the supper than it did to husk the corn.'"[11] Here customary gender roles encouraged an unequal distribution of work, thereby providing a greater amount of leisure time for men than women. By assigning women the roles of domestic, cook, and servant, men turned supposedly necessary labor gatherings into social events that served male preferences and prerogatives. As with leisure differences based in class, this pattern appeared natural, rather than artificial: men simply did male work, and women did female work. If the result meant more leisure for men than women, it might seem that this too, merely reflected the natural order of things. Though these examples have centered on agricultural workers, a similar case could be made for other sectors of the population as well.[12]

Women's Responses to the Unequal Distribution of Labor

How did women react to this system of allocating work and leisure? As one might expect, responses varied widely. Some women, like Jane Grey Swisshelm, resisted at every turn, pointing out the inequity of a system that granted men added leisure at the expense of women. Others attempted to escape an oppressive situation by removing themselves from it, either through geographical relocation, as in the case of farm girls who fled to cities, or by retreat into physical illness, as in the urban middle class who took water cures and other medical treatment at female spas and health resorts.[13] Many women, however, appear to have accepted this situation as the natural order of things, expressing little open bitterness about the uneven distribution of work and leisure or the gender roles that supported it.

The diary of Nancy Kendall, the wife of a relatively prosperous Fayette County farmer, demonstrates this point. Kendall's diary, which spans the period between late 1847 and mid-1849, offers a detailed account of a young farm wife's daily activities. Kendall recorded a constant round of burdensome household tasks: washing, scrubbing, starching, sewing, cleaning, rendering lard, and a seemingly endless amount of "beaking" [baking]. Kendall also noted her husband Isaac's activities, which were fairly typical for a middling farmer: mending fences, hauling wood, selling livestock, and so on. Like most farm families of this era, the Kendalls divided work into gender-specific tasks. Isaac undertook heavy physical labor and business dealings with the strangers, while Nancy saw to housework, the garden, and household manufacturing. This system of gender roles also characterized cooperative labor with others. In September, 1848, for example, Nancy noted that the men gathered apples while "Elmira and I have been sewing, chatting, & c." Similarly, in December, "Isaac has been helping his father butcher. E. K. and I done the cocking [cooking]. I done my ironing and finished my shirt also."[14]

Gender-based differences become evident when one examines the content and context of the couple's leisure activities. Nancy's leisure consisted largely of visiting with neighbors, friends, and family; trips to nearby towns and villages with Isaac to shop or attend church; and cooperative gatherings — sewing parties, quilting bees, and butchering frolics — with other women. On January 25, 1848, for example, Nancy noted that "I have been nocking around quite briskly this morning[.] Mother & EA Roher & Mrs. Smith came out today[;] I was vry much pleased to see them indeed[.] Papa brought little Mary on his horse. [T]hey have been quilting vry steady all day. [T]ook the skirt out before we went to bed. Mother K. & E. Kendall have been helping quilt this afternoon." In May of that year Nancy recorded: "Sabbath 14th. [Q]uite pleasant and cool. Isaac and I started for Brownfieldtown this morning[,] got along vry well[,] heard the Rev. Mr. Rossell preach a short sermon after which the sacrament was administered. Took dinner at Aunt Phillips[,] got home safe after which I went to Galleys [a neighbor] to see Anne[, who was feeling] quite poorly." In November, "Mother Kendall and I started for J. Coffmans [and] found a large company of married ladies[;] got lots of quilting done."[15] As these entries illustrate, Nancy's leisure revolved around home, church, and kin and was often linked to work of some kind.

Isaac's leisure presents a somewhat different picture. In addition to shared activities with Nancy, he hunted, fished, shot at marks, and attended militia parades and political rallies. Like Nancy, Isaac spent much time visiting with family and friends, but his social world was considerably larger than his wife's. Frequent business trips to nearby Measontown and Uniontown increased Isaac's interaction with the larger society and produced social contacts and leisure opportunities not circumscribed by home and family. Early in March 1848, for example, "Isaac started for New Salem about 11 o'clock as he is one of the mus[i]cians to attend an exhibition there this evening." Isaac's participation in politics and the militia, activities that largely excluded women, also expanded his leisure horizons. In May 1848, Nancy remained at home while Isaac attended "the general parade at Baltsinger's old stand"; in September, Isaac and a male companion attended the fall parade. A month later he traveled alone to Fairview to a large "Dunkards" meeting and heard a "vry good discourse." Isaac left Nancy at home again in July to attend a Whig meeting in Uniontown. Early the next year, he "started for Uniontown to see Old Zach Taylor" while Nancy remained home "sewing carpet filling." The following day Isaac returned home and regaled Nancy with tales of his trip, remarking that "he had the pleasure of seeing Old Rough and Ready."[16]

Kendall's diary demonstrates that the sexual division of leisure entailed more than just greater access to the larger society, however. Her account of daily activities also reveals the same pattern we noted in frolics and bees: men often played while women worked. Isaac frequently engaged in leisure activities with little or no instrumental value while Nancy toiled at home. On several occasions, Isaac attended fox hunts while Nancy worked at her usual chores: "Isaac has gone to C. Bradings to a Fox hunt. I have been beaking, churning & c. & c." Sometimes her diary illustrated both men's greater access to the larger society and their ability to control their free time: "I have been ironing all day[.] Isaac has gone to the Election after which he and C. L. Conner went out to kill muscrats. Conner & wife spent the night with us." Even in activities that both Nancy and Isaac enjoyed — visiting, for example — the burden of work was unevenly distributed, for Nancy had to cook and clean for guests Isaac might bring home. "Isaac started for Brownfield town this morning," Nancy wrote in February, 1848, "expecting a deer chase but got disappointed as it died.

[He] brought Aunt Phillips home with him[,] Wm Kendall at Brownfield Town also. I have been beaking[,] Scrubbing & c. & c."[17]

Did Nancy Kendall resent the unequal access to leisure that characterized her relationship with Isaac? On the surface, it would seem not. Nowhere in her diary does she express open resentment at him, or at her situation. On occasion she lamented being unable to travel to nearby towns for much anticipated church services or family visits: "I would very much like to be at Measontown this Evening as Mr. Orshum preaches ther[.] I feel quite melancholy about it." Her disappointment, however, seemingly stemmed more from being the victim of unforeseen circumstances — bad weather, for instance — than from having fewer leisure opportunities than her husband: "I was disappointed today as I expected to go to Uniontown but could not in consequence of the rain."[18] For the most part, she accepted and even enjoyed the leisure available to her, both in mixed company and all-female gatherings. Some hints of dissatisfaction did surface, however. When she juxtaposed accounts of her toils with Isaac's leisure activities, one suspects some awareness of, and comment upon, her situation. In February 1848, Nancy noted that "Isaac and AJA has gone to Genevia as they have a race after a deer. I have been beaking[,] *scrubbing*[,] *scouring* my *tinware* & c." One entry from 1848 captures this perhaps unintended irony more poignantly than others: "Friday 19th of May my Birthday. 25 years of my lifetime have rappidly passed away never more to return[.] I have been beaking[,] ironing[,] & c."[19]

Constraints on Women's Leisure Choices

The forgoing suggests some questions about women's leisure in nineteenth-century southwestern Pennsylvania. Was leisure less a realm of freedom for women than men, as feminist scholars have argued? Did "free" time pursuits constrain women through subordinating gender roles rather than allowing them choice and option?[20] Certainly, a persuasive case could be made along these lines. Jane Grey Swisshelm, for instance, found that her society deemed acceptable only those leisure activities that preserved women's roles as dutiful daughters and wives and disallowed pursuits that disrupted accepted notions of gender. Swisshelm used her talent for lacework and painting on velvet to help support her family after her father's death in 1823, thereby demonstrating her filial piety and personal industriousness. When she interested a patron in paying for further art education, the situation changed. If directed toward family nurturance or support, art was an acceptable and valued use of leisure. Pursuing it as an occupation, however, rendered it problematic. Strong familial and societal disapproval prevented Swisshelm from following her artistic interests. With the help of her patron, she might have developed a leisure pastime into a career, "had an artistic education, or any other education, been possible for a Western Pennsylvania girl in that dark age — the first half of the nineteenth century."[21]

Further evidence suggests that Swisshelm's experience was not uncommon. Typically, southwestern Pennsylvanians frowned upon any women's leisure activities that did not further the cause of hearth and home. Among working class women, as well as many farm wives like Nancy Kendall, leisure often involved labor that freed men from a variety of burdensome tasks related to hospitality, sociability, and housekeeping. In the middle and upper classes, a slightly different pattern prevailed. Money and servants eliminated some women's work, providing more free time that could, at least in theory, have been devoted to pastimes of a woman's choice.[22] In practice, freedom from the most onerous household tasks opened new avenues for linking women's leisure to the work of homemaking. The skills that made women good helpmeets and mothers went beyond mere cooking, cleaning, and household production and extended into the leisure sphere. Though not called upon to perform as much strenuous physical labor as their working class counterparts, middle and upper class women were expected to exhibit charm, refinement, and artistic accomplishment that would exert a salutary influence on their families. One list of the "Duties of Married Females" included self-cultivation to keep husbands happy and interested: "the pains she took to charm him before marriage, ought to be redoubled now; to render the home agreeable to him, to receive him with open arms, and cheerful looks." A variety of books, pamphlets, and lectures portrayed home as a refuge from the market and women as the creators and guardians of domestic bliss:

Yet here the virtues with their train of social joys resort
There health and peace and freedom reign,
Fair exiles from a court.
My loving partner in her turn,
Anticipates desire;
And oft, as if it would not burn,
She trims the blazing fire.[23]

Fulfilling this aspect of domestic obligation demanded refinement, education, and artistic attainment. Writers like Washington County's "Clarinda" portrayed the development of these qualities during leisure time as both the ideal and natural state of affairs. Writing in 1810, Clarinda inquired "wherein the true dignity and honor of the female sex consists." It consisted, she concluded, "in completely and fully answering the end and intention for which it was created."

> Now it is evident from the sacred pages, and from the concurring testimony of hundreds of generations that women were created for helpmeet, or companions for men. Hence it follows, that the true nobility and honor of every female consists in her being a complete helpmeet or companion for man, also that whatever has a tendency to make her a more agreeable companion for man is her proper and indeed her only proper employment.[24]

By cultivating her talents during leisure hours, a woman aided her husband by "dispers[ing] from his mind the settling gloom of continued reflection, and enliven[ing] his feelings from the languor of his necessary avocations." More than merely refreshing men from their worldly labors, women, by virtue of their superior morality and spirituality, could also foster a taste for the finer qualities of mind and soul in leisure hours: "Gay, sprightly and volatile, and susceptible to all the fine feelings; of all the exhilarating sentiments of the soul, and possessed of a person decorated with all the softer delicacies and tender attractions of grace and beauty, which give these qualities of her mind a more easy and enchanting access to the mind of man."[25]

Cultivated wives provided uplifting companionship and an alternative to the vicious pastimes to which men might otherwise be drawn: "Instead of wasting his nights in beerhouses, in drinking, revelries and carousing intercourses, he feels that as a member of the community he is looked upon to protect its morals and stay its influence." More than merely keeping men from the haunts of vice, accomplished ladies of leisure civilized the community. A poem that praised Miss Antoinette Brevost, the instructor at a Pittsburgh female seminary, explicitly linked womanly erudition, charm, and accomplishment to the progress of civilization:

> She called THE ARTS: The arts obey'd,
> And MANUFACTURES thither sped;
> MECHANICS too, and every TRADE
> Taught INDUSTRY to earn his bread.
> Invoked, the LIBERAL ARTS appear,
> The SOCIAL CHARMS, and every GRACE
> Which to the female mind are dear,
> Find now an undisputed place.[26]

Musical training was one leisure activity for women that fulfilled this civilizing function exceptionally well. Consider, for example, the opinion expressed about music in an enthusiastic account of the annual exhibition at Mrs. Baker's Pittsburgh school for young women in 1820. Music, one writer noted, was

> an accomplishment of which no young lady, especially those destined to move in the higher circles of polished society, should be destitute. Sent as guardian angels to soothe the cares, alleviate the sufferings, and moderate the violent passions of man, any advantage which may give them additional power, which may give zest to beauty and increased interest to lovely innocence, must be highly gratifying to all who are solicitous for the happiness of the human family.[27]

Not surprisingly, contemporaries valued musical women and endorsed concerts as uplifting family leisure. Pittsburghers, for example, remembered admiringly the Widow Collins, "a woman of charm [who] had many accomplishments, not the least of which was the old world talent of playing the harp." Pennsylvanians' love of music struck British traveler John Palmer, who noted in 1817 that Pittsburghers "are fond of music; in our evening walks, we were sure to hear performers on the violin, flute, and occasionally the piano-forte. Concerts are not unusual. The houses of the principal streets have benches in front, on which the family and neighbors sit and enjoy the placidity of their summer evenings."[28]

Music fostered a variety of desirable female qualities. As a solitary activity, it promoted discipline, morality, and personal development, albeit in the service of husband, children, and society. As a social activity, it facilitated moral and intellectual development in family and community leisure. Perhaps most importantly, musical training made women better mothers. By teaching their children to sing, for instance, women imparted the young with an appreciation for self-discipline, cooperation, and the arts. Catharine Beecher considered music an "elevating and delightful recreation for the young" that provided "not only a means of culture but also an amusement." Music's usefulness in Christian worship also recommended it to women, who were the supposed sources of religiosity in the household. Singing or playing hymns with the family represented both a pleasant diversion and a moral obligation for women.[29]

Women as Men's Leisure Commodity

One might expect that gender roles that linked women's leisure to family welfare and the progress of civilization in this fashion would enhance their status and enlarge their options. Such was not always the case. Middle and upper class anxiety about social climbing, status, and respectability sometimes turned women's free time into a contest among men to possess the most accomplished lady of leisure. Literary education, art instruction, and music lessons all required money, placing them beyond most of the working and some of the middle classes.[30] It was a short step to conclude that families that promoted women's leisure also fostered morality, thereby demonstrating their superior social and cultural status. In contrast to the working class, middle and upper class women represented more than labor sources that produced increased male leisure. Rather, they became supplements to male leisure that proclaimed men's ability to educate and cultivate their women. In short, gender roles that defined women's leisure in terms of its impact on men could and sometimes did turn women into objects of conspicuous consumption.[31]

This pattern is clearest in the upper class, which had the most money to spend on leisure. Like their middle class counterparts, upper class men groomed their women as sources of morality and respectability. But upper class women also served an artistic, intellectual, and ornamental role — they were, ideally, fashionable and accomplished as well as pious and virtuous. Upper class families could well afford the necessary literary, musical, and artistic training that prepared young women to be emblems of male status.[32] Possession of an artistically accomplished daughter, sister, or wife expressed symbolically upper class status and social power. The diaries of Charles Scully and Robert McKnight attest to the importance of female artistic and musical attainment in Pittsburgh's polite society. Charles Scully both admired and enjoyed female artistic accomplishment. In January 1843, he delighted in duets performed on the harp and piano by two daughters of the prestigious Denny family. In June Scully wrote approvingly of a painting on ivory by a Miss Rebecca Shields of nearby Sewickley. Scully's discussion of these women, however respectful, often centered on their desirability as fashionable and accomplished commodities — listings for the "Batchelors Directory." The same was true of Robert McKnight. He too attended and enjoyed leisure activities that involved women as intellectual and artistic ornaments. At a party given by his family, for instance, McKnight "pledged Miss Tyler in a glass of champagne and returning to the parlour danced with her[.] She is pretty, of fine figure and carriage, & a great coquette." McKnight's account of his engagement and marriage to Elizabeth O'Hara Denny, whom he discussed in almost reverential tones even in the privacy of his diary, revealed the desirability of these qualities for upper class men like himself.[33]

The best example of women as men's leisure commodities comes from the spa at Bedford Springs, a popular upper class haunt during the hot summer months. Men enjoyed field sports at the springs, but polite society considered such active pursuits to be unsuitable for women. Expected to be paragons of beauty and virtue, young women often found themselves consigned to expectant inactivity as dashing young men strove to pay them tribute. One participant recalled how women cultivated their charms and anxiously anticipated the men's return:

> How the girls waited in their rooms until midnight for the delicate dishes of fried trout, sure to be sent up to them with compliments of friends and

admirers who had caught them. Oh, the glory of having several dishes of such tribute. . . . We were a simpler-minded set of feminines in those days, fond of the good things of this life, which we took when offered without troublesome introspection.[34]

Clearly, the notion that women's leisure should serve men and the family, and not occasion any "troublesome introspection," constituted a powerful behavioral model.[35] Yet it represented only one of a number of competing ideological strains in antebellum American culture. Both Nancy Cott and Glenna Matthews argue convincingly, for example, that women gained status and authority within the domestic sphere during the early nineteenth century.[36] But women's efforts to extend their intellectual and social horizons to the public world of the marketplace suggest that they did not consider or accept the defense of hearth and home as the summum bonum of their existence. Domestic influence and moral authority became ideological prisons when they confined women to their homes. To truly expand the influence and status they earned within the domestic sphere, women strove to stake a claim to a public voice beyond the home.

Extending Female Influence and Activity Through Leisure

Leisure offered women a unique way to extend the ideological boundaries of female influence and activity both in the home and beyond it. Popular mores precluded a female role in formal political and civic debate, so women turned to leisure occasions and contexts as acceptable forms of public participation. Women could claim convincingly, for instance, that their presence exerted a moral influence on all kinds of public gatherings. If men were unwilling to admit women to strictly political or economic assemblies, they could hardly deny the desirability of a female presence on other public occasions, especially leisure events. This concession opened the door for women to make themselves heard indirectly, by using leisure to exploit contradictions in the gender roles proposed by their society. Taking greater liberties than expected or rejecting outright prescriptions for proper female behavior, women gained a measure of choice and self-determination. As we shall see, at communal gatherings, civic celebrations, and voluntary association meetings, women tested the boundaries of public and private spheres, using leisure to camouflage their challenge to a gender system that often attempted to marginalize them.

Sexual Segregation in Public Leisure

Yet convention often militated against women's efforts in this area, for sexual segregation in public leisure was common. At many public dinners and civic occasions, men welcomed women's presence only in spirit, remembering them in an obligatory final toast to the "absent fair." At a Washington dinner honoring Daniel Webster in 1833, for instance, the event's organizers toasted "The Ladies.—On such occasions ever absent, yet ever present—absent in person, present in remembrance."[37]

Even in activities deemed acceptable for both sexes, men determined women's participation, often relegating them to silence and passivity. In Westmoreland County, for example, the coeducational Robbstown Seminary sponsored a Fourth of July celebration in 1819. Both male and female students participated, but only males delivered orations and addresses: "It was highly pleasing to the audience, that females did not appear as speakers on this occasion." Robbstown notwithstanding, the question of women speaking in public rarely arose. Men reserved toasting, speech making, and debating for themselves, usually dismissing the women before the customary toasts or testimonials began. Women might lend beauty or decorum to the forgoing formal ceremonies, but men believed that the boisterous proceedings that often followed were too stimulating for the fair sex. A partisan Elizabethtown Fourth of July celebration in 1820 "was not a little enlivened by the presence of a number of young ladies, whose tender bosoms glowed with patriotism, and who joined in the celebration with pleasure." Glowing or not, tender bosoms had no place in the practice of politics, and after "dinner, the ladies retired to an arbor prepared for them" so that the partisan toasting could begin. This pattern of exclusion persisted throughout our period. In 1848, a militia-sponsored Fourth festivity at Amity, Washington County, welcomed women to the dinner, oration, and recitation of the Declaration of Independence. "The Ladies were then escorted back to their quarters in town, and on the return of the companies" the toasts commenced, and the male festivities began.[38]

Other leisure activities displayed similar arrangements, which, ostensibly, were aimed at shielding women from the potential embarrassment of unmediated contact with raucous or high-spirited men in public. Sexual segregation promised a respectable and nonthreatening leisure experience for presumably demure and retiring women. Typically, dance or art teachers held separate classes for men and women or catered to one sex exclusively. Mr. and Mrs. Collins, actors who visited Pittsburgh in the midteens, offered separate elocution lessons for boys and girls. A Uniontown dancing master also followed suit in 1817, advertising classes for ladies at 3 P.M. and for gentlemen at "early candle light." Though sexual segregation diminished as time passed, separate drawing and art classes persisted into the 1830s. Margaretta Reynolds offered piano lessons expressly to Pittsburgh's young ladies, while a Miss Crampton taught girls to play both the piano and pianoforte. Mr. Couse's dancing school at the Pittsburgh Concert Hall advertised separate classes and promised female students a respectable learning environment, emphasizing the establishment's commitment to the temperance cause. Division by sex also characterized the admission and seating policies of many commercial amusements, especially early in the century. In 1814 a Museum of Living Animals reserved 3 to 5 P.M. for the admission of ladies. At Mr. Collins's benefit night, the Pittsburgh theater's management announced that front seats "will be reserved for the ladies." Mr. Denniston, the proprietor of Pittsburgh's Columbian Inn, went a step further in 1823. Not only did he reserve the front seats for ladies who wished to view Mr. Nichol's dramatic monologues, but he assured potential patrons that "Christians of any denominations whatever, can find no objections to attending this exhibition."[39]

Sexual segregation in leisure often expressed gender roles that identified women with morality and the home and men with the market and outside world. Some men's activities, like Freemasonry, excluded women altogether, carving out an all-male preserve to foster business connections along with social ties. The proclivity for all-male leisure retreats apparently developed early in men's lives, particularly among the aspiring middle class.[40] Jefferson College's Franklin Literary Society, for example, prohibited female guests at its functions, despite the expectation that the "gloomy old cloisters would smile and brighten, to enclose such angelic visitants." In formal pronouncements, the Franklins evinced a high regard for the fair sex: "Thus the question — 'Is female modesty, natural or artificial?' being debated at one of the first meetings of the Society, it was decided, by acclamation, to be natural. The question, 'ought a man to whip his wife on any occasion?' was gallantly decided in the negative." But the Franklins also took pains to insure that the society would experience feminine influence only as a distant, salutary source of virtuous inspiration. By the 1840s they went so far as to show "no mercy to the poor unfortunate, who has launched his bark on the sea of matrimony — and for this one offense, debar[red] him from membership." Though the Franklins saw a role for women in male leisure, it was an indirect and secondary one, which assumed that women should be moral influences who stayed out of the bustle of public life and male leisure. Similar sentiments prevailed among Pittsburgh's Associated Singing Society. Though it did not admit women as members, the society did value their moral influence: "If the expenses of this institution, do not amount to the subscriptions, received by the Treasurer, the extra money shall be appropriated to charitable purposes; and a committee consisting of three Lady's shall be appointed by the Society, to dispose of the extra money in the manner specified."[41]

Women and Public Leisure

Despite this gender-based segregation, women were by no means absent from public leisure.[42] Women attended young men's clubs' anniversary dinners, firemen's parades, literary societies' activities, and Masonic addresses, sometimes in equal numbers with men. For example, of the 150 people who attended a supper for "Judge Gilmore and Lady" at Washington's Valentine House in 1850, one-half belonged to "the fair sex."[43] Reform-based leisure events provided obvious venues for female participation and influence. Temperance advocates noted that a woman could do much for the cause, "for the elements of her nature eminently fit her for labor in every benevolent work. . . . She can by her voice of persuasion, reach hearts that could never be touched by any other agent." Not surprisingly, soldiers of the Cold Water Army encouraged women to attend temperance functions: "Ladies, you are particularly requested to attend! Cheer us with your presence! Aid us with your influence!"[44] Precisely because southwestern Pennsylvanians of both sexes considered women to be a moral influence on society, they endorsed a female presence at a variety of public leisure activities.

Women's chances to exploit the possibilities of public leisure lay in this contradictory set of gender roles — one could not be both the home-bound guardian of domestic virtue and a moral influence on society at large. Since most southwestern Pennsylvanians expected women's presence to raise the tone of public leisure, promoting order and lending respectability to potentially unruly public occasions, female patrons could redeem even questionable amusements like theater. Writing in 1835, "Thalia" remarked admiringly that the Pittsburgh theater's "first tier of boxes presented a bright array of the beauty and fashion of the city." Women's presence apparently provided an incentive to actors and managers to behave properly, for theater companies realized that improprieties cost them patrons. After an embarrassing incident with a drunken actor in the mid-1830s, Francis Wemyss noted the abandonment of Pittsburgh theater by women, and thus by "every respectable citizen." For spectators and promoters alike, respectability (not to mention profitability) demanded that amusements be acceptable to female sensibilities. Puffing Mr. Hannington's exhibition in 1839 as a "Rational Entertainment and Extraordinary Novelty," for example, *Harris's Intelligencer* emphasized approval of the attraction by "our most moral and respectable ladies and gentlemen." In Washington as well, the presence of middle and upper class women at shows and lectures insured a favorable moral and intellectual climate. Mr. Sims's 1836 lectures on phrenology, for example, attracted a "majority of the literati of this place," but "what is better than all, the Ladies, those bright luminaries that light up the otherwise dark horizon of man's existence[,] turned out almost *en masse.*"[45]

Women appeared in other public leisure contexts as well. Many women owned or managed taverns and inns that hosted a variety of leisure activities. Local patrons enjoyed social drinking, conversation, and listening to others read aloud from newspapers and periodicals provided by the house. At the Pittsburgh Coffee Room, for instance, Mrs. Blair attracted patrons by stocking several newspapers that had been "selected with impartiality." Traveling performers and attractions also relied on taverns for exhibition space. In Washington, Mrs. McCammant's inn housed a traveling panorama of Rome along with the added attractions of waxworks, organ music, and a profile artist in 1818. That same year Mrs. Irwin's Pittsburgh tavern housed an array of amusements: a gallery of European paintings, a panorama and menagerie, and a ventriloquist.[46]

By the mid-nineteenth century, theaters and concert halls supplanted the makeshift facilities offered by taverns and inns as venues for traveling shows. This commercialization excluded women from many of their previous activities as purveyors of amusements and proprietors of exhibition spaces. Not only did most women lack the financial resources to build or operate formal exhibition halls, but the increasing imbeddedness of commercial leisure in market relations made it an unfit pursuit for the fair sex. Though their role in commercial leisure diminished, women continued to sponsor public leisure events, albeit of a different sort. Women retained a public role by turning to leisure events that were linked firmly to morality and religion, their undisputed area of expertise and influence. Later in our period women extended the moral authority they won in the domestic sphere beyond the home by organizing ladies' fairs, church bazaars, and similar social events to benefit charities and other good causes. Washington women held a "Ladies' Fair" for charity in 1836; four years later the Ladies' Sewing Society of St. Peter's Church solicited the "patronage of the friends of Religion and of the public in general" for their "Fair of Fancy and useful Articles." Similarly, the Female Benevolent Society of Christ Church in Brownsville, Washington County, organized a "sale of useful and fancy articles" in 1845. Devoted to the cause of sobriety, Pittsburgh's Martha Washington Society sponsored a temperance celebration on the Fourth of July in 1846. Four years later, the women of Washington's Cumberland Presbyterian Church scheduled their fair to coincide with the annual cattle show. To raise money for their church, they sold handmade articles and refreshments and offered visitors an inexpensive supper. Despite men's attempts to insulate them from economic activities and consign them to domestic pursuits, women entered the marketplace indirectly, using their leisure time to become fund-raisers under the aegis of religion and morality.[47]

Nor was this activity limited to white, middle class Protestants. Pittsburgh's African American women organized several "soirees" and social events during the year. In the summer months they sponsored picnics and festivals to benefit *The Mystery*, the city's only black newspaper. Black women also helped to organize First of August festivals, which commemorated West Indian independence, as well as church-sponsored leisure events. On July 2, 1848, the ladies of Allegheny City's "Colored Wesleyan Church" held a fair; two days later, their counterparts in Pittsburgh's African Methodist Episcopal Church offered a "grand entertainment" on the Fourth of July.[48]

Catholic women, too, organized leisure events for charity. Pittsburgh's Catholic women staged a "Ladies' Fair" in "Beale's Long Room" to benefit the Orphan Asylum as early as 1834. A similar event benefited Pittsburgh's hospital in 1847. In 1849, the "ladies, who are always foremost when any charitable or good work is to be performed," arranged a "miniature fair" on the grounds of Pittsburgh's St. Paul's Orphan Asylum to benefit the orphans. The *Gazette* encouraged attendance by all who wished "to enjoy in a pleasing manner our great national festival" with "the good things of this life, in the shape of dinner, refreshments, & c.," noting that they would "at the same time perform an act of charity."[49]

Women also performed in public leisure events. Professional actresses and singers toured southwestern Pennsylvania beginning early in the century. In 1806, for instance, Mrs. Smith, "formerly Miss Whitlock of the New York theater," entertained Pittsburghers with "theatrical exhibitions" in which she played opposite her husband. On July 4, 1816, the final night of the theater season, Pittsburghers enjoyed a "transparency of the Genius of Columbia crowning Washington with laurels and an address by Mrs. Turner as the Genius of America." Female performers ranged from the exotic to the prosaic. Southwestern Pennsylvanians attended the "Levees" of Ah Fong Moy, a Chinese woman who toured the United States during the 1830s, curious to hear her Chinese songs and view her bound feet. Attractions from closer to home sometimes elicited a more tepid response. In 1845, a Washington critic admitted to being "somewhat entertained" by the "vocal powers of a pair of Yankee girls (Misses Maccomber)."[50]

If some female performers failed to stir their patrons' imaginations, others outraged their sensibilities. Such was the reception of Abby Kelley, an abolitionist, women's rights advocate, and alleged disciple of Robert Dale Owen and Fanny Wright. Kelley's public lectures and outspoken support of radical causes shocked staid Washingtonians. Pittsburghers found their notions of sexual morality threatened in 1848, when a troupe of "Model Artists" visited the city. The artists, both male and female, formed a number of tableaux vivant clad only in flesh-colored tights. The troupe emphasized the artistic and cultural aspects of their presentation, but some Pittsburghers suspected that their protestations cloaked an appeal to prurience and lustfulness.[51]

Female amateurs, too, performed in public. While their participation differed markedly from that of their professional sisters, southwestern Pennsylvanian women displayed their talents nonetheless. Popular mores did structure and limit their participation, moving some activities beyond the pale of respectability. Most southwestern Pennsylvanians, for instance, considered theater an unsuitable activity for young women. Actor and manager Noah Ludlow recounted his difficulty procuring female extras to be "Virgins of the Sun" for a Pittsburgh production of *Pizarro* in 1815: "Virgins (of course I mean stage virgins) were not to be had in Pittsburgh in those days. Seamstresses and shoebinders would have as soon thought of walking deliberately into Pandemonium as to have appeared on the stage as 'supers' or 'corps de ballet.' "[52]

In general, demonstrations of literary or educational achievement received approval. Female seminaries held annual exhibitions of music and oratory throughout our period. In the teens, for instance, Mrs. Baker's Young Ladies' Seminary in Washington treated parents and friends to programs of pianoforte tunes and orations. In the 1840s, the Washington Female Seminary invited the public to attend student recitations and an exhibit of their paintings, while Westmoreland County's Classical Institute opened its female division's oral academic examinations to interested spectators. Women's participation in public leisure suggests that the behavioral prescriptions embodied in prevailing ideologies of gender did not completely restrict women to the home. It points, in fact, to other ways in which women used leisure to shape these gender roles and, when necessary, to resist their more oppressive features.[53]

Women's Education

Women's attempts to devote leisure to female education illustrate this resistance. Both sexes realized that women required some education to fulfill all the important roles that fell to them: homemaker, teacher of children, moral exemplar. Attaining the necessary moral and intellectual training to be guardians of hearth and home often entailed interaction with the public sphere through schools, seminaries, books and periodicals, or simply through contact with the broader world of ideas. Herein lay one of the contradictions of prevailing gender roles: men could hardly object to women's desire for education when school or music lessons clearly made them better wives and mothers. Advocates of female education argued that devoting leisure to learning and intellectual development allowed women to improve rather than merely waste their spare time. Though enthusiasts often justified female education by emphasizing its benefits for home and family, women recognized that intellectual development provided an opportunity to transcend the domestic world and enter, in a limited way, the larger society. Devoting their leisure to education allowed women to do this without offending those who believed that a woman's place was in the home.[54]

Yet concessions to female education were hard won. Even as men endorsed female education, they sought to limit and structure it to suit their own ends. To gain access to meaningful education, women exploited male fears about the effects of various kinds of education on the female character. Some men worried that perfunctory, charm school training would only produce vain, spendthrift wives who were unfit to raise children properly. Others also feared that fashionable wives would simply cost too much to win and maintain. Two equally undesirable scenarios presented themselves. Either the cost of courting a refined women would prevent poor men from marrying, or extravagant wives would bankrupt their husbands with the expensive tastes and habits they learned in school. Men liked to hark back to the "halcyon days" when a "wife was not only a comfort but a *help*" to her husband. By the late teens, "Jeremy Broadcloth" lamented that times were changing. Women now expected to live in luxury. "In short, Sir, a married woman, who would move in the first circles, . . . must have as much in her parlor, as would purchase a cargo of rum; and carry as many valuables about her person, as would load an Arabian camel." A suitable remedy, Broadcloth suggested, was to regard unmarried women as fashionable commodities and auction them off to the highest bidder. "The rich will pay a high price for the handsomest. The money thus received, should be bestowed as a portion on the more homely, whom the Auctioneer should present in their turns, asking if any one would accept of such a one with such a sum." The "second chop wives" would thus bring a dowry to support their own extravagance, "no one being obliged to accept a damsel except she brings the money with her."[55]

Much of the formal education available for young women was the charm school variety, and men feared that it might fill female heads with fantasies of a life devoted to leisure and fashion. In 1820, for instance, a Uniontown editor advised husbands to tell their wives "to study housekeeping more; dresses less. A good housewife is the first step toward making a good wife." Oroscor, a Pittsburgh humorist writing in 1828, agreed. He chided young ladies who were "more assiduous" at acquiring fashionable attainments than intellectual abilities. Oroscor's notion of women's intellectual capabilities must have been fairly narrow: he illustrated his concern by lambasting women who were "better acquainted with crimping and dancing than cooking and spinning."[56]

Male writers encouraged their readers to remember the true purpose of female education, and choose wisely any instruction given to daughters, sisters, and wives. Writing in 1823, a clergyman wondered if knowledge of dancing, however elegant and refined, would ever serve to "prepare *females* to be better wives and mothers, and to shine brighter in those virtues which are the true ornaments of their sex?" Other men expressed misgivings as well. Most agreed that a "well bred" young lady might learn the "fashionable arts." But they denied that the only end of education was "to make women of fashion dancers, singers, players, painters, actresses, sculptors, gilders, varnishers, engravers, and embroiderers." While female artistic accomplishment did embellish life and claim male admiration, overemphasizing it yielded only women who might "occasionally figure in a drawing room," rather than those fit to be a "help-mate to man; and 'to train up a child in the way he should go.' "[57]

Men were not always ready to eschew finishing school in favor of an academic education for women, however. Developing the female mind had pitfalls as well. Women might confront issues and ideas ill suited to their purportedly delicate constitutions and fragile intellects. In the early 1840s, for example, a Professor Bronson toured southwestern

Pennsylvania lecturing on human anatomy with the aid of a "Mannikin" depicting the human body. Bronson's lectures, or perhaps his mannikin, drew large crowds. In Washington he delivered public lectures and "24 lessons to private classes numbering near 100 ladies and gentleman." Not usually considered a fit subject for feminine contemplation, anatomy became a favorite of local women, especially when illustrated with Bronson's mannikin. Charles Scully noted the problems this interest posed for women's competing roles as seekers of knowledge and avatars of propriety. Commenting to his diary on Bronson's visit to Pittsburgh, Scully observed archly that ladies listened with interest to the lecture "(above the waist)" but would have fainted had the subject arisen in "polite society."[58]

Rigorous female education presented men with a prospect even more harrowing than exposing women to unsuitable ideas. The potent combination of leisure and education could produce wives who were intelligent enough to be discontented with their lot and insubordinate enough to air this dirty linen in public. Such must have been the case with Polly and Henry Barton. Early in 1801, the couple separated. As was the custom of the day, Henry placed an advertisement in a local newspaper to announce that Polly had "eloped from my bed and board without cause" and to disclaim any financial responsibility for debts the missing Polly might incur. Moreover, he threatened to "put the law in force" against anyone "harboring the said Polly Barton." Henry ran his advertisement again the following week, but this time he got an unexpected response. His estranged wife had printed a poem directly above *his* notice. Polly showed education and a poetic bent as she derided in verse her husband's claims and accusations. Lamenting Henry's broadcasting of their marital difficulties, Polly set the record straight:

> I never once did leave his bed,
> Nor from his board I never fled.
> What did he mean, the silly lad,
> He neither bed nor boarding had;
> He chose himself to take a scout,
> And from me ran in angry pout,
> And though the country takes his scope,
> Now judge you all who did elope.

Polly posted her errant husband as a ne'er-do-well, turning the tables on his concern about her unauthorized use of credit:

> How'er with him I'll have this bout,
> Pray trust him not on my account;
> For if you do, (hear what I say)
> One penny of it, I won't pay.
> With these remarks I now am free,
> To leave them to bold Henry.[59]

Leisure that cultivated literary skills in women proved particularly troubling to men, especially when female authors aspired to higher forms than Polly Barton's doggerel. A Pittsburgh reviewer's assessment of *Poems on Different Subjects* by "A Lady" of Boston illustrates this anxiety. Though unwilling to "snatch the quill from every fair hand," the male reviewer criticized women who abandoned their "interesting duties" as wives and mothers in order to "venture on the open field of literary glory." This said, he proceeded to demolish the work. "The rhyming was so faulty that the organs of the Boston-lady are verily diseased and require medical assistance. This circumstance, disagreeable as it is for her readers, must be still more so for her husband, if perchance she is sometimes scolding, as it would be impossible for her to hear the high key of her own voice." The reviewer execrated the lady's decision to "leave off the humble path of domestic virtues and domestic happiness" to write poetry. Worse, she was a scold and meddled in politics. In a poem critical of the Madison administration's pro-French policy, "her anger blazes forth in such a tremendous manner, that all our limbs were shaking on the perusal of it." Recovering from his brush with apoplexy, the reviewer continued to vent his indignation. "Heaven preserve us from female politicians! Much as we value mental accomplishments in the fair sex, we might almost prefer seeing them confined to the needle and spinning wheel, rather than sitting gravely in council on peace or war."[60]

For this writer as for other southwestern Pennsylvanian men, rigorous female education threatened to inspire women with ideas, ambitions, and discontents unsuited to their domestic lot. A variety of male voices advised caution lest female education produce uncontrollable viragos. "An early habitual restraint," the *Genius of Liberty* opined, "is peculiarly important to the future character and happiness of women. . . . Women who are so puffed up with the conceit of talents, as to neglect the plain duties of life, will not be frequently found to be women of the best abilities." Contentious wives, in particular, evoked fear for the very "natural" sexual order itself. "Dispute not with him," a Pittsburgh almanac admonished married women in 1838. Insisting on the "trifle of having your own will, or gaining the better in an argument" might "create a heart-burning which it is impossible to see the end of." But this writer did apparently see the end of female assertiveness: "Implicit submission in a man to his wife, is ever disgraceful to both."[61]

Beginning early in the century, women recognized these male concerns and cautiously turned them to their own advantage. Writing for a Washington County newspaper in 1810, "Clarinda" conceded that woman's primary function was to be a proper "companion" for man. But fulfilling this important role, Clarinda argued, required attention to intellectual development.

> Many, but far from all, of my sex have vainly imagined that happiness might be derived from another source, and that they might render themselves agreeable companions to the other sex, not only by cultivating their minds, but by beautifying and adorning the outside. . . . How foolish and absurd is the conduct of many females, who spare no expence in beautifying that part which nature left almost perfect, & neglect that part which nature left most rude; & strange to tell, that which they adorn, namely, their persons, is their least valuable part, and that which they leave neglected, viz. their mind is their most valuable part.

Developing the intellect rather than the appearance, Clarinda insisted, produced that "true happiness and pleasure we desire in a friend or companion," thereby fulfilling women's main duty in life.[62] To defuse any male anxieties about intellectual training for women Clarinda couched her argument in distinctly nonthreatening terms. She seconded male objections to female vanity, depicting feminine vainglory as the likely product of a mere finishing school education. Going further, she reassured her male readers that mental development served, rather than threatened, existing gender roles. In the process, she subtly staked a claim for more than superficial education for women.

Clarinda was not alone. A variety of female voices echoed similar messages. In 1828, "A," a member of Pittsburgh's Female Hesperian Society, addressed the topic of female education in the *Hesperus*, a men's literary journal. She began by rehearsing the standard arguments about women's role and natural capacities. The "province of women in society," she noted, "is clearly indicated by the delicacy of her constitution, her natural fitness for domestic avocations, and by her disposition to seclusion from the gaze of the world, and the active scenes of life." Rather than viewing these limitations as a "disparagement to our sex," the writer portrayed women's domestic role as socially important and personally satisfying, celebrating home as "the circumscribed sphere in which woman was destined to exert her influence." Having paid the requisite obeisance to the prevailing gender system, she proceeded to her main point: in order to exert a salutary influence on their homes, women needed more than the perfunctory education usually afforded them. Like Clarinda, she too dismissed the "superficial education" that neglected mental development in favor of fashionable accomplishment. At the same time, this woman insisted that rigorous intellectual training would better enable women to be dutiful mothers, wives, and daughters. Having allayed male anxieties about the rationale for female education, this female Hesperian felt bold enough to chide men for their inattention to this important matter. Despite some progress, she remarked pointedly, "there is a sensible defect in the manner of educating females in this section of our country."[63]

Reformer Emma Willard concurred with these sentiments. "In female education," she told the pupils of a Ligonier, Westmoreland County, female seminary in 1844, "chance and confusion reign." According to Willard, even rich girls rarely received a good education. Wealthy parents hurried their daughters "through the routine of boarding school instruction," only to introduce them prematurely "into the gay world," which became "thenceforth their only object of amusement." Waxing indignant, Willard contrasted the educations of boys to girls. While parents and teachers encouraged boys to "treasure up for future use the riches of ancient wisdom," they relegated their sisters to "gliding through the mazes of the midnight dance."[64]

Jane Grey Swisshelm's censure outmatched Willard's. She railed against charm schools that produced women who lounge around "reading novels, lisping about fashions and gentility, thumping some poor tired piano until it groans again, and putting on airs to catch husbands." Female seminaries — what passed for "good education" — taught girls only to play "a few tunes on the piano, talk about French and the 'ologies, and look genteel." Ultimately, she insisted, both family and society suffered from this inattention to proper education.

> After a while the piano-pounding simpleton captivates a tape-measuring, law-expounding, or pill-making simpleton. The two ninnies spend every cent that can be raised by hook or by crook — get all that can be got on credit, in broadcloth, satin, flowers, lace, carriage, attendance, &c. — hang their empty pockets on somebody's chair, lay their empty heads on somebody's pillow, and commence their empty life with no other prospect than living at somebody's expense — with no higher purpose than living genteely, and spiting the neighbors.[65]

Lest men be put off by the assertive, if not caustic tone of female educational advocacy, women took pains to present their opinions in deferential and reassuring tones. Typically, they emphasized the benefits to men, the family, and society of appropriating women's leisure to educational pursuits. "Nothing more clearly indicates rank, and education among females," opined *The Crystal*, a Pittsburgh women's magazine, "than the eveness of temper and a constant desire to please." In justifying its own existence, *The Crystal* portrayed itself as an aid to the "fond and intelligent *matron*," seeking more than "*oral* authority" to influence the "infantile intellect and tender faculties of the child." "A," whose views on female education we have already encountered, placated disturbed men by holding up as "an example of female excellence" a matron noted for her "dutiful deportment as a *daughter*, connubial attachment as a *wife*, and affectionate deportment as a *mother*." This matron, "A" assured her readers, illustrated "the manner in which I conceive females in general ought to be educated." Even Emma Willard took this tack. A "right education," Willard stressed, "enables us to be more efficient christians — makes us better in all the domestic relations — and enlarges our minds to comprehend, in our good desires, our sex, our country, and the world." Educated women, for example, would be better able to assume their proper role in child rearing. "Does not the right arrangement of society demand that while men provide for children, women should take the care of them? Men have neither the leisure nor the capacity for this which women possess; and in my opinion, common schools will not become what they should be until the village, as well as the family nursery, is faithfully watched by women."[66]

Women recognized that, once opened, the door to more extensive social participation would be difficult to close. If women exerted such a salutary effect in the home, they asked, would not their efforts also benefit society at large? "Why may not the ladies have a journal," asked *The Crystal*, "through which to communicate their thoughts and opinions to the world, as well as the 'lords of creation?' The efforts of female mind have not ended in useless or vapid results — but beautiful and brilliant have been the emanations, where the light of education has diffused its healthy influence over the soul." Emma Willard realized that using leisure for education satisfied men's domestic expectations *and* provided new alternatives for social action. "It undoubtedly behooves you," she told her Ligonier audience, "to perform well your duties in domestic life — to make your immediate circle happy, and to forward them in their heavenly course. Then, when these first duties are done, ask what part there is for you further to perform, which, while it advances the cause of your sex, may promote your country's prosperity, or hinder its decline."[67]

Religion: Linking Domestic Duties to Social Responsibilities

Southwestern Pennsylvanian women must have shared Willard's sentiment, for they sought ways to link domestic duties to social responsibilities. Using leisure for religious activities offered a neat solution to this problem. Reading the Bible or a tract in spare moments between household chores garnered praise from even the staunchest advocate of feminine domesticity, for it prepared women to exert a pious influence in the home. Religious women capitalized on this social approval to undertake organized religious work outside the home. If solitary meditation and scriptural study produced beneficial results, might not group efforts yield even greater spiritual returns? Many women believed so, for female prayer societies, Bible studies, religious lectures, and church groups gained wide popularity during our period. This reflected both the era's quickening religiosity and women's recognition of the possibilities leisure and religion offered for transcending the domestic sphere.[68] Even in activities overseen by men, women gained an irreproachable reason to leave their homes and venture into the public sphere. Westmoreland County women, for instance, gave Episcopal clergyman Sanson Brunot's "Female Bible Class" a warm reception in 1830. Brunot noted in his journal that "very unfavourable" weather marred the group's first meeting, "and only five members were present." The class grew to seventeen members, however, "and if the weather is favourable," Brunot opined, "the meeting on Wed. evening next will be quite large."[69]

The imprimatur of religion allowed women to use their leisure in unprecedented ways, many of which promoted personal autonomy and independence from men. Eliza Swift employed much of her leisure time in religious activities: reading tracts, attending a "Female Praying Society," participating in sewing circles, and acting as corresponding secretary for a missionary society that distributed "Bibles and Testaments" to the "part of this destitute region west of us." Swift considered the proper use of leisure as the key to self-improvement and social usefulness. "Do you in your leisure moments," she asked her sister Mary, "practice composition? I think you should do so[,] and as you are not at school[,] criticize it yourself or rather examine it attentively, and apply your own rules to your pieces. What if you at some future day be called on as a secretary to prepare a report? Read approved authors of good style just before you write and then express your ideas as they flow naturally."[70] Swift's message is clear. Leisure offered women an opportunity for intellectual development and a path to influence beyond the home. If Swift did not always relish her obligations as a minister's wife, she compensated for this frustration by embarking on religious work of her own.

Women used their leisure to prepare themselves for other religious activities as well. As we have already seen, women became quite active in the antebellum era's various temperance movements. Sometimes their participation was segregated, as with Martha Washington temperance societies. While this provided an autonomous sphere of action, it also relegated women to auxiliary roles. Even when male temperance societies included women in their activities, the female presence was often largely perfunctory. The Sons of Temperance, for instance, welcomed women to their parades and rallies, valuing the morality and piety female participants afforded the festivities. Actual female participation, however, ceased once a delegation of ladies presented a ceremonial Bible to the male officers.[71] Moral influence beyond the home, it seemed, could be a double-edged sword.

To avoid this pitfall, women who desired a more independent role in reform used their leisure to organize for direct action. Much to men's surprise, they sometimes did so without male supervision or guidance. Pittsburgh's *Hesperus* reported one such "delightful incident" in 1828. The journal's editor observed two "interesting females" who were "traversing different parts of the city, entering almost every house, and addressing themselves, with an air of earnest familiarity, to the children in the streets." This forward behavior astonished the locals, who speculated that the two were either "beside themselves" or strangers inquiring about "some particular acquaintance or friend." They turned out to be "pious young ladies" of the "first respectability, who in the character of *sunday school teachers*," endeavored to promote juvenile religious instruction. In another context, such behavior might have seemed inappropriate, if not scandalous. But because these "evidently importunate females" clothed their activities in morally respectable garb, the *Hesperus* could do little but approve. "We know not whether instances of this kind are rare in Pittsburgh," the editor remarked, "but they are certainly praiseworthy."[72]

For middle and upper class women like these two "respectable" Sunday school teachers, leisure promised substantial opportunities for autonomous action. In 1839, for example, a group of respectable women used their leisure time to form the Pittsburgh Ladies' Association. Members had to be respectable and possess sufficient financial means and leisure to be able to take time from domestic duties to devote it to charitable causes. The association's constitution defined its two major goals: "the encouragement of Industrious Indigent Women" and the "relief of the Helpless Poor." Some association members provided sewing for poor women, taking it upon themselves to "cut out all work," deliver it to authorized applicants, and "sell the made-up work." Organized like men's reform societies, the Ladies' Association illustrates how women used leisure to transcend customary gender roles. The association cultivated sedulously the image of female benevolence bolstering rather than threatening the prevailing gender system. Its bylaws provided that any "woman whose situation will admit of her being employed in family service, shall not receive work from this society." Poor, industrious women would not be drawn into the marketplace if more customary labor as domestic servants was available. Along with their support for feminine domesticity, the association promised to inculcate their charges with industry, cleanliness, and other appropriate values.

This deference to middle class values and prevailing gender roles masked association members' own departure from strictly domestic functions. By relieving the poor, the Ladies' Association carved out an area of influence beyond the confines of the home. Association "visitors" toured the city, inspecting and advising the recipients of their charity every two weeks. Visitors attempted to secure a poor family's confidence, ascertain the number of family members, and estimate their income, expenses, and financial prospects. In so doing, association members gained a sense of usefulness, self-esteem, and autonomy unavailable to most of their contemporaries. Leisure, they found, when used judiciously and cleverly, yielded options and opportunities that even the restrictive prescriptions of prevailing gender roles could not contain.[73]

By enlisting in worthy causes — religious activism, poor relief, temperance, and so on — women who possessed leisure time expanded the range of acceptable female behavior, making otherwise questionable assertiveness seem a logical and commendable extension of their domestic roles. Playing off a gender system that deemed them uniquely qualified to further piety and morality, women argued persuasively that their public efforts benefited society in ways impossible for men to duplicate. As mid-century approached, women engaged in church activities or reform efforts could also deflect criticism about the ease of housework and the idleness of wives. Especially in the middle class, the "pastoralization" of housework — its devaluation as productive and arduous labor — produced suspicions that homemakers had too much leisure and were prey to laziness and moral decay. When confronted with accusations that servants or labor-saving devices made housewives slothful, women could point to their undeniably productive uses of leisure. In the process, they could claim both an independent voice and a measure of social, as well as domestic, authority.[74]

Gaining a Public Voice

If Sunday School teachers and charity workers used leisure to transgress gender roles obliquely, other women did so more directly. Emboldened by the possibilities of leisure, women strove to gain a public voice throughout our period. Ceremonial occasions like dinners and civic celebrations provided an important venue for attempts at female self-expression, especially since custom and popular opinion proscribed public speaking by women. Women might be allowed to offer toasts, but only indirectly and with proper deference to male authority. When the men at a Uniontown Fourth of July celebration learned that "the ladies of the borough generally excited by a spirit of patriotism" had assembled nearby to celebrate, they decided to pay their respects. Appointing a committee "to wait on the ladies," they conveyed their "sentiments and congratulations" along with a toast: "The American Fair — May they frown on *traitors*, smile on *soldiers*, and wed *patriots*." The committee received "an appropriate answer" and a toast in return: "May the American fair pine in helpless love, if ever they fix their affections on any but true patriots." Though some recognition of female patriotism might be allowed, it was always somewhat patronizing and eschewed any direct public voice for women.[75]

Even women toasting each other at all-female gatherings raised eyebrows. In 1825, for instance, a Washington newspaper reported a female Fourth celebration, complete with toasts, which occurred in Alabama. "This is the first celebration of our Independence by the Ladies that we have seen," the paper explained, "and is therefore worthy of record." Sometimes the press ridiculed female pretensions to speak in public, publishing derisive parodies of women's celebrations. A Uniontown paper printed (in its "Poetry" column, no less) an account of a Fourth gathering by "a respectable body of spinsters: at the house of their 'lady president.'" In contrast to the solemnity with which newspapers depicted male celebrations, this parody portrayed women's efforts at speech making as ridiculous attempts to imitate men. The results merely revealed women's frivolity and preoccupation with catching a husband. "The day we celebrate," began the first toast, just as it would at a male dinner. But it continued on a strikingly different note than would a man's tribute to his country. "The fifty second birthday of American Independence — the first of the railroad, and, we hope, the last of our celibacy. *Tune — Nobody going to marry me.*"[76]

Some women resented this condescension and made their feelings known as best they could. In 1832, a Washington County woman expressed her frustration by sending a splenetic volunteer toast to a male Fourth of July celebration. In the newspaper account, her toast appeared as the first volunteer toast, immediately following the customary paean to woman in the final "regular" toast. Juxtaposed in this fashion, the two presented a sharp contrast.

> *The Ladies—* Place them as stars in the firmament, and they will make the face of nature so shine that all men will be in love with the night.

> Sent by a Lady. WOMAN — Expelled from public assemblies — denied the privilege of expressing her feelings of patriotism — but cherishing in her "heart of hearts" the purest love of country. — May the succeeding generation be better able to appreciate her worth, and by permitting her to occupy her proper station at national festivals, take the surest means of promoting order, and virtue, and happiness.[77]

As time passed, Southwestern Pennsylvanians' desire to avoid partisan strife on patriotic and civic occasions promoted female attendance at public celebrations. Capitalizing on the expectation that their presence would uplift the proceedings, women seized opportunities to make themselves heard. Though not common, toasts by women began to appear in accounts of dinners and social gatherings by the late 1830s. Some were coy, if not frivolous, and reinforced gender stereotypes. At an 1838 Washington's Birthday celebration in Middletown, Westmoreland County, the following exchange occurred.

> By a Lady. — May no one of the gentlemen present live the unhappy life of an old bachelor.

> By a Gentleman. — May none of the ladies present ever live the unhappy life of a scolding old maid.

Another woman attempted to raise the tone of female toasts:

> By a Lady. — The gentlemen of the Committee of Arrangement. To know them is but to perpetuate the memory of the man whose birth we celebrate.

The replying toast reflected continuing male disdain for assertive women, even respectful, deferential ones.

> By R. Woods.— Old Bachelors — Vilified and abused, yet the merriest of mankind.[78]

This example suggests that when women did toast, they often tried to downplay their unprecedented actions by reinforcing gender stereotypes. Whether innocent or calculated, a flippant toast about women's interest in marriage and husbands provoked less controversy than would an overtly political or partisan sentiment. At a Sabbath school Fourth of July in Claysville, Washington County, for example, a "Lady" raised her glass to "The single young men of this town and vicinity — May peace pervade among them, and love and matrimony unite them to us." A man responded: "The Fair Daughters of America — May they emulate the virtues and establish the precepts given by their ancestors, and thus secure the fairest gems that heaven can bestow — a loving husband."[79] By allowing themselves to be patronized, women seemed to conform to gender expectations while masking the significance of their departure from convention.

Once public speaking became more acceptable, women expanded the range of subjects on which they commented. Resisting a gender system that consigned them to purely domestic functions, women emphasized the necessity of extending their influence to patriotic occasions. To fulfil their maternal duties and educate future republicans, they argued, women must be allowed to participate more fully in patriotic exercises. "How would the countenance of the intelligent mother darken, and her voice falter," Emma Willard wondered, "should she attempt to teach her son to love a country that treats with contempt the rights of her sex!" At a Jackson Jubilee in 1844, a Washington "Lady" emphasized this theme in a toast. She praised Jackson's widowed mother, Elizabeth, as "lofty in soul, vigorous in intellect," and a prime example of patriotic motherhood. Seizing this chance to speak, another woman went further, offering a toast unrelated to female issues: "Gen. Jackson and the martial Law; the agent and the instrument in delivering the Country from her enemies."[80]

Though women might still mix self-deprecating levity with politics to diminish the shock of female toasting — in 1845 one woman told a Fourth of July gathering that "The Ladies are in favor of *annexation*, but not of Texas"[81] — they had by the mid-1840s staked their claim to a public voice. This voice went beyond toasting and took a number of forms, but a common thread ran through them all. Like the tactics women employed to advocate female education and inclusion at patriotic occasions, other stratagems used leisure contexts to transgress gender boundaries. Two very different examples — animal magnetism and a militia parade — illustrate how women used leisure to exploit the contradictions of female roles.

In a society that frowned on public displays of female authority, the chance for women to speak assertively and decisively appeared seldom if at all. The growing popularity in the 1840s of animal magnetism, a practice related to mesmerism and hypnosis, provided such an opportunity. Originally used as a medical treatment — an afflicted limb or body part would be "magnetized" to relieve pain or dysfunction — magnetic techniques also allowed adepts to place their subjects in a semiconscious trance state. Joseph Buffum, whom we have encountered earlier, avidly embraced both forms of magnetism as integral parts of his eclectic medical practice. "Miss Eliza Ramaley, whom I cured of the St. Vitus dance[,] I have magnetised daily for the most part of the time," he told his journal. Buffum treated a Mrs. Muldoon for a "very bad pain in her head" with a "few passes over her head." He also magnetized "Mrs. Dr. Riddle of the first Presbyterian Church for aberation of mind and melancholic and ghysterical affection."[82] Buffum's use of magnetism to induce a trance, rather than these more mundane operations, however, revealed its possibilities for modifying and challenging gender roles.

Magnetic trances appealed to nineteenth-century Americans both for their amusement and therapeutic value. Deep trances could soothe frayed nerves and relieve hysterical attacks, as they did for some of Buffum's patients. But they also entertained. Magnetists could induce entranced subjects to believe they were elsewhere, sings songs, play imaginary instruments, and perform a variety of acts, both comic and serious. Buffum cured Eliza Foyt of headaches, improving "her looks and appearance, [it] being much livelyer and gayer." He continued to magnetize her well after the symptoms disappeared, recording the interesting and amusing manifestations produced.

> I can make her follow me all over the house against her will: put her hands in any position and she cannot move them. Put them on the chair and she

cannot get them away; Put anything into her hands and she cannot get it out; can give her a piece of money and she will go to sleep looking at it just, or I can magnetise the looking glass and she will sleep looking in it. I can put her to sleep from another room. Pinch her ever so hard and she never would feel it; remembers nothing on being waked.[83]

At first glance, this might appear to be further evidence of male domination rather than female authority. The male magnetist directing a female subject to act "against her will," pinching her, and so on, doubtless had reassuring, if not titillating, effects on observers uncomfortable with assertive females. Once magnetists began to test the abilities of their subjects, however, a new pattern emerged. Entranced women exhibited clairvoyant and extrasensory abilities that amused and delighted observers, both in public exhibitions and private demonstrations. Buffum's account of his experiments on Foyt illustrates the link between leisure and female assertiveness. Because she was under the direction of another, the entranced Miss Foyt could do remarkable things while magnetized, without violating mores or challenging gender roles. She could, for instance, "tell some things accurately that she knew nothing about"[84] without worrying whether making authoritative pronouncements was an appropriate activity for women.

Other women demonstrated even more remarkable behavior while magnetized. "Mr. Alx. Scoot, a very fine man and a magnetiser" impressed Joseph Buffum with experiments on Scoot's sister-in-law, Almire Barber. Scoot magnetized Barber and "experimented on her cerebral organs," making her so sensitive that "she would jump if any one touched her as though one stuck needles in her. She said she was a very intense light like that of the sun." Buffum noted with relish the amusing aspects of the demonstration: "She, that is, Miss Barber, is a lively girl somewhat delicate. She sang songs and hymns under his influence. She thought she was playing the piano, also that she was stealing apples out of a tree, pretended she had the toothache and sent the pedlar out to get some clove oil and then she seemed to fill her pockets; besides many other laughable freaks too numerous here to mention." But there was more to Miss Barber than "laughable freaks." She "is a clairvoyant independent," Buffum noted, and had "directed Mr. S. how to operate upon [a] little girl[,] and the first time though they were looking for her to die she sat up in bed and laughed and talked."[85] Here, the tables had turned. Rather than receiving male direction, this woman instructed a man how to proceed in a life and death situation.

Buffum followed Scoot's lead. On New Year's Eve he magnetized a young woman named Eliza Wooster, throwing her "into a deep state." Under the magnetic influence, Wooster described distant scenes, asserting that she "could see Chambersburgh in some sort of a machine very swiftly. She did not know what it was. I asked her if she had never seen a [railroad?] car and she said no." Over the following two weeks, Buffum magnetized Wooster several more times in the company of friends and family. He solicited and received news of absent relatives and accounts of other cities. Wooster also revealed that Buffum's sometime girlfriend, Maria Ramaley, had turned down a rival's Christmas gift. "If this is true[,] and I think I can find out," he mused, "she can tell considerable."

Magnetized women *could* tell considerable, and they could tell it to men. In "their perfect state," magnetized subjects were influenced by a "vital fluid[,] a link between mind and matter more highly etherealized than electricity." That both men and women could mobilize this fluid provided a seemingly scientific basis for a limited sexual equality. Whether from conviction or avarice, lecturers and instructors did not discriminate against female inquirers. Mr. Spencer, a traveling magnetist in whose "magnetic class" Joseph Buffum enrolled, had "about 40 males, a few females" at his lectures. Spencer taught that anyone could magnetize, regardless of sex: "He says that ladies may magnetise ladies as well as gents." Anyone disturbed by female magnetists could be calmed by the reference to the "natural" basis of the practice: the supposedly scientific fluid theory of animal magnetism. The vital fluid, and not the woman herself, caused the manifestations that astonished onlookers. Because magnetized subjects were not consciously controlling their behavior, women could speak in public without incurring hostility from those shocked by female assertiveness.

Thus magnetic performances by entranced women — healing, advising men, describing places and events unknowable when conscious — allowed women to speak authoritatively without violating gender norms. Prevailing gender roles and expectations may have even facilitated this process. A historian of spiritualism has argued that trance speaking and mediumship were "closely identified with femininity."[86] Spiritualists believed that passivity, piety, and sensitivity, all supposedly female qualities, lent themselves to spirit communication. Though men or women might become mediums, the majority of trance speakers were women because they possessed the requisite qualities in abundance. Joseph Buffum's account of animal magnetism focuses on female subjects, suggesting that a similar dynamic may have operated. Miss Barber, for example, displayed both mental and physical sensitivity when entranced. Magnetic subjects, like mediums, spoke authoritatively in public by utilizing the ambiguities and tensions in the very gender roles that otherwise would have silenced them.

Women also found other, less arcane ways of speaking out in public. Sometimes they used leisure to strike at the very heart of the gender system that limited them. Even the volunteer militia parade, in many ways the epitome of class-differentiated, patriarchal leisure, was not immune to female resistance. In Fredrickstown, Washington County, the Jackson Reserve battalion gathered in October 1830 for its customary drill and parade. The unexpected "parade of the females of said village and vicinity, to a very considerable number, under a White Flag (the Banner of Peace) in honor of said Battalion," made this training day different from many others. For a number of reasons, this women's parade was remarkable. Women's participation in parades was rare to begin with, and usually involved only a minor or supporting role.[87] The juxtaposition of the Banner of Peace with the militant colors of the Jackson Reserve made the Fredrickstown women's action all the more remarkable. Rather than merely watch and applaud a male-dominated, class-differentiated celebration of martial prowess, the women discarded their expected passivity. Seizing this opportunity to assert themselves, they displayed values of their own: peace instead of war, and an undifferentiated procession of women in contrast to a hierarchical parade of men. In so doing, the women of Fredrickstown demonstrated how class and gender divisions established by and in leisure forms could be simultaneously exploited and transcended. Men expected women to be passive spectators but also active workers for piety and moral responsibility. In this contradictory set of roles lay the basis for action and a public voice. The men of the Jackson Reserve could do little but assent to the unaccustomed intrusion of women into their sphere. The battalion still reserved the last toast of the evening for the ladies, but it was a far cry from the usual paean to the absent fair: "The ladies who assembled in view of the parade and hoisted the Flag of Liberty, in honor of the Battalion entitled the Jackson Reserve, their conduct on the occasion entitles them to the grateful acknowledgement of our Battalion."[88] If hoisting the Flag of Liberty did not change these women's status permanently, it at least demonstrated their ability to question convention and transcend customary roles. By using leisure to exploit contradictions in the dominant gender ideology, they gained a public voice, and in the process, influenced the direction of cultural change.

7

The Reform of Leisure

Cooperation and Conflict

AS AN EXPRESSION OF VALUES, a source of cultural innovation, and a mode of social practice, leisure lent itself to conflict among various social and economic groups. Because of its creative and potentially subversive qualities, leisure was an obvious battleground for groups and individuals interested in promoting or imposing values and patterns of behavior on other elements of society. As Stephen and Eileen Yeo have observed of leisure in Britain, far "from being a neutral, free zone it was contested territory, with no party to the conflicts being in any danger of under-politicizing it up to and during the nineteenth century at least."[1] This was certainly true of southwestern Pennsylvania in the first half of the nineteenth century. Reform movements, church organizations, and voluntary associations all attempted in various ways to influence or prohibit targeted leisure activities ranging from drinking to theater attendance to blood sports.

Class-Based Social Control?

Many interpretations of nineteenth-century reform emphasize class issues as the key to understanding reformers' motivations and interests. Some historians of the early temperance movement, for example, have stressed status anxiety and middle class economic interests as the dynamic forces behind alcohol reform.[2] This type of analysis provides a useful and important perspective on reform, but too great a reliance on class as an explanatory category risks oversimplification. Though chapter 5 demonstrates how socioeconomic groups sought to use leisure to gain cultural ascendancy over others, it would be a mistake to assume that attempts at leisure reform were invariably efforts by one class to impose social control on another.[3] As scholars from a variety of theoretical and ideological viewpoints have argued, things were more complex than that. Lawrence Kohl, for example, has noted that in singling out moral and religious reform groups as agents of social control, historians imply that their activities were both unusual and, "given the common understanding of the term, . . . sinister." Gareth Stedman Jones has argued against a class-based interpretation of reform as social control in Marxist terms, contending that coercive action would have made more sense in the workplace, where more overt and effective controls were possible.[4]

Theoretical reservations aside, a class-based social control model of reform also fails to take seriously the middle and upper classes as *objects* as well as *initiators* of reform. Leisure reformers advocated "rational" amusements — those that uplifted, refreshed, and informed, thereby promoting individual virtue and social responsibility.[5] Ample evidence suggests that the upper as well as the lower ranks of society received reformers' attention, precisely because southwestern Pennsylvania's elite groups deviated from this ideal as often as did their supposed social inferiors. Disputes in churches over the amusements of prominent members were common, and drinking to excess among the region's clubs, lodges, and fraternities also presented an obvious problem.[6] Injunctions against immoral amusements and wasting free time applied equally to all classes and social groups and betrayed Americans' deep ambivalence about leisure itself. An 1824 letter to a Washington county newspaper, for instance, suggested that misspent leisure plagued people from all walks of life. Entitled "If I Had Leisure," the letter detailed the resolutions of a businessman, merchant, mechanic, farmer, and wheelwright to put their leisure to good use, revealing sarcastically that none had done so. Idleness, the author argued, often masquerades as leisure; to get something done, go to a busy person, not one in repose: "People are apt to be very much mistaken in this affair of 'leisure,' there are very few men who put every hour of their time to the best possible use. Often those who have the least to do don't half do that little, while those who are most engaged do everything thoroughly."[7]

Elite Abuses of Leisure

Reformers often focused on abuses of leisure among the elite, puncturing pretensions of moral superiority among the wealthy. Temperance reformers, for example, considered even moderate drinking by otherwise respectable citizens to be particularly invidious. In 1844 a Fayette County temperance convention concluded that "fashionable wine drinking at social parties and public entertainments is viewed by many of us as the greatest hindrance to our cause" because of the example it set for the rest of society. Upper class gambling troubled reformers as well. Commenting on shooting matches, those "hotbeds for intemperance, gambling, swearing, and every vice which follows in train," one reformer noted that "persons of an abandoned cast" could be expected as frequent participants. What shocked him, he added indignantly, was that he knew "men of standing in society who sanction them with their presence."[8] Revelations of private gambling also reflected unfavorably on the region's elites. Noah Ludlow recounted his experiences with a socially prominent Pittsburgh "general" who regularly invited visitors and strangers to his house under the pretext of a dinner party. These gatherings were actually opportunities for the general and his confederates ("all *gentlemen*, of course, — doctors, lawyers, bankers, bank officers, etc.") to "skin" unsuspecting guests at cards. Ludlow's opposition to gambling stood him in good stead (being ignorant of any card games, he insisted on betting on a cut of the deck and came out six hundred dollars ahead) but he could not contain his contempt for the leisure of the upper class:

> In the progress of time certain visitors who were in the habit of joining the general's card parties became poor and failed in business, while the general still to all appearances was prosperous, and kept up his custom of giving card-parties and suppers; and no one knew from whence the means came to support such hospitality except the initiated, who paid for their knowledge.[9]

Some critics associated leisured wealth with idleness and aristocratic decadence. On moral grounds, they urged, gentlemen who used leisure unwisely did not measure up to social inferiors who did. Thus an essayist contended in 1811 that "a decent and industrious mechanic" was far superior to "a supercilious, impertinent, blackguard dancing master," even though the latter might be a gentleman. In fact, designating someone a "man of leisure" might as easily be an insult as a sign of admiration. "Idleness," a Pittsburgh almanac reminded its readers, "is the badge of gentry, the bane of body and mind, the nurse of naughtiness, and the author of all mischief." George Bethune agreed, opining that "men of leisure, as they are termed, are rarely known to achieve greatness. Their time is frittered away in trifles, resolutions, and procrastination. They lack the habit of industry which occupation teaches, and are exposed to a thousand temptations men of business never know, the force of sluggishness being the worst of all."[10]

A series of vignettes published in 1838 revealed this distrust of the antebellum era's nascent leisure class. The author portrayed Mr. Inktin, the "man of Leisure," as a frivolous cad whose insensitivity and procrastination injured himself and those around him. Delaying promised aid in finding employment to a poor servant boy (" 'Not yet,' said the man of leisure, 'but there is time enough' ") resulted in the death of the boy's mother by starvation: "The man of leisure was shocked, and he gave the pale boy a dollar." In another episode, Inktin's interference in the courtship of housemaid Emma Roberts and her beau Harry Bertram, "a modest youth, thrown somewhat in the shade" by Inktin, culminated in Bertram's eventual marriage to another woman: "Harry, who was not a Man of Leisure, could not call for several days: when he did, Mr. Inktin 'dropped in' before him, and was twirling his watch-key with his cold wandering eyes, and the everlasting affirmatives." Inktin reached the height of insensitivity by offering Emma a piece of Bertram's wedding cake during his next visit. Ultimately, the Man of Leisure's character betrayed him and provided a lesson on the misuse of leisure for readers. On being taken ill, the Man of Leisure received at the urging of an "anxious friend" a clergyman who "spoke seriously but tenderly to the sufferer, of eternal truths." Procrastinating as usual, Inktin invited the clergyman to call the next day to discuss the matter further, but "that night the Man of Leisure died."[11] Even the upper class, it seemed, could claim no immunity to misusing leisure.

Middle Class Reformers

Similar attitudes prevailed in the middle class. Middle class reformers assuredly tried to impose their values on the upper and lower classes, but they often did so in the service of ideals shared by those groups, and with their aid and complicity. Furthermore, as much as anything else, middle class reformers sought to insure that their *own* leisure would be rational. Peter Levine has argued that antebellum middle class efforts to encourage sports and physical education as positive uses of leisure were not intended "to control the values of some inferior group or class" but, rather, were attempts "to shape the values of their own kind."[12] Further, middle class advocates of rational leisure directed warnings against the evils of the theater, intemperance, gambling, and other suspect practices as much to their own class as others. Even public displays of benevolence that used leisure activities to demonstrate middle class gentility and refinement drew fire. Thus one reformer from the Young Men's Society of Pittsburgh chided local ladies who held a "fancy fair for the benefit of the Orphan Asylum," an occasion "characterized by the usual accompaniments of these exceptional forms of pseudo-benevolence."[13]

Middle class reformers urged their charges not to be intimidated by upper class pretensions of intellectual and artistic superiority. Though some contended that the fine arts were "fit only for the amusement of men of leisure," middle class advocates argued that they were essential for social progress and thus the province of all classes. Much could be gained, they insisted, if the middle class adopted a taste for the arts and sciences and used its influence to promote them in the community at large. In this hope, reformers were often disappointed. The *Literary Casket*, a periodical designed for southwestern Pennsylvania's intelligentsia, bemoaned in 1842 the lack of a literary paper in Pittsburgh. Considering Pittsburgh's population, this reflected a lack of interest in the middle class: "In conclusion, we would ask, if the city of Pittsburgh, comprising a population amounting in round numbers to 50,000, will not sustain a periodical, devoted to Literary and Scientific subjects, requiring only six hundred subscribers to give it a permanent existence?"[14] Clearly, middle class Pennsylvanians who were in a position to foster institutional support for the arts and sciences were failing in their responsibility. The availability of commercial leisure lured even middle class citizens away from rational leisure. An 1849 letter to the *Washington Examiner* highlights reformers' frustration. The correspondent regretted the small attendance at a series of lectures on geology because of its implications for the town:

> Abroad Washington has the reputation of being a *literary place*, and when a stranger is told that there are two flourishing literary institutions here, he readily gives credence to the report. But what would be the impression created upon the minds of strangers, to see a lecturer upon some scientific or literary subject, compare *profits* with the manager of a menagerie, circus, or bear dance? Quite exalted, we opine — yes, very. Well so wags society, alias custom.[15]

The Buoyant Vitality of Disreputable Leisure

If leisure reform was merely a class-based attempt at social control, it left much to be desired. Despite the efforts of reformers, middle class and otherwise, disreputable and destructive leisure activities demonstrated a buoyant vitality throughout the period in question. Licensed taverns and liquor dealers provided ample opportunities for drunkenness, while doggeries, beer cellars, and disorderly houses added options for excessive drinking.[16] However much state legislators defended laws against "Tippling on the Sabbath," they realized the virtual impossibility of enforcing them. Of one such prohibition, in force since 1705, a special legislative committee on vice and immorality "freely admitted, that for a considerable time, the law had become almost inoperative owing to the deleterious influence of intoxicating drink" on "every city, town, and village in the land." All manner of traditional amusements and sports continued openly, even when divorced from productive labor and prohibited by law. The *Iron City* reported in 1842 that four young men were in the habit of meeting "behind a Doggery on Irwin St." on the "Sabbath, for the purpose of cockfighting." The paper suggested that they choose another day for "such cruel sport." Reports of other traditional pastimes frequently appeared in local newspapers: "loafers" playing cards in a church on Sunday; crowds engaging in cockfighting and dogfighting and betting on everything from horse races to elections. In 1835 one Washington County politico went so far as to offer in a newspaper advertisement to bet ten dollars with all comers on the outcome of a local election.[17]

The view of leisure reform as a class-based attempt at social control breaks down further when one considers the timing and impetus of many reform efforts. The custom of providing agricultural workers with whiskey as part of their pay is a good example. Since the settlement of south-western Pennsylvania, a "liberal supply of ardent spirits" was an expected part of an agricultural worker's wages, but this practice declined in the early nineteenth century. Much of this decline rested on the decisions of individual farmers, decisions often influenced by moral and religious rather than class or economic concerns. In 1812, for example, Ebeneezer Finley of Fayette County refused to provide the customary whiskey to workers at a barn raising because of moral reservations. Judge Charles Porter, another Fayette County temperance advocate, followed suit at harvest time. This was clearly more than an attempt by wealthy landowners to exploit their workers by cutting costs. Judge Porter paid extra wages rather than give whiskey to his harvest men, and Zachariah Connell, the founder of Connellsville in Fayette County, offered his workers a fifty cents a day raise in lieu of their whiskey ration. Likewise, Fayette County iron manufacturer Fidelio Hughes Oliphant banished whiskey from his establishment "almost from the start."[18]

These gradual changes, which commenced before the solidification of a self-conscious middle class, continued throughout our period. At a Washington County temperance meeting in 1830, farmer Alexander Reed "stated that all his farming operations had been and were now conducted without the use of ardent spirits, even the washing of his sheep, to the manifest advantage of all employed." Striking a similar note, the Cross Creek Temperance Society reported in 1837 that a "large portion of the farmers do not use spirits in their harvest fields as they formerly did." The idea and practice of temperance extended from farming to other social occasions. The Reverend Charles Wheeler wrote approvingly in 1830 that the hosts of a wedding at which he presided in Amwell Township, Washington County, served no liquor at the celebration following the ceremony. Wheeler considered this uncommon event to be highly admirable; serving liquor led to too many instances in which "the solemnities of that occasion [i.e., marriage] terminate in bacchanalian revelries." The temperance principle spread to other social groups and gatherings: Fourth of July celebrations, fire companies, even elections. Citizens of Buffaloe Township, Washington County, reported proudly in

1845 that their local elections had proceeded without whiskey for the first time in forty-nine years.[19]

A Response to Threatening Social Developments

If class-based social control does not explain adequately or completely the scope and conduct of leisure reform, what does? To answer this question, we must look again to the changing meaning of leisure in nineteenth-century culture. As chapter 1 discusses, leisure implied free time but not necessarily amusement in the early nineteenth century. It entailed responsibility as well as choice: leisure should not injure oneself or others, violate the dictates of religion or morality, or waste time and money. "Occasional relaxation from the fatigues and cares of life" was permissible, one writer observed, provided that one took care "to indulge in no recreations but what tend to promote the health of the body and vigor of the mind." This meant shunning amusements that might "stimulate the passions, excite impure emotions, or . . . corrupt the heart." As a general rule, leisure activities "should be moderate and innocent, and not take up too much time; we should never let our amusements interfere with our duties." In essence, commentators recommended a balance between work and leisure similar to the arrangement that characterized Anglo-American preindustrial society: amusement should always be linked to productive pursuits, facilitating but never threatening the accomplishment of necessary labor. This arrangement worked well in preindustrial society, for any potential or actual abuse could be easily regulated in relatively small, closely knit communities. People who chose to spend their leisure time on recreation, amusing diversions, or even excess did so in largely nonthreatening ways that did not usually interfere much with work.[20]

The Separation of Work and Play

Anxiety about leisure became acute in the early century because this balance between work and play seemed ever harder to maintain. As the ties that bound agricultural society together as a viable social system began to weaken in the early nineteenth century, Americans confronted increasing amounts of unsupervised discretionary time and a bewildering range of new ways to spend that time. The transformation of leisure examined in chapter 3 alarmed southwestern Pennsylvanians from all classes, social groups, and occupations. Most troubling was the divorce of amusement from productive labor. Commenting on this change, Solon and Elizabeth Buck noted that "In the rural districts the instinct for play found its expression most often in connection with church activities or with cooperative labor. In the towns, especially after 1800, amusement became an end in itself rather than a means incidental to the glory of God or the accomplishment of work."[21]

In this light, leisure reform is best seen as a response by all classes to new and threatening developments. Commenting on horse races in 1801, for instance, the *Pittsburgh Gazette* observed that they were fine in the rural setting of McKeesport but that Pittsburgh's growing population made races occasions for idleness, gambling, and lawlessness.[22] As leisure became more explicitly an opportunity for amusement and recreation, women and men from all socioeconomic classes, ethnic groups, and religious denominations expressed concern. Though an element of class-based social control may have been an unanticipated (or, for that matter, an intentional) result, there is no reason to believe that it was the predominant impetus to reform. True, many "respectable" citizens worried about the "lower orders" of society, and some of this concern manifested itself in paternalistic action by the wealthy and powerful. But this did not exhaust the possibilities of reform, for the problems associated with new patterns of leisure troubled everyone.

The Increasing Unsupervised Leisure of Youth

Both the cross-class character of leisure reform and its roots in anxiety over changing conditions manifested themselves forcefully in widespread concern for the leisure of youth, particularly that of young men. Parents and community leaders from all strata of society worried about the decreasing efficacy of family and communal supervision on young people's leisure. In rapidly changing circumstances, they feared, the problem of striking a balance between work and play rested increasingly on the shoulders of those whose age and inexperience made them least capable of resolving it.[23] Writing to a Pittsburgh paper in 1820, "A Pennsylvanian" asked indignantly:

What is the conduct of boys when dismissed from schools? Instead of returning quietly and peaceably to their families, do they not infest the streets
in the most disorderly manner, obstructing the pavements, and annoying
passengers, on foot or in carriages even with brick-bats and stones? . . . On
the approach of warm weather, are they not found on the wharves, on the
beach or in boats, in the face of the sun, naked, riotous and lewd, offending
every sense? . . . Parents, guardians and masters! What have ye to answer
for?[24]

Denunciations of youthful excess surfaced across the region. A
Greensburg resident remarked on the "alarming disorder in its streets" in
1823. It appeared "like a Bedlam," with "such noise, swearing, profane
and improper language: such blackguard, wicked expressions made me
doubt whether I was in a civilized part of the world." In Washington, too,
the situation seemed dire. By the middle 1830s, raucous young men had
begun to congregate on Washington's street corners in the evenings,
much to the alarm and dismay of local residents. Though Washingtonians
viewed young men's amusements — characterized by a local poet as
"Gaming, talking, swearing, drinking,/hunting, shouting, never thinking"— as a function of immaturity, their tolerance rested on the assurance
of community supervision to avoid excesses.[25] The rapid changes of the
early nineteenth century made community supervision and surveillance
more difficult and youthful excess more threatening. A Greensburg poet
wrote "High Life in Our Town" with this theme in mind: after telling a
stranger the "tale of wonders" in his altered town, he remarked on the
stranger's surprise at the troubling activity of young men in the streets.

> Knowing not, that in our town
> Such bloods as they, pace up and down,
> Each striving, still, to be seen the most
> Engaged; but never pass a post
> On which doth hang a friendly sign,
> Tend'ring its offices benign
> To thirsty mortals such as they,
> Fatigu'd by labors of the day.[26]

Unsupervised leisure could lead to appalling consequences, and
many feared that failure to oversee apprentices, students, and young workers consigned them to dissolute behavior and vice. In 1844 *Loomis's Mag-*

azine Almanac urged master mechanics to watch diligently over the "youth placed under [their] care and influence." Masters should know, the author insisted, where their charges "spend their leisure time, or in what society their evenings are passed." Dereliction of this duty could only lead to a young man's ruin, as an advertisement for the return of Thomas Davies, a runaway apprentice, attested. The notice described in graphic terms the consequences of increasing leisure and decreasing supervision: Davies, a nineteen-year-old, was "in the habit of staying out late at night — frequenting houses of doubtful character, and selecting his associates from the wicked and depraved." An 1844 essay, "Advice to Apprentices and Shop Boys," highlighted satirically the problem of regulating young workers' behavior in their leisure time. The essay advised young men to learn to chew tobacco ("no young man's education is complete without this accomplishment"), smoke, swear, avoid church ("Young men who work six days, should have the seventh for exercise and enjoyment. Therefore go ahead on Sundays. Stand on the corners of streets. — There is always a current of fresh air sweeping around the corner, and this is good for the lungs"), drink, and accost women ("After you have insulted them a dozen times, they will get quite used to it.").[27]

Unsupervised leisure posed a threat even to middle and upper class youth. Beginning early in the century, Washingtonians worried that gatherings of young men at Saturday night horse races, and the attendant "drinking, swearing and rioting," would blur the distinction between the community's college men and the "smutty-faced apprentice." At the very least, well-to-do young people might neglect productive work and fall prey to idleness or vice. This was the message of a spurious "Student's Journal," supposedly the diary of a young Washington College student. Though ostensibly at college to study, the young man spends more time sleeping late, socializing, hunting, and pursuing women than learning his Latin.[28] Critics expressed particular dismay at educated young men who abused leisure, for they might be expected to set a good example for their peers and the community in general.

This expectation was sometimes disappointed. An incident at Washington College in 1810 illustrates the difficulty of preserving the traditional patterns of leisure, even for the middle and upper classes. The college's students put on an annual examination and exhibition of their educational attainment to which the general public was invited. On September 17, 1810, the students advertised an exhibition of public speaking to be held on the morning of the twenty-seventh. Under most circumstances, college exhibitions won the approbation of all involved: they allowed young men to demonstrate and test their intellectual abilities while enlightening and uplifting the audience. If the students and audience were amused, all the better, for amusement wedded to learning strengthened individual and society alike.

The Washington College exhibition of 1810, however, crossed the line between informative amusement and corrupting frivolity. A scandalized citizen of Washington, writing as Bonus Homo, condemned the exhibition as immoral and irreligious. The students included performances of comedic scenes, fiddle music, satiric ethnic soliloquies ("An apish youth in German vogue / Just copies off the Dutchman's brogue"), burlesque sermons ("Thus one small youth a thousand lies, / (Not fearing vengeance from the skies) / With impious lips declares"), "polite" swearing, and exhibitions of boxing and fencing, along with the customary orations. Bonus questioned the competence of the college administration, doubted the quality of the curriculum, and awarded the students " 'the palm in the science of polite blackguardism.' "[29] The college's defenders took up Bonus's gauntlet, but their caustic replies betrayed a defensiveness and ambivalence about the inclusion of humor and bawdy entertainment in a supposedly educational exhibition. Though some of the speeches and satires were offensive, they claimed, the college was not at fault; any blame should be attributed to youthful high spirits.

> The pieces, dialogues, &c. on these occasions are generally the selections of the young men themselves, nor do they meet with more than a hasty, cursory examination from the faculty. . . . At such times the students themselves, freed "from college rules and common place book reason," feel an elasticity of spirits, that laughs at gravity of discipline, and frequently introduce into the arrangement of those days, things which serious propriety would perhaps have omitted.[30]

This reply did not quiet all doubters. One local wit, writing as John Buckskin, Jr., a student at Jefferson College in Canonsburgh, observed that he did not "like to hear so much said against the exhibition at Washington, for I am sure that if theirs was wrong ours was ten times worse and you know nothing that is bad would be approved by our doctors or by the religious people of Canonsburgh." Buckskin could not understand why "one of your most righteous men lost several nights sleep because his conscience was much hurted by the fiddle." Overall, Buckskin concluded, an exhibition like the one to which Bonus Homo objected could cause no lowering of moral and educational standards or social unrest:

> The people here took all these things in good humor, except a few foolish people who, as they had no rotten eggs in their pockets, had recourse to more petrifick materials and let fly a few stones at the trustees — but no harm was done. One grazed the head of a revd doctor, but if it had come in contact, it could not have done any injury to a head anointed with the oil of doctorship — No harm was done.

Using satire, this letter made the point more effectively than the high-minded moral criticism of Bonus Homo could. An imbalance of work and play — a misuse of leisure — led to disorder, disrespect, and the inevitable lowering of standards.[31]

Parents and community leaders worried that increasing amounts of unsupervised free time bred frivolous habits in young people and led them to value leisure more than work. Circumstances seemed to warrant their fear. Writing of the young middle class Pittsburghers he associated with during the 1840s and 1850s, William G. Johnston remembered that

> There seemed to be a prevailing impression among us that to maintain life properly, a considerable amount of recreation was essential, and we suffered ourselves to be controlled largely by this belief; and to use a homely expression, allowed no grass to grow under our feet. Certain it is that seldom was there a time when not in expectation, and there was accordingly an almost continual buzz and flutter.[32]

Many concerned Pennsylvanians feared that the "buzz and flutter" of unsupervised leisure might lead to a breakdown of morals, especially sexual morals, even among the sons and daughters of the region's best families. A widely circulated poem of the era, "Seasonable Admonitions," warned "Damsels white as snow" not to go sleighing with male friends after dark. During the early nineteenth century, sleighing occupied the same place among youthful vices that parking did in the mid-twentieth. Stopping at a tavern for a drink, "Just to warm her in the sleigh," a young woman might lose track of time

Till perhaps a storm may come
And all night she's forced to stay.
Then the youth she thought sincere
May her yielding heart betray
And she rues with many a tear
The mournful sequel of a sleigh.

Such warnings were not entirely unwarranted. Sleighing parties were popular, and unsupervised male-female interaction did sometimes lead to premarital sexual behavior. Robert T. Galloway, writing as Limerick Hotsepillar in the late 1820s, recounted in verse a "bundling" that occurred among a group of young people at the groom's house after a wedding:

On the 10th night of June 'twas at a wedding
So neatly laid the bedfellows and the bedding
'Twas then we split the apple to the core
And altogether bundled on the floor.
How pleasant was our little ride
When we rode with the groom and the bride
And all that night with them we staid
In a neat little pile on the floor we laid.

We there had bees and there had drones
Cushioned rumps and tight-laced bones
Elders' daughters and a deacon's son
Great mirth and abundance of fun.

Of us there were ten and a score
In less than a year there may be more
But it will come out' time everything shows
For me I think its fully time to close.

Later, Galloway responded in verse to threats from a church elder (presumably the one mentioned above) to jail him for circulating the poem:

A report from the Elder did proceed
That all who read mine [poetry] should go to jail
But now I'll let the good old elder know
That we are not willing there to go.

But if to jail the Elder makes us go
We'll tell him what he thinks we do not know
And if reading my lines he does forbid
Things then I'll bring to light he thought was hid.[33]

Pennsylvanians took the problem of youthful leisure seriously. If they allowed their sons and daughters to abuse leisure, they feared, the younger generation would not gain "an enlightened view of their own best interests" and become "the bulwark of our free institutions."[34] But concern for the abuses of youthful leisure mirrored a larger, more general cultural ferment. All the dangers and temptations that attended young people's use of free time applied to the rest of the population as well: more unsupervised leisure, a bewildering array of morally questionable new amusements, and the breakdown of older patterns of familial and communal surveillance. What would prevent people from abusing this newfound leisure, Pennsylvanians wondered, and engendering social chaos in the process? How could the ominous tide of drunkenness, gambling, prostitution, theater attendance, and novel reading be stemmed?

"Rational" Leisure

The desire to suppress objectionable or destructive leisure activities led reformers to emphasize what might be termed the instrumental aspects of leisure, those that served the interests of labor, moral and intellectual development, or the preservation of health. This emphasis reflects a continuity in attitudes toward play and amusement with traditional agricultural society. By encouraging people to spend their leisure time constructively or "rationally," reformers hoped to maintain the traditional equilibrium between work and play in the altered social and cultural circumstances in which they found themselves. Concerned citizens from all classes expressed positive as well as negative goals by advocating new, "rational" amusements. They attempted not merely to negate objectionable forms of leisure but also to create new, more positive amusements better suited to the realities of their industrializing, commercializing society.

Diverse social groups responded to new circumstances, often unsystematically and inconsistently, through leisure reform. Attempts to regulate, suppress, or offer alternative models of leisure are thus best viewed as points on a continuum of reform strategies. The continuum ranged from moral suasion on one end to coercion through vigilante action on the other. Between these endpoints were the provision of alternative forms of leisure, coercion through ostracism or social pressure, and coercion through legislation. These categories were not hard and fast divisions; specific attempts to regulate leisure often partook of more than one tactic. Such was the case in Pittsburgh during Francis Herron's pastorate at the First Presbyterian Church. Herron responded with alarm to a proposed ball sponsored by some of his congregation's younger members by offering an alternative amusement at his home. Herron's party, which excluded the morally dangerous practices of dancing and frivolous socializing, was open to all, especially the ladies. This might fall squarely into the category of alternative leisure were it not for Herron's announcement from the pulpit that there "would be a ball held by those who served the devil and he feared by some who professed to serve God." To the offer of an alternative, Herron added the coercive threat of disciplinary action before the church session for anyone who disregarded his warning. Herron's party was crowded; the ball failed miserably.[35]

Another reason to view the continuum as a heuristic device rather than a literal representation of reality was the difficulty in enforcing even the most stringent and coercive sanctions. As J. Thomas Jable has shown, local or state laws like the Pennsylvania "Act for the Prevention of Vice and Immorality" (1794) enjoyed little success in outlawing cock fighting, dice, billiards, or horse racing, even though they provided stiff penalties. At the level of enforcement, the application of legal sanctions was often selective, uneven, or nonexistent. In 1830, for example, the Pennsylvania legislature passed a bill aimed at reducing the number of drinking establishments in the state. The law required anyone applying for a tavern license to provide the signatures of twelve respectable citizens as character references and stipulated that no more licenses would be issued than were necessary for the accommodation of travelers. At the local level, this restriction had little effect in reducing the number of taverns or combatting drunkenness. Doggeries, beer cellars, and other unlicensed, illegal drinking establishments proliferated, and lax enforcement of the 1830 law undercut its restrictive intent. On June 18, 1842, an applicant for a tavern license appeared at the Pittsburgh courthouse and took a seat to wait his turn. Soon thereafter he "rolled off the chair, from absolute intoxication." As he hit the floor, a certificate of good repute signed by twelve citizens who attested to his "honesty and temperance" fell from under his hat.[36] Clearly, there was a considerable distance between the theory and practice of leisure reform in southwestern Pennsylvania.

Moral Suasion

These qualifications noted, we can begin examining leisure reform at one end of the continuum, with moral suasion. Denunciation of objectionable forms of leisure on moral grounds came from all sides in southwestern Pennsylvania and included exhortations by clerics and religious organizations, resolutions of moral reform groups, editorials by irate newspaper writers, and memorials sent by ad hoc groups of concerned citizens. For some, exhorting youth to use their free time wisely seemed the best course. "When serving your apprenticeship," wrote an advisor of youth in 1840, "you will have time and opportunity to stock your minds with useful information. The only way for a young man to prepare himself for usefulness," he continued, "is to devote himself to study in his leisure hours." Leisure could be a potent means of advancement if devoted to industry rather than frivolity: "Happy is the man, who in early life, has been taught by experience the blessed effects of honest industry and the inestimable value of time. Multiply time by industry and what is the result? Peace of mind; the innocent enjoyment of life, and every thing that can exalt human nature." Considering the stakes, a newspaper argued, it was "of the utmost importance to teach the youthful mind that enjoyment and self-satisfaction must be purchased by labor."[37]

Reformers tried to inculcate this lesson through example, parental admonition, and the encouragement of rational leisure. *Harris's Intelligencer* recounted in 1839 a "call in the office of one of our earliest and most respectable citizens, who is a practical mechanic with a large family." Much of the respectable mechanic's familial happiness rested on his large collection of books and subscription to eight "select" newspapers. This literary bent, Harris contended, was a "cheap and profitable way" of keeping the family at home and supervising their leisure.[38]

Moral suasionists also devoted much time and energy to promoting

Sabbatarianism and encouraging rational uses of the weekly respite from work. Unlike their more coercive-minded counterparts, voluntary Sabbatarians attempted to persuade others to keep the Sabbath holy by setting a good example and forming associations to plead their cause. In 1845 a Sabbath Convention convened in Greensburg, Westmoreland County, in the German church. The convention advocated voluntary Sabbatarianism, enjoining attendees to abstain from selling liquor and "lounging in public places" on Sunday. Sabbatarian organizations sprang up elsewhere in the region: enthusiasts established one in Washington, for example, at a Sabbatarian convention in November 1845.[39] By appealing to virtue and reason, these groups hoped to eliminate drinking, carousing, gambling, and other vices on Sundays.

Temperance, like Sabbatarianism, elicited much attention and interest from moral suasionists. Concerned citizens from all strata of society viewed with alarm the deleterious effects of liquor, and their reform efforts took various forms. Some supporters of sobriety formed temperance or total abstinence societies to provide fellowship and set an example for the rest of society.[40] Religious bodies like the Presbyterian Synod of Pittsburgh issued formal resolutions condemning the use of liquor and encouraging temperance. As early as 1817 the synod stated that it "cannot help but view the use of ardent spirits, except as a medicine, as a source of multiplied evils — injurious to the temporal and eternal interests of individuals, and subversive of the peace and happiness of families and of society in general." Secular commentators often relied on humor and sarcasm rather than moral injunction to make their point about the dangers of liquor. J. Heron Foster and William H. Whitney, the editors of Pittsburgh's *Iron City*, noted in 1842 that "It is a circumstance which ought to weigh with great force upon the mind of even the most temperate drinker, that among all the criminal cases which have been tried at the Court of Quarter Sessions now in setting in this city, not one has passed without the mention of the word 'WHISKEY' some time during its progress, as an immediate or remote cause of crime."[41]

Moral suasionists did not confine themselves to major social issues like the proper use of liquor and the Sabbath, however. They also preached morality to specific groups and attacked particular leisure practices. One outraged observer, writing in 1832, assailed indecorous celebrations of Washington's Birthday. In his opinion, the occasion called for dignified reflection on the contributions of a great American, not drunken revelry. Preparations for militia exercises and patriotic orations did not deceive him: "These suggestions, however different as to the commencement of the celebration, all lead to the same termination — military foolery and whiskey drinking." Some better manner of celebration should be conceived, he urged, perhaps by Congress.[42]

Some moral suasionists trained their sights on the social morality of various groups. Washington County suasionists, for instance, formed the Washington Bethel Association to Aid and Reform Boatmen and Sailors. Aimed at uplifting the predominantly lower class rivermen, the organization used moral and religious principles to reform dissolute, violent behavior that contrasted sharply with George Caleb Bingham's image of the Jolly Flatboatmen.[43] Others cast even broader nets, hoping through persuasion to improve the morality of society as a whole. Frequent objects of concern were parties and social occasions, especially those including both sexes. With the erosion of traditional patterns of work and play, socializing became an end in itself, much to the dismay of the champions of morality, reform, and religious piety. In 1818 the *Washington Examiner* published a dialogue between two pious young women, Christiana and Paulina, entitled "Parties of Pleasure, and Awful Moral Death." It condemned all manner of social occasions patronized by the fashionable set and their imitators: their "balls, their theatres, their Thespian corps, their gambling matches, their horse races &c.&c.," as wicked in their own right and subversive of piety and church discipline. Christiana and Paulina encouraged their readers to avoid such corrupting frivolity, noting that revivals "of true religion and fashionable amusements cannot progress together."[44] The dialogue thus objected not to socializing per se, but to fashionable amusement — that is, to leisure completely divorced from productive activity or communal supervision.

A similar message emerged in a series of columns by "Clarinda" in the early teens. Clarinda noted young people's fondness for parties that were intended to "promote love between the sexes." Conversations about love, recent marriages, and the like were fine, Clarinda allowed, but frequently these parties also included frivolous conversation and suspect amusements. Social gatherings as such were well within the sphere of propriety, but "unchaste" amusements fell beyond the pale. So long as the gatherings promoted a "productive" cause — in this case, the choice of marriage partners — they were permissible. Meetings for mere amusement, however, was morally and ethically dangerous. This attitude may be related to the tolerance of the traditional "kissing parties" and wedding feasts of agricultural society. No labor was performed on these occasions, but the "work" of matching and uniting prospective marriage partners was accomplished.[45]

Alternative Forms of Leisure

Recognizing the allure of amusements, fashionable and otherwise, some reformers supplemented moral suasion with alternative forms of leisure in order to make destructive activities less attractive. Churches, lay people, and religious organizations adopted this approach, sponsoring picnics, fairs, lectures, Sabbath school activities, and singing schools to prevent any straying from the fold. Religious discussion groups, for example, provided alternatives to secular debate clubs or literary societies, where frivolous or morally questionable topics might intrude. In 1822 a "few members of [Pittsburgh's] Reformed Presbyterian Church met at the house of Mr. Philip Mowry in order to organize a society for the purpose of discussing religious subjects." They established the Reformed Presbyterian Church Society to promote "the improvement of scriptural knowledge." The society offered its members an outlet for their desire to debate and deliver orations in an atmosphere that was beyond moral reproach. The group's first topic for discussion, for instance, was "How do the light of Nature and the Works of Creation prove the Existence of a Deity?"[46]

Though ostensibly devoted to enhancing their members' spiritual lives, these groups served leisure functions as well. Sponsoring churches recognized the importance of social interaction and stressed this aspect of the activity. The session of Westmoreland County's Poke Run Presbyterian Church, for instance, considered the "subject of social prayer meetings" in 1843. After some discussion, the session resolved to "earnestly recommend to the congregations to hold weekly social meetings for the glory of God and the edification of the people." The meetings, the session urged, should consist of between three and six families and be held in private homes. Proposed activities included singing psalms, reading scripture passages, and holding group prayer. Like the Reformed Presbyterian Church Society, the Poke Run session advocated discussions of scripture that were analogous to the debates and orations of secular literary societies: a "question of a religious nature" would be proposed, and "each member shall be invited to express his opinion."[47] By organizing a religious equivalent for a worldly pastime, churches provided a leisure alternative that excluded objectionable activities and influenced their members' use of discretionary time.

Often, churches and religious groups scheduled their alternative leisure activities to coincide with secular amusements that might otherwise lead the pious astray. Celebrations on or around holidays were prime examples. Female church members sponsored fairs on the Fourth of July, a day often given to excessive drinking. In this manner, the ladies could join in the celebration and provide an alternative to the raucous, destructive secular celebrations.[48] Reformers used this tactic on other occasions with the potential for destructive leisure practices as well. Too often, the religious press warned, people spent the Christmas season "in the gratification of their carnal inclinations, in vain amusements and Bacchanalian carousals and revellings," rather than in glorifying God. To provide celebratory options other than "the amusements of the theatre, the ballroom, or the billiard table," Pittsburgh's religious community offered more uplifting activities. In 1823, for example, the Pittsburgh Sabbath School Union held exercises on Christmas Day, offering a virtuous way for youthful participants and older spectators to spend the holiday. In the evening, the Allegheny Musical Society held a concert for the benefit of the Adelphia Free School in a local church. Reformers planned similar events for the following year, and others followed their lead. Washington's Sewing Society for Foreign Missions sponsored a public supper on Christmas Eve 1845, promising that besides "everything to tantalize the taste, there will be a galaxy of youth and beauty to delight the eye." As an alternative to the gambling, drinking, and carousing that accompanied the annual cattle show, the ladies of Washington's Cumberland Presbyterian Church held a fair of their own in the courthouse on the days of the exhibition, offering useful articles for sale, refreshments, and supper.[49]

Temperance societies also provided alternative amusements on holidays. Temperance Fourth of July celebrations were common by the 1840s.

The Cold Water Army, composed of groups of Sunday school students pledged to abstinence, often marched on Independence Day, as it did in Pittsburgh in 1842. Temperance activities around Christmas and New Year's also developed. Pittsburgh groups sponsored a temperance lecture on New Year's Day in 1830 that won such popular support it was repeated later in the month. The Buffaloe Township Temperance Society in Washington County held a meeting on Christmas Day, 1832; the Washington Female Temperance Society met on New Year's Eve in 1836. Temperance societies took the lead in providing entertainment as an additional draw to their alternative leisure offering. Brass bands rarely failed to draw crowds to temperance events, and as long as they bolstered the moral message of temperance, society organizers allowed that their amusing quality did not endanger virtue. Thus, in 1842, a temperance procession in Pittsburgh featured the music of the Scotch Hill Band, and a Union-town temperance convention offered two brass bands as an inducement to attendance.[50]

Moralists, reformers, and clerics realized that providing alternative forms of leisure could not be a sporadic undertaking if it was to have any practical effect. By the 1820s, calls for the permanent establishment of rational amusements sounded with increasing frequency and vigor from all quarters. As early as 1815, a traveling actor remarked that Pittsburgh had "no place or places or rational amusement open to the public, and men therefore congregated in beer-cellars, in eating-houses, gambling-houses, and other 'houses' to while away an evening." One Pittsburgher wrote in 1835 that the working classes "have no incentive held out to them, to mental exertion. . . . Men in their situations must have some relief from constant toil; and as no virtuous or profitable amusements are at hand, no useful mental relaxations, they fly to drinking houses to spend their money and time." Another pleaded for the provision of "improvement and innocent rational recreation" for youth, "upon many of whom the influence of both parents and teachers has ceased to operate." Suggestions included the establishment of a hall of science and a lecture series to attract young men who "after the labors of the day are over, pour into the streets to seek amusement. . . . Shall we leave them without any other places of amusement than the streets, the theatre, or the grog-shops?"[51]

Though class bias colored these exhortations, it was not the sole motivation for leisure reformers. As we have already seen, moralists considered the "fashionable" upper ranks of society to be just as culpable as the middle or lower, and equally in need of rational recreation and amusement. A citizen of Washington County noted in 1837 that he was a "detester of midnight street revellings, of back-room beer house gatherings, of suburb iniquities, and one who believes they can only be discarded by the introduction into the circles of the respectable, the good and the fashionable, a system of Rational Amusement."[52]

Artistic and Intellectual Recreation

Artistic and intellectual pursuits were prime examples of rational amusement and the constructive use of leisure. Though entertaining and diverting, art, music, literature, science, and rhetoric also served useful purposes in educating and uplifting participants. Societies to promote rational recreation through music emerged early in the century. "A Friend to Moral Society" advertised for a vocal teacher for New Geneva, Fayette County, in 1815, hoping to gain the civilizing influence of music for town residents. In Pittsburgh, the Harmonic Society began musical gatherings and outings as early as 1818; in Washington, a Musical Society was formed in 1825 to provide "Amateurs of Music" with the opportunity to select and perform musical pieces on the "Evening of the Week." This society, like some counterparts elsewhere, limited its membership and strove for small private meetings. Other groups chose to perform for the public, often to benefit a worthy charity. The Allegheny Musical Society, for example, presented periodic concerts of sacred music to benefit the local orphan asylum.[53]

Science, literature, rhetoric, and debate also provided rational recreation. Doctors and scientists lectured on scientific and quasi-scientific topics; and organizations like the Pittsburgh Horticultural Society offered the public both beauty and information at its annual exhibitions.[54] The younger generation, too, engaged in this kind of rational leisure. The Young Men's Society of Pittsburgh provided opportunities for learning, fellowship, and the development of good habits. Through participation in rational leisure, young men could set an example for the community. The Hesperus and Western Miscellany, for instance, was a literary periodical founded by the Hesperian Society in Pittsburgh in 1828. The society was "composed principally of young men who have united for the purpose, the sole purpose, of eliciting the literary energies, and stimulating the literary efforts, of the citizens in this portion of the West."[55] In addition, numerous announcements of grammar school, seminary, and college exhibitions and examinations invited the public to be entertained and enlightened by young people's rational amusements. Literary and debating societies also sponsored lecture series, public debates, and rational celebrations of various holidays. In Elizabeth, Allegheny County, for instance, the Frew Institute celebrated the Fourth of July, 1841, by listening to an original essay on the proper observance of the "National Jubilee" in the Methodist church: "All were pleased, as well with the exercises, as with the rational manner of spending the day — a day too often devoted to licentiousness and profanity."[56]

Nor was the working class exempted from the move toward rational leisure. Southwestern Pennsylvanians from all classes advocated the establishment of apprentice libraries, which would allow young men to spend leisure time in productive intellectual activity. In 1820, "An Apprentice" praised the library system of Boston and urged that a similar system be established in Pittsburgh, contending that of all institutions "for the relief of distresses, as for the promotion of literature," none were "more noble, none more deserving of praise" than the apprentice library association. Four years later, a group of Pittsburgh businessmen acted on this recommendation by founding the Pittsburgh Apprentice Library Company, a society intended to "afford that portion of the youth of our city, who are employed in its various manufacturing and mechanical establishments, an opportunity, by the perusal of well selected books, of acquiring useful information, cultivating their minds, and improving their morals, and of thus promoting their own welfare and the advantage of their employers."[57] Other towns and cities also promoted apprentice libraries. At a public meeting in Uniontown on April 14, 1831, citizens debated forming a society to "provide facilities for the youth of the place generally, and particularly to the young apprentices and mechanics, in acquiring a practical knowledge of the arts and sciences."[58]

Debating societies, amateur musical groups, and lecture series were hardly innovations in the early nineteenth century. What was new was the realization that these old forms of leisure could be adapted to altered circumstances. These activities, which had previously been the province of a relatively small, select group, could now be used to provide constructive leisure alternatives for society at large. The institutionalization of rational leisure extended to other areas as well. A primary example of this process was the Sons of Temperance, a quasi-secret order patterned after Freemasonry, which emerged in southwestern Pennsylvania in 1845. Despite general hostility in the region to secret societies of all sorts, the Sons of Temperance received enthusiastic support all over the area and persisted into the early 1850s. In March 1848 the Sons mounted a procession and exercises in Westmoreland County's Ligonier Valley; similar activities occurred in Greensburg two months later. A large meeting in Bellevernon, Fayette County, witnessed a procession and oration in May 1848; another sizable gathering took place in Youngstown, Westmoreland County, in March 1849. The order attracted members and spectators with extensive processions, elaborate regalia, and the allure of "secret" mysteries and ceremonies to which only the initiated were privy. Local chapters of the Sons sometimes planned their public displays to coincide with holidays that might otherwise lure young people to intemperance and immorality. Exercises consisted of parades with members in full regalia, orations on temperance and morality, and interaction with local women's and religious groups. The Sons demonstrated their piety and morality by having a deputation of local ladies present the order's officers with a Bible at the climax of the exercises. Because of the order's emphasis on temperance and morality, any stigma attached to the form of the organization was ignored or forgotten. Even secret societies could gain respectability if they were enlisted in the service of rational recreation and amusement.[59]

Commercial Leisure

This process extended to commercial leisure as well. The general insistence that leisure activities be rational — that they have some instrumental or productive function in addition to mere amusement — forced purveyors of commercial recreation to portray their offerings in this manner. Owners and promoters of theatricals, menageries, museums, and traveling performers found that local authorities were less hostile and local patrons more generous when they emphasized the educational and moral qualities of their wares. If they could transform questionable leisure into rational amusement, it qualified as an alternative to the destructive, morally reprehensible uses of free time so troubling to society.[60]

This casting of various amusements as rational occurred in nearly all aspects of leisure. Francis C. Wemyss, a British emigré and theatrical manager, assured prospective patrons on the opening of his Pittsburgh theater in 1833 that he had made every exertion "to render the THEATRE a place of Rational amusement." The owners of the Pittsburgh Museum took a similar tack three years later, asserting that they devoted their establishment to "Moral Amusement." Circus owners, conscious of the low reputation of traveling shows, took great pains to emphasize the educational and rational aspects of their exhibitions. They even stressed the circus performers' personal rectitude: Brown and Company's Circus promised its Washington County audiences in 1837 that the performers' "moral character will bear the strictest scrutiny." This tactic appears to have worked. Hannington's Grand Moving Dioramas and Italian Fantoccini, which visited Pittsburgh in 1839, billed itself as "Rational Entertainment and Extraordinary Novelty." A local newspaper editor concurred, recommending the exhibit to his readers and noting that he "saw a large number of our most moral and respectable ladies and gentlemen and children viewing it."[61]

In order to prosper, public facilities for leisure and amusement also had to become rational. Moralists often viewed establishments offering refreshments and space for socializing as objectionable because they promoted or tolerated destructive practices like drinking, swearing, and gambling. New businesses eliminated these vices, catering to the desire for socializing on a rational basis and emphasizing the high moral standards of their operations. Pittsburgh's Dravo Temperance House served ice cream and lemonade to its patrons, providing an alternative to the morally suspect tavern atmosphere. In like fashion, William Howe defended his Washington Bowling Saloon by stating that "Neither liquor, betting, nor any sort of gaming will be allowed in this establishment; the object being one of rational and innocent amusement, combined with healthful, physical exercise." Howe apparently began a fad, since his competitor, Haye's Bowling Saloon, promised that "no gaming is allowed — no betting — drinking of liquor — nor any swearing or boisterous language." The amusement at Haye's, its owner promised, was "innocent as well as health-ful." A further addition to the Washington bowling community, Koontz's Saloon, advertised that it too was "a pleasant place for recreation."[62]

Some leisure practices were easier to rationalize than others. If music was generally conceded to uplift as well as entertain, dancing was con-demned for its frivolity and lasciviousness. Debates about the morality and rationality of dancing raged throughout the period, usually inconclu-sively. As early as 1826, "Senex" defended dancing as "rational" amuse-ment in the Washington papers; despite frequent denunciation, dancing and dancing schools persisted throughout the period. Mr. Couse, an en-terprising dancing master, attempted to defuse the arguments against dancing by making it rational. His dancing school in the Pittsburgh Con-cert Hall advertised in 1839 that "this house being conducted on true Temperance principles, and located in the most quiet part of the city, will not be obnoxious to the prejudices existing against amusements of the kind."[63] Others used different strategies to depict dancing as an ac-ceptable alternative to other forms of leisure. In an 1846 letter to the *Washington Reporter*, "The Last Rose of Summer" defended dancing as a "varied, chaste and delightful amusement" in response to an earlier correspondent's criticism. Rose denied that dancing was impious, arguing that it served the rational end of socializing youth. She commented acidly that

> in this enlightened age, no amusements can be tolerated which will famil-iarize young people to the equalities of social life, soften and refine the manners, and give grace to their movements. No, the pleasures of refined communication, the cheerful and elegant courtesies, which formerly em-bellished society, are now deemed inconsistent with the most liberal Piety, though fed by the fountain of a conscience.[64]

In a less lofty vein, one Washington County dancing teacher defended his craft against narrow-minded people who "think that promiscuous dancing, balls, and theatrical amusements, are not so favorable to moral and intellectual improvement as reading, social conversations, Institute lectures, churchgoing &c. &c. I wish to enlighten them a little." People, he suggested, were divided into two classes: one with brains in their head, the other with brains in their heels. Intellectual amusement, he contended, does not work on the latter, adding archly: "Is it not philosophic — is it not natural — is it not right to educate that part of a man which can be educated?"[65]

Social Pressure and the Threat of Ostracism

While some reformers tried to steer people in the right direction by providing rational leisure alternatives, others took a different approach. They found that if social pressure could steer people toward some leisure forms, it could also steer them away from others. Social pressure and the threat of ostracism thus represented another point on the leisure reform continuum. Though often difficult to detect because it operated on an informal basis, social pressure was a very real aspect of leisure reform and regulation.

Coercion through ostracism or social pressure operated in a number of ways. At the simplest level, social groups penalized offenders informally for inappropriate behavior. Drinking whiskey, for example, was an indispensable part of many social occasions. "At weddings, corn-huskings, wood-choppings, log rollings, flax pullings, manure frolics, sheep washing, fish gigging, house and barn raisings," many participants considered it essential. Communal supervision and the threat of ostracism kept the situation in hand: despite widespread use of whiskey at harvests, "a drunken man in the harvest field was a rare occurrence and looked upon as very disgraceful conduct."[66]

Social pressure also operated through harangues in newspapers intended to use public opinion to alter behavior. In 1820 an outraged Pittsburgher railed against parents, clergy, police, and teachers for their laxity in controlling their young male charges.

> Conspicuous as Pittsburgh has been for the progress of the arts, and various improvements public and private, it is a matter of extreme regret, the conduct and morals of this city, have too generally been considered as of minor importance, and have been most shamefully neglected. . . . What is their [i.e., boys] deportment at night? assembled in groups, can a delicate female pass them without incurring a risque of insult? Can the sick, the infirm and the aged obtain rest or quiet? Does not every square resound with their oaths, their yells and their infernal orgies?[67]

By reminding adults in the strongest possible language of their responsibility to regulate the leisure of youth, this correspondent hoped to promote the reform of objectionable behavior.

Public recourse to social pressure also extended to the celebration of holidays. Reformers hoped not only to improve the celebration of holidays prone to abuse, like the Fourth of July and the New Year, but also to pressure people into observing approved holidays. In the 1840s, Pennsylvania governors began designating a Thanksgiving Day in November or December and encouraging religious and civic observance. At the local level, this was easier said than done. Merchants and businessmen were loath to close down on traditional holidays, so they needed special encouragement to forgo money-making opportunities on a fabricated holiday. Newspapers encouraged merchants and employers to close stores and businesses so that their employees and the public generally could join in a fitting communal day of thanks to God: "We trust that the people of this county are fully convinced of the propriety of co-operating in the suggestions of the Governor's Proclamation; that they will abstain from their worldly engagements, and be found acting the part of those who acknowledge their obligations to Him 'in whom we live, move, and have our being.'" Thanksgiving's advocates portrayed refusal to cooperate as mean-spirited and ungrateful and hinted that it would lead to some form of social ostracism or informal censure. This approach worked: by the late 1840s southwestern Pennsylvanians observed Thanksgiving "with appropriate religious exercises, and by a general closing of stores & c."[68]

Coercion through social pressure and ostracism also operated at a less public level. Informal social pressure exercised in families, groups of friends, and churches dictated, first, which leisure practices were acceptable, and second, the circumstances in which they could be indulged. In the middle and upper classes, respectable leisure entailed avoiding excessive drinking and shunning a variety of suspect groups. Charles Scully's aspiring middle class family, for example, berated him for remaining friends with a young man who got drunk at a sleighing party. Pittsburgh lawyer Robert McKnight noted disparagingly in his diary that one of his upper class contemporaries was arrested and fined by the city watch during a drunken party late one night in 1842. For McKnight, the proper use of leisure required careful scrutiny of one's associates as well as one's activities. Thus his Protestant bias led him to cast a jaundiced eye on the "Catholic Ball given at the Concert Hall, where was a mixture of black spirits & white &c. &c."[69]

As McKnight's comment illustrates, social groups used informal methods of coercion to discourage contact with anyone who participated in objectionable leisure, especially those perceived as outsiders. The treatment of anyone involved with the theater provided the best example of this process. Though respectable citizens might attend the theater, any contact with actors, managers, or other theatrical personnel was suspect, requiring constant vigilance to insure the moral propriety of all involved. Noah M. Ludlow, an actor and manager whose company performed in Pittsburgh in 1815, noted in his memoirs the difficulty he had finding lodgings. Most landlords hesitated to rent to actors because of their bad moral reputations, so Ludlow kept his profession a secret at first. After winning his landlady's respect with gentlemanly behavior, he learned "that, had she known I was a 'play actor,' she would not have allowed me to become a boarder in her house."[70]

Theater patrons insisted on strict morality or they would withdraw their financial support. During the season of 1833, two members of Francis C. Wemyss's company, Messrs. Green and Hubbard, appeared on stage drunk: "both so intoxicated, as to render it necessary to remove the first named from the theater; and the latter actually fell upon the stage during the performance." Wemyss lamented that the "theatre was filled with ladies, which I need scarcely add, did not occur again during the season," the result being that "every respectable citizen absent[ed] himself from the theatre."[71] As Wemyss's "respectable citizens" recognized, any involvement with questionable leisure practices or practitioners would have tainted their reputations and led to social ostracism.

Coercion through ostracism or social pressure worked for even established and approved forms of leisure. Communities tolerated volunteer fire companies, which acted both as public services and social clubs, because they linked the firemen's raucous play with necessary work. When the social function outweighed the service function, adjustment became necessary. Firemen racing their engines through narrow, crowded streets was a persistent problem. It became acute in Pittsburgh in the late 1830s, when public pressure forced companies to take action.

The Vigilant Fire Company passed resolutions in 1838 that condemned "the perilous practice of racing from fires and false alarms." More importantly, the company censured Charles Brown, a second engineer notorious for racing the Vigilant's engines. Brown resigned indignantly, arguing that he raced only because he thought it "necessary for the dignity and honor of this company." Brown opposed the resolutions against racing, he said, "thinking that they were calculated to do away with the spirit of rivalry that is necessary in fire Companys." After further investigation, the company decided that Brown had not deserved censure after all: they exonerated him and refused his resignation.[72] Here the threat of ostracism was enough to reform behavior (at least temporarily and outwardly) and restore the balance between work and play.

Pittsburgh's Neptune Fire Company also took action to clean up its public image. In 1835 it expelled John Milland from the "Company on account of his reported bad behavior at a late alarm of fire." Ten years later, problems persisted, and the Company moved again to correct them. In 1845 its members resolved to ignore alarms they knew to be false, and to "go to the scene of conflagrations with all possible speed but . . . return Decently & Orderly." Intoxicated firemen risked fines and expulsion, as did any member "guilty of having spirituous liquors brot to the engine house or to the apparatus of the Company at a fire or parade."[73]

Fire companies continued to be a target of informal social pressure. Drinking among firemen also concerned reformers. Drunken firemen were, at best, ineffective fire fighters and, at worst, dangers to the public safety because of fighting and racing. In the 1840s, there was "great jealousy between the several companies," noted one observer, "and frequently one company would start a *discussion* by *accidently* throwing water on another." This practice imperiled both the volunteers and the property they were supposed to be protecting. At a warehouse fire during the winter of 1848, water sprayed on each other by rival companies froze: "the appearance of the men was grotesque[,] as they were coated with ice and could hardly walk or work." By the early 1840s, Pittsburghers began pressuring the volunteers to alter their ways. In response to calls for the abolition of the volunteer system altogether, fire companies started taking the pledge en masse in 1842.[74] On Wednesday, October 5, 1842, the Vigilant Fire Company "unanimously resolved to sign the pledge, formed a procession, marched from their house to the Temperance Hall, where they signed the pledge in a body! Let the others follow their example, and let no man hereafter insult the Fireman of Pittsburgh by an offer of the intoxicating bowl." Public pressure for temperance reform apparently did motivate others to follow the Vigilant's example: the Uncle Sam Company signed the total abstinence pledge a few days later.[75]

Some Pennsylvanians preferred more organized methods of exerting social pressure in the interests of leisure reform. In this regard, church discipline was a primary means to regulate and reform people's leisure. Francis Herron, whom we have already encountered in our discussion of reform, frequently used the authority of the Presbyterian church to prohibit various leisure practices. The minutes of Herron's First Church record "numerous trials and stern disciplinary action taken against members convicted of such offenses as adultery, drunkenness, quarreling, assault, betting on elections, profanity, and Sabbath breaking." Though Herron censured transgressors perhaps more zealously than some, evidence suggests that clergy and laity frequently used church discipline to reform leisure. David T. Watson, remembering his boyhood in Washington County in the 1840s and 1850s, commented on the pervasiveness of this practice: "Secular amusements were then either denied, or at least largely disapproved. A dancing school, opened even after 1858, was thought to be very doubtful, or at least, not a desirable place; while from 1848 to, say, 1856, a line of cleavage was drawn between the circus and the animal show."[76]

As one might expect from Watson's reminiscence, many disciplinary actions involved proscribed leisure activities. In 1803 the Great Bethel Baptist Church in Uniontown, Fayette County, expelled Mary Brown for "drunkenness, and also using profane language"; Edward Jones received similar treatment in 1836 for "drinking excessively and using profane language." During 1829 the church inquired into Patrick Bradley's "propensity for missing services" and exhibiting "unchristion deportment in laying wagers, rabbet-hunting on Sunday & c." Salem Church, another Fayette County Baptist congregation, suspended James Adams for drunkenness and profanity in 1806, and in 1822 voted "Brother" Thomas Read and his wife Betsey "out of the Church for Dancin and Drunkenness."[77]

Punishment was only one side of the religious reform of leisure, however; reconciliation was the other. In contrast to religious caricatures that depict unforgiving bands of self-righteous hypocrites, real congregations usually attempted to reclaim rather than excommunicate transgressors. Ministers and elders imposed disciplinary measures flexibly, tailoring the punishment to fit the severity of the offense and the remorse displayed by the offender. If the sinning party admitted guilt, submitted to censure, or came forward voluntarily, the church might consider a stern rebuke or public admonition sufficient. At Great Bethel Church in 1814, for example, Benjamin Johnson stood accused of "being intoxicated"; he was "called in and admonished by all." Joseph Alexander, a member of Poke Run Presbyterian Church, confessed unprompted that "he had been once openly overcome since the last communion by too free use of ardent spirits." The penitent Alexander was "solemnly cautioned by the moderator and [allowed] to continue in the communion of the Church," and the affair was "published in the Congregation." Similar incidents occurred at Mount Moriah Baptist Church in Fayette County: in 1801 Brother Ashcroft admitted being sorry that he "drank rather too much," and Abraham Lot acknowledged that "he was overtaken in liquor and his language unbecoming." In 1807, Mount Moriah's records noted that "it appears by his own confession that [Nicholas Cross] follows frolickin and dancing." The minute books record no disciplinary action in these cases.[78]

Even members who had been denied fellowship might return to the fold if they manifested genuine remorse. Salem Baptist Church restored Betsey Read to full membership in 1824, despite reports that she had "tolerated Dansing" in her house and had taken "an active part therein." In 1840, two erring members of Poke Run Presbyterian Church petitioned for restoration of privileges after being suspended for intoxication, "the former on wine, and the latter on strong drink." The session approved one request but rejected the other, noting that evidence of the unsuccessful petitioner's "turning and repairing" from liquor was "unsatisfactory." Five years later, Poke Run's session declined to restore Benjamin Chambers to full membership. Though Chambers had "manifested contrition" and abstained from liquor for some time, the session believed that "immediate restoration would neither be conductive to the welfare of the individual nor the purity of the church." Only by insuring that Chambers would not return to his immoral ways could the session protect both church and individual from destructive leisure activities.[79]

To supplement formal church discipline, reformers founded quasi-religious moral societies and Sabbath associations. A moral society formed as early as the turn of the century in Elizabeth, Allegheny County; another sprang up in Pittsburgh in 1809.[80] These societies hoped to suppress vice through existing laws by bringing public pressure to bear on authorities for their enforcement. The Pittsburgh Moral Society stated that the "objects for which we associate are the suppression of vice — reformation from evil manners — and the increase of useful knowledge." The vices that prevented the realization of these goals were often identical with objectionable uses of discretionary time. The Washington Moral Society identified these vices in 1815 as "profane swearing, Sabbath breaking, intoxication, unlawful gaming, keeping a disorderly house," and the like.[81] More specialized groups might organize to combat specific vices,[82] but the goal was ultimately the same. By using the power of public opinion and social pressure, they hoped to reform leisure by linking its amusing aspects to work, the abandonment of "evil manners," and the acquisition of "useful knowledge."

Social Proscriptions Enacted as Law

Recognizing that social pressure was not as effective in rapidly changing towns and cities as in small, closely knit communities, concerned citizens in all parts of southwestern Pennsylvania gave social proscriptions the force of law. The Commonwealth of Pennsylvania passed the Act for the Prevention of Vice and Immorality in 1794 that forbade gambling, horse racing, cockfighting, and Sabbath breaking, but this law proved difficult to enforce in the shadow of the state house, let alone in the western reaches of the state.[83] Towns and cities attempted to supplement state laws with restrictive legislation at the local level. These local statutes frequently regulated the sale of liquor, forbade Sabbath breaking, and prohibited a number of traditional sports and amusements.

In Pittsburgh, for example, the borough passed an ordinance against the sport of throwing "bullets" in the public square or streets in 1809. The sport, which was popularized by soldiers stationed in Pittsburgh during the Revolution, involved throwing lead weights for distance. With increasing commerce and traffic in Pittsburgh streets, this practice became hazardous and was forbidden. Pittsburgh's incorporation in 1816 produced a spate of legislation regulating leisure activities. One ordinance prohibited nude bathing in the town's three rivers within city limits between sunrise and 8:30 p.m.; another, intended for the "Suppression of Nuisances," proscribed beating drums, ringing public bells, discharging firearms, constructing bonfires, and sounding false alarms of fire. An ordinance concerning "Plays, Shows, and Theatrical entertainments" stipulated that any exhibitions had to be "of a decent and moral tendency" and required an expensive license from the mayor. In addition, the ordinance required that the exhibitors pay a city constable to attend each exhibition to preserve "peace and good order, and prevent any outrage, or disturbance of the harmony of the citizens" and established a forty dollar fine for unauthorized use of minors or apprentices in any show.[84]

Pittsburgh was not alone in establishing ordinances regulating various leisure practices. In 1802 Canonsburgh, Washington County, imposed a fifty dollar fine on "Mounte-banks, play actors or managers of a puppet show"; by 1810, Washington had passed laws against Sabbath breaking and galloping horses through the town streets. The borough also passed laws regulating the sale of liquor, especially to minors. To stem the tide of student drunkenness, the Washington College Board of Trustees vowed in 1816 to use local laws to prosecute innkeepers who persisted in serving students.[85] As population and circumstances demanded, other localities in southwestern Pennsylvania passed restrictive ordinances as well. Greensburg enacted a statute in 1837 "For the suppression of immoral conduct." It targeted any "minor, apprentice, servant, or other person or persons" who behaved "in a noisy, outrageous or riotous manner," sang "any immodest or indecent song," or used "any impudent or indecent expressions." Uniontown passed new regulations for licensing taverns in 1838, the same year that a Pittsburgh citizens' meeting petitioned the Court of Common Pleas to limit the number of tavern licenses issued because of the deleterious effect that drinking establishments had on apprentices and the "rising generation."[86] Between state and local ordinances, southwestern Pennsylvania possessed ample statutory powers for the restriction and regulation of leisure.

Extralegal "Reforms" of Leisure

Despite the existence of the legal apparatus for correcting abuses or excesses of leisure, some reformers became frustrated with the efficiency of official reform and took matters into their own hands. Extralegal action to reform leisure was not uncommon in southwestern Pennsylvania, especially when population growth and ethnic diversity exacerbated existing problems. If this extralegal supervision of recreation served to eliminate flagrant abuses, it also expressed hostility toward specific groups stemming from fears and anxieties wholly unrelated to leisure.

Though ostensibly defenders of public safety and community morals, vigilantes often chose their targets selectively, directing their ire at minorities or strangers. This was especially true of attacks on African Americans in southwestern Pennsylvania. In 1843, for example, a mob of angry Allegheny City whites attacked Frank Johnston and his brass band after a concert at the Temperance Ark, a hall used for temperance activities. Johnston, a black musician of considerable talent and renown, agreed to play for the Washingtonians, a temperance group, presumably because of the good cause they championed. Despite this admirable action, "a large crowd of men and boys gathered about the doors and windows, and by their riotous conduct did all in their power to mar the entertainment of the evening." When Johnston and his band left the Ark after the concert, the mob attacked them with missiles and rotten eggs, slightly injuring Johnston. The authorities conducted a halfhearted inquiry into the affair, but "the ringleaders of the atrocious outrage upon these peaceful and unoffending colored citizens were permitted to escape the penalty of a broken law."[87] It was not the leisure activity itself — a temperance meeting or a brass band concert — to which the mob objected. Rather, it was the inclusion in that activity of an objectionable group. Leisure activities permissible for either blacks or whites separately were taboo if they involved interracial socializing. Considering the authorities' failure to punish the perpetrators of this extralegal "reform" of leisure, it would appear that the community as a whole concurred in this judgment.

Private action against objectionable social groups and practices had a long tradition in Britain and Europe. Charivaris and serenades were ways for small groups or entire communities to express disapproval for a variety of actions. Often these serenades involved claims of territory between social or ethnic groups or were attempts to intimidate individuals engaged in objectionable practices. This tradition found its way to southwestern Pennsylvania. Robert McKnight recorded one such serenade in his diary, noting that the drunken participants became so unruly that they were arrested and fined by the night watch. Holidays and special events were often occasions for serenades. A card published in the Greensburg papers in 1849 upbraided the town's night watch for not enforcing the law against wealthy as well as poor revellers "who were found 'making night hideous' by singing songs & c." during the Christmas season. In Fayette County, political differences often motivated partisans to chastise their opponents with a serenade. In Brownsville and Bridgeport, serenaders harassed their political opponents to celebrate a political victory in 1826.[88]

In Pittsburgh, the mayor's election day in early January was an annual occasion for extralegal action against various groups and leisure practices. In 1828, Pittsburgh witnessed a disturbance on election night "attended by riotous proceedings, such as shoutings, burning tar barrels, firing crackers, throwing fire balls, & c." In attempting to arrest the rioters the mayor and police "were violently assailed, and some of the officers badly hurt by missiles thrown by no boyish hands. . . . At one time the Court House was set on fire, by a flaming ball thrown on the roof." Commenting to his diary on the proceedings of election day 1843, Pittsburgh lawyer Charles B. Scully noted that "the whole city is ringing like a Bedlam with the 'feu de joie' of the Clay men, all the Engines are out and there's a 'd____d fuss generally.' — there is an 'interregnum,' and the whole City is rollicksome, the ordinances of peace and good order are pro tem suspended, & blackguardism is rampant everywhere." These descriptions seem to describe random, unrestrained mob action, or "blackguardism." Yet far from being anarchic, the mobs on election night had definite purposes, though their excesses often obscured their original goals. Before the institution of a professional police force, citizens enforced the law themselves, albeit in extralegal fashion. Election nights were set apart for "the destruction of houses of ill-fame": vigilantes burned these public nuisances with "skiffs filled with tar-barrels, and other combustible matter, which were deposited in the halls of the buildings thus purified by fire."[89] Mob action, then, served the interests of the community in that it eliminated objectionable leisure practices.

The nature of mob reform changed with the establishment of a permanent night watch in Pittsburgh. The watch proved "strong enough to prevent the destruction by the mob of such infamous haunts, [i.e., brothels] yet too weak, or perhaps unwilling, to suppress them themselves; under this system they flourished." But the citizens' frustration with the watch's inability to deter vice came to a head in early June 1842. On June first, at ten p.m., a fire alarm sounded, and a group of "energetic firemen" proceeded to a row of houses on Fourth Street known to the populace as "Aristocracy Row." The street, notorious for its brothels, doggeries, and disorderly houses, was occupied by Samuel Diehl, "commonly known as 'Blind Sam,' the fiddler . . . Polly Warner, the Latimores, and other degraded creatures,— and frequented by persons no less degraded."[90] Despite the fact that there was no fire, the volunteers hooked up their hoses and directed the stream of water through the front window of Blind Sam's establishment, drenching the inhabitants and ruining the property. Blind Sam tried to stop the dousing, "pouring on them [i.e., the firemen] a stream of curses as heavy as that of water which was directed against his dwelling. . . . 'The rascals are ruinin' all my property — I'll *see* about this tomorrow!'" The stream of water forced the inmates of Blind Sam's to exit through the back door, "several *en deshabille*." After the inhabitants' retreat, "the assailants retired, having rendered the building rather an uncomfortable dwelling place for its inmates."[91]

The following night the "energetic" firemen struck again, this time dousing the infamous Crow's Nest, a brothel in "Virgin Alley," known as a "haunt where the most depraved of all colors congregate." After giving the "smiling faces of Mrs. Murphy and Hannah Johnson" a "refreshing shower," the firemen proceeded to drench the building. "The door was then closed, and the whole nest, of all colors, fledged and unfledged, drunk and sober, took a flight the back way. The retreating squad was headed by a Maria Ramsey, in the ranks were old Mother Murphy, Hannah Reams, and Hannah Johnson, or Williams, while Henry Johnson, the husband of the last named, commonly known as the *Irish nagur*, (accompanied by a few 'nice young men;') brought up the rear!— The besieged thus effected a retreat with flying *colors*."[92]

Mob action did not end that night, even though the mayor arrived on the scene and persuaded the volunteers to desist. On the third, the disturbances spread to Pittsburgh's sister city: firemen attacked a brothel in Allegheny City and subjected it to the same treatment as Blind Sam's and the Crow's Nest. Without any real effort by city authorities to curb this "purification," the situation deteriorated even further.[93] "On Saturday night, or rather Sunday morning, we had the crowning scene of this mob purification, in the destruction of 17 buildings at the upper end of the Fifth Ward by the persons who assailed the Crow's Nest, for the purpose of punishing a Mrs. Turney who kept a disorderly house in the neighborhood." The city's firemen denied any participation or complicity in the attacks or the fire, claiming at a specially convened meeting that a band of rowdies had seized their engines and acted without their knowledge or approval.[94]

Attention to the details of these incidents reveals an attempt to link leisure reform (the "purification" of the city's morals) to the chastisement of minority groups. All the targets of the mob belonged to some suspect group: African Americans, the Irish, and those engaged in objectionable leisure practices. In addition to keeping a brothel, Blind Sam was also a performer involved in theater and exhibitions; he "acted as a musician to the old Fifth street Museum, when the 'Infernal Regions' were exhibited there."[95] A large part of the moral indignation attached to the Crow's Nest stemmed from its being an *interracial* brothel. By all accounts, Pittsburgh contained a number of brothels, but vigilantes singled out the Crow's Nest largely because it was "occupied by the Irish nagur and a degraded white woman, who lives with him as his wife, together with such females as can be induced to live in such a sink of filth and wretchedness — amalgamation and crime!"[96] We have already seen attitudes toward theater personnel and interracial leisure; the attacks on brothels were no more than extreme actions based on these prejudices. The mobs assaulted activities that seduced people away from approved leisure and toward vice, thereby threatening the community's morals. They also attacked groups that, by their very nature, were believed to pose a threat to rational leisure.

Anxiety About Change

What emerges from all these varied efforts at leisure reform is a profound sense of widespread anxiety about many of the changes that swept through southwestern Pennsylvanian society in the first half of the nineteenth century. Before then, traditional society had contained leisure's creative and subversive potential by linking it to work and limiting its exercise to specific times and situations, thereby imposing effective communal supervision on most people's discretionary time. With the gradual dissolution of the bonds of traditional community and the emergence of amusement and recreation as ends in themselves, all strata of southwestern Pennsylvania society voiced concern over the future of leisure in a changing world.

Though Pennsylvanians experienced commercialization, industrialization, and demographic change in a variety of social contexts, the transformation of leisure by these forces seemed a particularly blatant example of the passing of simpler, more appealing times. By undermining customary notions of family, community, and social order, new patterns of leisure threatened all members of society in one way or another. Not surprisingly, diverse groups of concerned citizens sought to meliorate the problems caused by expanding leisure time and the increasing separation of play and amusement from instrumental pursuits. The reform of leisure did not express solely or primarily class-based anxieties but, rather, an entire society's concern over the effects of rapid change on people's options and choices. In working class fire companies, middle class singing societies, and patrician literary associations alike, southwestern Pennsylvanians found themselves the agents and objects of reform. Rather than being attempts to exercise class-based social control, their efforts to reform existing leisure activities and create new ones reflected a recognition of altered social circumstances. In leisure and its reform, Pennsylvanians used cultural means to respond to and shape the course of their changing society.

8

Epilogue

Leisure in the 1850s and Beyond

BETWEEN 1800 AND 1850, the pattern and practice of leisure in south-western Pennsylvania changed dramatically and irrevocably. A young person growing up at midcentury would have had a vastly different experience of leisure than his or her counterpart of fifty years earlier. Like the rest of society, young people at the turn of the century gathered in community groups to share traditional holidays, necessary work with attendant play, and neighborly sociability; by 1850, different forms of amusement, recreation, and social interaction replaced this traditional pattern of leisure.

Formerly, the community or family had been the realm of leisure, but young people coming of age around 1850 encountered a much changed cultural landscape. Divisive political, economic, and religious issues, not to mention plain population growth, made unvarnished all-inclusive communal pastimes difficult to sustain, so that young people's leisure was often organized on more exclusive bases, like class, occupation, religion, and ethnicity. Nor was it as important by 1850 for amusement and recreation to be pursued in the public eye: private parties, discreet social calls, and exclusive recreation facilities filled the vacuum created by the erosion of communal leisure. Even the family could not retain its preeminent position in the provision of leisure: the intrusion of the market into heretofore noncommercial relationships offered young people a wide range of leisure options that did not depend on familial participation or, for that matter, approval. And increasingly, the very concept of leisure that a young person learned while growing up had changed by 1850. Leisure no longer meant time free from work that should be used for refreshment of mind and body, self-improvement, or some other useful purpose. By 1850, it connoted time for recreation, amusement, and fun.

This transition marked a major change in the locus of cultural experimentation and innovation. To be sure, familial and communal leisure were not extinct, and traditional patterns still coexisted with and in some areas prevailed over new cultural forms. But increasingly, the juxtaposition, inversion, and reordering of established social, cultural, and economic patterns and ideas characteristic of traditional leisure occurred in situations removed from the larger society. In southwestern Pennsylvania, this transformation proceeded through the trends toward fragmentation, privatization, and commercialization outlined in preceding chapters. During the second half of the century these trends continued and, in some areas, accelerated. Leisure remained contested cultural space and a source of cultural innovation, but its position and meaning in the nexus of southwestern Pennsylvania's social, economic, and political life was quite different in 1850 than it had been at the turn of the century. This change, and its implications for leisure beyond 1850, is best illustrated with a concrete example.

The Jenny Lind Incident

On April 25, 1851, Jenny Lind, the most celebrated songstress of the nineteenth century, arrived in Pittsburgh to give a concert for her numerous admirers. Eager to catch a glimpse of the adored diva, excited fans thronged the wharf to witness Lind's arrival aboard the steamboat *Messenger* from Cincinnati. After disembarking with her manager, the illustrious P. T. Barnum, the Swedish Nightingale slowly made her way through the immense crowd to a carriage that conveyed her to an appropriate lodging, the elegant Monongahela House.[1] All of southwestern

Pennsylvania looked forward to Lind's concerts that night and the next; Pittsburghers had gone as far as Cincinnati to hear Lind, and only frequent entreaties to Barnum from the region's press and private citizens secured an engagement in Pittsburgh. To provide an auditorium suitable to an artist of Lind's calibre, Barnum hired the handsome new Masonic Hall, recently erected on Fifth Avenue, for the two concerts. As was his standard practice, the showman auctioned the much coveted five dollar tickets the morning of his arrival, selling all 1,100 seats for both shows for "a sum which was very little short of $10,000";[2] the first ticket bringing fifty dollars from a visiting San Fransiscan. In accordance with the importance of the event, potential bidders were even willing to pay ten cents for admission to the auction.[3]

Unfortunately for Lind and her many admirers, the concert did not go well. Lind's popularity was so great that the 1,100 seats allotted for each concert could not begin to satisfy the public's demand to see and hear the Swedish Nightingale. Even worse, the high cost of tickets only exacerbated the situation. A "mass meeting" of seven to eight thousand "outsiders" gathered on Fifth Avenue around Masonic Hall attempting at least to hear the concert. As the *Post* put it, the "enormously high price of admission (averaging $7.50 a ticket) rendered it impossible for men in moderate circumstances to purchase their way into the hall," so they congregated in the street and on the roofs of surrounding buildings hoping to gain a good vantage point for listening to the dulcet tones emanating from the auditorium.[4]

Some of the mob evinced dissatisfaction with these arrangements: "the *hoi polloi* . . . expressed their opinions (or at least their low standard of courtesy) by stones and vocal insults." The *Post* reported indignantly that the "angel of goodness" was insulted by the "ruffian crowd, who, while the concert was going on, dashed in stones at the window of her dressing room, and applied to her, that she might hear them, the most shocking and degrading epithets." The *Morning Chronicle* also vented its spleen against the crowd, noting that the "howling in the street was terrific; those who indulged in it are mean scoundrels; low-bred, malicious ruffians."[5] This tumult understandably unnerved Lind, who became increasingly alarmed when the crowd failed to disperse after the concert's conclusion. After waiting for some time in the darkened theater, Lind and her entourage escaped through a hole in the fence behind Masonic Hall (the "liberal" owner of the property aided the group "for the consideration of five dollars"), and proceeded by a back street route "through a variety of dirty alleys and quaint lanes, and an abundant assortment of filth and fog"[6] to the Monongahela House. The incident so disturbed Lind that she took the first steamboat out of town the next morning, forgoing the promised second concert scheduled for that evening.

Despite the city's disappointment at losing a second opportunity to hear the diva, everyone involved tried to downplay the seriousness of the disturbances and their causes. Barnum, attempting to "glaze over the affront," explained in a card published in local papers that the excessive noise of the crowd had been a shock to the artiste's delicate constitution, forcing her to abandon her second concert; a future engagement was possible if "suitable arrangements" could be made. Joseph Caton, a Barnum employee and member of Lind's party, denied that any insults were uttered and revealed that the alleged rocks were in reality "small pebbles thrown by those behind at those immediately in front" to make them sit down so everyone could see.[7] Pittsburghers too sought to smooth over the affair, which threatened to reflect badly on their city. Mayor Guthrie denied any hostile intent in the crowd, noting that the "greatest noise that was produced was in consequence of some reckless hack and omnibus drivers attempting to force their vehicles through the dense mass of human beings on Fifth street," and the *Gazette* reported that the rumor of rock throwing was incorrect.[8]

A Society Struggling with Change

The Lind affair highlights many of the developments that transformed southwestern Pennsylvania society and leisure between 1800 and 1850. Far from the image of a close-knit agricultural community strengthened through common participation in traditional leisure pursuits, Lind's reception in 1851 revealed a society struggling with social and economic changes. These changes, and the conflicts they engendered, were powerfully represented and articulated in leisure forms and relations. Perhaps most striking was the incorporation of the region into larger cultural as well as economic networks. The advent of market intrusion into previously noncommercial relations transformed leisure and accelerated the concomitant trends toward community fragmentation and privatization. As we saw in chapters 3 and 4, commercial leisure and the financial capability to participate in it grew in importance as the antebellum years wore on. By the time that Jenny Lind visited Pittsburgh, the crowds pursuing commercial leisure were less members of a coherent community than individual consumers each eager to secure a portion of the available leisure commodities. Participation in commercial leisure no longer depended on membership in a community; in fact, as we saw in the discussion of the transformation of leisure, enjoyment of commercial attractions undermined older notions of communal sociability.[9]

Part of this process of fragmentation and privatization originated in the social and economic changes outlined in chapter 3. Without the economic and technological developments that made commercial leisure feasible (growing numbers of wage earners, better transportation, and so on), the social organization needed for moving leisure into the marketplace could not have emerged when or how it did. Traveling performers and exhibitions as well as leisure products were available early in the century, but their popularity and celebrity could not approach that of Jenny Lind, Olé Bull, Tom Thumb, or the plethora of inexpensive papers, books, and sheet music available by the 1850s. Cultural entrepreneurs like P. T. Barnum obviously understood and exploited the social and cultural preferences of people already hungry for entertainment and novelty, but their success depended on a communication network to spread the fame of products and attractions and on reliable transportation to deliver leisure goods and services. With the penetration of railroads into southwestern Pennsylvania in the 1850s and 1860s, the possibilities for commercial leisure — and the attendant communal fragmentation and privatization — increased exponentially.[10]

Class Concerns and Conflicts

Lind's visit to Pittsburgh presaged another development in southwestern Pennsylvania leisure: the increasing salience of class concerns and conflicts in leisure. Though Barnum and most Pittsburghers downplayed the disturbances that chased Lind from the city, evidence suggests that class tensions underpinned much of the crowd's raucous behavior. Barnum had apparently not anticipated the effect on crowd behavior of payday in a mining and industrial community. Pittsburgh workers "were scattered about, and entertaining no great respect for Temperance, had indulged in sundry of those agreeable potations which are rarely apt to strengthen the tendency to quietude or order." Consequently, they gave Lind and her party an unruly welcome when her carriage arrived at the theater.[11] The noise outside was due in part to a protest at their exclusion from the event by virtue of the high cost of tickets and Barnum's auction system, which favored the "batch of speculators" who purchased many of the available tickets and later scalped them.[12]

Far from overexuberant approval, the crowd's comments expressed anger and derision at the pretense and exclusivity of Lind's performance and its audience. Charles Rosenberg recounted that:

> Scarcely had the first notes of the overture been touched by them [the orchestra], than the disturbance began. Shouts, and cries, and cheers of every description were heard from the street. These blent with the music of the overture very successfully, and formed a perfectly hideous *charivari* of the most novel description. . . . Cock crowing, howling, and shouting of every description, filling the air and echoing on the startled ears of the auditors, who began to fear that they were doomed to enjoy this agreeable accompaniment during the whole of the evening. And, in truth, they were so doomed.[13]

Rosenberg's use of the term *charivari* was perhaps more prescient than he realized. Like its counterpart in earlier times, the Pittsburgh hoi polloi's protest at a social injustice used noise and group action to express disapproval and render enjoyment of the concert difficult: if we cannot hear the divine Jenny, they seemed to say, neither will you. This charivari, however, expressed predominantly class, rather than community, concerns.

More than elsewhere on Lind's tour, Pittsburgh demonstrated the emergence of class conflict in leisure. As private rather than group leisure activities grew in importance, leisure goods and services became commercial commodities as never before. That access to these commodities was distributed unevenly among the population was not lost on workers, or on the middle and upper classes who benefited from the prevailing arrangement. The "outsiders'" actions at the Lind concert were only one example of the vocal and insistent protest to inequality in leisure — and to the socioeconomic system graphically represented in leisure relations — that would continue throughout the century and into the next.[14]

The Lind incident also illustrated the continuing importance of leisure as contested cultural ground. Leisure offered many possibilities for comment and criticism: workers' reaction to their exclusion from the concert resonated with larger issues of class and gender. If Lind, the female "angel of goodness," imbued her audience with morality and refined sentiments, why were women excluded from so much of public life? Though commentators portrayed Lind as a "curious exception" to the "common human allotment" of talent and virtue, popular opinion held that all women shared these ennobling qualities, albeit in lesser measure. Why not use Lind's example to extend the salutary female influence in leisure to more of public life, rather than consigning women to the private sphere? In the decades following 1850, middle and upper class women pressed these questions as they continued to organize clubs, societies, and social activities that allowed them to claim a greater role and influence in public life.[15]

The universal approbation of Lind's moral example raised class issues as well. If the middle and upper class complained of the boorish and immoral behavior of the working class, why effectively exclude them from what all conceded to be an uplifting experience? Jenny's voice, which, like "Tamino's magic flute, might have quelled the beastly urges of the rabble if they could have heard her," was useless as long as it was "trapped inside the hall where she was barely audible." How could the region's elite claim that the only justifiable basis for cultural authority was an inherent tendency to gravitate toward the uplifting and refined, when it placed monetary barriers in the way of everyone else?[16] People took these questions and concerns seriously, for despite universal condemnation of the crowd's actions at the concert, popular disapproval of the event's handling seems to have achieved its purpose.

The Seeds of Cultural Democracy

When Lind finally returned to Pittsburgh in November 1851, her concerts proceeded without incident. By that time, she had politely jettisoned Barnum as her manager, lowered ticket prices, and abolished the auction system, thereby effectively opening her performances to a much broader audience. Lind also rebuffed wealthy Pittsburghers who offered expensive gifts to compensate for her previous experience in their town, explaining that she never accepted presents from gentlemen.[17] However strident and unpleasant the form of their protest, the city's leisure "outsiders" had resisted successfully attempts to exclude them from access to leisure commodities. If their demonstrations failed to achieve any immediate measure of socioeconomic democracy, they did plant a seed for the future and, at least for a moment, earn themselves a measure of cultural democracy.

Notes

Bibliography

Index

Notes

Chapter 1: Introduction

1. The Diary of Joseph C. Buffum, Sept. 13, 1847, to Oct. 30, 1854 (hereafter Buffum Diary), typescript, Pennsylvania Department, Carnegie Library of Pittsburgh, Sept. 13, 14, 1847.

2. Though Buffum never mentioned Benjamin Franklin explicitly in his diary, his language and references suggest familiarity with the *Autobiography* and correspondence. On December 31, 1847, for instance, Buffum recorded that he "bought a magic lantern today at auction for $0.60 but . . . paid dear for the whistle for it is not very good or is rather poor." He referred to a boyhood incident recounted in "The Whistle," one of Franklin's bagatelles, written in France as a letter to Mme. Brillon in 1779. Buffum may have been familiar with the edition of Franklin's writings published in Boston by Jared Sparks between 1836 and 1840. On "The Whistle," see Richard E. Amacher, *Franklin's Wit and Folly: The Bagatelles* (New Brunswick: Rutgers University Press, 1953), 44–47.

3. Buffum Diary, Sept. 14, 1847. On changes in Americans' perception of time during the nineteenth century, see Michael O'Malley, *Keeping Watch: A History of American Time* (New York: Penguin, 1990), especially 1–54.

Reflecting American culture's emerging consciousness of clock time, Buffum owned a watch and evinced fascination with its mechanism: "12th. Got a balance wheel put in my watch. . . . 13th. Sabbath, had a discussion about the verge and balance wheel of a watch. The verge is the wheel that plays backward and forward and the balance wheel works underneath and stands upright. Had also a discourse on poetry." Buffum Diary, Nov. 12, 13, 1847. On the importance of watches in nineteenth-century American culture, see O'Malley, *Keeping Watch*, 30, 151.

4. Buffum Diary, Sept. 13, 14, Dec. 22, 1847. Buffum not only participated in but also helped to organize a number of these activities. He filled several offices in his local Sons of Temperance division, aided in establishing a reformed medical society and periodical, and served as vice president for Pittsburgh's Phreno-magnetic Society. In addition, he maintained an informal medical practice, treating patients with magnetism and eclectic medical methods. See Buffum Diary, Sept. 13, Dec. 28, 1847, Jan. 4, Mar. 15 and 26, 1848.

5. Buffum Diary, Oct. 22, Nov. 17, 1847. Some health writers suggested that participation in leisure threatened health: crowded rooms, bad air, and late nights overexcited body and mind, leading to illness. See Harvey Green, *Fit for America:*

Health, Fitness, Sport and American Society (Baltimore: Johns Hopkins University Press, 1986), 19.

6. Buffum Diary, Oct. 17, 23, 1847.

7. The definition comes from *Entick's New Spelling Dictionary* (New York: Sidney's, 1810); the verse is from "An Epigram on Killing Time," *Patterson's Magazine Almanac for 1820* (Pittsburgh: Patterson and Lambdin, 1819), n.p. For background on preindustrial Anglo-American leisure, see Gary Cross, *A Social History of Leisure Since 1600* (State College, Pa.: Venture Publishing, 1990), 1–54.

8. George Bethune, "Leisure — Its Uses and Abuses; A lecture delivered before the New York Mercantile Library Association, March, 1839," in *Orations and Occasional Discourses* (New York: Putnam, 1850), 57, 58; T. Charlton Henry, D.D., *An Inquiry into the Consistency of Popular Amusements with a Profession of Christianity* (Charleston, S.C.: William Riley, 1825), 163. On leisure and its relation to work, see Daniel Rodgers, *The Work Ethic in Industrial America, 1850–1920* (Chicago: University of Chicago Press, 1978), 1–11, 103; O'Malley, *Keeping Watch*, 10–12; Foster Rhea Dulles, *A History of Recreation: America Learns to Play* (Englewood Cliffs, N.J.: Prentice Hall, 1965), 85–86, 88–91.

9. *The Richmond Alarm; A Plain and Familiar Discourse: Written in the Form of a Dialogue Between a Father and his Son* (Pittsburgh: Robert Ferguson & Company, 1815), 9, 83, 84, 131; *The Crystal and Ladies' Magazine* (Pittsburgh) 1, no. 1 (April 1828): 28–29.

10. "An Old Mercaant," *Pittsburgh Gazette*, July 5, 1839. Compare Buffum's activities with those advocated here. On advice about leisure, see O'Malley, *Keeping Watch*, 20–21; Rodgers, *Work Ethic*, 129–32.

11. Daniel Drake, *An Oration on the Intemperance of Cities: Including Remarks on Gambling, Idleness, Fashion, and Sabbath-Breaking, delivered in Philadelphia, January 24, 1831* (Philadelphia: n.p., 1831), 15, 14.

12. On traditional agricultural pastimes, see Dulles, *History of Recreation*, 22–43; Jack Larkin, *The Reshaping of Everyday Life 1790–1840* (New York: Harper and Row, 1989), 266–69. For a discussion of concerns about the erosion of traditional constraints on behavior, see Paul Boyer, *Urban Masses and Moral Order in America, 1820–1920* (Cambridge: Harvard University Press, 1978), 4–5, 22–33; Richard C. Wade, *The Urban Frontier: The Rise of Western Cities, 1790–1830* (Cambridge: Harvard University Press, 1959), 203, 308–309, 313, and Cross, *Social History of Leisure*, 57–70.

13. On concerns about popular amusements, consult O'Malley, *Keeping Watch*, 2–3, 21; Patricia C. Click, *The Spirit of the Times: Amusements in Nineteenth-Century Baltimore, Norfolk, and Richmond* (Charlottesville: University of Virginia Press, 1989), 61, 65–66; Dulles, *History of Recreation*, 88–91; and Karen Haltunnen, *Confidence Men and Painted Women: A Study of Middle Class Culture in America, 1830–1870* (New Haven: Yale University Press, 1982).

14. Boyer, *Urban Masses and Moral Order*, 6. For an examination of frontier leisure styles, see Wade, *Urban Frontier*, 121–24; and Elliott Gorn, " 'Gouge and

Bite, Pull Hair and Scratch': The Social Significance of Fighting in the Southern Backcountry," *American Historical Review* 90 (Feb. 1985): 18–43.

15. *An Address, together with the Constitution, By-Laws and Standing Rules of the Pittsburgh Young Men's Society, organized January 1, 1833* (Pittsburgh: n.p., 1833), 4. For a discussion of advice manuals that warned young men from the country about the snares and dangers of city vice, see Haltunnen, *Confidence Men and Painted Women,* 10–29. For more on the dangers to young men in antebellum cities, see Allan Stanley Horlick, *Country Boys and Merchant Princes: The Social Control of Young Men in New York* (Lewisburg, Pa.: Bucknell University Press, 1975), especially 45–64, 147–78.

16. See, for example, Ronald G. Walters's discussion of perceived threats to America's moral order in his *American Reformers 1815–1860* (New York: Hill and Wang, 1978), 6, 8, 10; Boyer, *Urban Masses and Moral Order,* 70–76; Wade, *Urban Frontier,* 122–24, 218–19, 287–91. On concerns about drinking, see W. J. Rorabaugh, *The Alcoholic Republic: An American Tradition* (New York: Oxford University Press, 1979).

17. On the symbolic importance of leisure in general, see Timothy H. Breen, "Horses and Gentlemen: The Cultural Significance of Gambling Among the Gentry of Virginia," *William and Mary Quarterly* 34 (April 1977), 3d series: 239–57; and Rhys Isaac, *The Transformation of Virginia* (Chapel Hill: University of North Carolina Press, 1982). For the nineteenth century, see Click, *Spirit of the Times,* 34–56, which discusses fears of social disintegration as elites lost control of leisure activities like gambling and horse racing. On other aspects of this issue, consult Lawrence W. Levine, *Highbrow/Lowbrow: The Emergence of Cultural Hierarchy in America* (Cambridge: Harvard University Press, 1988); Bruce A. McConachie, "Pacifying American Theatrical Audiences, 1820–1900," in *For Fun and Profit: The Transformation of Leisure into Consumption,* ed. Richard Butsch (Philadelphia: Temple University Press, 1990), 47–70; Sean Wilentz, "Artisan Republican Festivals and the Rise of Class Conflict in New York City, 1788–1837," in *Working Class America: Essays on Labor, Community, and American Society,* ed. Michael H. Frisch and Daniel J. Walkowitz (Urbana: University of Illinois Press, 1983), 37–77; Scott C. Martin, "The Fourth of July in Southwestern Pennsylvania, 1800–1850," *Pittsburgh History* 75, no. 2 (summer 1992): 58–71.

18. Alexis de Tocqueville, *Democracy in America,* 2 vols., ed. Phillips Bradley (New York: Knopf, 1945), 2:152; Michel Chevalier, *Society, Manners, and Politics in the United States* (1839; reprint, New York: Augustus M. Kelly, 1966), 169; *Loomis's Magazine Almanac for 1836* (Pittsburgh: Luke Loomis, 1836), 70. Chevalier also lamented Americans' aversion to pleasant diversions: "Of little moment are the disgust and disappointment that a European of delicate nerves may have to encounter, if, for the purpose of killing time, he ventures upon a western steamboat, or into a western tavern; so much the worse for him, if he has fallen into a country where there is no place for an idle tourist, seeking only amuse-

ment!" (175). On these points, see also Rodgers, *Work Ethic*, 5–6; Dulles, *History of Recreation*, 87–88.

19. Philadelphius, *The Moral Plague of Civil Society; or, The Pernicious Effects of the Love of Money on the Morals of Mankind: Exemplified in the Encouragement Given to the Use of Ardent Spirits in the United States, with the Proper Remedy for the Cure of this National Evil* (Philadelphia: n.p., 1821), 2. On Americans' attitudes toward the dangers of money-making and prosperity, see Fred Somkin, *Unquiet Eagle: Memory and Desire in the Idea of American Freedom, 1815–1860* (Ithaca: Cornell University Press, 1967), 16–34; Green, *Fit for America*, 15–16.

20. Samuel Nott, Jr., "Leisure in the Midst of Business," *Loomis's Magazine Almanac for 1836* (Pittsburgh: Luke Loomis, 1836), 48, 49, 51–52, 57, 51, 53.

21. Bethune, "Leisure," 65, 69, 70. Many Americans looked to leisure to mitigate the effects of overwork and acquisitiveness. John Sears has argued that nineteenth-century tourist attractions served as "sacred places" for Americans and acted as a "cultural check on aggressive fantasies of exploiting America's resources to the fullest extent possible." See his *Sacred Places: American Tourist Attractions in the Nineteenth Century* (New York: Oxford University Press, 1989), 8. On anxieties about overwork, see Peter Levine, "The Promise of Sport in Antebellum America," *Journal of American Culture* 2, no. 4 (1980): 623–34; Green, *Fit for America*, 21–22; Click, *Spirit of the Times*, 103.

22. Drake, "Oration," 13; A. H. Saxon, *P. T. Barnum: The Legend and the Man* (New York: Columbia University Press, 1989), 12, see also 105–107. See also Neil Harris, *Humbug: The Art of P. T. Barnum* (Chicago: University of Chicago Press, 1973).

23. On the rejection of European cultural models, consult Joseph J. Ellis, *After the Revolution: Profiles of Early American Culture* (New York: Norton, 1979), especially 3–38; Harris, *Humbug*, especially 59–90; and Carl Bode, *The American Lyceum: Town Meeting of the Mind* (New York: Oxford University Press, 1956).

24. My view of leisure owes much to the work of Victor Turner. Linking leisure to the liminality and antistructure of ritual, Turner asserts that it is "potentially capable of releasing creative powers, individual or communal, either to criticize or buttress the dominant social structural values" ("Liminal to Liminoid in Play, Flow, Ritual," in *From Ritual to Theatre: The Human Seriousness of Play* [New York: Performing Arts Journal Publications, 1982], 37). For more on Turner's view of ritual and its implications for leisure, see his *The Ritual Process: Structure and Anti-Structure* (Chicago: Aldine, 1969); and "Frame, Flow, and Reflection: Ritual and Drama as Public Liminality," in *Process, Performance, and Pilgrimage: A Study in Comparative Symbology* (New Delhi, India: Concept, 1979), 94–120.

25. For discussions of leisure as a cultural mediator of identity formation and change, see Kathy Peiss, *Cheap Amusements: Working Women and Leisure in Turn-of-the-Century New York* (Philadelphia: Temple University Press, 1986), especially 3–10; Christine Stansell, *City of Women: Sex and Class in New York*,

1789–1860 (Chicago: University of Illinois Press, 1986), especially her discussion of youth culture on the Bowery, 89–101; Stephen Hardy, *How Boston Played: Sport, Recreation, and Community, 1865–1915* (Boston: Northeastern University Press, 1982); Click, *Spirit of the Times*, 72–86.

26. Buffum Diary, June 24, July 21, 1848.

27. On the history of the region, see any of the county histories available. Though no synthetic work discusses adequately the region as a whole during the early nineteenth century, many works on Pittsburgh also include material on the surrounding area. For background on the region, consult R. Eugene Harper, *The Transformation of Western Pennsylvania, 1770–1800* (Pittsburgh: University of Pittsburgh Press, 1991); Catherine M. Reiser, *Pittsburgh's Commercial Development, 1800–1850* (Harrisburg: Pennsylvania Historical and Museum Commission, 1951); Wade, *Urban Frontier*, 7–13; and the essays in Samuel P. Hays, ed., *City at the Point: Essays on the Social History of Pittsburgh* (Pittsburgh: University of Pittsburgh Press, 1989), especially Edward K. Muller's "Metropolis and Region: A Framework for Enquiry into Western Pennsylvania," 181–211.

28. For a useful collection of traveler's accounts, see John Harpster, *Crossroads: Descriptions of Early Western Pennsylvania, 1720–1829* (Pittsburgh: University of Pittsburgh Press, 1938).

29. Charles Sellers has suggested that "market revolution" is a better description than "transportation revolution" of the changes that swept over the early republic. See his *The Market Revolution: Jacksonian America, 1815–1846* (New York: Oxford University Press, 1991).

Chapter 2: Cohesion and Diversity in Southwestern Pennsylvania Leisure

1. Albert Bushnell Hart, "The Pennsylvania Pioneer," in Boyd Crumrine, ed., *The Centennial Celebration of the Incorporation of the Borough of Washington, PA, in Its Old Home Week of October 2–8, 1910* (Washington, Pa.: Washington County Historical Society, 1912), 77.

2. J. A. Caldwell, *Caldwell's Illustrated Historical, Centennial Atlas of Washington County, Pennsylvania* (Conduit, Ohio: J. A. Caldwell, 1876), 9; James Veech, *The Monongahela of Old, or Historical Sketches of South-Western Pennsylvania to the Year 1800* (Pittsburgh: n.p., 1910), 106.

3. The quotation is from Joffre Dumazedier, "Leisure," in *International Encyclopedia of the Social Sciences*, ed. David Sills (New York: Macmillan, 1968), 9:248. See also Dumazedier's *Toward a Society of Leisure* (New York: Free Press, 1967).

4. Henrietta Galley and J. O. Arnold, M.D., *History of the Galley Family with Local and Old-Time Sketches in the Yough Region* (Philadelphia: Philadelphia Printing and Publishing, 1908), 190; "Summer Fades," *Pittsburgh Commonwealth*, Oct. 26, 1808; "A Winter's Song," *Washington Reporter*, Feb. 13, 1809.

5. "Winter Evenings," *Loomis's Magazine Almanac for 1835* (Pittsburgh: Luke Loomis, 1835), 62–63; "Useful Rules for Farmers and Mechanics," *Loomis's Magazine Almanac for 1837* (Pittsburgh: Luke Loomis, 1837), 32–33.

6. "Winter," *Western Literary Messenger* (Pittsburgh) 1 (April 1841): 11, 85; W. G. Lyford, *The Western Address Directory* (Baltimore: n.p., 1837), 17.

7. Thomas Ashe, *Travels in America Performed in 1806* (New York, n.p., 1811), 30–31. For more on traditional agricultural society, see Joseph Doddridge, *Notes on the Settlement and Indian Wars of the Western Parts of Virginia and Pennsylvania* (Albany: Joel Munsell, 1876); Solon J. Buck and Elizabeth H. Buck, *The Planting of Civilization in Western Pennsylvania* (Pittsburgh: University of Pittsburgh Press, 1939), especially chap. 15, "Community Life"; and Stevenson Fletcher, *Pennsylvania Agriculture and Country Life 1640–1840* (Harrisburg: Pennsylvania Historical and Museum Commission, 1950). For background on these issues, see Robert Malcolmson, *Popular Recreations in British Society, 1700–1850* (Cambridge: Cambridge University Press, 1973); and Dulles, *History of Recreation*, especially 22–43, 67–83.

8. Both quotations are from Samuel B. Jones, *Pittsburgh in the Year 1826* (Pittsburgh: Johnston and Stockton, 1826), 43. Jones was referring to the period before 1816, when Pittsburgh was not incorporated as a city.

9. John McDowell, Esq., "Address on Agriculture," in *The Centennial Celebration of the Organization of Washington County, Pennsylvania*, Washington Historical Society (Washington, Pa.: E. E. Crumrine, 1881), 64; Fletcher, *Pennsylvania Agriculture*, 119; Sally Hastings, *Poems on Different Subjects* (Lancaster, Pa.: William Dickson, 1808), 200.

10. *Washington Reporter*, Nov. 11, 1816; *Greensburg Gazette*, July 4, 1828.

11. John S. Van Voorhis, *The Old and New Monongahela* (Pittsburgh: Nicholson, 1893), 14. See also Emma D. A. Morris, "Old Springhill" (master's thesis, University of Pittsburgh, 1938), 60–64; and Harry C. Gilchrist, *History of Wilkinsburg, Pennsylvania* (Wilkinsburg, Pa.: n.p., 1927), 72–75; *Washington Reporter*, Nov. 11, 1822; Earle R. Forrest, *History of Washington County, Pennsylvania* (Chicago: S. J. Clarke, 1926), 374–76.

12. Fletcher, *Pennsylvania Agriculture*, 439–49; (Uniontown) *Genius of Liberty*, Aug. 8, 1828; Forrest, *History of Washington County*, 376.

13. *Pittsburgh Gazette*, Jan. 29, 1813; *Pittsburgh Mercury*, Sept. 28, 1814; J. C. McClenathan et al., *Centennial History of the Borough of Connellsville, Pennsylvania, 1806–1906* (Columbus, Ohio: Champlin, 1906), 194.

14. J. Ritchie Garrison, "Battalion Day: Militia Muster and Frolic in Pennsylvania Before the Civil War," *Pennsylvania Folklife* 26 (1976–77): 2–12; McClenathan et al., *Centennial History of Connellsville*, 193–95; George W. F. Birch, *Our Church and Our Village* (New York: Ward and Drummond, 1899), 157.

Sally Hastings is quoted from her *Poems on Different Subjects*, 201. See also Morris, "Old Springhill," 65.

15. Walter S. Abbott and William E. Harrison, *The First One Hundred Years*

of McKeesport (McKeesport, Pa.: *McKeesport Times*, 1894), 15; Hastings, *Poems on Different Subjects*, 205; *Pittsburgh Tree of Liberty*, Sept. 20, 1800; *Washington Reporter*, Nov. 27, 1809; *Genius of Liberty*, Sept. 10, 1814. For a discussion of gambling, horse racing, and the law in the antebellum South, see Click, *Spirit of the Times*, 57–71.

16. Henry Marie Brackenridge, *Recollections of Persons and Places in the West* (Philadelphia: Lippincott, 1868), 62.

17. See, for example, Thomas B. Searight's account of tavern-based racing along the National Pike in his *The Old Pike: A History of the National Road* (Uniontown, Pa.: n.p., 1894), 220–24.

18. *Washington Examiner*, Oct. 7, 1822, Nov. 4, 1823; see also Dec. 29, 1832, for a poem, "The Twin Sisters," that depicts the social and courtship aspects of the fair. For more on agricultural fairs generally, see Forrest, *History of Washington County*, 699–704; Crumrine, *Incorporation of the Borough of Washington, Pennsylvania*, 472–74; James Hadden, *A History of Uniontown* (Akron, Pa.: New Werner Company, 1913), 604; *Pittsburgh Mercury*, Jan. 7, 1820, Nov. 6, 1822, Nov. 25, 1823; *Pittsburgh Gazette*, Nov. 7, 1823; *Genius of Liberty*, Nov. 5, 1812, Nov. 3, 1823.

19. *Tree of Liberty*, May 8, 1802; Hastings, *Poems on Different Subjects*, 207; Birch, *Our Church*, 166–67; Galley and Arnold, *History of the Galley Family*, 231; Gilchrist, *History of Wilkinsburg*, 76–78. See also *Tree of Liberty*, Oct. 23, 1802; B. F. Vogle, *Greensburg and Greensburg Schools* (Greensburg, Pa.: Vogle and Winsheimer, 1899), 114–15; *Farmer's Register*, May 2, 1801; *Genius of Liberty*, June 7, 1815.

20. Obviously it is a contrivance to talk of "women's" leisure as if it were a unitary phenomenon: race, ethnicity, religion, class, and related factors shaped the ways in which individual women experienced and used free time, just as they did for men. Yet few southwestern Pennsylvania women described their perceptions of leisure time in diaries, journals, or memoirs, hampering comparative analysis. Generalizations about women's leisure are thus necessary; if treated as heuristic devices rather than immutable principles, they point the way to a better understanding of the varieties of gendered leisure. This difficulty is compounded by the paucity of historical studies of women's leisure, which might have provided a framework for comparative analysis. Though some progress has already been made in filling this gap, broad statements will continue to be unavoidable until detailed accounts of the leisure experiences of various groups of women are available. See chapter 6 for a more detailed account of women, gender, and leisure. For recent work on women and leisure, see Peiss, *Cheap Amusements*; and Joan D. Hedrick, "Parlor Literature: Harriet Beecher Stowe and the Question of 'Great Women Artists,'" *Signs* 17, no. 2 (1992): 275–303.

21. Brackenridge, *Recollections*, 60.

On the history of housework, see Susan Strasser, *Never Done: A History of American Housework* (New York: Pantheon, 1982); Ruth Schwartz Cowan, *More*

Work for Mother: The Ironies of Household Technology from the Open Hearth to the Microwave (New York: Basic, 1983); Glenna Matthews, *"Just a Housewife"; The Rise and Fall of Domesticity in America* (New York: Oxford University Press, 1987); and Jeanne Boydston, *Home and Work: Housework, Wages, and the Ideology of Labor in the Early Republic* (New York: Oxford University Press, 1990).

22. The quotation is from *Centennial Celebration of the Organization of Washington County*, 64; John N. Boucher, *The Old and New Westmoreland* (New York: American Historical Society, 1918), 2:463.

See, for example, Samuel Young's account of a visit by his mother and sisters to a family in Sharpsburg, a short distance from Pittsburgh, in *The History of My Life, Being a Biographical Outline of the Events of a Long and Busy Life* (Pittsburgh: n.p., 1890), 23.

23. Richard T. Wiley, *Elizabeth and Her Neighbors* (Butler, Pa.: Zeigler, 1936), 314; Searight, *The Old Pike*, 229, 267.

On the varying amounts of free time among wives versus unmarried women, see Nancy F. Cott, *The Bonds of Womanhood: "Woman's Sphere" in New England, 1780–1835* (New Haven: Yale University Press, 1977), 14–15, 40, 52–53.

24. Joseph E. Walker, ed., *Pleasure and Business in Western Pennsylvania: The Journal of Joshua Gilpin, 1809* (Harrisburg: Pennsylvania Historical and Museum Commission, 1975), 34; Peregrine Prolix (Philip H. Nicklin), *Journey Through Pennsylvania, 1835, By Canal, Rail, and Stage Coach* (York, Pa.: American Canal and Transportation Center, 1978), 54–55; Boucher, *Old and New Westmoreland*, 2:511.

25. *Pittsburgh Gazette*, Jan. 3, 1812; Boucher, *Old and New Westmoreland*, 2:461.

26. William Baker, Jr., *Canonsburg, Pennsylvania 1773–1936* (Canonsburg: n.p., 1936); Birch, *Our Church*, 154, 145; Helen E. Vogt, *Westward of Ye Laurel Hills, 1750–1850* (Parsons, W. Vir.: McClain Printing Co., 1976), 66; Searight, *The Old Pike*, 220–21; Noah M. Ludlow, *Dramatic Life as I Found It* (1880; reprint, New York: Benjamin Blom, 1966), 58–60; Boucher, *Old and New Westmoreland*, 2:461; *Pittsburgh Commonwealth*, June 23, 1813.

27. Searight, *The Old Pike*, 332; Young, *History of My Life*, 33; James Flint, *Letters from America (1818–1820)* (orig. published in 1822), in *Early Western Travels, 1748–1846*, ed. Reuben G. Thwaites (Cleveland: A. H. Clark, 1904), 9:87; Searight, ibid., 270.

28. On this point, see Paul Goodman, *Towards a Christian Republic: The Great Transition in New England, 1826–1836* (New York: Oxford University Press, 1988), 54–79, 82–84. Mark Carnes claims that secret ritual itself was the major attraction of this all-male activity. See his *Secret Ritual and Manhood in Victorian America* (New Haven: Yale University Press, 1989).

29. Buck and Buck, *Planting of Civilization*, 350; Charles W. Dahlinger, *Pittsburgh, A Sketch of Its Early Social Life* (New York: Putnam, 1916), 95–96; Alfred Creigh, *History of Washington County* (Washington, Pa.: n.p., 1870), 341;

"Journal of Uria Brown (1816)," *Maryland Historical Magazine* 10 (1915): 283; *Centennial Anniversary of the Founding of Monongahela City, 1892* (Monongahela City, Pa.: Hazzard, 1895), 200–201; (Greensburg) *Farmer's Register*, June 14, 1800; *Westmoreland Republican*, May 23, 1818. For more on Freemasonry in Pittsburgh and Allegheny County, see Frederick C. Rommel, *History of Lodge #45, F. & A.M., 1785–1910* (Pittsburgh: Republic Bank Note Company, 1912); and Frank W. Powelson, "History of Freemasonry in Allegheny County" (typescript, 1960, in Collection of the Pennsylvania Department, Carnegie Library of Pittsburgh). For an excellent discussion of the leisure aspects of Masonry, see Goodman, *Toward A Christian Republic*, especially 45–49.

30. *Tree of Liberty* (Pittsburgh), Jan. 23, 1802; Fortescue Cuming, *Sketches of a Tour to the Western Country, Through the States of Ohio and Kentucky* (Pittsburgh: Cramer, Speer, and Eichbaum, 1810), 82; *Pittsburgh Mercury*, March 2, 1814; Cuming, *idem.*, 81; Brackenridge, *Recollections*, 90–91; *Pittsburgh Gazette*, March 1, 1800, Oct. 30, 1801; Creigh, *Washington County*, 353.

31. Boucher, *Old and New Westmoreland*, 463; *City of Greensburg, A History* (Greensburg, Pa.: Westmoreland County Historical Society, 1949), 20; Sol Smith, *Theatrical Management in the West and South for Thirty Years* (New York: Harper and Brothers, 1868), 31.

32. Buck and Buck, *Planting of Civilization*, 366–67; *Washington Reporter*, March 16, 1812; Henry Marie Brackenridge, "Pittsburgh in the Olden Time," in *The Literary Casket* (Pittsburgh) 3, no. 1 (July 1842): 12.

33. Buck and Buck, *Planting of Civilization*, 368; *Pittsburgh Gazette*, Oct. 10, 1808, July 13, 1810, Nov. 2, 1814. Similarly, the Pittsburgh theater reserved separate seats for ladies. See the *Gazette*, Nov. 8, 1814.

34. *Pittsburgh Commonwealth*, Dec. 16, 1811; *Pittsburgh Gazette*, Jan. 17, 1812, July 23, 1813; *Pittsburgh Statesman*, Jan. 5, 1820. For more on lectures as entertainment, see Bode, *The American Lyceum*; and Click, *Spirit of the Times*, 28–31.

On music, dance, and fencing teachers, see *Pittsburgh Commonwealth*, July 22, 1815; *Genius of Liberty*, Jan. 9, 1812, Jan. 4, 1817. For more on early leisure services, see the *Pittsburgh Gazette*, Jan. 4, 1800, Jan. 5, 1808; *Tree of Liberty*, March 26, 1803; *Washington Reporter*, March 9, 1812; *Pittsburgh Commonwealth*, June 30, 1812.

35. David T. Watson, "Early School Day Recollections," in *The Centennial Celebration of the Incorporation of the Borough of Washington, PA*, ed. Boyd Crumrine (Washington: Washington County Historical Society, 1912), 85.

36. *Pittsburgh Statesman*, July 15, 1829; *Iron City*, May 25, 1844; *Allegheny Democrat*, March 24, 1835; *Pittsburgh Gazette*, July 7, 1849; *City of Greensburg*, 251.

37. F. A. Michaux, *Travels to the West of the Allegheny Mountains, in the States of Ohio, Kentucky, and Tennessee* (London, 1805), vol. 3 in *Early Western Travels 1748–1846*, ed. Reuben G. Thwaites (Cleveland: A. H. Clark, 1904), 152; Flint, *Letters from America*, 80.

As early as 1840, a Mr. S. Barrett opened a gymnasium "on German principles" in Pittsburgh; German Turners were extremely active in promoting the
establishment of gymnasia in the early 1850s. See the *Pittsburgh Mercury*, July
29, 1841; and Soeren Stewart Brynn, "Some Sports in Pittsburgh During the National Period, 1775–1860," *Western Pennsylvania Historical Magazine* 52 (Jan.
1969): 65–66. On German Turnvereine, see Augustus J. Prahl, "The Turner," 79–
110 in A. E. Zucker, ed., *The Forty-Eighters: Political Refugees of the German
Revolution of 1848* (New York: Columbia University Press, 1950).

38. *The Diary of Lucy Ann Higbee, 1837* (Cleveland: n.p., 1924), 22; *Pittsburgh
Gazette*, July 14, 1848.

The *Greensburg Sentinel*, April 16, 1841, noted the removal of a German
music teacher from Pittsburgh to Greensburg; the *American Manufacturer* (Pittsburgh), April 29, 1832, contains a notice for a German concert at Lutz's Coffee
House.

39. *Pittsburgh Gazette*, Dec. 24, 1802; *Pittsburgh Mercury*, March 29, 1817;
Pittsburgh Gazette, March 21, 1823.

40. For accounts of both celebrations, see the *Pittsburgh Commonwealth*,
March 25, 1807.

41. *Iron City*, April 9, 1842; *Pittsburgh Telegraph*, April 24, 1847; *The Mystery*
(Pittsburgh), Dec. 16, 1846. For material on black Masonic lodges, see William
Muraskin, *Middle Class Blacks in a White Society: Prince Hall Freemasonry in
America* (Berkeley and Los Angeles: University of California Press, 1975).

42. *Washington Reporter*, Aug. 25, 1823; *Proceedings of the Second Annual
Meeting of the Pittsburgh Temperance Society of the Coloured People of the City
of Pittsburgh and Vicinity* (Pittsburgh: n.p., 1839). Donald Yacovone's "The Transformation of the Black Temperance Movement, 1827–1854: An Interpretation,"
Journal of the Early Republic 8: 281–97, provides a good overview of black temperance activities during the period.

43. Hugh Henry Brackenridge, *Gazette Publications* (Carlisle, Pa.: Alexander
& Phillips, 1806), 269; *Pittsburgh Statesman*, Feb. 1, 1832.

44. (Pittsburgh) *Spirit of the Age*, July 4, 1843; (Greensburg) *Farmer's Register*,
Oct. 24, 1801; *Pittsburgh Telegraph*, July 17, 1847; Dorothy Sterling, *The Making
of an Afro-American, Martin Robinson Delany, 1812–1885* (New York: Doubleday,
1971), 83.

45. Buck and Buck, *Planting of Civilization*, 353–56; Birch, *Our Church and
Our Village*, 156. Lenore W. Bayus, *Beulah Presbyterian Church, 1784–1984* (Pittsburgh: Davis and Warde, 1984), 46.

46. Buck and Buck, *Planting of Civilization*, 353–54; *Records of the [Pres-
byterian] Synod of Pittsburgh from its First Organization September 29, 1802 to
October 1832, Inclusive* (Pittsburgh: Shyrock, 1852), 130–33; Bayus, *Beulah Presbyterian Church*, 46; *Centennial Volume of the First Presbyterian Church of Pittsburgh, Pennsylvania, 1784–1884* (Pittsburgh: William G. Johnston, 1884), 76.

47. For trade processions and the "Snag Marines," a group of Pittsburgh

steamboat captains who sponsored an annual winter parade of boats mounted on runners through the icy streets, see William G. Johnston, *Life and Reminiscences from Birth to Manhood of William G. Johnston* (New York: Knickerbocker, 1901), 40–41, 51; for professional groups see, for example, an account of the Western Medical Society, a debate club for doctors, in the *Pittsburgh Gazette*, Dec. 9, 1815.

48. Robert Bruce, *The National Road* (Washington, D.C.: National Highways Association, 1916), 59; Searight, *The Old Pike*, 220–21, 225; ad for "Pratt's Fashionable Hair Dressing" in Jones, *Pittsburgh in 1826*; Young, *History of My Life*, 2–4, 31.

49. *Pittsburgh Post*, Jan. 18, 1859, quoted in S. Kussart, "Navigation on the Monongahela River," in "Kussart Scrapbooks," vol. 2, 88, in collection of the Pennsylvania Department, Carnegie Library of Pittsburgh; Timothy Flint, *Recollections of the Last Ten Years in the Valley of the Mississippi*, ed. George R. Brooks (1826; reprint, Carbondale: Southern Illinois University Press, 1966), 15. For more on the boatman's life generally, see chap. 4, "The Boatmen," in Leland Baldwin, *The Keelboat Age on Western Waters* (Pittsburgh: University of Pittsburgh Press, 1941); James M. Miller, *The Genesis of Western Culture: The Upper Ohio Valley, 1800–1825* (Columbus: Ohio State Archaeological and Historical Society, 1938), 140–41, and Michael Allen, *Western Rivermen, 1763–1861: Ohio and Mississippi Boatmen and the Myth of the Alligator Horse* (Baton Rouge: Louisiana State University Press, 1990).

50. On Mike Fink, see Charles H. Ambler, *A History of Transportation in the Ohio Valley* (Glendale, Calif.: Arthur Clark, 1932), 53–58; Young, *History of My Life*, 21–22; *Pittsburgh Monthly Museum and Record of the Times* 1, no. 9 (Nov. 1846): 141; *Iron City*, May 28, 1842. Elliott Gorn offers an interpretation of frontier violence that includes the boatmen in "Gouge and Bite, Pull Hair and Scratch," 18–43.

Mrs. Houston is quoted from her *Hesperos: Or, Travels in the West*, 2 vols. (London: J. W. Parker, 1850), 265; the historian of Sewickley is Franklin Taylor Nevin, *The Village of Sewickley* (Sewickley, Pa.: n.p., 1929), 30.

51. Henry B. Fearon, *Sketches of America*, 2d. ed. (London: Longman, Hurst, Rees, Orme and Brown, 1818), 297; Morris Birkbeck, *Notes on a Journey in America* (1818; reprint, Ann Arbor: University Microfilms, 1966), 40; *Pittsburgh Gazette*, June 3, 1831, March 20, 1832; *Washington Reporter*, Jan. 22, 1848.

52. John Palmer, *Journal of Travels in the United States of North America and in Lower Canada, Performed in the Year 1817* (London: Sherwood, Neely, Jones, 1818), 52; Flint, *Letters from America*, 88; Birkbeck, *Notes on a Journey in America*, 41. For domestic accounts of the leisure of laborers and the lower class generally, see the *Pittsburgh Morning Chronicle*, Sept. 20, 1841, and the police reports that appeared regularly in the *Iron City* during the 1840s.

53. On the self-definition of various groups through leisure, cf. Click, *Spirit of the Times*, 19, 83–85.

On the role of leisure in resisting dominant stereotypes and ideologies see, for example, Rhyss Isaac's work on the Baptists' challenge to the prerevolutionary Virginia gentry through rejection of deference and elite leisure, in *The Transformation of Virginia*. In addition, see Stuart Hall and Tony Jefferson, *Resistance Through Rituals: Youth Subcultures in Post-War Britain* (London: Hutchinson, 1976), for explorations of how working class youth in twentieth-century Britain have used leisure to resist dominant norms.

Chapter 3: The Transformation of Leisure: Commercialization, Fragmentation, and Privatization

1. Jones, *Pittsburgh in 1826*, 42, 44.

2. Hugh Cunningham has made a similar point for the case of nineteenth-century British leisure, criticizing Robert Malcolmson's contention that the period was one of decline and decay for traditional amusements. See Cunningham's *Leisure in the Industrial Revolution* (New York: St. Martin's, 1980), especially 9–14; and Malcolmson's *Popular Recreations*. For a more theoretical discussion of the process of change in traditional societies, see Joseph R. Gusfield, "Tradition and Modernity: Misplaced Polarities in the Study of Social Change," *American Journal of Sociology* 72 (1966): 351–62.

3. On developments in transportation, see George Rogers Taylor's classic *The Transportation Revolution*, vol. 4 of *The Economic History of the United States* (White Plains, N.Y.: M. E. Sharpe, 1951). On the market revolution, see Sean Wilentz, "Society, Politics, and the Market Revolution, 1815–1848," in *The New American History*, ed. Eric Foner (Philadelphia: Temple University Press, 1990), 51–71; Harry Watson, *Liberty and Power: The Politics of Jacksonian America* (New York: Noonday, 1990), especially 17–41; and Sellers, *The Market Revolution*.

4. U.S. Census, statistical summary, 1820, 1840. For more on the commercial growth of the region, see Reiser, *Pittsburgh's Commercial Development*; and chap. 1 of Michael Holt's *Forging a Majority: The Formation of the Republican Party in Pittsburgh, 1848–1860* (New Haven: Yale University Press, 1969).

5. Holt, *Forging a Majority*, 17–22. For more on the industrial development of southwestern Pennsylvania, see also the various U.S. Census reports that detailed manufacturing; for example, Book 2 of the 1820 Census, *Digest of the Accounts of Manufacturing Establishments in the United States and of Their Manufactures* (Washington: Gales and Seaton, 1823); or the Census of 1860's *Manufactures of the United States in 1860; Compiled from the Original Returns of the Eighth Census* (Washington: Government Printing Office, 1865).

6. *Pittsburgh Gazette*, Feb. 27, 1824.

7. On the William Penn and Lincoln Highways, see William Shank, *Indian Trails to Super Highways*, 2d ed. (York, Pa.: American Canal and Transportation Center, 1974), 20–25; Robert Bruce, *The Lincoln Highway in Pennsylvania* (Washington, D.C.: American Automobile Association, 1920), esp. 12–22; George Swet-

nam, *Pennsylvania Transportation*, Pennsylvania Historical Studies, No. 7 (Gettysburg: Pennsylvania Historical Association, 1964), 16.

8. Searight, *The Old Pike*, 264, 273; James Hadden, *A History of Uniontown* (Uniontown, Pa.: n.p., 1913), 424; Bruce, *The National Road*, 73; Forrest, *History of Washington County*, 736–61. See also Norris F. Schneider, *The National Road, Main Street of America* (Columbus: Ohio Historical Society, 1975).

9. Robert McCullough and Walter Leuba, *The Pennsylvania Main Line Canal* (Martinsburg, Pa.: Morrison's Cove Herald, 1962), 86; William Shank, *The Amazing Pennsylvania Canals*, 4th ed. (York, Pa.: American Canal and Transportation Center, 1981), 13–16, 19–24.

10. Mrs. Houston, a British traveler in the 1840s, described the trip from Uniontown to Pittsburgh by road and steamer in *Hesperos*, 255–61. For a general overview of the emergence of tourism, see Horace Sutton, *Travelers: The American Tourist from Stagecoach to Space Shuttle* (New York: Morrow, 1980); and Sears, *Sacred Places*.

11. Shank, *Amazing Pennsylvania Canals*, 39. One illustration of this dissemination was the advertisement of leisure goods and services, especially bookstores, in distant cities. By the 1840s, for example, newspapers and almanacs from Washington and Pittsburgh contained advertisements for stores in both cities.

12. Philip D. Jordan, *The National Road* (New York: Bobbs-Merrill, 1948), 327; Searight, *The Old Pike*, 229–31.

13. Boucher, *Old and New Westmoreland*, 463; Jordan, *National Road*, 253, 333; see also Forrest, *History of Washington County*, 924.

14. On the emergence and development of minstrelsy, see Robert Toll, *Blacking Up: The Minstrel Show in Nineteenth Century America* (New York: Oxford University Press, 1974); Dulles, *History of Recreation*, 128–31; and Russell B. Nye, *The Unembarassed Muse: The Popular Arts in America* (New York: Dial, 1970), 162–67. On the class and racial dynamics of blackface minstrelsy, see Alexander Saxton's "Blackface Minstrelsy and Jacksonian Ideology," *American Quarterly* 27 (March 1975): 3–28; and his *The Rise and Fall of the White Republic: Class Politics and Mass Culture in Nineteenth-Century America* (London: Verso, 1990), 165–82; and Eric Lott, *Love and Theft: Blackface Minstrelsy and the American Working Class* (New York: Oxford University Press, 1993).

15. Jordan, *National Road*, 335–41; Ambler, *Transportation in the Ohio Valley*, 183; Johnston, *Reminiscences*, 45.

16. On this point, see Roy Rosenzweig, *Eight Hours for What We Will: Workers and Leisure in an Industrial City, 1870–1920* (Cambridge: Cambridge University Press, 1983), 179–80; Joseph S. Zeisel, "The Workweek in American Industry, 1850–1896," in *Mass Leisure*, ed. Eric Larrabee and Rolf Meyersohn (Glencoe, Ill.: Free Press, 1958), 145–53. For British leisure, consult James Walvin, *Leisure and Society 1830–1950* (New York: Longman, 1978), 60–64; and Hugh Cunningham, *Leisure in the Industrial Revolution*, 148–51. For a survey of leisure, commercialization, and work, see Cross, *Social History of Leisure*, 73–84, 123–39.

17. Buffum Diary, Nov. 4, 1847.

18. *Our Country* (Washington County), Aug. 9, 1837.

19. Buffum Diary, Dec. 27, 30, 1847.

20. Margaret C. Golden, "Directory of Theater Buildings in Pittsburgh, PA, since Earliest Times" (master's thesis, Carnegie Institute of Technology, Pittsburgh, 1953), 13; *Pittsburgh Gazette*, July 24, 1849. See also Edward G. Fletcher, "Records and History of Theatrical Activities in Pittsburgh, Pennsylvania, from Their Beginnings to 1861, in Two Volumes" (Ph.D. diss., Harvard University, 1931). In her study of amusements in the upper South, Patricia Click noted similar developments in newspaper advertising of leisure activities during the 1840s and 1850s. See her *Spirit of the Times*, 3, 92.

21. *Pittsburgh Statesman*, Aug. 29, 1818; *Greensburg Gazette*, June 25, 1824; *Westmoreland Republican*, Feb. 6, 1824; *Pittsburgh Statesman*, April 14, 1830. For an overview of the commercial development of leisure in Pittsburgh, see Alfred McClung Lee, "Trends in Commercial Entertainment in Pittsburgh as Reflected in the Advertising in Pittsburgh Newspapers (1790–1860)" (master's thesis, University of Pittsburgh, 1931).

22. *Pittsburgh Gazette*, April 24, 1818; *Pittsburgh Statesman*, July 25, 1818, July 2, 1828; *Pittsburgh Gazette*, Jan. 11, 1830, Nov. 5, 1831, July 10, 1832; *Harris's Intelligencer*, Nov. 11, 1837; *Pittsburgh Mercury*, March 21, 1838; *Allegheny Democrat*, Aug. 19, 1834; *Weekly Advocate and Statesman* (Pittsburgh), May 21, 1836; *Harris's Intelligencer*, Dec. 15, 1838; *Spirit of the Age* (Pittsburgh), May 2, 1844. Some of these attractions traveled all over the United States. Ah Fong Moy, for example, also toured the South; see Click, *Spirit of the Times*, 26, for an account of her visits to southern cities.

23. *American Manufacturer*, April 23, 1842. The appeal of seeing "Chaldean Miracles Exposed" may have had something in common with what Neil Harris has called the "operational aesthetic." See his *Humbug*, 59–90.

24. *Genius of Liberty* (Uniontown), June 20, 1831; *Washington Reporter*, July 17, 1847; *Washington Examiner*, Sept. 18, 1847; *Pennsylvania Argus*, Dec. 8, 1848. *Genius of Liberty* (Uniontown), Sept. 23, 1829; *Washington Examiner*, July 5, 1834; *Greensburg Sentinel*, Sept. 18, 1840; Jordan, *National Road*, 335–41; *Genius of Liberty*, Feb. 15, 1837; *Washington Examiner*, Oct. 5, 1818; *Our County* (Washington), Feb. 25, 1836; *Washington Examiner*, Jan. 25, 1845; *Pennsylvania Argus* (Greensburg), June 19, 1846.

25. *Pittsburgh Statesman*, Sept. 18, Nov. 3, 1833; *Allegheny Democrat*, April 14, 1834; *Pennsylvania Argus*, June 19, 1846; *Washington Examiner*, May 19, 1849.

26. Johnston, *Reminiscences*, 200; *Pittsburgh Gazette*, April 15, 1831; *Harris's General Business Directory of the Cities of Pittsburgh and Allegheny* (Pittsburgh: A. A. Anderson, 1841), 60; *American Manufacturer*, Aug. 7, 1841; *Pittsburgh Statesman*, July 22, 1829. See also *Pittsburgh Gazette*, Dec. 20, 1811; *Genius of Liberty*, June 6, 1831; and an 1831 broadside, "Books Published and for Sale to the Trade, at the Annexed Prices, by Luke Loomis & Co., Wood Street, Pittsburgh Penn-

sylvania," for more on bookstores. The Loomis broadside, which is in the collection of the American Antiquarian Society in Worcester, Massachusetts, contains a handwritten note to Mr. Kaufman, a Canton, Ohio, printer. Loomis offered to exchange books he printed for some of Kaufman's products, reflecting the expansion of markets for leisure commodities.

27. *Pittsburgh Gazette*, April 2, Nov. 8, 1819, Jan. 18, 1822; Erasmus Wilson, *Standard History of Pittsburgh* (Chicago: H. R. Cornell and Co., 1898), 867; *Harris's General Business Directory of the Cities of Pittsburgh and Allegheny* (1841), 60–61; *Harris's Intelligencer*, Oct. 21, 1837; *Genius of Liberty*, July 18, 1844.

28. *Pittsburgh Statesman*, July 23, 1828, Feb. 3, June 23, 1830; *Pittsburgh Gazette*, April 6, April 13, July 16, July 27, 1830; *American Manufacturer*, Nov. 27, 1841.

29. *Washington Reporter*, Aug. 26, 1816, April 28, 1817; *Genius of Liberty*, Oct. 10, 1831; *Pennsylvania Argus*, Nov. 28, 1834; *Pittsburgh Gazette*, April 18, April 25, 1823; *Genius of Liberty*, May 20, 1820; *Harris's Intelligencer*, March 10, 1838. On the popularity and prevalence of singing schools, see Fletcher, *Pennsylvania Agriculture*, 460; Carl Bode, *The Anatomy of American Popular Culture, 1840–1861* (Westport, Conn.: Greenwood, 1983), 36–37; Larkin, *Reshaping of Everyday Life*, 208, 254.

30. Rev. Richard Lea, *Reminiscences of Sixty Years of Presbyterianism in Western Pennsylvania* (Pittsburgh: n.p., 1886), 3; *Washington Examiner*, Aug. 5, 1822.

31. As used here, *fragmentation* does not connote the destruction or irrevocable loss of community but, rather, its redefinition along less inclusive and unified lines. As Thomas Bender notes in *Community and Social Change in America* (New Brunswick: Rutgers University Press, 1978), historians have recorded the loss of community in nearly every decade of American history, and yet the concept still has meaning and validity in discussing U.S. society.

32. Jones, *Pittsburgh in 1826*, 42. Population figures from U.S. Census Reports, 1800–1850.

33. Jones, *Pittsburgh in 1826*, 42; Rev. John Wrenshall, "Farewell to Pittsburgh and the Mountains, 1818," annotated by Isaac Craig, *Pennsylvania Magazine of History and Biography* 9, no. 1 (1885): 89–101, quoted from p. 96; *Harris's General Business Directory of the Cities of Pittsburgh and Allegheny* (1839), 2. The population figure of 60,000 included the city of Allegheny and the surrounding area along with Pittsburgh's population.

Cf. Click, *Spirit of the Times*, 52, on the impact of expanded theater options in the upper South during the 1840s.

34. The classic study is Robert Gray Gunderson, *The Log Cabin Campaign* (Lexington: University of Kentucky Press, 1957). For two differing perspectives on campaign tactics, see Michael F. Holt, "The Election of 1840, Voter Mobilization, and the Emergence of the Second Party System: A Reappraisal of Jacksonian Voting Behavior," and Jean H. Baker, "The Ceremonies of Politics: Nineteenth-Century Rituals of National Affirmation," both in *A Master's Due: Essays in*

Honor of David Herbert Donald, ed. William J. Cooper, Jr., Michael F. Holt, and John McCardell (Baton Rouge: Louisiana State University Press, 1985).

35. *Genius of Liberty,* Aug. 8, Aug. 27, 1828.

36. Hadden, *History of Uniontown,* 618, 695.

37. For examples of Whig log cabin and pole raisings, see Hadden, *History of Uniontown,* 618; *Genius of Liberty,* July 25, 1844; Johnston, *Reminiscences,* 226, 257.

38. *Allegheny Democrat,* May 6, May 9, 1834.

39. *Pennsylvania Argus,* July 6, 1838.

40. John N. Boucher, *History of Westmoreland County, Pennsylvania,* 2 vols. (New York: Lewis, 1906), 1:491; see also Boucher, *Old and New Westmoreland,* 461–62.

41. *Pittsburgh Gazette,* March 8, 1811.

42. *Pittsburgh Gazette,* Feb. 24, 1832; *Pittsburgh Statesman,* Feb. 21, Feb. 29, 1832; see also Johnston, *Reminiscences,* 40–41, for an eyewitness account of the trades procession. On the cultural importance of nineteenth-century parades, see Mary P. Ryan, "The American Parade: Representations of the Nineteenth-Century Social Order," in *The New Cultural History,* ed. Lynn Hunt (Berkeley and Los Angeles: University of California Press, 1989), 131–53; Wilentz, "Artisan Republican Festivals," 37–77; Susan Davis, *Parades and Power: Street Theater in Nineteenth-Century Philadelphia* (Philadelphia: Temple University Press, 1986).

43. *Pittsburgh Mercury,* March 1, 1837; *Our Country,* Feb. 1, Feb. 8, Feb. 22, March 1, 1837; *Washington Examiner,* March 4, 1837.

For background on Washington County antislavery, see Whitfield J. Bell, "Washington County, Pennsylvania, in the Eighteenth-Century Antislavery Movement," *Western Pennsylvania Historical Magazine* 25 (Sept.-Dec. 1942): 135–42.

44. *Pittsburgh Mercury,* March 6, 1839; *Iron City,* March 8, 1845; *Pittsburgh Gazette,* Jan. 24, 1832; Charles B. Scully Diary, Darlington Library, University of Pittsburgh, Feb. 22, 1843 (hereafter Scully Diary).

45. *Washington Examiner,* Feb. 15, 1840; Feb. 22, 1840.

46. Steven Nissenbaum noted a similar trend in the creation of Christmas and New Year's Day as privately celebrated holidays in early national New York City. To avoid boisterous crowds, New York's elite established new, more private patterns of holiday commemoration and celebration. See Nissenbaum, "Revisiting 'A Visit from St. Nicholas': The Battle for Christmas in Early Nineteenth-Century America," in *The Mythmaking Frame of Mind: Social Imagination and American Culture,* ed. James Gilbert et al. (Belmont, Calif.: Wadsworth, 1993), 25–70.

47. See Haltunnen, *Confidence Men and Painted Women;* Levine, *Highbrow/Lowbrow;* John Kasson, *Rudeness and Civility: Manners in Nineteenth-Century Urban America* (New York: Hill and Wang, 1990); and Richard L. Bushman, *The Refinement of America: Persons, Houses, Cities* (New York: Knopf, 1992).

48. Patricia Click also notes that privatization occurred in leisure during this period but views it as primarily an upper-class phenomenon. See Click, *Spirit of the Times*, 55, 84.

49. Jones, *Pittsburgh in 1826*, 29–30; *The Literary Casket* (Pittsburgh) 3, no. 1 (July 1842): 5–6.

50. "Women," *Genius of Liberty*, Oct. 18, 1809; John Armstrong, "The Duties of Married Women," *Patterson's Magazine Almanac for 1820* (Pittsburgh: Patterson and Lambdin, 1819). For more on domesticity and leisure, see Cross, *Social History of Leisure*, 103–09.

51. James M'Henry, "Home," in *The Pleasures of Friendship, A Poem in Two Parts; to Which are Added a Few Original Irish Melodies* (Pittsburgh: n.p., 1822), 67. Interestingly enough, M'Henry allowed the market to infiltrate even this vision of domestic delight:

> Whenever my sum of contentment is low,
> When a bankrupt in bliss, and embarrass'd with wo!
> At home I still find in the charms that are there,
> A fund that o'erpays, and discharges my care.

52. *Iron City*, Jan. 29, Feb. 5, Feb. 26, April 2, July 16, 1842; *Pittsburgh Gazette*, July 5, July 12, 1848, July 10, 1849.

On elite responses to this problem of increasingly fractious public leisure in the later decades of the nineteenth century, see chap. 3, "Order, Hierarchy, and Culture," in Levine, *Highbrow/Lowbrow*, 171–242.

53. Diary of Robert McKnight, Darlington Library, University of Pittsburgh (hereafter cited as McKnight Diary), Jan. 14, April 7, 1842.

54. *Iron City*, Oct. 1, 1842; Fearon, *Sketches of America*, 209; McKnight Diary, Dec. 14, 1846; *Pittsburgh Statesman*, Nov. 6, 1833. See also Levine, *Highbrow/Lowbrow*, 24–30, 178–83; Click, *Spirit of the Times*, 34–56; and Claudia D. Johnson, "That Guilty Third Tier: Prostitution in Nineteenth Century American Theaters," in *Victorian America*, ed. D. W. Howe (Philadelphia: University of Pennsylvania Press, 1976), 111–20.

55. *Washington Examiner*, July 11, 1835; *Harris's Intelligencer*, Aug. 25, 1838; *Iron City*, July 16, 1842.

56. *Iron City*, May 28, 1842; Scully Diary, March 30, 1843; *Genius of Liberty*, June 20, 1831.

57. Scully Diary, March 11, 17, June 2, 1843.

58. Cf. Roy Rosenzweig's account of the erosion by movies of ethnic culture among second- and third-generation Americans in *Eight Hours for What We Will*, 219–21.

59. *Harris's Intelligencer*, July 20, 1839. The *American Manufacturer*, May 11, 1842, contains a letter that addressed the issue of theater prices excluding people from performances; on volunteer fire companies and the working class, see Charles Dawson, ed., *Our Firemen: The History of the Pittsburgh Fire Department*

from the Village Period Until the Present (Pittsburgh: n.p., 1889), 23, 57, 60–61; Johnston, *Reminiscences*, 211–12; James Waldo Fawcett, "Quest for Pittsburgh Fire Department History," *Western Pennsylvania Historical Society Magazine* 49, no. 1 (Jan. 1966): 47–48; cf. Bruce Laurie, "Fire Companies and Gangs in Southwark: The 1840s," in *The People of Philadelphia: A History of Ethnic Groups and Lower Class Life, 1790–1840*, ed. Allen F. Davis and Mark H. Haller (Philadelphia: Temple University Press, 1973), 71–87.

Chapter 4: The Fourth of July in Southwestern Pennsylvania

1. Merle Curti, *The Roots of American Loyalty* (New York: Atheneum, 1968), 138–39; Bender, *Community and Social Change*, 98. See Steven J. Ross, *Workers on the Edge: Work, Leisure and Politics in Industrializing Cincinnati, 1788–1890* (New York: Columbia University Press, 1985), 23, for another account of the Fourth as a unifying communal event.

2. Charles Warren, "Fourth of July Myths," *William and Mary Quarterly* 2, no. 3, 3d series (July 1945): 254. See also Diane Carter Applebaum, *The Glorious Fourth: An American Holiday in American History* (New York: Facts on File, 1989), 34–49.
     William H. Cohn, "A National Celebration: The Fourth of July in American History," *Cultures* 3, no. 2 (1976): 146, 147.

3. Almost all Fourth of July observances included a procession, a reading of the Declaration of Independence, several orations, a dinner, and numerous toasts. For a discussion of the standard celebratory format, see Applebaum, *Glorious Fourth*, 36–43.

4. *Spirit of the Age*, July 4, 1843.

5. *Pittsburgh Statesman*, July 18, 1818. *Westmoreland Republican*, July 11, 1823.

6. *Westmoreland Intelligencer*, July 19, 1839.

7. Miller, *Chronicles of Families, Houses and Estates*, iii, 50–51, 26; Harvey B. Gaul, "The Minstrel of the Alleghenies," *Western Pennsylvania Historical Magazine* 34 (March 1951): 1, 5–6.

8. *Washington Reporter*, July 30, 1810.

9. On Jeffersonian political economy, see Drew R. McCoy, *The Elusive Republic: Political Economy in Jeffersonian Virginia* (New York: Norton, 1980).
     For more on this type of celebration and on preindustrial festivals in general, see Malcolmson, *Popular Recreations*; Fletcher, *Pennsylvania Agriculture*; Galley and Arnold, *History of the Galley Family*; Rev. Joseph Doddridge, *Notes on the Settlement and Indian Wars of the Western Parts of Virginia and Pennsylvania from 1763 to 1783, inclusive, together with a review of the Society and Manners of the first settlers of the Western Country* (1824; reprint, Pittsburgh: Rittenour and Lindsey, 1912).

10. "Manufacturers Dinner," *Pittsburgh Mercury*, July 8, 1823.

11. See the *Pittsburgh Statesman*, July 7, 1830, and July 6, 1831, for accounts of Snag Marine celebrations.

12. *Pittsburgh Mercury*, July 12, 1826. The artillery's reply was: "By the Company — 'The Society of Journeyman Shoemakers — May they ever receive the rewards due to benevolence.'" See the *Pittsburgh Gazette*, July 1, 1835, and the *Statesman*, June 23, 1830, for information on celebrations by artisans and mechanics.

13. *Pittsburgh Mercury*, July 13, 1836.

14. Rev. Sanson Brunot, "The Journal of the Reverend Sanson Brunot; A Partial Account of his Ministry at Blairsville and Greensburg, PA from the time of his Ordination May 9, 1830 until January 3, 1831," typescript, Carnegie Library of Pittsburgh, July 4, 1830.

For more on Sabbatarianism, see Richard R. John, "Taking Sabbatarianism Seriously: The Postal System, the Sabbath, and the Transformation of American Political Culture," *Journal of the Early Republic* 10, no. 4 (winter 1990): 517–67.

15. "Celebration Not Celebrated," *Washington Examiner*, July 16, 1821; *Washington Examiner*, July 22, 1822.

16. *Washington Reporter*, July 15, 1843. Anne Boylan's *Sunday School: The Creation of an American Institution, 1790–1880* (New Haven: Yale University Press, 1988), examines the historical development of Sabbath schools.

17. "Celebration by the Sons of Temperance," *Washington Examiner*, July 10, 1847. For other examples of temperance celebrations, see Westmoreland County's *Pennsylvania Argus*, July 11, 1845; and Fayette County's *Genius of Liberty*, July 7, 1842.

18. On the separate women's celebration in Greensburg, see the *Farmer's Register*, July 11, 1801.

On the family Fourth, see *Pittsburgh Statesman*, July 18, 1818. Even this family celebration was not all-inclusive. The gathering seems to have excluded young men, who met separately.

On the Canton Township celebration, see the *Washington Reporter*, July 19, 1845.

19. On the Monongahela River party, see the *Pittsburgh Statesman*, July 11, 1818.

On the Washington College students' meeting, see the *Washington Reporter*, July 17, 1815. For other student celebrations, see the *Washington Reporter*, July 7, 1817, and July 20, 1818.

On the Tusculum Association feast, see *Our Country*, July 14, 1836.

20. *Washington Report*, July 18, 1825, contains the derisive satire of a black Fourth celebration. The African Methodist Episcopal Church celebration is reported in the *Pittsburgh Daily Dispatch*, July 1, 1848.

21. *Iron City* and *Pittsburgh Weekly Chronicle*, July 9, 1845; *Pittsburgh Weekly Telegraph*, July 10, 1847.

22. *Pittsburgh Statesman*, July 18, 1818.

23. *Washington Reporter*, Aug. 7, 1820; Gaul, "Minstrel of the Alleghenies," 4.

24. "The Fourth of July, 1819," poem by Henry Sterling in Sterling Papers, Folder 6, Darlington Library, University of Pittsburgh (hereafter Sterling Papers).

25. Young, *History of My Life*, 22. *Allegheny Democrat*, July 7, 1835.

26. *Washington Reporter*, July 15, 1843.

27. *Genius of Liberty*, July 12, 1815.

28. For the Burgettstown celebration, see the *Washington Examiner*, July 17, 1823; on the Ligonier festivities, see the *Pennsylvania Argus*, July 10, 1840; for the comments of Uniontown Democrats, see the *Genius of Liberty*, June 22, 1840, July 13, 1840.

29. *Westmoreland Intelligencer*, July 11, 1834. William T. Barry was a Kentucky lawyer appointed to Jackson's cabinet as postmaster general on the merits of his unswerving loyalty to the president, rather than his administrative ability. See Watson, *Liberty and Power*, 99, 125.

30. For Craig's Antimasonic blast, see the *Pittsburgh Gazette*, July 9, 1835. See the *Pittsburgh Gazette*, July 24, 1835, for a glowing account of the Antimasonic Fourth. For the comments on Joseph Ritner, see the *Westmoreland Intelligencer*, July 10, 1835.

31. *Greensburg Gazette*, July 25, 1828.

32. *Pittsburgh Statesman*, July 1, 1829.

33. On the Working Men's celebration, see the *Pittsburgh Mercury*, July 9, 1835. A similar celebration took place in Washington, Pennsylvania; see *Our Country*, July 9, 1835.

On the competing celebration led by Richard Phillips, see the *Pittsburgh Mercury*, July 2, 1835.

34. *Pittsburgh Gazette*, July 24, 1837.

35. *Pittsburgh Statesman*, June 29, 1831.

36. *Pittsburgh Statesman*, July 6, 1831. For their part, the Jacksonians responded blandly: "The Tariff of 1828 — the rallying point of the friends of Domestic Industry."

37. *Pittsburgh Daily Dispatch*, July 4, 1848.

38. Letter from Milo A. Townsend, New Brighton, Pa., in Pittsburgh's *Spirit of Liberty*, July 15, 1842. By the late 1830s, antislavery societies, as well as colonization societies, routinely met on the Fourth, adapting the celebration of political independence to a plea for racial independence.

39. "Constitution of the Pittsburgh Antislavery Society, 1833," McClelland Family Papers, Series 2, Box 2, Folder 1, in collection of Western Pennsylvania Historical Society; Searight, *The Old Pike*, 223–24; *Pittsburgh Gazette*, July 8, 1848.

40. See the *Washington Reporter*, July 17, 1820, for a plea from Jefferson College's Modern Forum for a more "grateful remembrance" of the day; see the *Washington Reporter*, July 1, 1843, for an editorial on the loss of community in Fourth celebrations.

On the militia celebration in Westmoreland County, see the *Westmoreland Intelligencer*, July 19, 1839.

41. *Genius of Liberty*, July 13, 1840; *Washington Examiner*, July 10, 1847; *Spirit of Liberty*, July 9, 1842.

42. "The Fourth," *Pittsburgh Morning Chronicle*, July 1, 1843.

43. This pattern in southwestern Pennsylvania contradicts Diane Carter Applebaum's contention that Sunday school, temperance, and abolitionist celebrations "remained auxiliary events, not the central celebration of Independence Day." See Applebaum, *Glorious Fourth*, 72.

44. *Spirit of the Age*, July 4, 1843; *Pittsburgh Daily Aurora*, July 8, 1843; *Washington Reporter*, July 8, 1843.

45. *Pennsylvania Argus*, July 10, 1847.

46. "The Fourth in Birmingham," *Pittsburgh Weekly Telegraph*, July 10, 1847.

47. See, for example, Greensburg's *Pennsylvania Argus*, July 10, 1846; and the *Pittsburgh Telegraph*, July 10, 1847.

48. Scully Diary, July 4, 1843; McKnight Diary, July 4, 1842, and July 4, 1846. *Morning Chronicle*, July 4, 1842.

49. Vigilant Fire Company Minute Book, June 18, 1838, in Vigilant Fire Company Papers, 1838–1888, Pennsylvania Department, Carnegie Library of Pittsburgh; *Washington Reporter*, June 19, 1842; *Pittsburgh Morning Dispatch*, July 1, 1848; *Pittsburgh Morning Chronicle*, July 1, 1850; Buffum Diary, July 4, 1848.

50. "The Glorious Fourth," *Washington Reporter*, July 1, 1843.

51. William Cohn notes this transition in his study of the Fourth but contends that it occurred at a much later date. Roy Rosenzweig also notes that the "rough" elements of the working class inclined toward recreation rather than reflection on the Fourth by the late nineteenth century. See Rosenzweig, *Eight Hours for What We Will*, 67–76. Patricia Click notes that amusements generally changed from edifying to entertaining events during the nineteenth century. See her *Spirit of the Times*, esp. 1–5, 21–33.

52. Buffum Diary, June 24, 1848; *Pittsburgh Gazette*, July 3, 1849; *Pittsburgh Gazette*, July 1, 1848.

53. *Pittsburgh Gazette*, June 29, 1835; July 8, 1835; *Harris's Intelligencer*, July 6, 1839.

54. See advertisements and notices in the *Spirit of the Age*, July 4, 1843; *Pittsburgh Gazette*, June 19–July 5, 1846; and *Pittsburgh Morning Chronicle*, July 1–July 10, 1846; Buffum Diary, July 4, 1848.

55. *Pittsburgh Gazette*, June 27, 1849.

56. *Pittsburgh Spirit of the Age*, July 4, 1843; Scully Diary, June 30, 1843. Note here too the subordination of the military celebration to a religious cause.

57. *Pittsburgh Morning Chronicle*, July 2, 1844; *Pittsburgh Gazette*, July 4, 1846; *Weekly Telegraph*, July 10, 1847; *Pittsburgh Morning Chronicle*, July 3, 1847.

58. *Pittsburgh Daily Dispatch*, July 4, 1848; Scully Diary, July 4, 1843. *Pittsburgh Gazette*, July 2, 1849; *Pittsburgh Daily Dispatch*, July 3, 1848.

For civic concerns about fireworks, see the *Pittsburgh Weekly Telegraph*, July 10, 1847.

59. *Pittsburgh Morning Chronicle*, July 2, 1844. *Pittsburgh Gazette*, July 2, 1849. *Pittsburgh Daily Dispatch*, July 3, 1848. *Pittsburgh Morning Chronicle*, July 3, 1847.

60. Gaul, "Minstrel of the Alleghenies," 3. See also the editor's suggestion that businesses be closed on the Fourth to enable artisans and mechanics to celebrate the day, in the *Washington Examiner* of July 4, 1835; or the letter from an "Old Merchant" recommending that stores be closed on the Fourth, in the *Pittsburgh Morning Chronicle*, July 4, 1844.

61. *Pittsburgh Daily Gazette*, July 2, 1839.

62. *Harris's Intelligencer*, June 29, 1839.

63. Gaul, "Minstrel of the Alleghenies," 3, 4. *Harris's Intelligencer*, July 6, 1839. *Morning Chronicle*, June 30, 1842. *Iron City and Pittsburgh Weekly Chronicle*, July 13, 1844.

64. *Iron City and Pittsburgh Weekly Chronicle*, July 2, 1845; *Pittsburgh Post*, July 8, 1850. The cricket match, played on the Allegheny Commons, was apparently a great attraction, drawing a large number of spectators.

65. *Pittsburgh Morning Chronicle*, July 3, 1847.

66. "The Celebration," *Pittsburgh Evening Telegraph*, July 10, 1847.

Chapter 5: Leisure, Culture, and the Creation of Class

1. Negotiating different approaches to class remains a problem for historians, as no one definition or theory will satisfy all critics or apply in every case. Some scholars emphasize wealth or occupation as the determining factor, while others focus on political power or control of the factors of production. For a useful discussion of the various approaches to class, see Nigel Thrift and Peter Williams, "The Geography of Nineteenth-Century Class Formation," in Thrift and Williams, eds., *Class and Space: The Making of Urban Society* (London: Routledge Kegan Paul, 1987), 1–24; see especially 2–12.

2. On this point, see Edward Pessen, *Riches, Class, and Power Before the Civil War* (Lexington, Mass.: D. C. Heath, 1973), especially 165–67. On southwestern Pennsylvania's working class, see Richard Oestreicher, "Working Class Formation, Development, and Consciousness in Pittsburgh, 1790–1860," in *City at the Point: Essays on the Social History of Pittsburgh*, ed. Samuel P. Hays (Pittsburgh: University of Pittsburgh Press, 1989), 111–50. Oestreicher defines class *development* as the "gradual development of common values, symbols, modes of thought and language, behavior, day-to-day living patterns, and formal institutions among the members of an economic class as a result of association or common experiences; that is the development of a working class culture or a social class," (111–12). I am attempting to discern through the examination of leisure practices

this process of class development not only for the working class but for the middle and upper classes as well.

3. See the (Pittsburgh) *Literary Messenger* 1, no. 4 (Sept. 1840): 29, for a discussion of antebellum notions of class division.

4. Brackenridge, *Recollections*, 66. For more on Pittsburgh's founders, see Joseph Rishel, *Founding Families of Pittsburgh: The Evolution of a Regional Elite, 1760–1910* (Pittsburgh: University of Pittsburgh Press, 1990). On patterns of land ownership in early southwestern Pennsylvania, see Harper, *Transformation of Western Pennsylvania.*

5. Cuming, *Sketches of a Tour*, 71. Samuel Jones, *Pittsburgh in 1826* (Pittsburgh: n.p., 1826), 28.

6. For a description of working class formation in the Pittsburgh area, see Oestreicher, "Working Class Formation," 112–18. On working class leisure in this period, see Bruce Laurie, *Working People of Philadelphia, 1800–1850* (Philadelphia: Temple University Press, 1980); Paul Faler, "Cultural Aspects of the Industrial Revolution: Lynn, Massachusetts, Shoemakers and Industrial Morality, 1826–1860," in *Labor History* 15: 367–94; Richard Stott, *Workers in the Metropolis: Class, Ethnicity and Youth in Antebellum New York City* (Ithaca: Cornell University Press, 1990); Ross, *Workers on the Edge;* Stansell, *City of Women,* especially 77–100.

7. Cuming, *Sketches of a Tour*, 70.

8. Jones, *Pittsburgh in 1826*, 43; Young, *History of My Life*, 27.

9. Cuming, *Sketches of a Tour*, 70; Flint, *Recollections of the Last Ten Years*, 18.

10. Jones, *Pittsburgh in 1826*, 29–30.

11. Elizabeth Simpson (Darragh) Bladen, *Old Bedford* (n.p., n.d.), 55.

12. Cuming, *Sketches of a Tour*, 86–87.

13. Jones, *Pittsburgh in 1826*, 43.

14. On the importance of style for class differentiation, see Stuart Ewen, *All Consuming Images: The Politics of Style in Contemporary Culture* (New York: Basic, 1988), especially 24–40.

15. *The Diary of Lucy Ann Higbee*, 25–28 (June 6, 7, 8, 1837).

16. (Pittsburgh) *Literary Messenger* 1, no. 4 (Sept. 1840): 29.

On upper class solidarity and separateness from those below, see Miller, *Chronicles of Families, Houses and Estates,* iii, 5, 9–10, 15–17, 24–28, 48–51, 101–103.

17. Mrs. Ellen Blythe, Letters to Her Brother, John C. Green, Esq. Letter #2, June 9, 1835, in Pennsylvania Department, Carnegie Library of Pittsburgh.

18. Brackenridge, *Recollections*, 55.

On the wartime tax, see the *Genius of Liberty*, Feb. 8, 1815.

The dashing set is chronicled in the *Tree of Liberty*, March 26, 1803; *Commonwealth*, Sept. 7, 1814, July 22, 1815; *Pittsburgh Mercury*, Oct. 12, 1814.

19. Scully Diary, July 13, 1843. Annie Clark Miller noted that Homewood "had the reputation of being the most fashionable and aristocratic country-seat in Western Pennsylvania" and that it was "a record of the intelligence, culture, and refinement of a great Pittsburgher," in her *Chronicles of Families, Houses and Estates*, 101.

McKnight Diary, vol. 1, Oct. 21, 1842, March 25, 1847. See also Miller, *Chronicles of Families, Houses and Estates*, 15.

20. Buffum Diary, Nov. 25, Dec. 27, Nov. 16, 1847, Feb. 24, 1848.

21. The point here is not that economic and financial power was unimportant for differentiating the classes but, rather, that the ideological justification of economic inequality stemmed in part from social distinctions based in leisure practices. If the middle (or working) class could acquire the requisite social "graces" through participation in genteel leisure, they too could claim cultural authority and place economic inequities as determinants of class in high relief.

22. *Pittsburgh Mercury*, March 8, 1817.

23. McKnight Diary, Sept. 8, 29, 1842, typescript pp. 223–28, 247. Advertisements for schools and teachers were numerous throughout the period. See, for example, *Pittsburgh Commonwealth*, June 3, 1811, Oct. 6, 1812; *Harris's Intelligencer*, March 10, Nov. 10, 1838, July 16, 1839.

24. Letter from "Oroscor," in *The Hesperus and Western Miscellany* (Pittsburgh) 1, no. 4 (March 29, 1828): 28; *The Friend*, April 2, 1835.

25. Brian Harrison, *Drink and the Victorians* (Pittsburgh: University of Pittsburgh Press, 1971), and Brian Harrison, "Religion and Recreation in Nineteenth-Century England," *Past and Present* 38 (1967): 98–125; Brian Harrison, "Pubs," vol. 1, *The Victorian City: Images and Realities*, ed. H. J. Dyos and Michael Wolff (London: Routledge & Kegan Paul, 1973), 161–90.

For more on the Young Men's Society, see, for example, *The Friend*, Jan. 1 and 8, 1835.

26. *Pittsburgh Mercury*, Oct. 26, 1816, Jan. 25, 1817.

27. McKnight Diary, Aug. 6, 1846.

28. *Our Country*, Nov. 12, 1835.

29. *Greensburg Sentinel*, Jan. 8, 1841. For more on sleighing, see Fletcher, *Pennsylvania Agriculture*, 449.

30. Jane Grey, "Summer and Winter," *Western Literary Magazine* 4, no. 5 (Feb. 1844): 111.

31. "Who Did It?" *American Manufacturer*, May 11, 1842.

32. Francis Courtney Wemyss, *Theatrical Biography: or The Life of an Actor and Manager* (Glasgow: R. Griffin and Co., 1848), 194.

33. Young, *History of My Life*, 2, 3, 4–5, 31.

34. Jones, *Pittsburgh in 1826*, 28–29.

35. David S. Roediger and Philip S. Foner, *Our Own Time: A History of American Labor and the Working Day* (Westport, Conn.: Greenwood, 1989), 22, 36, 59–62.

36. Johnston, *Reminiscences*, 40–41. See also *Pittsburgh Gazette*, Feb. 24, 1832. On workers' processions, see Davis, *Parades and Power*, especially 113–53.

37. *Pittsburgh Mercury*, March 1, 1837. *Iron City*, April 2, 1842; *American Manufacturer*, March 26, 1842.

38. *Pittsburgh Statesman*, Aug. 19, 1829. On public leisure space as contested ground, see Davis, *Parades and Power*, 23–48; Francis G. Couvares, *The Remaking of Pittsburgh: Class and Culture in an Industrializing City, 1877–1919* (Albany: State University of New York Press, 1984), especially 105–119.

39. *City of Greensburg*, 251.

40. Johnston, *Reminiscences*, 200; *Pittsburgh Mercury*, Aug. 7, 1827.

41. "Our Public Square," *Washington Reporter*, April 29, 1843. "A Green House Novelty," *Washington Reporter*, Aug. 12, 1843.

42. Ludlow, *Dramatic Life*, 59; *City of Greensburg*, 251; Young, *History of My Life*, 40–41.

43. *Pittsburgh Mercury*, June 15, 1816; *Pittsburgh Gazette*, June 3, 1831; March 20, 1832.

44. Miller, *Chronicles of Families, Houses and Estates*, 39.

45. Cuming, *Sketches of a Tour*, 67. On the alleged health benefits available to wealthy patrons of the springs, see articles in *Cramer's Magazine Almanac for the Year of Our Lord 1808* (Pittsburgh: Zadock Cramer, 1808), 50; and *Cramer's Magazine Almanac for the Year of Our Lord 1824* (Pittsburgh: Zadock Cramer, 1824), 66–70.

46. *Iron City*, Aug. 13, 1842, July 13, 1844.

47. Bladen, *Old Bedford*, 53.

48. Ibid., 54–55.

49. *Harris's Intelligencer*, Nov. 11, 1837.

50. *Genius of Liberty*, May 11, 1840; *Iron City*, Aug. 6 and 13, 1845. *Washington Examiner*, Aug. 4, 1849. See also *Pittsburgh Gazette*, July 19, 1837; *Our Country*, July 2, 1835; *Washington Examiner*, July 29, 1837; *Washington Reporter*, July 1, 1848, July 24, 1850, for more on Frankfurt Springs. Scully Diary, Aug. 4–18, 1843; McKnight Diary, July 26, 1846.

51. For information on Summerville Springs, Baily's Springs, and Scully's Springs, see the *Allegheny Democrat*, March 22, 1835, June 29, 1838; *Pittsburgh Weekly Advocate*, June 29, 1838. Johnston, *Reminiscences*, 160. See also *American Manufacturer*, May 18, 1842, for more on Mt. Emmet.

52. *Pittsburgh Statesman*, June 1, July 6, 1831. *Pittsburgh Gazette*, July 1, 1848, June 27, 1849. *Pittsburgh Mercury*, June 13, 1838. *Washington Reporter*, July 24, 1850.

53. John G. Cawelti, *Apostles of the Self-Made Man* (Chicago: University of Chicago Press, 1965), 60. This theme continued to resonate in the work of Horatio Alger and other success writers after the war.

54. Cuming, *Sketches of a Tour*, 81–82; *Pittsburgh Statesman*, July 18, 1818.

55. Minutes of the Washington Musical Society (1825), Washington County Historical Society, Washington, Pennsylvania.

56. On the Associated Singing Society, see Constitution and Treasurer's Report of the Associated Singing Society (1820), Folder 1, Sterling Papers.

Charles Scully is quoted from the Scully Diary, June 12, 1843.

57. Richard Wade has noted that these clubs "were quasi-academic in purpose, but their main function was to maintain class ties," in his *Urban Frontier*, 209. See also Pessen, *Riches, Class, and Power*, 221–47.

58. *Constitution and By-Laws of the Pittsburgh Horticultural Society* (Pittsburgh: n.p., 1834); *Constitution and By-Laws of the Pittsburgh Horticultural Society* (Pittsburgh: n.p., 1848), 3, 6.

59. W. T. Wiley, "Anniversary Address, delivered before the Apollonian Literary Society of Madison College, Uniontown, Pennsylvania, February 22, 1842," in "Addresses Delivered Before the Schools and Colleges of Pennsylvania," in Pennsylvania Department, Carnegie Library of Pittsburgh.

60. *Literary Messenger* 1, no. 1 (June 1840): 5.

On the Philological Institute, see *Harris's Intelligencer*, Dec. 14, 1839; *Harris's Pittsburgh and Allegheny Directory* (Pittsburgh: n.p., 1839), 199.

On the Wirt Institute, see the *Literary Messenger* 1, no. 6 (Nov. 1840): 45; *American Manufacturer*, Jan. 15, 1842.

61. Neptune Fire Company Minutes, July 15, 1845, in Historical Society of Western Pennsylvania; *Constitution and By-Laws of the Young Men's Mercantile Library and Mechanic's Institute of Pittsburgh, Pennsylvania* (Pittsburgh: n.p., 1847), 3, 5–6. Pittsburgh's black community supported a literary society as well. The Theban Literary Society, founded by Martin R. Delany and others in the early 1830s, emerged from a desire to associate for "intellectual and moral improvement." See Sterling, *Martin Robinson Delany*, 39.

62. *American Manufacturer*, Feb. 19, Feb. 26, 1842.

63. On the Tilghman Literary Society, see the *Literary Messenger* 11, no. 5 (Oct. 1841): 37.

The newspaper piece on literary societies is "Literary Associations," *Iron City*, June 8, 1844.

On the Philological Institute meeting, see *Harris's Intelligencer*, Nov. 11, 1837.

On the Marshall Institute, see *Harris's Intelligencer*, Aug. 17, 1839.

64. *Pittsburgh Mercury*, Feb. 13, 1839.

65. *Pittsburgh Mercury*, Feb. 13, 1839.

66. Cawelti, *Apostles of the Self-Made Man*, 43–46. On the ideology of social mobility, see Eric Foner, *Free Soil, Free Labor, Free Men: The Ideology of the Republican Party* (New York: Oxford University Press, 1970).

67. *Genius of Liberty*, May 30, Aug. 1, Sept. 26, Oct. 10, 17, 31, 1831; *Washington Examiner*, March 13, 1847.

68. *Constitution and By-Laws of the Young Men's Mercantile Library and Mechanic's Institute of Pittsburgh* (Pittsburgh: n.p., 1847), 23.

69. Jane Elizabeth Hobbs, "Old Jefferson College" (master's thesis, University of Pittsburgh, 1929), 71; Brackenridge, *Recollections*, 90. See also Frederick J. Frank, "Student Life in Selected Colleges in the Early Nineteenth Century" (Ph.D. diss., University of Pittsburgh, 1975), 101–105, 268–86.

70. Sterling Papers, Folder 5, "PQ Society." Sterling's affection for his own wit, not his background, stood in the way of social advancement. In response to a sarcastic poem by Sterling concerning a Fourth of July outing, prominent Pittsburgher J. B. Butler wrote "I am an enthusiastic admirer of *females* and allways [*sic*] feel pride and satisfaction in defending them against the aspersions of a malignant snake." Butler completed his response with some verse of his own:

A misanthrope I hate in my heart.
That Sterling is one there's no doubt,
Or why does he take such a part
And of trifles make such a damnable rout?"

(Folder 6, Sterling Papers).

71. On Robert Galloway, see the Galloway Family Papers, Historical Society of Western Pennsylvania, Pittsburgh (hereafter Galloway Papers), Series 3, Robert Galloway: Folder 1, Play and Poetry, 1826; Folder 2, Poetry by Limerick Hotsepillar; Folder 5, Cookstown Debating Society, 1837.

On Samuel Young, see his *History of My Life*, 27. Students of the Western University of Pennsylvania, the precursor of the University of Pittsburgh, originally established the Marshall. Young later joined not the patrician Philo Institute or Tilghman Society, but the Franklin Literary Society. See *Harris's Business Directory for 1844* (Pittsburgh: n.p., 1844), 68.

72. A similar point could be made about race. Martin Delany's biographer, writing of Delany and his contemporaries in 1830s Pittsburgh, noted that "it was, perhaps to the literary society of Pittsburg [*sic*], resembling that formed by Franklin and his young associates, that the germ of their usefulness first came forth." Sterling, *Martin Robinson Delany*, 39.

73. *Pittsburgh Commonwealth*, Dec. 22, 1813; *Our Country*, Jan. 4, March 8, 1837.

74. *Allegheny Democrat*, May 24, June 24, 1825.

75. Dawson, *Our Firemen*, 26. Cf. Laurie, "Fire Companies and Gangs in Southwark: The 1840s."

76. Johnston, *Reminiscences*, 212, 211; Dawson, *Our Firemen*, 57.

77. Dawson, *Our Firemen*, 60–61; Johnston, *Reminiscences*, 209–11.

78. Scully Diary, Feb. 6, 1843; McKnight Diary, vol. 2, Aug. 30, 1846.

On Mose, see Walter J. Meserve, *Heralds of Promise: The Drama of the American People During the Age of Jackson, 1829–1849* (Westport, Conn.: Greenwood, 1986), 120–27; on firemen's political influence, see Scott C. Martin, "The

Great Brothel Dousing: Leisure, Reform, and Urban Change in Antebellum Pittsburgh," in *American Cities and Towns: Historical Perspectives*, ed. Joseph Rishel (Pittsburgh: Duquesne University Press, 1992), 26–38, especially 33–35.

79. J. Blan van Urk, *The Story of Rolling Rock* (New York: Scribner's Sons, 1950), xviii; Alfred Aversa, Jr., "Foxhunting: A Patrician Sport," *Review of Sport and Leisure* 6, no. 2 (1981): 83–100; John R. Betts, *America's Sporting Heritage 1850–1950* (Reading, Mass.: Addison-Wesley, 1974), 15.

80. See, for example, an advertisement for a proposed hunt in the *Washington Examiner*, Jan. 27, 1827.

81. *Washington Examiner*, Feb. 10, 1827.

82. *Pennsylvania Argus*, March 18, 1842; see also March 25, 1842.

See, for example, *Washington Examiner*, Feb. 9, 1828; *Westmoreland Intelligencer*, Feb. 14, March 28, 1834; *Pennsylvania Argus*, March 18 and 25, 1842, March 2, 1849, for more on disorder and attempts at control at circular hunts.

83. The historian quoted is van Urk, *Rolling Rock*, 50–51.

The Westmoreland County hunt is described in the *Pennsylvania Argus*, Feb. 21, 1840.

See Johnston, *Reminiscences*, 152.

84. *Genius of Liberty*, Oct. 18, 1815; Morris, "Old Springhill"; *City of Greensburg*, 195. Patricia Click found a similar pattern in the antebellum upper South. Once the upper class lost control of horse racing, they withdrew their support and participation. See her *Spirit of the Times*, 57–71.

85. Brynn, "Some Sports in Pittsburgh During the National Period, 1775–1860," 361, 59; Miller, *Chronicles of Families, Houses and Estates*, 24–25; Mrs. S. Kussart, *Early History of the Fifteenth Ward, City of Pittsburgh* (Pittsburgh: n.p., 1925), 40–41; Henry Oliver Evans, "Life in Pittsburgh in 1845," *Western Pennsylvania Historical Magazine* 28 (March-June 1945): 21.

86. Brynn, "Some Sports in Pittsburgh During the National Period, 1775–1860," 361. Trotting may have developed differently in other regions. John R. Betts argues that trotting was "first engaged in by the social aristocracy," (*America's Sporting Heritage*, 15). In the upper South, Patricia Click found that the lower and middle classes popularized trotting (*Spirit of the Times*, 69–70). Steven A. Reiss, on the other hand, suggests that the sport originated among the middle class and was taken over by wealthy urban sportsmen (*City Games: The Evolution of American Urban Society and the Rise of Sports* (Urbana: University of Illinois Press, 1989), 32–34).

87. *Pittsburgh Statesman*, Sept. 14, 1831, Nov. 21, 1832. See also John R. Betts, "Agricultural Fairs and the Rise of Harness Racing," *Agricultural History* 28 (1954): 71–75.

88. Joseph T. Holmes, "The Decline of the Pennsylvania Militia, 1815–1870," *Western Pennsylvania Historical Magazine* 57 (April 1974): 215, 213.

89. *Washington Reporter*, Sept. 30, 1811, June 15, 1812. Van Voorhis, *The Old and New Monongahela*, 380; McKnight Diary, Oct. 6, 1842.

90. "Brigade Orders," *Tree of Liberty*, March 7, 1801, Jan. 10, 1801. On the symbolic importance of militia uniforms, see Davis, *Parades and Power*, 61–62, 70.

91. *Tree of Liberty*, Nov. 4, 1801.

92. Tradition has it that Butler had the last word, instructing that a hole be cut in his coffin so that his queue could hang out. On the Butler-Wilkinson dispute, see Theodore J. Crackel, *Mr. Jefferson's Army: Political and Social Reform in the Military Establishment, 1801–1809* (New York: New York University Press, 1987), 116–19; and Miller, *Chronicles of Families, Houses and Estates*, 10–11; *Tree of Liberty*, March 27, 1802; *Washington Reporter*, Nov. 25, 1811.

93. *Pittsburgh Mercury*, Aug. 3, 1814; *Washington Reporter*, Aug. 28, 1815; *Pennsylvania Argus*, June 16, 1846.

94. On the cornstalk militia, see Fletcher, *Pennsylvania Agriculture*, 456; Garrison, "Battalion Day," 2–12; Davis, *Parades and Power*, 81, 84, 96.

95. *Iron City*, May 7, 1842. *Iron City*, May 28, 1842.

96. "Military Elections," *American Manufacturer*, June 11, 1842.

97. Garrison, "Battalion Day," 10–12. For a selection of Turner's work, see *The Ritual Process*, and *From Ritual to Theatre*. On "communitas," see Victor and Edith Turner, *Image and Pilgrimage in Christian Culture: Anthropological Perspectives* (New York: Columbia University Press, 1978), 250–55.

98. "The Encampment," *Iron City*, Sept. 10, 1842.

99. "Fun at the Encampment," *Iron City*, Sept. 10, 1842.

100. For an excellent account of burlesque militia parades in Philadelphia, see Davis, *Parades and Power*, 77–96.

101. "A Tall Animal — That Giraffe!" *Iron City*, Sept. 17, 1842.

102. "Fun at the Encampment," *Iron City*, Sept. 10, 1842.

Chapter 6: Engendering Leisure

1. Eliza Swift to Mrs. Keturah Young, Hanover, New Jersey, Folder 8 in Swift Family Papers (hereafter Swift Papers), Record Group 252, Box 1, Presbyterian Historical Society, Philadelphia, Pennsylvania.

2. On this point, see Christine Griffin, Dorothy Hobson, Sue MacIntosh, and Trisha McCabe, "Women and Leisure," in *Sport, Culture, and Ideology*, ed. Jennifer Hargreaves (London: Routledge Kegan Paul, 1982), 88–116; Eileen Green, Sandra Hebron, and Diana Woodward, *Women's Leisure, What Leisure?* (London: Macmillan, 1990); and the essays in Erica Wimbush and Margaret Talbot, eds., *Relative Freedoms: Women and Leisure* (Milton Keynes, U.K.: Open University Press, 1988). For more on feminist approaches to leisure, see Karla A. Henderson, "Broadening an Understanding of Women, Gender, and Leisure," *Journal of Leisure Research* 26, no. 1 (1994): 1–7; Susan Shaw, "Gender, Leisure, and Constraint: Toward a Framework for the Analysis of Women's Leisure," *Journal of Leisure Research* 26, no. 1 (1994): 8–22; and Karla A. Henderson, M. Deborah Bialeschki, Susan Shaw, and Valerie Freysinger, *A Leisure of One's*

Own: A Feminist Perspective on Women's Leisure (State College, Pa.: Venture Publishing, 1989).

3. Eliza Swift to Keturah Young, May 14, 1820, Swift Papers, Folder 18.

4. See Wimbush and Talbot, *Relative Freedoms*, xiv; and Cowan, *More Work for Mother*, 14.

5. To a lesser degree, this was also true of men's leisure. Fishing or hunting, for example, produced social enjoyment and camaraderie but also yielded useful commodities. The point is that a much higher proportion of men's leisure lacked any clear instrumental or productive purpose.

6. Cowan, *More Work for Mother*, 11; Catharine E. Beecher, *A Treatise on Domestic Economy for the Use of Young Ladies at Home and at School* (New York: Harper Brothers, 1845), 184–85; Eliza Swift to Lucy McComb, Nov. 27, 1825, Swift Papers, Folder 9.

7. Jane Grey Swisshelm, *Half A Century*, 3d ed. (Chicago: Jansen, McClurg and Co., 1880), 78. An excellent family history from Fayette County noted that "The welfare of the family depended on the success of home industries, and consequently the wife had much less leisure than the husband" (Galley and Arnold, *History of the Galley Family*, 162). On the magnitude and difficulty of women's housework, see Boydston, *Home and Work*, 75, 95–96; Cowan, *More Work for Mother*, 42–43.

8. Fletcher, *Pennsylvania Agriculture*, 107–22; Galley and Arnold, *Galley Family*, 179; Swisshelm, *Half a Century*, 45–46.

9. Fletcher, *Pennsylvania Agriculture*, 371; Jane Grey Swisshelm, *Letters to Country Girls* (New York: John C. Riker, 1853), 103; Swisshelm, *Half a Century*, 45–46. Ruth Schwartz Cowan and Jeanne Boydston suggest that a similarly unequal division of labor and leisure also characterized the lives of urban women. See note 22, below.

10. Galley and Arnold, *History of the Galley Family*, 198. One historian suggests that the sexual division of labor and leisure at frolics and bees differed among ethnic groups. German butchering frolics, for example, appear to have divided work more evenly between men and women than did their Scots-Irish equivalents. See Fletcher, *Pennsylvania Agriculture*, 442–43.

11. Galley and Arnold, *History of the Galley Family*, 202.

12. On the "naturalness" of women's roles, see Boydston, *Home and Work*, 48; and Diana Woodward and Eileen Green, " 'Not Tonight Dear!' The Social Control of Women's Leisure," in *Relative Freedoms: Women and Leisure*, ed. Erica Wimbush and Margaret Talbot (Milton Keynes, U.K.: Open University Press, 1988), 131–46. On men's and women's work in the urban middle class, see Cowan, *More Work for Mother*, 14. For a useful discussion of these issues in late twentieth-century Great Britain, see John Clarke and Chas Critcher, *The Devil Makes Work: Leisure in Capitalist Britain* (Urbana: University of Illinois Press, 1985), 160–61.

13. Swisshelm, *Letters to Country Girls*, 131–34; Linda Borish, "Forsaking

'Clothes Thumping' for 'Piano Thumping': Farmers' Daughters Quitting the Homestead in Antebellum New England" (paper delivered at the 1991 American Historical Association meeting, Chicago); Katherine Sklar, *Catharine Beecher: A Study in American Domesticity* (New Haven: Yale University Press, 1973), 205.

14. Diary of Nancy J. Kendall (hereafter Kendall Diary), typescript, in the collection of the Historical Society of Pennsylvania, Philadelphia, Sept. 27, Dec. 19, 1848.

15. Kendall Diary, Jan. 25, May 14, Nov. 1, 1848.

16. Kendall Diary, March 3, May 9, June 4, July 24, 1848; Feb. 21, 22, 1849.

17. Kendall Diary, Feb. 23, March 16, 1849. For Isaac's attendance at fox hunts, see March 20, 1848, Jan. 26, 1849.

Kendall Diary, Feb. 26, 27, 1848; see also Jan. 21, 1848.

18. Kendall Diary, June 12, May 26, 1848. Nancy Osterud's study of gender and labor patterns in New York state's Nanticoke Valley later in the nineteenth century suggests that women's acceptance, even enjoyment, of their work relationship to men was not uncommon. According to Osterud, under some economic and social structural conditions, women sought mutuality with men rather than a separate culture. See her " 'She Helped Me Hay It as Good as a Man': Relations Among Women and Men in an Agricultural Community," in *To Toil the Livelong Day: America's Women at Work 1780–1980*, ed. Carol Groneman and Mary Beth Norton (Ithaca: Cornell University Press, 1987), 87–97, and her *Bonds of Community: The Lives of Farm Women in Nineteenth-Century New York* (Ithaca: Cornell University Press, 1991).

19. Kendall Diary, Feb. 19, May 19, 1848.

20. On this point, see Woodward and Green, " 'Not Tonight Dear!' " 131; Griffin et al., "Women and Leisure"; Peiss, *Cheap Amusements*.

21. Swisshelm, *Half a Century*, 20.

22. See Matthews, *Just a Housewife*, 11–17. Jeanne Boydston and Ruth Schwartz Cowan contend that women did *not* have more free time. While tasks may have changed, they argue, women's work actually increased during the first half of the nineteenth century. See Boydston, *Home and Work*, 76–80; Cowan, *More Work for Mother*, 42–43.

23. Armstrong, "Duties of Married Females"; "Home," *Genius of Liberty*, March 30, 1819.

24. *Washington Reporter*, July 16, 1810.

25. "Women," *Genius of Liberty*, Oct. 18, 1809.

26. *Pittsburgh Mercury*, Aug. 1, 1817.

27. Account of the annual exhibition of Mrs. Baker's Pittsburgh school for girls, *Genius of Liberty*, Nov. 14, 1820.

28. Larkin, *Reshaping of Everyday Life*, 249; Miller, *Chronicles of Families, Houses and Estates*, 48; Palmer, *Journal of Travels*, 51.

29. Beecher, *Treatise on Domestic Economy*, 252–53; Catharine E. Beecher and Harriet Beecher Stowe, *The American Woman's Home* (New York: J. B. Ford,

1869), 296–97; Bode, *Anatomy of American Popular Culture*, 21–24. As the nineteenth century progressed, sacred music became a standard part of worship in most Protestant denominations, furthering its influence in the home. See Larkin, *Reshaping of Everyday Life*, 251–56.

30. The Belle Vernon Academy, for example, which William G. Johnston mentioned in his memoirs, charged $1.50 per week for board and $8 per session for tuition in "the balmy air, fresh from the hand of heaven" in contrast to the "atmosphere of the smoky and pent up city." With clothing and transportation figured in, an education at the academy became out of the question for working class or lower middle class girls. See Johnston, *Reminiscences*, 148–50; *Pittsburgh Spirit of the Age*, July 4, 1843. Another school for young women, the Western Collegiate Institute, in the "picturesque environs" of Laceyville, near Pittsburgh, charged thirty-eight dollars per term, with music, French, art, or dancing lessons extra. See the broadside, "Western Collegiate Institute for Young Ladies, Will Commence Its 19th Term on the 27th of February, 1837," in the collection of the American Antiquarian Society, Worcester, Massachusetts.

31. The classic formulation of this concept is Thorstein Veblen, *The Theory of the Leisure Class* (1899; reprint, New York: Penguin, 1986).

32. Edgeworth Seminary, conducted by an English couple at the "Mansion" at Braddock's Fields, was an exclusive school for upper class young women. Its rates were eighty dollars for twenty-two weeks, with an additional charge of twenty-four dollars for music instruction and five dollars for singing lessons. See Miller, *Chronicles*, 125; *Loomis's Magazine Almanac for 1839* (Pittsburgh: Luke Loomis, 1839); Swisshelm, *Half a Century*, 21–28.

33. Scully Diary, Jan. 17, June 20, Sept. 27, Feb. 17, 1843.

Diary of Robert McKnight (hereafter McKnight Diary) Darlington Library, University of Pittsburgh, Jan. 21, 1847; on the courtship, see Jan. 11, 1847, to May 27, 1847, especially March 1.

34. Bladen, *Old Bedford*, 53–54.

35. This behavioral model is related to what Barbara Welter, Nancy Cott, and others have dubbed the cult of true womanhood, the ideology of domesticity, and the doctrine of separate spheres. Clearly, evidence both supporting and questioning their tenets is readily available. My purpose here is not to affirm or contradict their usefulness as interpretive strategies. Rather, I am suggesting that however valid they are heuristically, these ideas did not dictate, nor necessarily describe, uniform behavior. Nor should they preclude the scholarly reconstruction and articulation of alternative and antagonistic cultural and ideological formations. On true womanhood, separate spheres, and domesticity, see Nancy Cott, *Bonds of Womanhood*; Barbara Welter, "The Cult of True Womanhood, 1820–1860," in *The American Family in Social-Historical Perspective*, ed. Michael Gordon (New York: St. Martin's, 1978), 313–33; and Linda Kerber, "Separate Spheres, Female Worlds, Woman's Place: The Rhetoric of Women's History," *Journal of American History* 75, no. 1 (June 1988): 9–39.

36. Cott, *Bonds of Womanhood*, especially 200–201; Matthews, *Just a Housewife*, 35–65.

37. *Washington Examiner*, July 13, 1833.

38. *Westmoreland Republican*, July 10, 1819; *Pittsburgh Mercury*, July 18, 1820; *Washington Examiner*, July 15, 1848.

39. *Pittsburgh Gazette*, Jan. 28, 1815; *Uniontown Genius of Liberty*, Jan. 4, 1817; *Pittsburgh Times*, Nov. 8, 1837; *Pittsburgh Gazette*, June 3, 1831, March 23, 1832; *Harris's Intelligencer*, Sept. 17, 1839; *Pittsburgh Mercury*, Oct. 26, 1814; *Pittsburgh Gazette*, Nov. 8, 1814, June 18, 1823.

40. Rural society also displayed patterns of all-male sociability. In nearby Bedford County, for instance, farm men held stag husking bees: "The whiskey bottle goes round, the story, the laugh and the rude songs . . . sometimes the frolic ends with a stag dance; that is, men and boys, without females, dance like mad devils in good humor to the time of a neighbor's cat-gut and horse-hair." Thomas Gordon, *Gazetteer of the State of Pennsylvania* (Philadelphia: T. Belknap, 1832), 33; quoted in Fletcher, *Pennsylvania Agriculture*, 442.

41. Rev. W. A. Passavant, *Address delivered before the Franklin Literary Society, of Jefferson College, at its Semi-Centennial Anniversary, November 14th, 1847* (Washington, Pa.: John Bausman, 1848), 10; "Constitution of the Associated Singing Society," Sterling Papers.

42. Recently, historians have reconsidered women's participation in the public sphere, concluding that a female presence was more common than has been imagined. See Mary P. Ryan, *Women in Public: Between Banners and Ballots, 1825–1880* (Baltimore: Johns Hopkins University Press, 1990); and Glenna Matthews, *The Rise of Public Woman: Woman's Power and Woman's Place in the United States, 1630–1970* (New York: Oxford University Press, 1992).

43. *The Friend* (Pittsburgh), Jan. 1, 1835; *Harris's Intelligencer*, Oct. 6, 1838; *Literary Messenger* (Pittsburgh) 1, no. 10 (March 1841); *Washington Examiner*, March 2, 1850.

44. *Washington Banner* (Pittsburgh), Dec. 17, 1842; *American Manufacturer* (Pittsburgh), Dec. 18, 1841.

45. *Pittsburgh Mercury*, May 14, 1835; Wemyss, *Theatrical Biography*, 196–97; *Harris's Intelligencer*, Sep. 21, 1839; *Our Country*, Feb. 25, 1836.

46. *Pittsburgh Commonwealth*, May 7, 1810; *Washington Reporter*, Oct. 4, 1818; *Pittsburgh Statesman*, July 25, Oct. 31, Nov. 24, 1818.

47. *Our Country*, June 23, 1836; *Genius of Liberty*, June 22, 1840; *Washington Reporter*, July 5, 1845; *Pittsburgh Gazette*, July 1, 1846; *Washington Reporter*, Oct. 3, 1849.

48. Sterling, *Martin Robinson Delany*, 83; *Pittsburgh Telegraph*, April 24, 1847; *Pittsburgh Dispatch*, July 1, 1848.

49. *Allegheny Democrat*, Dec. 30, 1834; *Pittsburgh Telegraph*, April 24, 1847; *Pittsburgh Gazette*, July 3, 1849.

50. *Pittsburgh Commonwealth*, Feb. 5, 1806; Edward G. Fletcher, "Records and History of Theatrical Activities in Pittsburgh," 23; *Pittsburgh Weekly Advocate and Statesman*, May 21, 1836; *Washington Examiner*, July 12, 1845. On actresses in nineteenth-century America, see Claudia D. Johnson, *American Actress: Perspectives on the Nineteenth Century* (Chicago: Nelson-Hall, 1984), and Faye E. Dudden, *Women in the American Theatre: Actresses and Audiences, 1790–1870* (New Haven: Yale University Press, 1994).

51. *Washington Reporter*, May 9, 1846; Fletcher, "Records and History of Theatrical Activities in Pittsburgh," 137–44. On Abby Kelley, see Dorothy Sterling, *Ahead of Her Time: Abby Kelley and the Politics of Antislavery* (New York: Norton, 1991).

52. Ludlow, *Dramatic Life*, 57, 64–65.

53. *Washington Reporter*, Nov. 2, 1812, Oct. 11, 1813, April 19, 1845; *Westmoreland Intelligencer*, April 27, 1849.

On separate spheres and other ways of conceptualizing gender roles, see Kerber, "Separate Spheres, Female Worlds, Woman's Place."

54. On female education and its relationship to woman's "sphere," see Cott, *Bonds of Womanhood*, 101–25.

55. Letter from "Jeremy Broadcloth," *Washington Reporter*, Aug. 24, 1818; originally printed in the *New Haven Herald*.

56. On the low quality of antebellum female education, see Ann Douglas, *The Feminization of American Culture* (New York: Avon, 1972), 65–70; and Cott, *Bonds of Womanhood*, 104–107.

Quotations in this paragraph are from the *Genius of Liberty*, May 30, 1820; *The Hesperus and Western Miscellany* (Pittsburgh) 1, no. 4 (March 29, 1828): 28. See also Cott, *Bonds of Womanhood*, 110–11, for a discussion of middle class opposition to female education on these grounds.

57. "On Dancing," *Pittsburgh Recorder* 2, no. 3 (Feb. 7, 1823): 41–42; "On Female Education," *The Hesperus and Western Miscellany* (Pittsburgh) 1, no. 15 (Aug. 30, 1828): 120.

58. *Washington Examiner*, July 15, 1843; see also *Washington Reporter*, July 15, 1843; Scully Diary, March 13, 1843.

59. *Farmer's Register* (Greensburg), March 28, April 4, 1801. See also Buck and Buck, *The Planting of Civilization*, 328.

60. Anonymous review of "Poems on Different Subjects" by a Lady [Nancy Sproat] (Boston: West and Richardson, 1813), in *The Western Gleaner, or Repository for the Arts, Sciences and Literature* (Pittsburgh) 1, no. 4 (Jan. 1814): 119–20, 123–24, 125.

61. *Genius of Liberty*, March 2, 1819; *Loomis's Magazine Almanac for 1838* (Pittsburgh: Luke Loomis, 1838), 30.

62. *Washington Reporter*, July 23, 1810.

63. "The Ladies' Garland," *The Hesperus and Western Miscellany* (Pittsburgh) 1, no. 8 (May 24, 1828): 64.

64. Emma Willard, *Address to the Pupils of the Washington Female Seminary* (Pittsburgh: 1844), 7.

65. Swisshelm, *Letters to Country Girls*, 130, 149, 132–33.

66. *The Crystal and Ladies' Magazine* (Pittsburgh) 1, no. 1 (April 1828): 30, 31; *The Hesperus and Western Miscellany* (Pittsburgh) 1, no. 8 (May 24, 1828): 64; Willard, *Address*, 23, 22.

67. *The Crystal and Ladies' Magazine* 1, no. 1 (April 1828): 31; Willard, *Address*, 4–5. The curriculum at female seminaries may have come to reflect this dual emphasis. The Western Collegiate Institute in Laceyville, for example, having "in view the after respectability and usefulness of its subjects," offered courses in science, languages, and literature, as well as "Needle and Fancy Work, Drawing, Painting, Musick, Dancing, and the Principles of social intercourse." See the broadside, "Western Collegiate Institute."

68. On this and related points, see Cott, *Bonds of Womanhood*, 126–59.

69. "Journal of the Reverend Sanson Brunot," Dec. 13, 1830.

70. Eliza Swift, letter to Mary Young, Hanover Neck, New Jersey, Feb. 28, 1824, in Folder 9, Swift Papers.

71. On women and temperance, see Ian Tyrell, *Sobering Up: From Temperance to Prohibition in Antebellum America* (Westport, Conn.: Greenwood, 1979) and "Women and Temperance in Antebellum America, 1830–1860," *Civil War History* 28 (1982): 128–52; and Barbara Epstein, *The Politics of Domesticity* (Middletown, Conn.: Wesleyan University Press, 1981). For women at Sons of Temperance parades, see the *Washington Examiner*, July 10, 1847; and Buffum Diary, Dec. 4, 1847.

72. *The Hesperus and Western Miscellany* (Pittsburgh) 1, no. 4 (March 29, 1828): 30.

73. *Constitution and By-Laws of the Pittsburgh Ladies' Association, instituted in January, 1839* (Pittsburgh: n.p., 1839), 3, 5, 7, 9. Note the similarity in the strategic affirmation of domestic values in poor reform and the encouragement of female education. Both argued implicitly that an unprecedented expansion of female influence and activity would strengthen, rather than endanger, family, home, and society.

74. The concept of "pastoralized" housework comes from Boydston, *Home and Work*, 140–46. See also Cowan, *More Work for Mother*, 42–43; Rodgers, *Work Ethic*, 186; O'Malley, *Keeping Watch*, 190–91.

75. *Genius of Liberty*, July 12, 1815.

76. *Washington Examiner*, Aug. 20, 1825; *Genius of Liberty*, Aug. 27, 1828. Another possible message of the spinster Fourth was that women who assumed their proper role as wives and mothers would have little time or interest in this ridiculous affair.

77. *Washington Examiner*, July 14, 1832.

78. *Washington Examiner*, March 17, 1838. It is unclear whether the ladies in question actually read or spoke their own toasts or had a man do it for them.

Either way, their presence and the inclusion of their sentiments was a marked change in practice.

79. *Washington Examiner*, July 23, 1842. Major Peden, the next speaker, apparently had more serious things on his mind: "May the sons of freedom ever preserve their country from the power of darkness, and the fair daughters of Columbia ever be preserved from the foul stain of amalgamation with the sable sons of Africa."

80. Willard, *Address*, 13; *Washington Examiner*, March 23, 1844.

81. *Washington Examiner*, Aug. 2, 1845.

82. Buffum Diary, Oct. 17, 1847, March 9, 1848.

83. Ibid., Oct. 17, 1847.

84. Ibid., Sept. 14, 1847.

85. Ibid., Dec. 29, 1847.

86. Ann Braude, *Radical Spirits: Spiritualism and Women's Rights in Nineteenth-Century America* (Boston: Beacon, 1989), 23. For more on animal magnetism and mesmerism, consult Robert C. Fuller, *Mesmerism and the Cure of American Souls* (Philadelphia: University of Pennsylvania Press, 1982).

87. On this point, see Ryan, "The American Parade," 131–53.

88. *Washington Examiner*, Oct. 23, 1830.

Chapter 7: The Reform of Leisure:
Cooperation and Conflict

1. Eileen Yeo and Stephen Yeo, "Ways of Seeing: Control and Leisure Versus Class and Struggle," in *Popular Culture and Class Conflict 1590–1914: Explorations in the History of Labour and Leisure*, ed. Yeo and Yeo (Atlantic Highlands, N.J.: Humanities, 1981), 150.

2. See, for example, Joseph Gusfield, *Symbolic Crusade: Status Politics and the American Temperance Movement* (Urbana: University of Illinois Press, 1986); Paul E. Johnson, *A Shopkeeper's Millenium: Society and Revivals in Rochester, New York, 1815–1837* (New York: Hill and Wang, 1978); Joseph Rumbarger, *Profits, Power and Prohibition: Alcohol Reform and the Industrializing of America, 1800–1930* (Albany: State University of New York Press, 1989).

3. See Malcolmson, *Popular Recreations*, for a classic example of this type of analysis. Cf. Peter Bailey, "A Mingled Mass of Perfectly Legitimate Pleasures: The Victorian Middle Class and the Problem of Leisure," *Victorian Studies* 21, no. 1: 7–28.

4. Lawrence F. Kohl, "The Concept of Social Control and the History of Jacksonian America," *Journal of the Early Republic* 5 (spring 1985): 28; Gareth Stedman Jones, "Class Expression Versus Social Control? A Critique of Recent Trends in the Social History of 'Leisure,'" *History Workshop* 4 (autumn 1977): 163–70. See also William A. Muraskin, "The Social-Control Theory in American History: A Critique," *Journal of Social History* 9 (summer 1976): 559–80; Lois

Banner, "Religious Benevolence as Social Control: A Critique of an Interpretation," *Journal of American History* 60 (June 1973): 23–41; Boyer, *Urban Masses and Moral Order*, 57–61; and Levine, *Highbrow/Lowbrow*, 206–207.

5. *The Friend*, a Pittsburgh newspaper published by the Young Men's Society, for example, contrasted a noisy, drunken, brawling Fourth of July celebration with a rational festival organized on temperance principles (May 7, 1835). Click, *Spirit of the Times*, 2–3, discusses prevailing attitudes toward rational amusements; Teresa Murphy explores working class attitudes toward rational leisure in "Work, Leisure, and Moral Reform: The Ten Hour Movement in New England, 1830–1850," in *Worktime and Industrialization: An International History*, ed. Gary Cross (Philadelphia: Temple University Press, 1988), 59–76. Peter Bailey examines rational leisure in England in *Leisure and Class in Victorian England: Rational Recreation and the Contest for Control, 1830–1885* (Buffalo, N.Y.: University of Toronto Press, 1978). See also Cross, *Social History of Leisure*, 87–101.

6. W. W. McKinney, *Early Pittsburgh Presbyterianism* (Pittsburgh: Gibson, 1938), 145–46; see also Dahlinger, *Pittsburgh*.

7. *Washington Examiner*, July 24, 1824.

8. *Genius of Liberty*, Aug. 15, 1844; *The Friend*, Jan. 22, 1835.

9. Ludlow, *Dramatic Life*, 284.

10. "A Short Essay," *Washington Reporter*, Sept. 2, 1811; *Loomis's Magazine Almanac for 18339* (Pittsburgh: Luke Loomis, 1839), 55; George Bethune, "Leisure — Its Uses and Abuses," in *Orations and Occasional Discourses* (New York: Putnam, 1850), 76. On distrust of men of leisure generally, and of slave owners as a particular species of this group, see Rodgers, *Work Ethic*, 15, 31; and Click, *Spirit of the Times*, 15–16.

11. *Westmoreland Intelligencer*, May 4, 1838, reprinted from the *Southern Rose*.

12. Levine, "The Promise of Sport in Antebellum America," 634.

13. *The Friend*, Jan. 15, 1835. On contemporary discussions of middle class leisure, see the *Pittsburgh Statesman*, Aug. 4 and Sept. 8, 1830, for an exchange with the editor of the *Christian Herald* on the theater; and the *Pittsburgh Mercury*, Dec. 10, 1822, for a piece against gambling. Daniel Walker Howe has suggested that middle class evangelical attempts to control other elements of antebellum society were linked to their own efforts at self-discipline. A similar process may be at work in leisure reform. See Howe's "The Evangelical Movement and Political Culture in the North During the Second Party System," *Journal of American History* 77, no. 4 (March 1991): 1216–39.

14. *Pittsburgh Gazette*, July 9, 1849; *The Literary Casket* 3, no. 1 (July 1842): 17.

15. *Washington Examiner*, Aug. 4, 1849. See also Aug. 18 for further comments on attendance at the lectures.

16. See the file of Pittsburgh tavern license applications in the Carnegie Library of Pittsburgh. The *Pittsburgh Mercury* of June 8, 1836, reported that Al-

legheny City had forty taverns for a population of approximately seven thousand; illegal establishments undoubtedly added to this total. By 1838, Pittsburgh's Mayor's Court licensed 158 taverns, while the county approved 203 applications (*Pittsburgh Times*, Feb. 21, 1838). Notices of prosecutions for public drunkenness and selling without a license were common in local newspapers, attesting to the magnitude of drunkenness. See, for example, *Pittsburgh Gazette*, July 1, 1848, and June 27, 1849; and *Washington Reporter*, May 30, 1849, for judicial action against doggeries.

17. *Report of the Committee on Vice and Immorality, Relative to the Repeal of the Law of Seventeen Hundred and Five, which Prohibits Persons from Tippling on the Sabbath* (Harrisburg: n.p., 1844), 3.

Iron City, April 2, 1842; *Iron City*, Jan. 29 and Feb. 5, 1842; *Pittsburgh Telegraph*, April 17, 1847; *Our Country*, Sept. 3, 1835.

18. Stevenson Fletcher is quoted on a "liberal supply of ardent spirits" from his *Pennsylvania Agriculture*, 120–21.

On refusing to provide whiskey to workers, see William H. Cooke, *Recollections of James Guthrie Johnson* (Uniontown, Pa.: Uniontown Library Association, 1929), 28–29.

Also see McClenathan et al., *Centennial History of Connellsville*, 46; Franklin Ellis, ed., *History of Fayette County, Pennsylvania* (Philadelphia: Everts, 1882), 587.

19. *Washington Examiner*, Jan. 2, 1830; *Our Country*, June 28, 1837; *Washington Examiner*, Oct. 3, 1829; *Washington Reporter*, Oct. 18, 1845.

20. "Recreations," *Loomis's Magazine Almanac for 1847* (Pittsburgh: Luke Loomis, 1847), 31. E. P. Thompson has shown that for English workers, choice was important and not always dictated by necessity: some chose fewer work hours for less pay over increased income to preserve their discretionary time. See "Time, Work Discipline and Industrial Capitalism," *Past and Present* 38: 56–97. Douglas Reid's examination of St. Monday, "The Decline of St. Monday, 1766–1876," *Past and Present* 71: 76–101, gives an example of a preindustrial use of leisure time that involved excess but did not threaten the accomplishment of work.

21. Buck and Buck, *Planting of Civilization*, 353.

22. *Pittsburgh Gazette*, Oct. 16, 1801.

23. On attempts to use schoolbooks and children's literature to demonstrate the perils of idleness, see O'Malley, *Keeping Watch*, 20–22; and Rodgers, *Work Ethic*, 129–32. Boyer, *Urban Masses and Moral Order*, discusses the problem of youth in general (34–53) and young men in particular (109–12), as does Haltunnen, *Confidence Men and Painted Women*, 10–20, 27–28, and Cross, *Social History of Leisure*, 112–20.

24. *Pittsburgh Gazette*, May 1, 1820.

25. *Greensburg Gazette*, April 30, 1823; *Washington Examiner*, July 11, 1835; *Washington Reporter*, Sept. 2, 1811, April 16, 1810.

26. *Greensburg Gazette*, Jan. 20, 1823.

27. *Loomis's Magazine Almanac for 1844* (Pittsburgh: Luke Loomis, 1844), 48; *Our Country*, July 26, 1837; *Washington Examiner*, June 1, 1844.

28. *Washington Examiner*, July 11, 1835, Aug. 6, 1817. See also Frederick J. Frank, "Student Life in Selected Colleges in the Early Nineteenth Century," for a discussion of "A Student's Journal."

29. *Washington Reporter*, Sept. 17, 1810, Oct. 8, 1810. Bonus Homo's description of the exhibition appeared in poetic form, "The Genius of the West," in the *Washington Reporter*, Oct. 22, 1810.

30. *Washington Reporter*, Oct. 8, 1810. See also Oct. 22, 1810, Nov. 19, 1810, and Nov. 26, 1810, for more volleys in the war of letters.

31. *Washington Reporter*, Nov. 5, 1810. In a wry comment on the poor grammar of the letter, and thus the education provided by institutions condoning raucous exhibitions, the editor of the *Reporter* appended "[Copy-Punctuatum et literatum]" to the letter.

32. Johnston, *Reminiscences*, 281.

33. "Seasonable Admonitions," *Washington Reporter*, Jan. 29, 1816. Galloway Papers, 1809–1875, Folder 11.

34. *Harris's Intelligencer*, Oct. 27, 1838.

35. McKinney, *Early Pittsburgh Presbyterianism*, 144.

36. J. Thomas Jable, "Aspects of Reform in Early Nineteenth-Century Pennsylvania," *Pennsylvania Magazine of History and Biography* 102, no. 3 (1978): 344–63.

See the letter from "A Citizen" in the *Washington Examiner*, Feb. 19, 1831, praising the new legislation on tavern licenses as a boon to the supporters of sobriety and order.

The intoxicated tavern license applicant is described in *Iron City and Pittsburgh Weekly Chronicle*, June 25, 1842.

37. *Loomis's Magazine Almanac for 1840* (Pittsburgh: Luke Loomis, 1840), 54–55; *Genius of Liberty*, April 5, 1815.

38. "An Intelligent Family," *Harris's Intelligencer*, July 20, 1839.

39. *Pennsylvania Argus*, Aug. 29, 1845; *Washington Reporter*, Nov. 1 and Nov. 15, 1845. On Sabbatarianism, see John, "Taking Sabbatarianism Seriously."

40. Local newspapers during our period abounded with notices of temperance society meetings. See, for example, the formation of the Canonsburgh Temperance Society, *Washington Examiner*, Nov. 8, 1828; the Rostraver Township (Westmoreland County) Temperance Society, *Greensburg Gazette*, April 3, 1829; and the Pittsburgh Fourth Ward Total Abstinence Society, *Pittsburgh Gazette*, July 26, 1841. For general treatments of temperance, see Tyrell, *Sobering Up*; and Jack S. Blocker, Jr., *American Temperance Movements: Cycles of Reform* (Boston: Twayne, 1989), 1–61.

41. *Records of the [Presbyterian] Synod of Pittsburgh*, 130 (Oct. 8, 1817). *Iron City* and *Pittsburgh Weekly Chronicle*, Jan. 8, 1842.

42. *Pittsburgh Gazette*, Jan. 24, 1832.

43. *Our Country*, Jan. 18, 1836. A similar organization existed in Pittsburgh. See issues of *The Friend* from 1836 for information on the Pittsburgh association to aid boatmen. For a description of the objectionable leisure practices of boatmen, see "The Boatmen," chap. 4 in Baldwin's *The Keelboat Age on Western Waters*. On George Caleb Bingham's depiction of western boatmen, see Elizabeth Johns, *American Genre Painting: The Politics of Everyday Life* (New Haven: Yale University Press, 1991), 81–89.

44. *Washington Examiner*, April 13, 1818.

45. *Washington Reporter*, May 28, 1810. On kissing parties, see Buck and Buck, *Planting of Civilization*, 355.

46. Reformed Presbyterian Church Society Papers, Sterling Papers, Folder 2.

47. Records of the Poke Run Presbyterian Church, Westmoreland County, Pennsylvania, 1840–1863. Typescript in Pennsylvania Department, Carnegie Library of Pittsburgh.

48. Ladies' fairs on or around the Fourth were numerous and usually advertised and reported in local newspapers. See, for example, Uniontown's *Genius of Liberty*, June 22, 1840, for a fair being planned by the Ladies' Sewing Society of St. Peter's Church for the Fourth.

49. *Pittsburgh Recorder* 2, no. 47 (Dec. 19, 1823): 750; *Allegheny Democrat*, Dec. 21, 1824; *Washington Reporter*, Dec. 20, 1845, and Oct. 3, 1849.

50. *American Manufacturer*, July 2, 1842; *Pittsburgh Gazette*, Jan. 22, 1830; *Washington Examiner*, Dec. 22, 1832; *Our Country*, Dec. 28, 1836.

Iron City, Oct. 1, 1842; *Genius of Liberty*, Oct. 6, 1842.

51. The traveling actor is Noah Ludlow, *Dramatic Life*, 58.

On working class amusements, see "Sketch of Pittsburgh, No. 2," *The Friend*, April 9, 1835.

On suggestions for innocent recreation, see *Harris's Intelligencer*, Oct. 20, 1838.

52. *Our Country*, June 21, 1837.

53. *Genius of Liberty*, April 15, 1815; *Pittsburgh Statesman*, July 18, 1818; Minutes of the Washington Musical Society; *Pittsburgh Mercury*, Oct. 5, 1836. On music in Pittsburgh, see Leland D. Baldwin, *Pittsburgh: The Story of A City* (Pittsburgh: University of Pittsburgh Press, 1937), 256.

54. *Allegheny Democrat*, June 23, 1835. Science lectures ranged from talks on chemistry and anatomy to demonstrations of phrenology and nitrous oxide. See, for example, Mr. Riddell's lectures in Pittsburgh's Lambdin's Museum, *Pittsburgh Gazette*, March 6, 1832; an exhibition of nitrous oxide, *Pittsburgh Gazette*, Oct. 14, 1833; Mr. Sims's lectures on phrenology in Washington County, *Our Country*, Feb. 25, 1836; and Dr. Derby's lecture series on phrenology and physiology in the Greensburg courthouse, *Westmoreland Republican*, Nov. 23, 1849.

55. For the Young Men's Society, see *Pittsburgh Statesman*, Jan. 16, 1833; *Allegheny Democrat*, Dec. 30, 1834; and *The Friend*, Jan. 1, 1835. *The Hesperus and Western Miscellany* (Pittsburgh) 1, no. 1 (Feb. 16, 1828), 5.

56. *The Literary Messenger* 2, no. 3 (Aug. 1841): 20.

57. *Pittsburgh Gazette*, March 23, 1820, July 16, 1824. See *Pittsburgh Mercury*, June 15, 1824, for a letter endorsing an apprentice library.

58. *Genius of Liberty*, April 18, 1831. The meeting appears to have resulted in the establishment of a Mechanics' Institute, which sponsored lectures at Madison College (May 30, 1831, provides an example). See also Murphy, "Work, Leisure, and Moral Reform," especially 68–72.

59. Abbot and Harrison, *The First Hundred Years of McKeesport*, 89; *Pennsylvania Argus*, Feb. 18, May 5, May 19, 1848, March 9, 1849; Van Voorhis, *The Old and New Monongahela*, 375, 381; *Westmoreland Republican*, March 9, 1849. For a description of a Sons of Temperance procession in Pittsburgh, see the McKnight Diary, vol. 2, May 20, 1846. On the Sons as alternative leisure, see Click, *Spirit of the Times*, 81.

60. In this process at the national level, as in most areas of commercial leisure, P. T. Barnum led the way. He portrayed his museum and exhibitions as instructive and harmless alternatives to drinking and gambling. See Saxon, *P. T. Barnum*, 12, 16.

61. *Pittsburgh Statesman*, July 17, 1833; *Pittsburgh Mercury*, Sept. 7, 1836; *Our Country*, July 26, 1837; *Harris's Intelligencer*, Sept. 14, Sept. 21, 1839.

62. *Pittsburgh Gazette*, June 29, 1841; *Washington Examiner*, July 7, July 28, 1849; March 23, 1850.

63. *Washington Examiner*, July 29, 1826; *Harris's Intelligencer*, Sept. 7, 1839.

64. *Washington Reporter*, Feb. 7, 1846.

65. *Washington Reporter*, Dec. 20, 1845.

66. Van Voorhis, *The Old and New Monongahela*, 14, 12.

67. *Pittsburgh Gazette*, May 1, 1820.

68. *Pennsylvania Argus*, Dec. 15, 1843. *Washington Reporter*, Dec. 23, 1843; Nov. 22, Nov. 29, 1845; *Washington Examiner*, Dec. 14, 1850.

69. Scully Diary, Feb. 25, 1843; McKnight Diary, May 30, 1842.

70. Ludlow, *Dramatic Life*, 57, 64–65.

71. Wemyss, *Theatrical Biography*, 196, 197.

72. Minutes for March 26, 1838, Vigilant Fire Company Minute Book, Vigilant Fire Company Papers, Pennsylvania Department, Carnegie Library of Pittsburgh.

73. Neptune Fire Company Minute Books, 1833, 1845–54, in the collection of the Historical Society of Western Pennsylvania, Pittsburgh.

74. Reuben Miller III is quoted from his "Events in the Course of an Active Life," (n.p., n.d.), manuscript in the collection of the Historical Society of Western Pennsylvania.

See the *Iron City*, Aug. 13, 1842, for an editorial on the proposed abolition of volunteer companies in favor of a paid professional company. The November 5 edition of this paper gave an indignant account of the frequent disturbances — false alarms, fighting, racing — that characterized the Vigilant and Allegheny Companies' existence.

75. *Iron City*, Oct. 8, Oct. 15, 1842. See also the file of newspaper clippings in the Vigilant Fire Company Papers in the Pennsylvania Department, Carnegie Library of Pittsburgh.

76. Herron is discussed in McKinney, *Early Pittsburgh Presbyterianism*, 145. See Watson, "Early School Day Recollections," 87–88. See also Marian Silveus, "Churches and Social Control on the Western Pennsylvania Frontier," *Western Pennsylvania Historical Magazine* 19 (1936): 123–34; Buck and Buck, *Planting of Civilization*, 442–46.

77. James Allie Davidson, ed., "Source Materials for Baptist History in Western Pennsylvania," typescript, Pennsylvania Department, Carnegie Library of Pittsburgh, vol. 1, Great Bethel Baptist Church Minute Book, June 11, 1803, April 6, 1836, Oct. 3, 1829; vol. 2, Salem Baptist Church Minute Book, June 14, 1806, April 20, 1822.

78. Ibid., Great Bethel Baptist Church Minute Book, Jan. 1, Feb. 5, 1814; "Records of Poke Run," Oct. 15, 1840; Davidson, "Source Materials," vol. 2, Mount Moriah Minutes, May 9, June 13, 1801, Nov. 31, 1807.

79. Davidson, "Source Materials," Salem Baptist Church Minutes, Aug. 14, 1824, Aug. 26, 1820; "Records of Poke Run," May 3, 1845.

80. Buck and Buck, *Planting of Civilization*, 446–47; McKinney, *Early Pittsburgh Presbyterianism*, 118–19; Wade, *Urban Frontier*, 122–24.

81. *Pittsburgh Gazette*, Aug. 16, 1809; *Washington Reporter*, April 17, 1815. See the *Genius of Liberty*, Aug. 18, 1842, for an article on the Fayette County moral society.

82. In 1842, for example, the Pittsburgh Sabbath Association met to send a memorial requesting Sabbatarian legislation to Congress (*Iron City*, Jan. 22, 1842). Similarly, concerned citizens held a public meeting in 1838 to petition the Court of Common Pleas to reduce the number of tavern licenses granted in Manchester, a town on the Allegheny River, and in Allegheny County generally (*Harris's Intelligencer*, March 10, 1838).

83. For a discussion of the commonwealth's efforts at leisure reform, see Jable, "Aspects of Reform in Early Nineteenth-Century Pennsylvania."

84. On throwing bullets, see the *Pittsburgh Gazette*, Aug. 17, 1809. On leisure ordinances, see the *Pittsburgh Mercury*, Aug. 31, Sept. 14, Sept. 28, 1816.

85. Blaine Ewing, ed., *Canonsburg Centennial 1802–1902* (Pittsburgh: Pittsburgh Printing Co., 1903), 18; *Washington Reporter*, April 30, 1810; Minutes of the Board of Trustees, Washington College, Dec. 2, 1816, quoted in Frank, "Student Life in Selected Colleges," 127.

86. On the Greensburg statute, see the *Genius of Liberty*, Dec. 14, 1838; *Westmoreland Intelligencer*, June 2, 1837.

On the Uniontown regulations, see the *Pittsburgh Times*, March 14, 1838.

87. John E. Parke, *Recollections of Seventy Years and Historical Gleanings of Allegheny, Pennsylvania* (Boston: Rand, Avery, and Co., 1886), 76.

88. McKnight Diary, May 30, 1842.

For criticisms of the Greensburg night watch, see the *Pennsylvania Argus*, March 9, 1849. Cf. street disturbance around Christmas in Davis's *Parades and Power*.

On the serenades of the political victors, see the *Genius of Liberty*, Oct. 24, 1826.

89. On the election night disturbance in Pittsburgh, see the *Greensburg Gazette*, Nov. 7, 1828; piece reprinted from the *Pittsburgh Gazette*.

Scully Diary, Jan. 10, 1843.

On destroying houses of ill-fame on election nights, see the *Iron City*, June 4, 1842.

90. *Pittsburgh Morning Chronicle*, June 3, 1842. For more on the brothel attacks, see Martin, "The Great Brothel Dousing."

91. *Iron City*, June 4, 1842.

92. *American Manufacturer*, June 11, 1842; *Pittsburgh Morning Chronicle*, June 4, 1842. The *Chronicle* was not alone in its emphasis on the interracial character of the Crow's Nest. The *American Manufacturer* of June 11, 1842, reported that "The mob was again successful, and made Molly Murphy the 'Irish Nigger,' the 'Bay Nigger,' & every other kind of niggers fly from the premises in quick time."

93. *Pittsburgh Morning Chronicle*, June 6, 1842. The *Morning Chronicle* of June 15, 1842, reported "on good authority" that "a member of the Select Council, who was present at the late attack on the 'Crow's Nest,' spoke in favor of giving the inmates of that house 'a good drenching,' and that the Mayor of the city objected *only* to the throwing of stones at the house, and not to the original flooding that it received."

94. *American Manufacturer*, June 11, 1842.

See the *Pittsburgh Morning Chronicle*, June 10 and June 13, 1842, for an account of the specially convened firemen's meeting.

95. *Pittsburgh Morning Chronicle*, June 3, 1842.

96. *Iron City*, June 11, 1842.

Chapter 8: Epilogue: Leisure in the 1850s and Beyond

1. Most histories of Pittsburgh contain an account of Lind's visit to the city. See Baldwin, *Pittsburgh*, 256–57; Wilson, *Standard History of Pittsburgh*, 871; Henry Oliver Evans, *Iron Pioneer: Henry W. Oliver, 1840–1914* (New York: Dutton, 1942); George B. Fleming, "Jenny Lind in Pittsburgh," *Pittsburgh Gazette-Times*, Nov. 7, 1920. For more on Jenny Lind, see C. G. Rosenberg, *Jenny Lind in America* (New York: Stringer and Townsend, 1851); Joan Bulman, *Jenny Lind, A Biography* (London: J. Barrie, 1956); Gladys Denny Schultz, *Jenny Lind, The Swedish Nightingale* (Philadelphia: Lippincott, 1962); W. Porter Ware and Thaddeus C. Lockard, Jr., *P. T. Barnum Presents Jenny Lind: The American Tour of the Swedish Nightingale* (Baton Rouge: Louisiana State University Press, 1980).

2. Rosenberg, *Jenny Lind in America*, 215; Bulman, *Jenny Lind*, 244–45.

3. *Pittsburgh Gazette*, April 24, 25, 1851; *Pittsburgh Post*, April 26, 1851.

4. *Pittsburgh Post*, April 28, 1851.

5. Baldwin, *Pittsburgh*, 257; *Pittsburgh Post*, April 28, 1851; *Pittsburgh Morning Chronicle*, April 28, 1851.

6. Rosenberg, *Jenny Lind in America*, 218; Bulman, *Jenny Lind*, 275–76.

7. Rosenberg, *Jenny Lind in America*, 219; *Pittsburgh Post*, April 28, 29, 1851.

8. *Pittsburgh Post*, April 28, 1851. These accounts had much support, at the time and subsequently (see, for example, George Swetnam, "Who Threw the Rock at Jenny Lind?" *Pittsburgh Press Magazine*, Nov. 30, 1969, 4–5), but they fail to explain several salient points. The windows to Lind's dressing room were boarded over: what was there for those in the back to see? And why was Lind so upset by *this* supposedly innocuous crowd, when her concerts routinely drew large, raucous mobs of fans? If the gun battle and near riot that attended her appearance in Cincinnati several weeks earlier had failed to chase Lind, why was she so upset by the supposedly nonhostile Pittsburgh demonstration? See the *Post*, April 19, 1851, for an account of her Cincinnati engagement.

9. See chap. 3. Cf. Roy Rosenzweig's discussion of the effect of motion pictures on ethnic working class cultures in Worcester, Massachusetts, during the early twentieth century. Rosenzweig contends that the movies and the celebration of consumption they promoted made inroads into but did not destroy working class culture at once, but that by the second and third generations of ethnic workers, commercial leisure did take ethnic workers away from traditional communal patterns of ethnic culture. See *Eight Hours for What We Will*, especially 218–21.

10. On Barnum's use of advertising, the media, and transportation, see Harris, *Humbug*.

11. Rosenberg, *Jenny Lind in America*, 216; Bulman, *Jenny Lind*, 275.

12. Rosenberg, *Jenny Lind in America*, 215; Schultz, *Jenny Lind*, 274–75; Ware and Lockard, *P. T. Barnum Presents*, 91. Joan Bulman contends that Barnum became concerned, soon after Lind's arrival in the United States, that "she would be entirely monopolized by the *beau monde*, which he felt would be against her interests" (*Jenny Lind*, 243).

13. Rosenberg, *Jenny Lind in America*, 217.

14. For a discussion of some aspects of class-based leisure later in the century, see Rosenzweig, *Eight Hours for What We Will*; Couvares, *The Remaking of Pittsburgh*; Ross, *Workers on the Edge*; Levine, *Highbrow/Lowbrow*; Betts, *America's Sporting Heritage*, especially 15–31; Neil Harris, "Four Stages of Cultural Growth: The American City," in *Indiana Historical Society Lectures, 1971–1972: History and the Role of the City in American Life* (Indianapolis: Indiana Historical Society, 1972), 24–49.

15. By 1850, working class women in southwestern Pennsylvania had already taken the initiative in publicly influencing leisure issues. In 1846, female textile

mill operatives in Pittsburgh and Allegheny City agitated for the ten-hour day, an issue that, workers contended, was crucial to their having enough leisure for learning and improvement. Female defense of their families' leisure time even turned violent, when "women and girls" made "an irruption" into the Penn cotton factory to drive out workers and damage equipment. See Henry Mann, ed., *Our Police: A History of the Pittsburgh Police Force, Under the Town and City* (Pittsburgh: n.p., 1889), 81; Roediger and Foner, *History of American Labor and the Working Day*, 11–14, 59–62.

16. Nathaniel Parker Willis, quoted in Bulman, *Jenny Lind*, 251; Ware and Lockard, *P. T. Barnum Presents*, 91, see also 28–29 for a discussion of Lind's moral influence and virtuous example. On the quality and range of Lind's voice, see Bulman, *Jenny Lind*, 52–53. Lawrence Levine addresses similar issues in his discussion of late nineteenth-century attempts to create and preserve "highbrow" art and music as a badge of elite status, while still having to include the working class in these activities. See his *Highbrow/Lowbrow*, especially the last two chapters.

17. Ware and Lockard, *P. T. Barnum Presents*, 114.

Bibliography

Primary and Manuscript Sources

An Address, together with the Constitution, By-Laws and Standing Rules of the Pittsburgh Young Men's Society, organized January 1, 1833. Pittsburgh: n.p., 1833.

Armstrong, John. "The Duties of Married Women." *Patterson's Magazine Almanac for 1820.* Pittsburgh: Patterson and Lambdin, 1819.

Ashe, Thomas. *Travels in America Performed in 1806.* New York: n.p., 1811.

Beecher, Catharine E. *A Treatise on Domestic Economy for the Use of Young Ladies at Home and at School.* New York: Harper Brothers, 1845.

Beecher, Catharine E., and Harriet Beecher Stowe. *The American Woman's Home.* New York: J. B. Ford, 1869.

Bethune, George. *Orations and Occasional Discourses.* New York: Putnam, 1850.

Birkbeck, Morris. *Notes on a Journey in America.* 1818. Reprint, Ann Arbor: University Microfilms, 1966.

Bladen, Elizabeth Simpson (Darragh). *Old Bedford.* N.p., n.d.

Blythe, Mrs. Ellen. Letters to Her Brother, John C. Green, Esq. Pennsylvania Room, Carnegie Library of Pittsburgh.

"Books Published and for Sale to the Trade, at the Annexed Prices, by Luke Loomis & Co., Wood Street, Pittsburgh, Pennsylvania." Broadside. Pittsburgh, 1831.

Brackenridge, Henry Marie. "Pittsburgh in the Olden Time." In *The Literary Casket* (Pittsburgh) 3, no. 1 (July 1842): 12.

———. *Recollections of Persons and Places in the West.* Philadelphia: Lippincott, 1868.

Brackenridge, Hugh Henry. *Gazette Publications.* Carlisle, Pa.: Alexander and Phillips, 1806.

Brown, Uriah. "Journal of Uria Brown (1816)." *Maryland Historical Magazine* 10 (1915).

Brunot, Rev. Sanson. "The Journal of the Reverend Sanson Brunot; A Partial Account of his Ministry at Blairsville and Greensburg, PA from the time of his Ordination May 9, 1830 until January 3, 1831." Typescript, Pennsylvania Dept., Carnegie Library of Pittsburgh.

Buffum, Joseph C. Diary. Typescript. Pennsylvania Dept., Carnegie Library of Pittsburgh.

By-Laws and Ordinances of the City of Pittsburgh, 1828. Pittsburgh: n.p., 1828.

Chevalier, Michel. *Society, Manners, and Politics in the United States.* 1839. Reprint, New York: Augustus M. Kelly, 1966.

Constitution and By-Laws of the Pittsburgh Horticultural Society. Pittsburgh: n.p., 1848.

Constitution and By-Laws of the Pittsburgh Ladies' Association, instituted in January, 1839. Pittsburgh: n.p., 1839.

Constitution and By-Laws of the Young Men's Mercantile Library and Mechanic's Institute of Pittsburgh, Pennsylvania. Pittsburgh: n.p., 1847.

Coxe, Tench. A *Statement of the Arts and Manufactures of the United States for the Year 1810.* Philadelphia: A. Cornman, Jr., 1814.

Cuming, Fortescue. *Sketches of a Tour to the Western Country, Through the States of Ohio and Kentucky.* Pittsburgh: Cramer, Speer, and Eichbaum, 1810.

Davidson, James Allie, ed. "Source Materials for Baptist History in Western Pennsylvania." Typescript, Pennsylvania Dept., Carnegie Library of Pittsburgh.

A *Digest of Ordinances of the City of Pittsburgh.* Pittsburgh: n.p., 1846.

Doddridge, Rev. Joseph. *Notes on the Settlement and Indian Wars of the Western Parts of Virginia and Pennsylvania from 1763 to 1783, inclusive, together with a review of the Society and Manners of the first settlers of the Western Country.* 1824. Reprint, Pittsburgh: Rittenour and Lindsey, 1912.

Drake, Daniel. *An Oration on the Intemperance of Cities: Including Remarks on Gambling, Idleness, Fashion, and Sabbath-Breaking, delivered in Philadelphia, January 24, 1831.* Philadelphia: n.p., 1831.

Entick's New Spelling Dictionary. New York: Sidney's, 1810.

Fearon, Henry B. *Sketches of America.* 2d ed. London: Longman, Hurst, Rees, Orme and Brown, 1818.

Flint, James. *Letters from America (1818–1820)* (orig. published in 1822), vol. 9. In *Early Western Travels, 1784–1846,* ed. Reuben G. Thwaites. Cleveland: A. H. Clark, 1904.

Flint, Timothy. *Recollections of the Last Ten Years in the Valley of the Mississippi,* ed. George R. Brooks. 1826. Reprint, Carbondale: Southern Illinois University Press, 1966.

Galloway Family Papers, Historical Society of Western Pennsylvania, Pittsburgh.

Gordon, Thomas. *Gazetteer of the State of Pennsylvania.* Philadelphia: T. Belknap, 1832.

Halsey, J. F. *An Appeal to Patriots, Philanthropists and Christians, in Behalf of the Temperance Reform, Delivered in the First Presbyterian Church, at the Anniversary of the Allegheny County Temperance Society, January 1, 1830.* Pittsburgh: n.p., 1830.

Harris's General Business Directory of the Cities of Pittsburgh and Allegheny, 1841. Pittsburgh: Isaac Harris, 1841.

Harris's General Business Directory of the Cities of Pittsburgh and Allegheny, 1844. Pittsburgh: Isaac Harris, 1844.

Harris's Pittsburgh and Allegheny Directory, 1839. Pittsburgh: n.p., 1839.

Hastings, Sally. *Poems on Different Subjects*. Lancaster, Pa.: William Dickson, 1808.

Henry, T. Charlton, D.D., *An Inquiry into the Consistency of Popular Amusements with a Profession of Christianity*. Charleston, S.C.: William Riley, 1825.

Higbee, Lucy Ann. *The Diary of Lucy Ann Higbee, 1837*. Cleveland: n.p., 1924.

Houston, Mrs. J. *Hesperos: Or, Travels in the West*. 2 vols. London: J. W. Parker, 1850.

Jones, Samuel B. *Pittsburgh in the Year 1826*. Pittsburgh: Johnston and Stockton, 1826.

Kendall, Nancy B. Diary. Typescript, Historical Society of Pennsylvania, Philadelphia.

Ludlow, Noah M. *Dramatic Life as I Found It*. 1880. Reprint, New York: Benjamin Blom, 1966.

Lyford, W. G. *The Western Address Directory*. Baltimore: J. Robinson, 1837.

McClelland Family Papers, Historical Society of Western Pennsylvania, Pittsburgh.

McKnight, Robert. Diary. Typescript, Darlington Library, University of Pittsburgh.

M'Henry, James. "Home." In *The Pleasures of Friendship, A Poem in Two Parts; to Which are Added a Few Original Irish Melodies*. Pittsburgh: n.p., 1822.

Michaux, F. A. *Travels to the West of the Allegheny Mountains, in the States of Ohio, Kentucky, and Tennessee* (originally published in London, 1805), vol. 3 in *Early Western Travels 1748–1846*, ed. Reuben G. Thwaites. Cleveland: A. H. Clark, 1904.

Miller, Reuben, III. "Events in the Course of an Active Life." Manuscript in the collection of the Historical Society of Western Pennsylvania, Pittsburgh.

Minutes of the Washington Musical Society (1825), Washington County Historical Society, Washington, Pennsylvania.

Neptune Fire Company Papers, in the collection of the Historical Society of Western Pennsylvania, Pittsburgh.

Palmer, John. *Journal of Travels in the United States of North America and in Lower Canada, performed in the Year 1817*. London: Sherwood, Neely, Jones, 1818.

Passavant, Rev. W. A. *Address delivered before the Franklin Literary Society, of Jefferson College, at its Semi-Centennial Anniversary, November 14th, 1847*. Washington, Pennsylvania: John Bausman, 1848.

Patterson's Magazine Almanac for 1820. Pittsburgh: Patterson and Lambdin, 1819.

Philadelphius. *The Moral Plague of Civil Society; or, The Pernicious Effects of the Love of Money on the Morals of Mankind: Exemplified in the Encouragement Given to the Use of Ardent Spirits in the United States, with the Proper Remedy for the Cure of this National Evil*. Philadelphia: n.p., 1821.

Pittsburgh Tavern License Applications, Carnegie Library of Pittsburgh.

Proceedings of the Second Annual Meeting of the Pittsburgh Temperance Society of the Coloured People of the City of Pittsburgh and Vicinity. Pittsburgh: n.p., 1839.

Proceedings of the Second Annual Meeting of the Temperance Society of the Coloured People of the City of Pittsburgh and Vicinity; Together with the Constitution and Standing Rules, and Annual Report. Pittsburgh: n.p., 1837.

Prolix, Peregrine (Philip H. Nicklin). *Journey Through Pennsylvania, 1835, By Canal, Rail, and Stage Coach.* York, Pa.: American Canal and Transportation Center, 1978.

Records of the Poke Run Presbyterian Church, Westmoreland County, Pennsylvania, 1840–1863. Typescript in Pennsylvania Dept., Carnegie Library of Pittsburgh.

Records of the [Presbyterian] Synod of Pittsburgh from its First *Organization September 29, 1802 to October 1832, Inclusive.* Pittsburgh: Shyrock, 1852.

Report of the Committee on Vice and Immorality, Relative to the Repeal of the Law of Seventeen Hundred and Five, which Prohibits Persons from Tippling on the Sabbath. Harrisburg: n.p., 1844.

The Richmond Alarm; A Plain and Familiar Discourse: Written in the Form of a Dialogue Between a Father and his Son. Pittsburgh: Robert Ferguson & Company, 1815.

Rosenberg, C. G. *Jenny Lind in America.* New York: Stringer and Townsend, 1851.

Scully, Dennis B. Diary. Manuscript, Darlington Library, University of Pittsburgh.

Sterling Papers. Darlington Library, University of Pittsburgh.

Swift Family Papers. Presbyterian Historical Society, Philadelphia.

Swisshelm, Jane Grey. *Letters to Country Girls.* New York: John C. Riker, 1853.

de Tocqueville, Alexis. *Democracy in America.* 2 vols. Ed. Phillips Bradley. New York: Knopf, 1945.

Vigilant Fire Company Papers. Pennsylvania Dept., Carnegie Library of Pittsburgh.

Walker, Joseph E., ed. *Pleasure and Business in Western Pennsylvania: The Journal of Joshua Gilpin, 1809.* Harrisburg: Pennsylvania Historical and Museum Commission, 1975.

Wemyss, Francis Courtney. *Theatrical Biography: Or, The Life of an Actor and Manager.* Glasgow: R. Griffin and Co., 1848.

"Western Collegiate Institute for Young Ladies, Will Commence Its 19th Term on the 27th of February, 1837." Broadside. Pittsburgh, 1837.

Wiley, W. T. "Anniversary Address, delivered before the Apollonian Literary Society of Madison College, Uniontown, Pennsylvania, February 22, 1842." In "Addresses Delivered Before the Schools and Colleges of Pennsylvania," in the Pennsylvania Dept., Carnegie Library of Pittsburgh.

Willard, Emma. *Address to the Pupils of the Washington Female Seminary.* Pittsburgh: n.p., 1844.

Wrenshall, Rev. John. "Farewell to Pittsburgh and the Mountains, 1818." Annotated by Isaac Craig. *Pennsylvania Magazine of History and Biography* 9, no. 1 (1885): 89–101.

Secondary Sources

Abbott, Walter S., and William E. Harrison. *The First One Hundred Years of McKeesport.* McKeesport, Pa.: McKeesport Times, 1894.

Allen, Michael. *Western Rivermen, 1763–1861: Ohio and Mississippi Boatmen and the Myth of the Alligator Horse.* Baton Rouge: Louisiana State University Press, 1990.

Amacher, Richard E. *Franklin's Wit and Folly: The Bagatelles.* New Brunswick: Rutgers University Press, 1953.

Ambler, Charles H. *A History of Transportation in the Ohio Valley.* Glendale, Calif.: Arthur Clarke, 1932.

Applebaum, Diane Carter. *The Glorious Fourth: An American Holiday in American History.* New York: Facts on File, 1989.

Aversa, Alfred, Jr. "Foxhunting: A Patrician Sport." *Review of Sport and Leisure* 6, no. 2 (1981): 83–100.

Bailey, Peter. *Leisure and Class in Victorian England: Rational Recreation and the Contest for Control, 1830–1885.* Buffalo, N.Y.: University of Toronto Press, 1978.

———. "A Mingled Mass of Perfectly Legitimate Pleasures: The Victorian Middle Class and the Problem of Leisure," *Victorian Studies* 21, no. 1: 7–28.

Baker, Jean H. "The Ceremonies of Politics: Nineteenth-Century Rituals of National Affirmation." In *A Master's Due: Essays in Honor of David Herbert Donald,* ed. William J. Cooper, Jr., Michael F. Holt, and John McCardell. Baton Rouge: Louisiana State University Press, 1985.

Baker, William, Jr. *Canonsburg, Pennsylvania 1773–1936.* Canonsburg: n.p., 1936.

Baldwin, Leland D. *The Keelboat Age on Western Waters.* Pittsburgh: University of Pittsburgh Press, 1941.

———. *Pittsburgh: The Story of a City.* Pittsburgh: University of Pittsburgh Press, 1937.

Banner, Lois. "Religious Benevolence as Social Control: A Critique of an Interpretation." *Journal of American History* 60 (June 1973): 23–41.

Bayus, Lenore W. *Beulah Presbyterian Church, 1784–1984.* Pittsburgh: Davis and Warde, 1984.

Bell, Whitfield J. "Washington County, Pennsylvania, in the Eighteenth-Century Antislavery Movement." *Western Pennsylvania Historical Magazine* 25 (Sept.-Dec. 1942): 135–42.

Bender, Thomas. *Community and Social Change in America.* New Brunswick: Rutgers University Press, 1978.

Betts, John R. "Agricultural Fairs and the Rise of Harness Racing." *Agricultural History* 28 (1954): 71–75.

————. *America's Sporting Heritage 1850–1950*. Reading, Mass.: Addison-Wesley, 1974.

Birch, George W. F. *Our Church and Our Village*. New York: Ward and Drummond, 1899.

Blocker, Jack S., Jr. *American Temperance Movements: Cycles of Reform*. Boston: Twayne, 1989.

Bode, Carl. *The American Lyceum: Town Meeting of the Mind*. Carbondale: Southern Illinois University Press, 1956.

————. *The Anatomy of American Popular Culture, 1840–1861*. Westport, Conn.: Greenwood, 1983.

Borish, Linda. "Forsaking 'Clothes Thumping' for 'Piano Thumping': Farmers' Daughters Quitting the Homestead in Antebellum New England." Paper delivered at the American Historical Association meeting, Chicago, 1991.

Boucher, John N. *History of Westmoreland County, Pennsylvania*. 2 vols. New York: Lewis, 1906.

————. *The Old and New Westmoreland*. 2 vols. New York: American Historical Society, 1918.

Boydston, Jeanne. *Home and Work: Housework, Wages, and the Ideology of Labor in the Early Republic*. New York: Oxford University Press, 1990.

Boyer, Paul. *Urban Masses and Moral Order in America, 1820–1920*. Cambridge: Harvard University Press, 1978.

Boylan, Anne. *Sunday School: The Creation of an American Institution, 1790–1880*. New Haven: Yale University Press, 1988.

Braude, Ann. *Radical Spirits: Spiritualism and Women's Rights in Nineteenth-Century America*. Boston: Beacon, 1989.

Breen, Timothy H. "Horses and Gentlemen: The Cultural Significance of Gambling Among the Gentry of Virginia." *William and Mary Quarterly*, 3rd ser., 34 (April 1977): 239–57.

Bruce, Robert. *The Lincoln Highway in Pennsylvania*. Washington, D.C.: American Automobile Association, 1920.

————. *The National Road*. Washington, D.C.: National Highways Association, 1916.

Brynn, Soeren Stewart. "Some Sports in Pittsburgh During the National Period, 1775–1860." *Western Pennsylvania Historical Magazine* 51: 345–63; 52: 57–79.

Buck, Solon J., and Elizabeth H. Buck. *The Planting of Civilization in Western Pennsylvania*. Pittsburgh: University of Pittsburgh Press, 1939.

Bulman, Joan. *Jenny Lind, A Biography*. London: J. Barrie, 1956.

Bushman, Richard L. *The Refinement of America: Persons, Houses, Cities*. New York: Knopf, 1992.

Butsch, Richard, ed. *For Fun and Profit: The Transformation of Leisure into Consumption*. Philadelphia: Temple University Press, 1990.

Caldwell, J. A. *Caldwell's Illustrated Historical, Centennial Atlas of Washington County, Pennsylvania*. Conduit, Ohio: J. A. Caldwell, 1876.

Carnes, Mark. *Secret Ritual and Manhood in Victorian America*. New Haven: Yale University Press, 1989.

Cawelti, John G. *Apostles of the Self-Made Man*. Chicago: University of Chicago Press, 1965.

Centennial Anniversary of the Founding of Monongahela City, 1892. Monongahela City, Pa.: Hazzard, 1895.

The Centennial Celebration of the Organization of Washington County, Pennsylvania. Washington, Pa.: E. E. Crumrine, 1881.

Centennial Volume of the First Presbyterian Church of Pittsburgh, Pennsylvania, 1784–1884. Pittsburgh: William G. Johnston, 1884.

Clarke, John, and Chas Critcher. *The Devil Makes Work: Leisure in Capitalist Britain*. Urbana: University of Illinois Press, 1985.

Click, Patricia. *The Spirit of the Times: Amusements in Nineteenth-Century Baltimore, Norfolk, and Richmond*. Charlottesville: University of Virginia Press, 1989.

Cohn, William H. "A National Celebration: The Fourth of July in American History." *Cultures* 3, no. 2 (1976), 141–56.

Cooke, William H. *Recollections of James Guthrie Johnson*. Uniontown, Pa.: Uniontown Library Association, 1929.

Cott, Nancy F. *The Bonds of Womanhood: "Woman's Sphere" in New England, 1780–1835*. New Haven: Yale University Press, 1977.

Couvares, Francis G. *The Remaking of Pittsburgh: Class and Culture in an Industrializing City, 1877–1919*. Albany: State University of New York Press, 1984.

Cowan, Ruth Schwartz. *More Work for Mother: The Ironies of Household Technology from the Open Hearth to the Microwave*. New York: Basic, 1983.

Crackel, Theodore J. *Mr. Jefferson's Army: Political and Social Reform in the Military Establishment, 1801–1809*. New York: New York University Press, 1987.

Creigh, Alfred. *History of Washington County, Pennsylvania*. Washington, Pa.: n.p., 1870.

Cross, Gary. *A Social History of Leisure Since 1600*. State College, Pa.: Venture Publishing, 1990.

Crumrine, Boyd, ed. *The Centennial Celebration of the Incorporation of the Borough of Washington, Pennsylvania, in its Old Home Week of October 2–8, 1910*. Washington, Pa.: Washington County Historical Society, 1912.

Cunningham, Hugh. *Leisure in the Industrial Revolution*. New York: St. Martin's, 1980.

Dahlinger, Charles W. *Pittsburgh, A Sketch of Its Early Social Life*. New York: Putnam, 1916.

Davis, Susan. *Parades and Power: Street Theater in Nineteenth-Century Philadelphia*. Philadelphia: Temple University Press, 1986.

Dawson, Charles, ed. *Our Firemen: The History of the Pittsburgh Fire Department from the Village Period Until the Present.* Pittsburgh: n.p., 1889.

Douglas, Ann. *The Feminization of American Culture.* New York: Avon, 1972.

Dudden, Faye E. *Women in the American Theatre: Actresses and Audiences, 1790–1870.* New Haven: Yale University Press, 1994.

Dulles, Foster Rhea. *A History of Recreation: America Learns to Play.* Englewood Cliffs, N.J.: Prentice Hall, 1965.

Dumazedier, Joffre. "Leisure." In *International Encyclopedia of the Social Sciences,* ed. David Sills. Vol. 9, 248–54. New York: Macmillan, 1968.

————. *Toward A Society of Leisure.* New York: Free Press, 1967.

Dyos, H. J., and Michael Wolff, eds. *The Victorian City: Images and Realities.* London: Routledge & Kegan Paul, 1973.

Ellis, Franklin, ed. *History of Fayette County, Pennsylvania.* Philadelphia: Everts, 1882.

Ellis, Joseph J. *After the Revolution: Profiles of Early American Culture.* New York: Norton, 1979.

Epstein, Barbara. *The Politics of Domesticity.* Middletown, Conn.: Wesleyan University Press, 1981.

Evans, Henry Oliver. *Iron Pioneer: Henry W. Oliver, 1840–1914.* New York: Dutton, 1942.

————. "Life in Pittsburgh in 1845." *Western Pennsylvania Historical Magazine* 28 (March-June 1945): 20–25.

Ewen, Stuart. *All Consuming Images: The Politics of Style in Contemporary Culture.* New York: Basic, 1988.

Ewing, Blaine, ed. *Canonsburg Centennial 1802–1902.* Pittsburgh: Pittsburgh Printing Co., 1903.

Faler, Paul. "Cultural Aspects of the Industrial Revolution: Lynn, Massachusetts, Shoemakers and Industrial Morality, 1826–1860." In *Labor History* 15: 367–94.

Fawcett, James Waldo. "Quest for Pittsburgh Fire Department History." *Western Pennsylvania Historical Magazine* 49, no. 1 (Jan. 1966): 39–55.

Fletcher, Edward G. "Records and History of Theatrical Activities in Pittsburgh, Pennsylvania, from Their Beginnings to 1861, in Two Volumes." Ph.D. diss., Harvard University, 1931.

Fletcher, Stevenson. *Pennsylvania Agriculture and Country Life, 1640–1840.* Harrisburg: Pennsylvania Historical and Museum Commission, 1950.

Foner, Eric. *Free Soil, Free Labor, Free Men: The Ideology of the Republican Party.* New York: Oxford University Press, 1970.

Forrest, Earle R. *History of Washington County, Pennsylvania.* Chicago: S. J. Clarke, 1926.

Frank, Frederick J. "Student Life in Selected Colleges in the Early Nineteenth Century." Ph.D. diss., University of Pittsburgh, 1975.

Fuller, Robert C. *Mesmerism and the Cure of American Souls*. Philadelphia: University of Pennsylvania Press, 1982.

Galley, Henrietta, and J. O. Arnold, M.D. *History of the Galley Family with Local and Old Time Sketches in the Yough Region*. Philadelphia: Philadelphia Printing and Publishing, 1908.

Garrison, J. Ritchie. "Battalion Day: Militia Muster and Frolic in Pennsylvania Before the Civil War." *Pennsylvania Folklife* 26 (1976–1977): 2–12.

Gaul, Harvey B. "The Minstrel of the Alleghenies." *Western Pennsylvania Historical Magazine* 34 (March 1951): 1–22.

Gilchrist, Harry C. *History of Wilkinsburg, Pennsylvania*. Wilkinsburg: n.p., 1927.

Golden, Margaret C. "Directory of Theater Buildings in Pittsburgh, PA, since Earliest Times." Master's thesis, Carnegie Institute of Technology, Pittsburgh, 1953.

Goodman, Paul. *Towards A Christian Republic: The Great Transition in New England, 1826–1836*. New York: Oxford University Press, 1988.

Gorn, Elliott. " 'Gouge and Bite, Pull Hair and Scratch': The Social Significance of Fighting in the Southern Backcountry." *American Historical Review* 90 (Feb. 1985): 18–43.

Green, Eileen, Sandra Hebron, and Diana Woodward. *Women's Leisure, What Leisure?* London: Macmillan, 1990.

Green, Harvey. *Fit for America: Health, Fitness, Sport and American Society*. Baltimore: Johns Hopkins University Press, 1986.

Griffin, Christine, Dorothy Hobson, Sue MacIntosh, and Trisha McCabe. "Women and Leisure." In *Sport, Culture, and Ideology*, ed. Jennifer Hargreaves, 88–116. London: Routledge Kegan Paul, 1982.

Groneman, Carol, and Mary Beth Norton, eds. *To Toil the Livelong Day: America's Women at Work 1780–1980*. Ithaca: Cornell University Press, 1987.

Gunderson, Robert Gray. *The Log Cabin Campaign*. Lexington: University of Kentucky Press, 1957.

Gusfield, Joseph. *Symbolic Crusade: Status Politics and the American Temperance Movement*. Urbana: University of Illinois Press, 1986.

———. "Tradition and Modernity: Misplaced Polarities in the Study of Social Change." *American Journal of Sociology* 72 (1966): 351–62.

Hadden, James. *A History of Uniontown*. Akron, Pa.: New Werner Company, 1913.

Hall, Stuart, and Tony Jefferson. *Resistance Through Rituals: Youth Subcultures in Post-War Britain*. London: Hutchinson, 1976.

Haltunnen, Karen. *Confidence Men and Painted Women: A Study of Middle Class Culture in America, 1830–1870*. New Haven: Yale University Press, 1982.

Hardy, Stephen. *How Boston Played: Sport, Recreation, and Community, 1865–1915*. Boston: Northeastern University Press, 1982.

Hargreaves, Jennifer, ed. *Sport, Culture, and Ideology*. London: Routledge & Kegan Paul, 1982.

Harper, R. Eugene. *The Transformation of Western Pennsylvania, 1770–1800.* Pittsburgh: University of Pittsburgh Press, 1991.

Harpster, John. *Crossroads: Descriptions of Early Western Pennsylvania, 1720–1829.* Pittsburgh: University of Pittsburgh Press, 1938.

Harris, Neil. "Four Stages of Cultural Growth: The American City." In *Indiana Historical Society Lectures, 1971–1972: History and the Role of the City in American Life,* 24–49. Indianapolis: Indiana Historical Society, 1972.

———. *Humbug: The Art of P. T. Barnum.* Chicago: University of Chicago Press, 1973.

Harrison, Brian. *Drink and the Victorians.* Pittsburgh: University of Pittsburgh Press, 1971.

———. "Pubs." In *The Victorian City: Images and Realities,* ed. H. J. Dyos and Michael Wolff. London: Routledge & Kegan Paul, 1973.

———. "Religion and Recreation in Nineteenth-Century England." *Past and Present* 38 (1967): 98–125.

Hays, Samuel P., ed. *City at the Point: Essays on the Social History of Pittsburgh.* Pittsburgh: University of Pittsburgh Press, 1989.

Hedrick, Joan D. "Parlor Literature: Harriet Beecher Stowe and the Question of 'Great Women Artists.'" *Signs* 17, no. 2 (1992): 275–303.

Henderson, Karla A. "Broadening an Understanding of Women, Gender, and Leisure." *Journal of Leisure Research* 26, no. 1 (1994): 1–7.

Henderson, Karla A., M. Deborah Bialeschki, Susan Shaw, and Valerie Freysinger. *A Leisure of One's Own: A Feminist Perspective on Women's Leisure.* State College, Pa.: Venture Publishing, 1989.

Hobbs, Jane Elizabeth. "Old Jefferson College." Master's thesis, University of Pittsburgh, 1929.

Holmes, Joseph T. "The Decline of the Pennsylvania Militia, 1815–1870." *Western Pennsylvania Historical Magazine* 57 (April 1974): 199–217.

Holt, Michael F. "The Election of 1840, Voter Mobilization, and the Emergence of the Second Party System: A Reappraisal of Jacksonian Voting Behavior," 16–58. In *A Master's Due: Essays in Honor of David Herbert Donald,* ed. William J. Cooper, Jr., Michael F. Holt, and John McCardell. Baton Rouge: Louisiana State University Press, 1985.

———. *Forging a Majority: The Formation of the Republican Party in Pittsburgh, 1848–1860.* New Haven: Yale University Press, 1969.

Horlick, Allan Stanley. *Country Boys and Merchant Princes: The Social Control of Young Men in New York.* Lewisburg, Pa.: Bucknell University Press, 1975.

Howe, Daniel Walker. "The Evangelical Movement and Political Culture in the North During the Second Party System." *Journal of American History* 77, no. 4 (March 1991): 1216–39.

Isaac, Rhys. *The Transformation of Virginia.* Chapel Hill: University of North Carolina Press, 1982.

Jable, J. Thomas. "Aspects of Reform in Early Nineteenth-Century Pennsylvania." *Pennsylvania Magazine of History and Biography* 102, no. 3 (1978): 344–63.

John, Richard R. "Taking Sabbatarianism Seriously: The Postal System, the Sabbath, and the Transformation of American Political Culture." *Journal of the Early Republic* 10, no. 4 (winter 1990): 517–67.

Johns, Elizabeth. *American Genre Painting: The Politics of Everyday Life.* New Haven: Yale University Press, 1991.

Johnson, Claudia D. *American Actress: Perspectives on the Nineteenth Century.* Chicago: Nelson-Hall, 1984.

———. "That Guilty Third Tier: Prostitution in Nineteenth Century American Theaters." In *Victorian America*, ed. D. W. Howe, 111–20. Philadelphia: University of Pennsylvania Press, 1976.

Johnson, Paul E. *A Shopkeeper's Millenium: Society and Revivals in Rochester, New York, 1815–1837.* New York: Hill and Wang, 1978.

Johnston, William G. *Life and Reminiscences of William G. Johnston from Birth to Manhood.* New York: Knickerbocker, 1901.

Jones, Gareth Stedman. "Class Expression Versus Social Control? A Critique of Recent Trends in the Social History of 'Leisure.'" *History Workshop* 4 (autumn 1977): 163–70.

Jordan, Philip D. *The National Road.* New York: Bobbs-Merrill, 1948.

Kasson, John. *Rudeness and Civility: Manners in Nineteenth-Century Urban America.* New York: Hill and Wang, 1990.

Kerber, Linda. "Separate Spheres, Female Worlds, Woman's Place: The Rhetoric of Women's History." *Journal of American History* 75, no. 1 (June 1988): 9–39.

Kohl, Lawrence F. "The Concept of Social Control and the History of Jacksonian America." *Journal of the Early Republic* 5 (spring 1985): 21–34.

Kussart, Mrs. S. *Early History of the Fifteenth Ward, City of Pittsburgh.* Pittsburgh: n.p., 1925.

———. "Navigation on the Monongahela River." In "Kussart Scrapbooks" collection of the Pennsylvania Dept., Carnegie Library of Pittsburgh.

Larkin, Jack. *The Reshaping of Everyday Life, 1790–1840.* New York: Harper and Row, 1989.

Laurie, Bruce. "Fire Companies and Gangs in Southwark: The 1840s." In *The People of Philadelphia: A History of Ethnic Groups and Lower Class Life*, ed. Allen F. Davis and Mark H. Haller, 71–87. Philadelphia: Temple University Press, 1973.

———. *Working People of Philadelphia, 1800–1850.* Philadelphia: Temple University Press, 1980.

Lea, Rev. Richard. *Reminiscences of Sixty Years of Presbyterianism in Western Pennsylvania.* Pittsburgh: n.p., 1886.

Lee, Alfred McClung. "Trends in Commercial Entertainment in Pittsburgh as Reflected in the Advertising in Pittsburgh Newspapers (1790–1860)." Master's thesis, University of Pittsburgh, 1931.

Levine, Lawrence. *Highbrow/Lowbrow: The Emergence of Cultural Hierarchy in America.* Cambridge: Harvard University Press, 1988.

Levine, Peter. "The Promise of Sport in Antebellum America." *Journal of American Culture* 2, no. 4 (1980): 623–34.

Lockard, Thaddeus C., Jr., and W. Porter Ware. *P. T. Barnum Presents Jenny Lind: The American Tour of the Swedish Nightingale*. Philadelphia: Lippincott, 1962.

Lott, Eric. *Love and Theft: Blackface Minstrelsy and the American Working Class*. New York: Oxford University Press, 1993.

McClenathan, J. C., et al. *Centennial History of the Borough of Connellsville, Pennsylvania, 1806–1906*. Columbus, Ohio: Champlin, 1906.

McConachie, Bruce A. "Pacifying American Theatrical Audiences, 1820–1900." In *For Fun and Profit: The Transformation of Leisure into Consumption*, ed. Richard Butsch, 47–70. Philadelphia: Temple University Press, 1990.

McCoy, Drew R. *The Elusive Republic: Political Economy in Jeffersonian Virginia*. New York: Norton, 1980.

McCullough, Robert, and Walter Leuba. *The Pennsylvania Main Line Canal*. Martinsburg, Pa.: Morrison's Cove Herald, 1962.

McKinney, W. W. *Early Pittsburgh Presbyterianism*. Pittsburgh: Gibson, 1938.

Malcolmson, Robert. *Popular Recreations in British Society, 1700–1850*. Cambridge: Cambridge University Press, 1973.

Mann, Henry, ed. *Our Police: A History of the Pittsburgh Police Force, Under the Town and City*. Pittsburgh: n.p., 1889.

Martin, Scott C. "The Fourth of July in Southwestern Pennsylvania, 1800–1850." *Pittsburgh History* 75, no. 2 (summer 1992): 58–71.

———. "The Great Brothel Dousing: Leisure, Reform, and Urban Change in Antebellum Pittsburgh." In *American Cities and Towns: Historical Perspectives*, ed. Joseph Rishel, 26–38. Pittsburgh: Duquesne University Press, 1992.

Matthews, Glenna. *"Just A Housewife": The Rise and Fall of Domesticity in America*. New York: Oxford University Press, 1987.

———. *The Rise of Public Woman: Woman's Power and Woman's Place in the United States, 1630–1970*. New York: Oxford University Press, 1992.

Meserve, Walter J. *Heralds of Promise: The Drama of the American People During the Age of Jackson, 1829–1849*. Westport, Conn.: Greenwood, 1986.

Miller, Annie Clark. *Chronicles of Families, Houses and Estates of Pittsburgh and Its Environs*. Pittsburgh: n.p., 1927.

Miller, James M. *The Genesis of Western Culture: The Upper Ohio Valley, 1800–1825*. Columbus: Ohio State Archaeological and Historical Society, 1938.

Morris, Emma D. A. "Old Springhill." Master's thesis, University of Pittsburgh, 1938.

Muller, Edward K. "Metropolis and Region: A Framework for Enquiry into Western Pennsylvania." In *City at the Point: Essays on the Social History of Pittsburgh*, ed. Samuel P. Hays, 181–211. Pittsburgh: University of Pittsburgh Press, 1989.

Muraskin, William A. *Middle Class Blacks in a White Society: Prince Hall Free-*

masonry in America. Berkeley and Los Angeles: University of California Press, 1975.

———. "The Social-Control Theory in American History: A Critique." *Journal of Social History* 9 (summer 1976): 559–80.

Murphy, Theresa. "Work, Leisure, and Moral Reform: The Ten Hour Movement in New England, 1830–1850." In *Worktime and Industrialization: An International History*, ed. Gary Cross, 59–76. Philadelphia: Temple University Press, 1988.

Nevin, Franklin Taylor *The Village of Sewickley*. Sewickley, Pa.: n.p., 1929.

Nissenbaum, Steven. "Revisiting 'A Visit from St. Nicholas': The Battle for Christmas in Early Nineteenth-Century America." In *The Mythmaking Frame of Mind: Social Imagination and American Culture*, ed. James Gilbert et al., 25–70. Belmont, Calif.: Wadsworth, 1993.

Nye, Russell B. *The Unembarassed Muse: The Popular Arts in America*. New York: Dial, 1970.

Oestreicher, Richard. "Working Class Formation, Development, and Consciousness in Pittsburgh, 1790–1860." In *City at the Point: Essays on the Social History of Pittsburgh*, ed. Samuel P. Hays, 111–50. Pittsburgh: University of Pittsburgh Press, 1989.

O'Malley, Michael. *Keeping Watch: A History of American Time*. New York: Penguin, 1990.

Osterud, Nancy. *Bonds of Community: The Lives of Farm Women in Nineteenth-Century New York*. Ithaca: Cornell University Press, 1991.

———. " 'She Helped Me Hay It as Good as a Man': Relations Among Women and Men in an Agricultural Community." In *To Toil the Livelong Day: America's Women at Work 1780–1980*, ed. Carol Groneman and Mary Beth Norton, 87–97. Ithaca: Cornell University Press, 1987.

Parke, John E. *Recollections of Seventy Years and Historical Gleanings of Allegheny, Pennsylvania*. Boston: Rand, Avery, and Co., 1886.

Peiss, Kathy. *Cheap Amusements: Working Women and Leisure in Turn-of-the-Century New York*. Philadelphia: Temple University Press, 1986.

Pessen, Edward. *Riches, Class, and Power Before the Civil War*. Lexington, Mass.: D. C. Heath, 1973.

Powelson, Frank W. "History of Freemasonry in Allegheny County." Typescript in collection of the Pennsylvania Dept., Carnegie Library of Pittsburgh, 1960.

Prahl, Augustus J. "The Turner," 79–110 in *The Forty-Eighters: Political Refugees of the German Revolution of 1848*, ed. A. E. Zucker. New York: Columbia University Press, 1950.

Reid, Douglas. "The Decline of St. Monday, 1766–1876." *Past and Present* 71: 76–101.

Reiser, Catherine M. *Pittsburgh's Commercial Development, 1800–1850*. Harrisburg: Pennsylvania Historical and Museum Commission, 1951.

Reiss, Steven A. *City Games: The Evolution of American Urban Society and the Rise of Sports.* Urbana: University of Illinois Press, 1989.

Rishel, Joseph. *Founding Families of Pittsburgh: The Evolution of a Regional Elite, 1760–1910.* Pittsburgh: University of Pittsburgh Press, 1990.

Rodgers, Daniel. *The Work Ethic in Industrial America, 1850–1920.* Chicago: University of Chicago Press, 1978.

Roediger, David S., and Philip S. Foner. *Our Own Time: A History of American Labor and the Working Day.* Westport, Conn.: Greenwood, 1989.

Rommel, Frederick C. *History of Lodge #45 F. & A. M., 1785–1910.* Pittsburgh: Republic Bank Note Company, 1912.

Rorabaugh, W. J. *The Alcoholic Republic: An American Tradition.* New York: Oxford University Press, 1979.

Rosenzweig, Roy. *Eight Hours for What We Will: Workers and Leisure in an Industrial City, 1870–1920.* Cambridge: Cambridge University Press, 1983.

Ross, Steven J. *Workers on the Edge: Work, Leisure and Politics in Industrializing Cincinnati.* New York: Columbia University Press, 1985.

Rumbarger, Joseph. *Profits, Power and Prohibition: Alcohol Reform and the Industrializing of America, 1800–1930.* Albany: State University of New York Press, 1989.

Ryan, Mary P. "The American Parade: Representations of the Nineteenth-Century Social Order." In *The New Cultural History,* ed. Lynn Hunt, 131–53. Berkeley and Los Angeles: University of California Press, 1989.

———. *Women in Public: Between Banners and Ballots, 1825–1880.* Baltimore: Johns Hopkins University Press, 1990.

Saxon, A. H. *P. T. Barnum: The Legend and the Man.* New York: Columbia University Press, 1989.

Saxton, Alexander. "Blackface Minstrelsy and Jacksonian Ideology." *American Quarterly* 27 (March 1975): 3–28.

———. *The Rise and Fall of the White Republic: Class Politics and Mass Culture in Nineteenth-Century America.* London: Verso, 1990.

Schneider, Norris F. *The National Road, Main Street of America.* Columbus: Ohio Historical Society, 1975.

Schultz, Gladys Denny. *Jenny Lind, The Swedish Nightingale.* Philadelphia: Lippincott, 1962.

Searight, Thomas B. *The Old Pike: A History of the National Road.* Uniontown, Pa.: T. B. Searight, 1894.

Sears, John F. *Sacred Places: American Tourist Attractions in the Nineteenth Century.* New York: Oxford University Press, 1989.

Sellers, Charles. *The Market Revolution: Jacksonian America, 1815–1846.* New York: Oxford University Press, 1991.

Shank, William. *The Amazing Pennsylvania Canals.* 4th ed. York, Pa.: American Canal and Transportation Center, 1981.

———. *Indian Trails to Super Highways.* 2d ed. York, Pa.: American Canal and Transportation Center, 1974.

Shaw, Susan. "Gender, Leisure, and Constraint: Toward a Framework for the Analysis of Women's Leisure." *Journal of Leisure Research* 26, no. 1 (1994): 8–22.

Silveus, Marian. "Churches and Social Control on the Western Pennsylvania Frontier." *Western Pennsylvania Historical Magazine* 19 (1936): 123–34.

Sklar, Katherine. *Catharine Beecher: A Study in American Domesticity.* New Haven: Yale University Press, 1973.

Smith, Sol. *Theatrical Management in the West and South for Thirty Years.* New York: Harper and Brothers, 1868.

Somkin, Fred. *Unquiet Eagle: Memory and Desire in the Idea of American Freedom, 1815–1860.* Ithaca: Cornell University Press, 1967.

Stansell, Christine. *City of Women: Sex and Class in New York, 1789–1860.* Chicago: University of Illinois Press, 1986.

Sterling, Dorothy. *Ahead of Her Time: Abby Kelley and the Politics of Antislavery.* New York: Norton, 1991.

———. *The Making of an Afro-American: Martin Robinson Delany, 1812–1885.* New York: Doubleday, 1971.

Stott, Richard. *Workers in the Metropolis: Class, Ethnicity and Youth in Antebellum New York City.* Ithaca: Cornell University Press, 1990.

Strasser, Susan. *Never Done: A History of American Housework.* New York: Pantheon, 1982.

Sutton, Horace. *Travelers: The American Tourist from Stagecoach to Space Shuttle.* New York: Morrow, 1980.

Swetnam, George. *Pennsylvania Transportation.* Pennsylvania Historical Studies, No. 7. Gettysburg: Pennsylvania Historical Association, 1964.

———. "Who Threw the Rock at Jenny Lind?" *Pittsburgh Press Magazine,* Nov. 30, 1969, 4–5.

Swisshelm, Jane Grey. *Half a Century.* 3d ed. Chicago: Jansen, McClurg and Co., 1880.

Taylor, George Rodgers. *The Transportation Revolution.* Vol. 4 of *The Economic History of the United States.* White Plains, N.Y.: M. E. Sharpe, 1951.

Thompson, E. P. "Time, Work Discipline and Industrial Capitalism." *Past and Present* 38: 56–97.

Thrift, Nigel, and Peter Williams, eds. "The Geography of Nineteenth-Century Class Formation." In *Class and Space: The Making of Urban Society.* London: Routledge Kegan Paul, 1987.

Toll, Robert. *Blacking Up: The Minstrel Show in Nineteenth Century America.* New York: Oxford University Press, 1974.

Turner, Victor. *From Ritual to Theatre: The Human Seriousness of Play.* New York: Performing Arts Journal Publications, 1982.

———. *Process, Performance, and Pilgrimage: A Study in Comparative Symbology.* New Dehli, India: Concept, 1979.

———. *The Ritual Process: Structure and Anti-Structure.* Chicago: Aldine, 1969.

Turner, Victor, and Edith Turner. *Image and Pilgrimage in Christian Culture: Anthropological Perspectives*. New York: Columbia University Press, 1978.

Tyrell, Ian. *Sobering Up: From Temperance to Prohibition in Antebellum America*. Westport, Conn.: Greenwood, 1979.

———. "Women and Temperance in Antebellum America, 1830–1860." *Civil War History* 28 (1982): 128–52.

van Urk, J. Blan. *The Story of Rolling Rock*. New York: Scribner's Sons, 1950.

Van Voorhis, John S. *The Old and New Monongahela*. Pittsburgh: Nicholson, 1893.

Veblen, Thorstein. *The Theory of the Leisure Class*. 1899. Reprint, New York: Penguin, 1986.

Veech, James. *The Monongahela of Old, or Historical Sketches of South-Western Pennsylvania to the Year 1800*. Pittsburgh: n.p., 1910.

Vogle, B. F. *Greensburg and Greensburg Schools*. Greensburg, Pa.: Vogle and Winsheimer, 1899.

Vogt, Helen E. *Westward of Ye Laurel Hills, 1750–1850*. Parsons, W. Vir.: McClain, 1976.

Wade, Richard C. *The Urban Frontier: The Rise of Western Cities, 1790–1830*. Cambridge: Harvard University Press, 1959.

Walters, Ronald G. *American Reformers 1815–1860*. New York: Hill and Wang, 1978.

Walvin, James. *Leisure and Society 1830–1950*. New York: Longman, 1978.

Ware, W. Porter, and Thaddeus C. Lockard, Jr. *P. T. Barnum Presents Jenny Lind: The American Tour of the Swedish Nightingale*. Baton Rouge: Louisiana State University Press, 1980.

Warren, Charles. "Fourth of July Myths," *William and Mary Quarterly* 2, no. 3, 3d series (July 1945): 237–72.

Watson, David T. "Early School Day Recollections." In *The Centennial Celebration of the Incorporation of the Borough of Washington, PA*, ed. Boyd Crumrine. Washington: Washington County Historical Society, 1912.

Watson, Harry. *Liberty and Power: The Politics of Jacksonian America*. New York: Noonday, 1990.

Welter, Barbara. "The Cult of True Womanhood, 1820–1860." In *The American Family in Social-Historical Perspective*, ed. Michael Gordon, 313–33. New York: St. Martin's, 1978.

Wilentz, Sean. "Artisan Republican Festivals and the Rise of Class Conflict in New York City, 1788–1837." In *Working Class America: Essays on Labor, Community, and American Society*, ed. Michael H. Frisch and Daniel J. Walkowitz, 37–77. Urbana: University of Illinois Press, 1983.

———. "Society, Politics, and the Market Revolution, 1815–1848." In *The New American History*, ed. Eric Foner, 51–71. Philadelphia: Temple University Press, 1990.

Wiley, Richard T. *Elizabeth and Her Neighbors*. Butler, Pa.: Zeigler, 1936.

Wilson, Erasmus. *Standard History of Pittsburgh*. Chicago: H. R. Cornell and Co., 1898.

Wimbush, Erica, and Margaret Talbot, eds. *Relative Freedoms: Women and Leisure*. Milton Keynes, U.K.: Open University Press, 1988.

Woodward, Diana, and Eileen Green. " 'Not Tonight Dear!' The Social Control of Women's Leisure." In *Relative Freedoms: Women and Leisure*, ed. Erica Wimbush and Margaret Talbot, 131–46. Milton Keynes, U.K.: Open University Press, 1988.

Yacovone, Donald. "The Transformation of the Black Temperance Movement, 1827–1854: An Interpretation." *Journal of the Early Republic* 8: 281–97.

Yeo, Eileen, and Stephen Yeo. "Ways of Seeing: Control and Leisure Versus Class and Struggle." In *Popular Culture and Class Conflict 1590–1914: Explorations in the History of Labour and Leisure*, ed. Yeo and Yeo. Atlantic Highlands, N.J.: Humanities, 1981.

Young, Samuel. *The History of My Life, Being a Biographical Outline of the Events of a Long and Busy Life*. Pittsburgh: n.p., 1890.

Zeisel, Joseph S. "The Workweek in American Industry, 1850–1896." In *Mass Leisure*, ed. Eric Larrabee and Rolf Meyersohn, 145–53. Glencoe, Ill.: Free Press, 1958.

Newspapers, 1800–1850

Allegheny Democrat
American Manufacturer (Pittsburgh)
Farmer's Register (Westmoreland County)
The Friend (Pittsburgh)
Genius of Liberty (Uniontown, Fayette County)
Greensburgh Gazette (Westmoreland County)
Greensburg Sentinel (Westmoreland County)
Harris's Intelligencer (Pittsburgh)
Iron City and Pittsburgh Weekly Chronicle
The Mystery (Pittsburgh)
Our Country (Washington County)
Pennsylvania Argus (Greensburg, Westmoreland County)
Pittsburgh Commonwealth
Pittsburgh Daily Aurora
Pittsburgh Daily Dispatch
Pittsburgh Daily Gazette
Pittsburgh Gazette
Pittsburgh Gazette-Times
Pittsburgh Mercury
Pittsburgh Morning Chronicle
Pittsburgh Post

Pittsburgh Statesman
Pittsburgh Telegraph
Pittsburgh Times
Pittsburgh Weekly Telegraph
Spirit of Liberty (Pittsburgh)
Spirit of the Age (Pittsburgh)
Tree of Liberty (Pittsburgh)
Washington Banner (Pittsburgh)
Washington Examiner
Washington Reporter
Weekly Advocate and Statesman (Pittsburgh)
Westmoreland Intelligencer
Westmoreland Republican

Periodicals, All Published in Pittsburgh, 1800–1850

The Crystal and Ladies' Magazine
The Hesperus and Western Miscellany
The Literary Casket
Literary Messenger
Loomis's Magazine Almanac
Patterson's Magazine Almanac
Pittsburgh Magazine Almanack for the Year of Our Lord 1809
Pittsburgh Monthly Museum and Record of the Times
The Western Gleaner, or Repository for the Arts, Sciences and Literature
Western Literary Magazine

Index